The scandal of particularity
incarnating universality connects
Christ with the Christian mission of
colleges + institutions.

Number One:
Issues in Religion and Higher Education

Professing in the Postmodern Academy

Faculty and the Future of Church-Related Colleges

Edited by

Stephen R. Haynes

A Markham Press Fund Publication from

Baylor University Press
Waco, Texas

This volume is the thirty-ninth published by the Markham Press Fund of Baylor University Press, established in memory of Dr. L. N. and Princess Finch Markham of Longview, Texas, by their daughters, Mrs. R. Matt Dawson of Waco, Texas, and Mrs. B. Reid Clanton of Longview, Texas.

Library of Congress Cataloging-in-Publication Data

Professing in the postmodern academy : faculty and the future of church-related colleges / edited by Stephen R. Haynes.
    p. cm. — (Issues in religion and higher education ; no. 1)
Includes bibliographical references.
  ISBN 0-918954-82-7 (alk. paper)
  1. Church colleges—United States. 2. College teachers—United States—Attitudes. 3. Educational surveys—United States. I. Haynes,
Stephen R. II. Series.
  LC427 .P75 2002
  378'.071'0973—dc21
                              2002004604

Printed in the United States of America on acid-free paper.

CONTENTS

PART FOUR: PEDAGOGY AND PRAXIS

PART FIVE: MISSION AND CURRICULUM

AFTERWORD

ACKNOWLEDGEMENTS

The authors wish to thank all the persons and institutions who contributed to the completion of this book, especially Lilly Endowment Inc. By funding and cultivating the Rhodes Consultation on the Future of the Church-Related College since 1995, the Endowment has made a significant contribution to church-related higher education and to the lives and careers of Consultation participants. Craig Dykstra, Vice President of the Religion Division at Lilly, has been a strong advocate for this work and a mentor for many of the participants. Jeanne Knoerle, SP, former Program Officer at the Endowment, deserves much credit for the Rhodes Consultation's success. Before her retirement in 1999, Jeanne fashioned and nurtured the Consultation in important ways. Her encouragement of younger scholars, her guidance and leadership, and her faith in the spirituality of conversation have left their mark on each of us. We dedicate this volume to her, in appreciation of her friendship and support.

PREFACE

Scholars have employed a number of images to describe the problems and possibilities associated with American church-related higher education. Charles McCoy (1972) speaks of an identity crisis, an image that foregrounds the struggles which accompany maturation and social change. Merrimon Cuninggim (1994) refers to "uneasy partners," an image that captures the shifting relationship between church and college and the intellectual chafing that results from the unequal yoking of institutions. Studies by George Marsden (1994) and James Tunstead Burtchaell (1991; 1997)—along with other recent works on higher education that have its religious dimensions in view—traffic in images of declension. They plot the history of higher education in America as a fall from grace, a diminishment of soul, an exile from pristine origins.

"Professing in the postmodern academy" is the metaphor we have selected to guide our reflections on the identity and role of the church-related college. The image of professing in the postmodern academy commends itself to us for several reasons. First, it accentuates the faculty voice on an issue where it is often silent or silenced. Second, by foregrounding the authors' institutional locations—which include colleges and universities affiliated with a variety of Protestant (Presbyterian, Methodist, Baptist, Lutheran, Episcopal and Mennonite) and Roman Catholic traditions (Norbertine, Lasallian, Benedictine, Dominican, Jesuit, and Sisters of Holy Cross)—it emphasizes the faculty role in articulating and embodying religious identity. Third, while the academic vocation calls us to be *professors*, we are aware of professing in a world and an academy that are in the midst of change. The "postmodern" environment emerging in the American academy may be one that is friendly to religious professions—as George M. Marsden and others have suggested. In any case, if claims of church-relatedness at our institutions are to be taken seriously amid the welter of competing methodologies and truth claims, an articulate and committed faculty voice is required.

THE RHODES CONSULTATION

Who are these junior scholars who dare to speak about the importance of church-relatedness at this juncture in the history of American higher education? The twelve contributors to this volume are the original members of the Rhodes Consultation on the Future of the Church-Related College, a project funded since 1995 by Lilly Endowment Inc.[1] The Rhodes Consultation began as an attempt to convene outstanding junior faculty at church-related colleges and universities to reflect together on the future of our institutions and the role of faculty in shaping that future. The authors were selected from among 130 applicants to the first round of the Consultation. Because interest in the project was so great, a second round of conversations was initiated in 1997. Forty-two new participants were selected, again from well over one hundred applicants. A third round of the Consultation, which included thirty-six new faculty members, was launched in 1999. To this point, ninety faculty representatives from ninety institutions have participated in the Rhodes Consultation, and as the project has evolved a majority of participants in the first two rounds have remained involved in some capacity.

When an institution becomes part of the Consultation, the first step is initiation of a series of formal campus discussions dealing with issues of church-relatedness. These faculty discussions typically move from the general to the specific, and often utilize the college's own history as a case study. Every attempt is made to represent the various attitudes toward church affiliation to be found on college faculties, with the goal of establishing the sort of open and respectful dialogue that is often lacking around this issue. The campus conversations sponsored by the Consultation yield further discussions, revision of mission statements, strategic planning documents, and plans for new initiatives. These developments are institutionalized in the second step of the Consultation, which calls for participants to develop "Institutional Renewal Grant" proposals. The Consultation's IRG program funds projects designed by faculty to reclaim creatively the institution's religious tradition. Programs initiated under the IRG banner have included faculty orientation seminars, mentoring programs, institutional history projects, and curriculum development (e.g., courses in "Religion and Education" and Catholic Studies programs). The ultimate goal of both campus discussions and IRGs is long-term institutional change. Indeed, after a full year of formal discussion and two years of a project specifically designed to enhance the viability of the religious tradition on campus, the very character of the college can be affected.

This volume represents another contribution of the Rhodes Consultation to the future of church-related higher education. Between 1996 and 1998, the twelve original members of the Consultation met regularly to discuss the situation on their campuses, their own identity and vocation as scholars, and the issues affecting church-related higher education about which they felt most strongly. After undertaking research projects and writing, revising, and editing together for two years, the group produced this manuscript. It represents the reflections of junior teacher-scholars who are religiously committed and deeply concerned with the future of their institutions. It does not represent the official view of any college, church, or denomination, but it does capture the spirit of the Rhodes Consultation, whose aim has been to provoke genuine conversation about the issues we care about and the institutions to which we are called.

ORIGINS

How did the Rhodes Consultation come to be? Its origins go back a decade to an episode that is symbolic of the tensions that animate many church-affiliated institutions. At Rhodes College, during the opening faculty meeting of the 1991–1992 academic year, a newly hired professor of Political Science was introduced. Following his official welcome by the Dean, he asked to address the faculty. The prestigious scholar, whom the college had lured away from a leading research university, walked to the podium and proclaimed that it had long been his dream to teach at a place like Rhodes. "I am happy to be at a Christian college finally," he announced, "for my professional work is thoroughly informed by my faith." As these words reached his audience, an awkward embarrassment became palpable.

I was in that audience, and though ten years have passed, I remember the episode as if it were yesterday. For it launched me on a path of concerted reflection and permanently altered my professional life. Why, I wondered, had faculty at a college with a century-long formal alliance with the Presbyterian Church registered such visible discomfort at this expression of Christian identity? The truth was that I had felt uncomfortable too, despite being a Presbyterian who just a year earlier had been ordained to teach at the college. But while I was a practicing Presbyterian, I was also a faculty member in Religious Studies who had been well prepared to survive in the secular academy. In graduate school I had been socialized to embrace a "two-realm theory of truth" that dichotomized private faith and public knowledge and effectively banished confessional statements from academic space. In this respect I represented the major cultural trends affecting religion and higher education in the twentieth century. Since 1950 in particular, the exile of faith from academic life had steadily affected church-related colleges as teachers trained at the nation's leading graduate schools brought rationalistic and naturalistic conceptions of knowledge to historically Christian institutions, and as administrators competing for recognition and resources encouraged loyalty to the standards of a national professoriate.[2]

When I undertook a survey of American church-affiliated colleges in 1994, questions about the distinctiveness of Christian higher education were very much on my mind.[3] As responses from over three hundred institutions were tabulated, a broad portrait of the church-related college began to emerge. Many features of this portrait are as paradoxical as the faculty meeting described above. For instance, the survey revealed that it is not unusual for colleges to claim a "strong" or "moderate" connection with an affiliated church body while stating that less than a quarter of the school's students and faculty are members of this denomination, or that the college's "religion requirement" can be satisfied with just one course in Religion or Philosophy. This evidence suggested to me that a great many church-related colleges had lost a sense of themselves as "recognizably Christian," and I wondered whether the trends leading them in this direction were reversible.

In April 1995, I was invited by Jeanne Knoerle, SP of Lilly Endowment Inc., to participate in a gathering of grantees in the Endowment's Religion and Higher Education Initiative. As an observer, I was struck by several points on which participants seemed to agree. First, the cultural and intellectual conditions under which current views of the relationship of religion and higher education had evolved were in the process of changing. Second, this process was widely understood as a response to something called the "postmodern."[4] Third, the religious identities at church-related institutions were being eroded by the market forces shaping higher education. Fourth, as the role of religion in the academy and the relationship between faith and learning were under reconsideration, it was clear that the way forward was not a return to the past.

As I began to develop a proposal for studying the future of American church-related colleges, my thinking was sharpened by recent works on religion and higher education by George M. Marsden, James Tunstead Burtchaell, and Douglas Sloan. Each of these authors details the sacrifices—both institutional and intellectual—made by Christians seeking to find space for faith under the conditions of modernity. Marsden and Burtchaell trace the path to secularization navigated by well-meaning Christians at the helms of church-affiliated institutions of higher learning, while Sloan relates the story of leading Protestant thinkers who embraced a naturalist epistemology in order to gain a hearing for belief in the wider culture. These authors communicate a similar message: In their rush to conform to the demands of modernity in a post-Christian world, American Christians sacrificed both relevance and identity.

My interaction with Lilly staff and grantees and my reflection on these published studies began to illumine a compelling question regarding the church-related college's future: Given the steady rise of the postmodern and the church's un- successful attempt to preserve its identity and relate its mes- sage on terms set by the modern secular academy, what was likely to be the identity and societal role of church-related lib- eral arts colleges in the twenty-first century? With this ques- tion in mind, in 1995 I submitted a proposal for the Rhodes Consultation to the Lilly Endowment. The project I proposed would initiate a national discussion on the peculiar challenges facing the church-related liberal arts college, a discussion that would convene teacher-scholars who wished to see their col- leges make a singular contribution to the future of American higher education. The project was funded and the Rhodes Consultation on the Future of the Church-Related College was launched in the Spring of 1996. Since that time the Consulta- tion has engaged nearly a hundred teacher-scholars on the fac- ulties of American church-related liberal arts colleges who are committed to the future of these institutions, scholars who are poised to make lasting contributions to this segment of Ameri- can higher education.

A PORTRAIT OF THE AMERICAN CHURCH-RELATED COLLEGE

What do we know about the church-related college as it exists today? The decline and demise of the church-affiliated college was predicted as early as 1900, was reiterated in the 1960s and 1970s, and was forecast as recently as 1990.[5] And yet these in- stitutions remain a visible part of the American academic land- scape. How has this aspect of the landscape changed over time; and what does an early twenty-first-century portrait reveal?

It is estimated that fewer than two hundred church colleges existed in 1860, that by 1900 that number had grown to nearly a thousand, and that between the Civil War and World War I over eight hundred church-affiliated institutions were founded.[6] However, the first inventory of church-related col- leges was not taken until around 1960. Writing in 1964, Myron F. Wicke could identify 528 four-year and 137 two-year church- related colleges.[7] Based on the total number of institutions of higher learning in the country at that time, Wicke concluded that about one-third of all degree-granting and two-year colleges maintained some relationship to a church body. The Danforth Commission Study of 1966, whose authors addressed inquiries to 1,189 independent institutions, found 817 colleges and universities they "identified as having relationships of sufficient significance to be considered church-sponsored institutions."[8] By 1974 that number apparently had dwindled to 717.[9] The next comprehensive count of American church-affiliated colleges was undertaken in the early 1990s, when Merrimon Cuninggim published a list of 725 church-sponsored institutions (alphabetically and by affiliated church body), over two hundred of them Roman Catholic.[10]

Assuming a general reliability for these numbers, they relate an undramatic tale. Despite the fact that many institutions founded in the hey-day of the church-related college did not survive into the second half of the twentieth century, over the past three decades there has been no significant diminishment in their numbers. Using the totals arrived at by the Danforth study in 1966 and Cuninggim in 1994, we find a net loss of fewer than one hundred institutions over thirty years. This represents a rate of closure, merger, or secularization of about three colleges per year—an unfortunate trend, though not one to indicate the demise of the church-related college.

A useful portrait of these institutions, of course, must depict more than the relative stability of their numbers. A national questionnaire administered in 1994 helps to flesh out our picture. In response to the author's invitation, 317 church-related institutions completed written questionnaires designed to ascertain information on various manifestations of church-relatedness. One item asked: "Does the college have a Religion or Bible requirement?" and another inquired about the "strength" of the college's church affiliation. Other items asked whether an institution required faith statements from students or faculty, and what percentage of each group belonged to the sponsoring denomination.

Overall, the survey results do not inspire confidence in the capacity of church-related colleges to provide a distinctive educational experience. Perhaps the most encouraging finding is that 82% of respondents reported some sort of Religion or Bible requirement for students, with about 30% requiring at least one course in Bible. Among the 238 respondents who described the extent of this requirement, the average was 2.4 semester courses.[11] Thus, it appears that at a majority of church-related colleges the curriculum is still distinctive to some degree. On the other hand, even assuming that required courses in "Religion" have the effect for which they were instituted—providing students with a favorable indoctrination into the Christian tradition—at most institutions they comprise a very meager portion of a student's academic experience (typically, about six of 120 credit hours). Further, these "Religion" requirements are often met with elective courses that bear no meaningful relation to the college's founding tradition. Finally, it is increasingly the case that those who teach religion and philosophy courses at church-affiliated institutions have little stake in (and perhaps little knowledge of) the college's tradition. They are less likely than in the past to be ordained ministers or active church members, and may be indistinguishable professionally from their counterparts at public universities.

If we cannot be sure that students are sympathetically introduced to the Christian tradition even at church-related colleges that retain a religion requirement, then we are left to doubt whether there is anything to distinguish the church-related college curriculum as a whole.[12] Indeed, questionnaire responses revealed that most church-affiliated institutions no longer require any formal religious requirement for faculty membership and that "faith statements" are quite rare as a condition for hiring or enrollment. Surely the current academic job market exacerbates the problem. When small colleges can attract promising young scholars who hail from the best graduate schools, religious affiliation quickly becomes a secondary consideration in hiring. In any case, only 16% of responding colleges reported having such a requirement for faculty, and only 12% required student assent to a faith statement. More revealing is that 61% of responding colleges reported that fewer than half their faculty were members of the related church, while another 31% noted that fewer than a quarter of their teachers were members. The numbers are similar for students:

at 63% of church-related colleges fewer than half of students are members of the founding church, while at 34% less than a quarter of students are church members.

Ultimately, of course, church relationship is not a function of numbers. The critical question is not "how many church-affiliated students and teachers does a church-affiliated college need?"; but "do church-affiliated colleges possess the will to insure the existence on campus of a critical mass of persons favorably disposed toward the college's founding tradition?" There is much evidence that they do not. When the statistics cited here are combined with the fact that the prominent characteristics of the church-sponsored college of fifty or one hundred years ago—mandatory chapel services, clergy presidents, major financial support from sponsoring churches, chaplains with faculty appointments, and the capstone course in "moral philosophy"—have largely vanished, it is a fair question whether the academic and social life at American church-related institutions is different in any discernible way from that to be found at small private colleges without church affiliations.

The portrait of the American church-related college drawn here comprises a challenge for the authors of this volume. We are challenged to explore how church-affiliated institutions can remain critically faithful to their cherished traditions, fulfill their missions to the church and the world, insure that their curricula possess a meaningful core, and take seriously how our colleges participate in the moral and spiritual formation of our students; all the while remembering that we are in an increasingly postmodern intellectual environment that acknowledges and embraces pluralism. In addition, we are challenged to consider how each of us can contribute to making our institutions' religious commitments a more visible aspect of their identities in the future.

✠

PART ONE

Introduction

A Review of Research on Church-Related Higher Education

Stephen R. Haynes

In 1944, Albea Godbold began a study of "church colleges in the old South" with a note of deep concern. "Many are asking," he wrote, "can the church college survive? Does it have a place in the American system of higher education? Can it, or dare it, be Christian?"[1] In 1953, Winthrop Hudson lamented that denominational colleges had long since lost any significant religious heritage.[2] In 1969, Charles S. McCoy wondered "what roles and functions are appropriate to [church colleges] in this age of the public college and federal-grant university? Do they have a future? Should the relation between church and college be severed?"[3] More recently, in 1991, James Tunstead Burtchaell asked: "In what form can these colleges survive," and "What role will they play in American higher education in the future?" The consistency in these expressions of concern indicates that certain critical questions—can church-related colleges and universities survive, and can they remain relevant and distinctive—have been with us for at least half a century. In the chapters that follow, junior teacher-scholars at church-related colleges and universities who are participants in The Rhodes Consultation on the Future of the Church-Related College address these very questions. As an introduction to their work, this chapter offers a brief history of American church-related higher education and a review of twentieth-century scholarship dealing with the phenomenon.

A HISTORICAL OVERVIEW

THROUGH THE NINETEENTH CENTURY

The first American colleges were founded to serve the welfare of their communities. Though it is sometimes claimed that these colleges existed for the sole purpose of educating clergy, in fact they prepared graduates for all the professions. These colleges dominated the American scene during the colonial and early national periods. In fact, Robert Pace notes, "from the mid-seventeenth century to the mid-twentieth century, higher education was mainly private and mainly Protestant."[4]

The years between 1820 and 1870 saw an explosion of denominational schools and colleges, an eruption accompanied by a high mortality rate. The surviving schools were more sectarian than their colonial predecessors and less committed to serving the public good. Among the conditions that encouraged the emergence of the denominational college in the nineteenth century were westward expansion, flexible academic standards, and Protestantism's disposition to fragmentation. Another factor was the "Dartmouth" Supreme Court case of 1819, which assured that private institutions could remain free from state interference. Yet because college founding was "undertaken in the same spirit as canal-building, cotton-ginning, farming and gold-mining,"[5] many institutions were exceedingly fragile:

> Often when a college had a building, it had no students. If it had students, frequently it had no building. If it had either, then perhaps it had no money, perhaps no professors; if professors, then no president, if a president, then no professors. Perhaps as many as seven hundred colleges tried and failed before the Civil War.[6]

The rapid appearance and extinction of denominational colleges in the nineteenth century contributed to a chaotic educational environment and, ironically, fueled suspicion regarding experiments in public higher education. In fact, by late in the century the "diversity of sects, religious conservatism, and the American insistence upon radical separation of church and state created a suspicion of tax-supported higher education and an active opposition to it."[7] After the Morrill Act of 1862, however, the American public began to embrace the notion of public higher education. This embrace was aided in the twentieth century by the ideological shift from elite to democratic notions of education, a shift that gradually moved from the secondary to post-secondary level. Meanwhile, the emerging state universities were often as religious as the denominational colleges with which they were in competition.

In the last third of the nineteenth century, American higher education was further diversified by a new kind of private university initiated and financed by wealthy industrialists such as Johns Hopkins, Leland Stanford, and John D. Rockefeller. Newly established state universities shared with these private institutions a "vision of mind as being in the service of society."[8] The influx of new money into American higher education from public and private sources brought significant changes: its center of gravity shifted westward from New England, the number of students attending college grew dramatically, businessmen replaced clergymen as trustees, laymen replaced ministers as college presidents, and both the liberal arts ideal and the influence of denominational colleges was eroded.[9]

Perhaps the most significant new feature to appear on the academic landscape between the Civil War and World War I was application of a German pattern of university education, distinguished by its emphases on academic freedom and "scientific" research. The first Germanized institution to flourish in American soil was Johns Hopkins University, founded in 1876. Up to this time American colleges and universities generally conformed to the English collegiate model that placed emphasis on "teaching rather than on study; on students, rather than scholars; on order and discipline, rather than learning."[10]

Following the Civil War, American church colleges were forced to respond to a series of actual and predicted changes in higher education that threatened their identity and their existence. Among the defensive actions taken in the postbellum period was a struggle to preserve the classics against the advocates of the scientific curriculum.[11] By the end of the nineteenth century, church colleges faced further challenges:

increased competition for resources and support, waning public influence, and enrollment of a shrinking proportion of the student population. As we shall see, these challenges were the seeds of a lingering identity crisis that would beset church-affiliated colleges throughout the twentieth century.[12]

EARLY TWENTIETH CENTURY

As the twentieth century commenced, the educational landscape became even more inhospitable for church colleges and the pressure to adapt intensified. Although the proportion of students in private institutions was still considerably greater than that enrolled in public institutions (the numbers would not be in balance until 1950), a series of notable educators predicted the imminent demise of the small liberal arts college. The most influential was William Rainey Harper, whose *Prospects of the Small College* (1900) delineated the forces he believed would impede the development of smaller institutions. Among these were the rise of the state university, the tendency toward specialization, the difficulty of keeping strong faculty from departing for larger institutions, and the decline of the "sectarian spirit." Harper lamented neither these changes nor the extinction, consolidation, and redefinition they were sure to bring. Yet he firmly believed that, having passed through a struggle which only the fittest institutions would survive, small colleges would eventually contribute to "a system of higher education . . . the lack of which is sadly felt in every sphere of educational activity." For Harper, the term "system" was crucial, for it denoted organization, sharp distinctions, and recognized standards.[13] Harper's conception of religion's role in American higher education is also pivotal. For he was an advocate of the university's messianic role in spreading a "religion of democracy."[14]

Around the turn of the century, amid prodigious growth in American higher education, transformative forces were at work, including the rise of vocationalism, the separation of graduate study from undergraduate work, the implementation of an elective system, and the establishment of entrance exams and accrediting agencies. Also fateful for the future of denominational colleges were well-funded efforts to systematize American higher education. During the century's first decade, Andrew Carnegie and John D. Rockefeller set aside several hundred million dollars to forge "a comprehensive system of higher education." In its dissemination of these funds, The Carnegie Foundation for the Advancement of Teaching's faculty pension program openly discriminated against colleges under denominational control;[15] and though the Rockefeller-supported General Education Board sought to assist high quality denominational schools, its advocacy of national standards in higher education had the effect of diminishing colleges' connections with their denominations and encouraging their gradual secularization.[16]

Thus, as the twentieth century began to unfold, it was not clear whether American church colleges could survive in an educational environment increasingly dominated by the large public university, the research ideal, secularism, and competition for foundation funds.

INTERWAR PERIOD

Following World War I, the troubles facing traditional centers of higher education "multiplied and intensified."[17] "Orthodox doctrine, Victorian mores, and traditional piety" were coming under attack;[18] the fundamentalist/modernist controversy brought conflict to some college campuses; a national wave of student-led protests assailed the tradition of required chapel; unordained men were elected to the presidencies of flagship Protestant-founded universities; and there was a precipitous decline in clergy presence on boards of trust.[19] For church-sponsored institutions, these forces were exacerbated by other developments, including waning denominationalism, the shrinking proportion of American students educated at church colleges, meager financial resources (in some cases, debt outstripped endowment), and "overburdening" (the existence of more colleges than a denomination could effectively support).

Characterizing American higher education between 1919 and 1946, Merrimon Cuninggim highlights the themes of institutional self-examination, curricular experimentation, vocationalism, retrenchment, and rising secularism.[20] However, despite the growing difficulties facing church colleges, there were signs of religious vibrancy in American higher education. For instance, the interwar period saw a series of national conventions on the vocation of the Christian college (e.g., at Princeton in 1928 and Chicago in 1930), an ecumenical and international student Christian movement, the beginnings of a "theological renaissance" that would leave a lasting impression on Protestant Christianity, attempts to promote the academic study of religion at colleges and universities, and the founding of new organizations and initiatives—including the National Council of Religion in Higher Education (1922), its Kent Fellows program for college graduates interested in professional work in higher education (1924), the University Christian Mission (1938), the United Student Christian Council (1942), and the Faculty Committee on Religion and Higher Education (1944).[21]

Writing in 1947, Cuninggim observed that during the interwar period the "undiluted optimism" of the turn of the century gradually had been replaced by "chastened confidence." Studies of church-related higher education written between the wars confirm Cuninggim's analysis by evincing both a vague dread of the future and soul-searching exploration of the meaning and purpose of the church college. Yet despite the changes that were underway during the first half of the century, church-related colleges remained a major feature on the landscape of American higher education, and a major asset of the church. The vast majority of mainstream Protestant ministers and a great many other professionals were graduates of these institutions.[22]

POSTWAR PERIOD

Beginning about mid-century, the notorious decline of mainline denominations—along with loyalty to these denominations among the populace—exacerbated all the problems reviewed thus far. In addition, World War II brought into view a new array of societal ambiguities with implications for higher education. On the one hand, secularism was on the offensive: The Harvard Report entitled *General Education in a Free Society* (1945) concluded ominously that "whatever one's views, religion was not now for most colleges a practicable source of intellectual unity."[23] On the other hand, postwar America was in the midst of a resurgence of popular piety. Together with the theological renaissance that had been underway since the 1930s, this revival of religious sentiment fueled a general interest in the connection of faith and higher education.

This interest was expressed in conferences, organizations such as The Commission on Christian Higher Education, and publications like *The Christian Scholar* which appeared in 1953. In a special issue of the journal devoted to the "Christian College," the editor noted that "church-related colleges are discovering new vitality as they seek to bring the Christian faith and understanding to bear upon their total life. . . ."[24] This issue of the journal looked toward the First Quadrennial Convocation of Christian Colleges to be held at Denison University in June 1954, "the first major effort of the Christian colleges to meet together across denominational frontiers for a consideration of their unique responsibility in the total educational scene." Supplemental issues published the proceedings of the Convocation, and those of the Second Quadrennial at Drake University in 1958.[25] Both Convocations were ecumenical and international in focus, and both emphasized the Christian college's contribution to higher education; the participants were applauded for their willingness to take up "the serious intellectual tasks facing the church in higher education."[26]

In 1952 the Danforth Foundation initiated a summer seminar for college faculty, while the Hazen Foundation's work in the area included cosponsorship of several "Faculty Consultations on Religion in Higher Education" between 1945 and 1949, and publication of a series of pamphlets dealing with the place of religion in higher education.[27] Another measure of postwar interest in the connection of religion and education was the so-called Christian University Movement, a broad group of individuals and organizations which during the 1940s and 1950s sought to critique the intellectual basis of higher education on Christian grounds.[28] Works associated with the movement—for instance, Sir Walter Moberly's *The Crisis in the University* (1949) and Alexander Miller's *Faith and Learning*

(1960)—proclaimed a new opportunity for faith in the university.

The result of these paradoxical tendencies seems to have been the emergence of an identity crisis within church-affiliated education as a whole. Bradley Longfield and George Marsden argue that already by the 1940s American theological pluralism had created such a crisis among church-related schools.[29] According to Dorothy Bass, by mid-century church-related colleges "began to report haziness of purpose and to conduct studies into their identity."[30] Douglas Sloan adds that "by the beginning of the 1960s . . . the role of the church-related college . . . seemed as elusive as ever."[31] Though "the main contours of the contemporary situation were already in place during the middle years of this century,"[32] perception of the crisis developed slowly. Recognition accompanied growth in the federal government's involvement in higher education (the "GI Bill" of 1944, the National Defense Act of 1958, the Higher Education Act of 1965, and the Education Amendments of 1972), expansion in public education, and shrinkage in the proportion of students educated at church-related colleges.

Perhaps the most accurate measure of the growing identity crisis among American church-related colleges is the number of studies of this sector of higher education that appeared between 1950 and 1980, most of which attempted to restore the prestige, vigor, and clarity of purpose that seemed to be steadily eluding Christian liberal arts education as the twentieth century wore on.

1960S AND BEYOND

Identity crises, of course, can lead to self-examination; and this is precisely what happened among church-related colleges in the 1960s and following. Ben C. Fisher has referred to the period between 1960 and 1980 as an "era of reexamination and reappraisal of the church-related college in America."[33] The reasons for this mood of reappraisal were spiritual (e.g., the crisis within mainline denominations regarding their role in a pluralistic society), economic (e.g., the steady diminishment of funds flowing between denominations and their colleges),[34] and social (e.g., the emergence of the community college, waning denominational loyalty, and disenchantment with higher education generally as campuses became hotbeds of social agitation.)[35] If these forces provided the rationale for self-scrutiny among church-related colleges, the Danforth Foundation provided both encouragement and means. Led by its able director Merrimon Cuninggim, the foundation exercised a profound influence on the self-understanding and self-confidence of church-affiliated colleges during the 1960s and 1970s.[36]

Nevertheless, Robert Wood Lynn has called the history of church-related colleges since the mid-1970s "an unraveling fabric." The disintegration connoted by this phrase is in part a result of the Protestant cultural hegemony's demise and a growing sense of church-related higher education's minority status relative to the public sector.[37] But other factors have been at work as well, including the collapse of the University Christian Movement in 1969, the demise of the Faculty Christian Fellowship about the same time, the disappearance of "Religion and Higher Education" programs at Yale and other leading graduate schools in the 1970s, Danforth's decision to concentrate the foundation's efforts and resources in St. Louis, and the bewildering variety of schools that over time have come to call themselves church-related.[38] Exacerbating all these trends have been increasing financial pressures and growing competition from public education. Among the various responses to these forces are renewed calls for "excellence," reminders of the college's role in the "integration" of faith and learning, and pleas for a return to the distinctively "Christian college," a term that, along with "Protestant college," had fallen into disuse since the 1960s.[39]

For reasons that are not entirely clear, the last decade or so has brought a rekindling of interest in the role of religion in American higher education.[40] Several high-profile studies published during the 1990s analyzed the process of secularization in American society and its implications for higher learning. Douglas Sloan, George Marsden, and James Tunstead Burtchaell each described how faith had been displaced from the center of American intellectual life and gradually propelled to the margins during the first half of the twentieth century as a naturalist ethos became ascendant in the country's leading universities. Furthermore, each of these authors called   atten-tion to an important irony: throughout the twentieth century religion's cultural displacement was expedited by Christian leaders who chose to sacrifice religious identity at the altar of relevance and acclaim. Though they do not directly address the contemporary situation of the church-related college, these studies remind advocates of church-sponsored higher educa-tion that its privileged societal role could not be regained any more than the Christian cultural hegemony could be reestab-lished. Before we look more closely at these recent studies, we shall review American scholarship on church-related higher education.

SCHOLARSHIP ON CHURCH-RELATED HIGHER EDUCATION

1930s AND 1940s

One of the first scholarly studies of church-affiliated col-leges in America was Leslie Karr Patton's *The Purposes of Church-Related Colleges* (1940).[41] Striking the chord of uncer-tainty that had come to resonate through the world of higher education after World War I, Patton observed that "the church-related college in the United States today appears to be stand-ing at the parting of the ways." The self-assured past was gone, Patton observed, and he wondered if the future would reveal a clear and viable role for the church in higher education. Patton was particularly concerned by the fact that the relative unanimity concerning collegiate "aims" that had reigned un-til the Civil War had been replaced by "much confusion . . . as to the aims and purposes of the church-related college."

Patton's study was both descriptive and programmatic. He wished to determine what functions church-related colleges were claiming, as well as which were most fitting. Of the nine major aims commonly cited by church colleges in the 1930s, Patton could endorse only three—preparation for citizenship, attention to the individual, and the development of charac-ter—as appropriately "Christian." In fact, he concluded that most of the institutions in his sample did "not emphasize their church relationship," with many of them taking "great pains to stress their nonsectarian policies and practices."[42] In some ways Patton's study exuded the pieties of liberal Protestantism: he tended to equate "Christian" with "reverence for personality" and believed that Christian character should express itself primarily through social leadership. Nevertheless, much of what he observed in 1940 has perennial significance. For instance, Patton showed that the rhetoric of "Christian character" could be defined quite variously, or not at all. He noted that many of the things church-related institutions profess to offer students are not distinctively "Christian," being claimed by every liberal arts college and many large universities. And Patton was critical of the accommodations church-related institutions were making to modern secular trends in higher education.

One other book-length study from the interwar period deserves mention. In *The Church Follows its Students* (1938), Clarence P. Shedd drew attention to a trend that had been evident for some time—the focus of the church's ministry at public institutions of higher learning. Observing that the first student YMCAs were founded at state universities in the 1850s, Shedd noted that "beginning about 1900 the church awoke to the fact that the majority of its students were in tax-supported institutions . . . [and] evolved through a process of trial and error a wholly new student ministry, the university pastorate."[43] Shedd chronicled the origins of this movement, which he regarded as "equal in importance and significance to the church-related college."[44] If Shedd's assessment were correct, then it raised a serious question for the church: Where should it direct its limited resources in higher education? Shedd and other progressive thinkers of his time pushed the church to consider rethinking its educational role in a changing society. Yet the notion that Christians should concentrate their resources to establish vital ministries at secular colleges and universities further diminished the prospects that church colleges would survive in their old form.[45]

Postwar Period

The first major postwar work to assess the religious situation as it related to church-affiliated institutions was Merrimon

Cuninggim's *The College Seeks Religion* (1947). This book
unmistakably reflected the optimism of the postwar period
with regard to religion's role in American society. Cuninggim
suggested, in fact, that the secularization of higher education
was on the wane (having peaked during the century's second
decade) and that religion occupied "a larger place in the colleges' thinking and practice than at any time in the twentieth
century."[46] With reference to the church-related college,
Cuninggim perceived a gradual shift "from defense to affirmation," evident in a new note of confidence in the statements
of college presidents. Cuninggim celebrated both the demise
of "sectarianism" and the birth of a more ecumenical and liberal spirit at church-related institutions.

During the 1950s many observers concurred that a *kairos* for
church-related higher education had arrived. One was Howard
Lowry, President of the Presbyterian-affiliated College of
Wooster, whose book *The Mind's Adventure* has been called "the
most significant work about the church college produced with
the full backing of an old-line denomination during the 1950s."
Lowry endeavored to resuscitate a principle declared moribund
in the 1945 Harvard report: "Christianity gives meaning and
ultimate unity to all parts of the curriculum, indeed to the
whole life of the college."[47] Lowry acknowledged the new pluralism in America, but denied that it necessitated the end of
Protestant leadership in higher education. Instead, he invoked
the unifying power of "religion," and appealed to the "Hebraic-
Christian tradition" as a source of continuity in American life.[48]
Similarly emboldened by the ongoing "religious revival,"
Alexander Miller assailed the modern university's failure to
locate a principle of order and provide students with a coherent life philosophy. Miller opined that "the Community of Faith
and the Community of Learning are coming to a new self-con-
sciousness," and envisioned "the possibility of a new and fruit-
ful encounter between Faith and Learning."[49]

Naturally, these works "stirred new interest in the nature
and purpose of the specifically church-related college and . . .
inspire[d] new hopes for its future."[50] Yet it is important to note
that during this time there were less promising words being
spoken regarding the future of the church college. For instance,

an editorial appearing in *The Christian Century* in 1951 entitled "Church Colleges in Trouble" assessed the situation with brutal honesty.[51] The colleges were "communities of apprehensive and often distracted men and women," the author warned. The "grim facts of life" which they had to face were sharp declines in enrollments (in part due to the diminishment of students enjoying GI benefits), shrinking income investments, spreading red ink, and a superfluity of church colleges, many of which were losing their distinctive character due to their acceptance of financial salvation from the government and armed forces. The trouble had "been a long time growing" and began with the rise of the state universities, the author continued; "scores of them are doomed," unless consolidation among these colleges is actively pursued.

The same year, Thorton W. Merriam, while acknowledging that the atmosphere in higher education was more favorable to religion than in the recent past, was forced to admit that some things had changed forever. According to Merriam, it is

> this acute awareness of all-enveloping and uncontrolled social forces and bafflement as to how religion and education ought to be related to them which mark a major difference between the attitude of the sensitive religious educator today and his predecessor of a quarter-century ago. What then looked like a land of promise, to be laid under cultivation by hard work and good will, now seems like a land of doom.[52]

Ultimately, optimism would not be a sufficient response to the emerging crisis: As Robert Wood Lynn writes of Howard Lowry, his heroic efforts to preserve a place at the center of American higher education for the recognizably Protestant college could not reverse its "actual drift toward the margins."[53]

1960s

As we turn to the 1960s, we once again begin our survey of scholarship on church-affiliated higher education with Merrimon Cuninggim, who in 1961 published *The Protestant Stake in Higher Education*. In this book Cuninggim was interested in assessing the church-related college's academic "quality," particularly in the areas of teaching and research. He expressed "serious concern" for the future of Christian higher education and inquired as honestly as possible, How good are the church-related colleges? Although he acknowledged "marks of vigor," Cuninggim concluded that as a group these colleges "lie somewhere between the middle and the end of the academic procession, closer to the end than to the middle."[54] Perhaps the book's most damning judgment was that Protestant colleges ranked "only fair or poor on items that are most often used as their raison d'être": great teaching, the study of religion, encouragement of campus religious life, and the virtues of smallness. Cuninggim's overall conclusion was unflinching: "Protestant church-related colleges as a group are not quality institutions. They are not as good as we think they are; they are not as good as they claim to be; they are not as good as they ought to be; they are not good."[55] Cuninggim's plan for helping the church reclaim its stake in higher education required Protestantism once again to assume its role as "the conscience for the totality of American higher education."[56]

Myron F. Wicke's *The Church-Related College* (1964) reported the results of a questionnaire completed by two hundred college administrators. Wicke's chief concern was "whether or not the church-related college [had] in fact a unique and essential role to play in American higher education."[57] Answering this question was difficult, he found, because as a group these colleges had not maintained clear identities.[58] Having analyzed their purpose statements, Wicke was not convinced that church colleges were committed to intellectual growth, and he warned that Bible or chapel requirements should not bear the burden of a distinctive undergraduate education. Wicke opined that the future of church colleges depended in part upon their ability to define clearly their mission in the future.

The Danforth Foundation's landmark contribution to assessing the situation of religiously affiliated colleges was a "systematic assessment of church-related higher education in the United States" directed by the Danforth Commission on Church Colleges and Universities and published in 1966.[59] Extending Cuninggim's assessment of collegiate quality, the "Danforth Study" reached the striking conclusion that by and large church colleges were stronger academically than they were religiously! The authors lamented, in fact, that "the intellectual presuppositions which actually guide the activities of most church colleges are heavily weighted in the secular direction." The study commented, as others had, on the success of church-sponsored colleges in preparing students for graduate and professional studies. But it noted colleges' lack of awareness regarding a distinctive educational role and criticized the "institutional imitation" of prestigious secular schools. The Commission identified the fundamental problem facing these colleges as the unstable foundation for religiously oriented educational programs represented by the shifting sands of American culture.

The Danforth Study indicated that by the middle of the 1960s the prospect of secularization had become the central focus for advocates of the church-related college. But not everyone perceived secularization as an unmitigated threat to the church or to its work in higher education. In fact, by 1968 one student of religion and higher education—influenced by the secularity movement in contemporary theology—was welcoming secularization as a sign of the university's inevitable coming of age. In *Secularization and the University* Harry E. Smith utilized the work of German interwar theologians Friedrich Gogarten and Dietrich Bonhoeffer to clarify the concept of "secularization," and applied their insights to the field of higher education.[60] Smith observed that the radical shift in American higher education away from religious domination was "not to be deplored . . . but welcomed as an integral part of the process in which modern man has 'come of age.'"[61] Christians should not give up on higher education, Smith counseled; rather, they ought to view it "not as a realm to be captured and exploited for religious purposes . . . but as a matter of worldly concern equally accessible to Christians and non-Christians."[62] Eschewing normative images of higher education forged in the past, the church should seek a new understanding of its role in higher education. For

> if secularization is interpreted as a historical process of reorientation in man's understanding of the world, God, and himself, a process for which biblical insights are in large part responsible, then the task of the church in higher education is not to belittle

its advent but to understand its roots and accept it, on the one hand, and to prevent its perversion into secularism, on the other.[63]

Smith noted four areas of university life where the church could affirm secularity while remaining critical of secularism: receptivity to all forms of truth, respect for the relative autonomies of university disciplines, concern for faculty and student freedom and responsibility, and respect for diversity in institutional forms and goals. With this relatively favorable assessment of secularization, Smith could interpret prominent twentieth-century trends in higher learning—the rise of experimentation and research, the expansion and revision of the curriculum, the increase of responsibility and freedom among faculty and students, and the decline of denominational control—as "basically liberating" and as signs of maturity for the university that could be embraced by the church.

In 1969, a new perspective on the American church-related college was provided by Andrew M. Greeley's *From Backwater to Mainstream: A Profile of Catholic Higher Education*.[64] Up to this time, and unfortunately to the present moment, the term "church-related college" was used as shorthand for colleges founded and maintained by Protestant denominations. But *From Backwater to Mainstream*, written under the auspices of the Carnegie Commission, presented a portrait of American higher education that featured Catholic institutions' distinctive histories, their special problems and challenges, and their unique contributions toward an innovative future for American higher learning. Drawing on the work of Philip Gleason (and other pioneers in the area) and on a broad statistical picture of Catholic colleges, Greeley illumined the atmosphere and mission of these colleges at the end of the 1960s.

Greeley emphasized the tremendous diversity within the group of 350 America colleges and universities affiliated with the Roman Catholic Church and used this diversity to slay the myth of the American Church as a "massive, smoothly organized and efficiently operating monolith." To reinforce his point that the Catholic higher educational "system" possessed neither organizational nor ideological unity, Greeley observed that some schools have barely heard that there was a Second Vatican Council, and others are preparing for the day when they can have major influence at Vatican III. Some are seeking academic excellence with so great a hunger that they can almost taste it, and others are quite content to produce docile, upper-middle-class parishioners. Some are bent on being as secular as possible, while others are terrified that hiring even one non-Catholic faculty member may threaten their right to be called a Catholic college. Some of their faculty (and particularly the non-Catholic faculty) are enthusiastic and loyal to their schools, while others are openly critical and content that the idea of a Catholic college is a contradiction in terms. . . . Almost all the schools are in financial difficulty, but some face the future with hope and optimism and others with the grim conviction that their days are numbered, and they may well be. [65]

Greeley anchored this diverse reality in the history of American Catholic colleges and universities, which tended to be founded more recently than their Protestant counterparts (about three-fourths of them in the twentieth century), generally in order to serve the Catholic immigrant population. Greeley also treated more recent trends—for instance, the fantastic rate of expansion in the 1940s, the "quest for excellence" in the 1950s and 1960s, and the push toward "secularization" (which in the Catholic sphere referred to laicization and professionalization on campuses)—and argued that Catholic education was then reflecting the last stages of the American acculturation process affecting Catholicism as a whole.

It is instructive to note that, despite Greeley's limited focus, the problem areas he identified at Catholic institutions were many of the same being described in studies of Protestant colleges: imitation of secular schools, financial strain, faculty recruitment, church-college relations, resistance to compulsory religious exercises, and lack of inter-institutional cooperation.

1970s

To date the most prolific decade for studies of church-affiliated higher education has been the 1970s, when trends inside and outside American higher education led to a serious reassessment of the identity and future of church-related colleges.

In 1970 a volume entitled *The Contribution of the Church-Related College to the Public Good* assumed a defeatist attitude before the specter of secularization, and asked quite candidly whether it might be in "the public good that church-related institutions go out of business and become either Christian institutions in the broader sense or go totally secular."[66] Charles McCoy's contribution to this volume, entitled "The Church-Related College in American Society," went straight to the point: "What will be lost to American society and the churches if church-related colleges sever their denomination ties?" In pursuit of an answer to this question, McCoy observed that the quest to describe some unique function that only church-related colleges can perform is illusory, and may even subvert Christian purposes; rather, these colleges ought to be asking "what is the common good? And how can we contribute to it?" According to McCoy, the church colleges' principle contribution to the common good will lie in fighting the deadly tendency toward sameness in American higher education by safeguarding its diversity, in part through pioneering new approaches to teaching and learning and through inter-college cooperation. McCoy added that in 1970 the state, not the church, represented the major threat to both freedom and diversity in American higher education.[67]

In 1972 McCoy published *The Responsible Campus: Toward a New Identity for the Church-Related College*, in which he complained about diminished quality and inadequate leadership in this sector of higher education, and pointed out that a far smaller proportion of students attended church-related colleges than had been the case in 1900. McCoy expressed ambivalence regarding the future of church-related college. On the one hand, he proclaimed that just when church-related institutions had been pronounced moribund they "unexpectedly began to show signs of life." On the other hand, he acknowledged a pervasive sense of uncertainty on many campuses and foresaw the arrival of "an agonizing time of reappraisal." All this resulted, McCoy claimed, from a crisis of identity in the church-related college that derived from the tension "between its sectarian past and its public present." For some colleges, McCoy opined, the tension created by this role diffusion was being "elevated into agonizing awareness."[68]

The same year also saw the appearance of C. Robert Pace's *Education and Evangelism*. Pace's Carnegie-funded study of eighty Protestant colleges conducted between 1966 and 1970 was "explorative and descriptive" and motivated by recurrent and troubling questions. To the familiar issue of collegiate quality Pace added another persistent concern: whether there exists a unique Protestant college environment. To answer this question, Pace statistically assessed several dimensions of campus environment: *scholarship* (intellectuality and scholastic discipline), *awareness* (concern about and emphasis on personal, poetic and political meaning), *community* (campus friendliness and cohesiveness), *propriety* (politeness and considerateness), and *practicality* (enterprise, organization, material benefits, and social activities). Pace's data included questionnaire responses and observations made during short visits to the campuses under study.

Pace's study merits attention because it differed in important ways from most of those that preceded it. First, it gave considerable attention to the experiences and values of Protestant colleges' students and graduates. Second, Pace was the first to deal systematically with an issue that was of growing interest in the 1970s—the differences between "mainline" and "evangelical" Protestant colleges. Not surprisingly, Pace concluded that institutions affiliated with evangelical or fundamentalist groups were more distinctive than their mainline-affiliated counterparts. However, he also determined that these colleges were "undifferentiated from mainline Protestant colleges with regard to scholarship and awareness, a fact indicating that education and evangelism are not incompatible."[69] As McCoy had done, Pace identified signs of life on Protestant college campuses. He remarked, for instance, that four of the schools he visited had new and impressive chapel buildings. Overall, though, Pace's conclusions regarding the distinctiveness of Protestant colleges were less than encouraging. The environments at some of these schools were frankly "tepid," leading Pace to ask:

> Is there a Protestant college environment that is in any way dis-
> tinctive? If all one knew about a liberal arts college was its asso-
> ciation with a mainline Protestant denomination, the only thing
> one could say about it with any assurance is that its general at-
> mosphere will be friendly, supportive, and congenial.[70]

The number of books and articles dealing with American church-related colleges and universities diminished noticeably in the second half of the 1970s, although a few organizations and agencies were still conducting studies dealing with this segment of higher education. One example is *A Dialogue on Achieving the Mission of Church-Related Institutions of Higher Learning*, published by the American Association of Colleges in 1977.[71] The dialogue referred to in the book's title took place in 1976 at Rockhurst College and involved about fifty admin-istrators (and a few faculty members) from twenty-seven church-affiliated colleges and universities. The dialogue began with a series of questions that had become familiar to advocates of church-related higher education. They included, "What does it mean to be a Christian college or university to-day? Have any of us lost our mission? Has Christian higher education been compromised by the exigencies of a secular world?"[72] The ensuing discussion affirmed the "special role" of Christian colleges in American higher education, but did little to clarify that role. It did, however, raise questions that had been largely ignored in previous scholarship: "What is the importance of faculty influence on individual students, on curriculum, on religious life and perspective? How can fac-ulty members be encouraged to share actively in the Christian mission of the college?"[73]

The major study to appear in the second half of the 1970s was a multi-author volume entitled *Church-Related Higher Edu-cation: Perceptions and Perspectives.* The book addressed well-publicized issues ("problems of purpose, self-doubt, support, even survival") and posed familiar questions: "Do the church-related colleges have a distinctive contribution to make to the churches? To the enrichment of higher education? To the qual-ity of life in America?"[74] What distinguished this volume from previous studies, aside from its sponsorship by the National Council of Churches, was its emphasis on pluralism within

American higher education and within the church-related sector. Section One—Merrimon Cuninggim's "Varieties of Church-Related Higher Education"—included a typology of church relatedness featuring the descriptors *consonant, proclaiming,* and *embodying*. This typology took into consideration the way a school's church relatedness may change over time, but Cuninggim stressed that movement between his categories need not signify a greater or lesser degree of church-relatedness.

Cuninggim's contribution to the volume also included a chapter on the "essentials of church-relatedness." Cuninggim began with the observation that to be church-related, a college must want to be, and know why it wants to be:

> There must be on the part of the college a conscious intention to achieve and maintain a continuing relationship with a church or perhaps churches and a significant measure of congruence among the constituent groups of the college in their understanding of the intention.[75]

Further essentials of church-relatedness mentioned by Cuninggim included making provision for religion in all its dimensions, and putting its values and those of its church into recognizable operation in every aspect of the college's life, including the campus ethos.

In a chapter entitled "An Overview of Current Denominational Policies and Studies in Higher Education," Robert Rue Parsonage observed that the various problems cited in denominational studies of church-related colleges "seem to be rooted in a larger identity crisis: what is the present and future mission of the church-related college, and what is or ought to be its relationship to the church?" The book also included an insightful article by James H. Smylie which explored how the American church-related college had arrived at its present position. Smylie noted how much American higher education had changed, recalling that while state-supported institutions were on the defensive in the early nineteenth century, presently church-related institutions were having to justify their very existence! Looking toward the future, Smylie concluded that "the road ahead does not look easy."[76]

1980s

The culmination of the 1970s' considerable output of scholarship on church-related higher education actually appeared in 1980. It was a series of four volumes (in pamphlet form, but averaging around two hundred pages per volume) entitled *Church and College: A Vital Partnership.*[77] The series was published by The National Congress on Church-Related Colleges and Universities, "a cooperative effort of twenty-three denominations to examine the issues facing their institutions of higher education." Launched by Executives for Church-Related Higher Education, the Congress carried out a two-part program: 1) sponsorship of events to educate the public about church-related colleges, and 2) examination of salient issues and the way denominations and institutions could deal with them. The series of books sponsored by the Congress was quite diverse. It included papers and addresses from national meetings held in 1979 and 1980, summaries of other conference sessions, studies of legal, social, and policy issues facing church-related colleges, a self-study inventory, and extensive bibliographical materials. But it is of interest mainly because it represents a transition between the high-profile and high-quality studies of the 1960s and 1970s and the denominationally funded and poorly circulated works produced during the 1980s.

In fact, a chief feature of discussions on church-related higher education during the 1980s is scholarly silence.[78] When the silence was occasionally broken, the old malaise was very much in evidence. For instance, in 1988 Richard G. Hutcheson, Jr.'s article in *The Christian Century* temporarily resurrected the moribund debate on the identity of church-related institutions by recounting, anecdotally and otherwise, the Protestant college's decline and offering a vision of rejuvenation for Christian higher education in general.[79] Hutcheson summarized the situation at many church-sponsored colleges:

> Beyond having a historical tie to a particular denomination, offering some religion courses and some elective extracurricular activities, they would be hard-pressed to demonstrate how their church relationship affects their academic program or campus life.[80]

As with many earlier critics, Hutcheson's plan for helping the church college discover an identity recalled a time of certainty before these colleges had lost their way. Colleges that proclaim the sovereign God incarnate in Jesus Christ, that offer courses that reflect a Christian worldview and faculty committed to Christian values and lifestyle, and that promote an unfettered pursuit of truth, Hutcheson maintained, would "add to American culture and higher education a distinctively Christian world view and value system."[81] A published response to Hutcheson's article by F. Thomas Trotter called the discussion back to harsh realities, including the necessity of meeting criteria for government funding.[82] Trotter's rebuttal demonstrated that by the late 1980s even supporters of church-related higher education were in considerable disagreement as to whether the Christian liberal arts college remained a feasible entity.

But while the debate over the future of mainline institutions appeared at an impasse, another sort of Christian college was gaining strength and self-confidence. Indeed, most serious studies of church-related higher education published during the 1980s evince an interest in the history and character of the evangelical college. William Ringerberg's *The Christian College* (1984), *Making Higher Education Christian* (1987), edited by Joel A. Carpenter and Kenneth W. Shipps, and Ben C. Fisher's *The Idea of a Christian University in Today's World* (1989) all reflect this growth of scholarly interest in "Christian colleges," with or without denominational ties.[83]

1990s

The 1990s saw a renewal of interest in the history and future of church-related institutions. Some of the studies in this area focused on the stories of particular colleges and universities, while others traced the process of secularization within denominations.[84] Among the many articles that treated large segments of the church-related population were Robert Wood Lynn's "'The Survival of Recognizably Protestant Colleges': Reflections on Old-Line Protestantism, 1950–1990" (1992), and Dorothy Bass's "Church-Related Colleges: Transmitters of Denominational Cultures?" (1993).[85] Bass paid special attention to the "new authority of university standards and values to shape perceptions," particularly with regard to faculty professionalization. She answered the question stated in her subtitle by concluding that most church-related colleges were not effective agents for the transmission of denominational identity. But she did not find this particularly lamentable, given the "ecumenical consensus" that this is not their primary role, as well as the new identity of many of these institutions as first-rate colleges of the liberal arts.

Several book-length studies dealing specifically with church-related higher education appeared during the 1990s. The first was *Reclaiming a Mission* (1990) by Arthur J. de Jong, president of Whitworth College and veteran leader of religiously affiliated institutions.[86] Despite the author's knowledge and experience, however, *Reclaiming a Mission* suffered from the superficial analyses and vague prescriptions too often associated with the public statements of college presidents. De Jong wrote with the intention of helping advocates of church colleges to grasp the new cultural context in which these schools operated. But in diagnosing changes in American society since World War II and the influence of the public university, de Jong took refuge in attacks on "value-free education," "pluralism," and "secularism"; and offered vague generalizations concerning "a crisis in direction and meaning in nation and individual" and the importance of treating every member of the college community as a "whole person."

De Jong saw his chief contribution to the future of church-related higher education in an analysis of the complementarity between Christian tenets and postmodernism. He described the wane of the "Cartesian-Newtonian paradigm" in American higher education and its slow replacement by "the post-modern science paradigm." De Jong perceived in postmodernism a friendly development for church-affiliated institutions since, in his analysis, it emphasized "integration and wholeness, interdependence and connectedness," and was open to transcendence, and thus to transcendent authority. But De Jong's reading of recent changes in science led him to a sanguine and ultimately superficial understanding of the postmodern and its potential impact on the church-related college.

Another monograph to appear during the early 1990s was Merrimon Cuninggim's *Uneasy Partners: The College and the Church* (1994). Surveying the landscape of religiously affiliated higher education toward the century's end, Cuninggim discovered distinct signs of promise. He observed that since the 1950s many church-related colleges had fared better than their denominations, and his prognosis for these colleges' future was decidedly upbeat. He noted that their leadership was better trained and more able than previously, their resources stronger and getting more so, and their sense of heritage less sentimental and more genuine than ever before. Cuninggim ascribed much recent criticism of church colleges—from educational and ecclesiastical leaders, secularists and neoconservatives—to a stubborn refusal to let these colleges "grow up." For his own part, Cuninggim celebrated a steady evolution in the church-college relationship and identified three stages in this maturing process: at the end of the nineteenth century the church was senior partner and the college junior partner; then, sometime between the 1930s and World War II the relationship became more balanced; more recently, the college had assumed the primary position and could now act as senior partner in the relationship. Cuninggim commented that "this is the time frame we are still in, of course, and are likely to stay."[87]

As this summary suggests, Cuninggim's evolutionary understanding of Christian higher education, in which he traces a "maturing process" across the twentieth century, is unapologetically old liberal.[88] In fact, *Uneasy Partners* reveals the extent to which his view of these colleges is rooted in the Protestant era whose failures George Marsden, Douglas Sloan, and others have so convincingly demonstrated.[89] Cuninggim recognizes that American church-related colleges have changed dramatically since World War II. Yet his awareness that a new day has dawned does not deter him from interpreting these colleges and their critics on the basis of solidly modernist cultural assumptions. Cuninggim perceives in the evolution of church-affiliated colleges a "steadily growing maturity." But where is this newly matured college heading? Cuninggim's own prescriptions for the future are decidedly vague or platitudinous. No one would deny that the church-college relationship must be "credible and mutually understood," or that the college must remain "loyal to its values." But none of this is very useful in helping the church-related college face the future.

To displace the stereotypes forged in a previous era, Cuninggim suggests a new archetype for the church-related college with three requisites: an appreciation of its past, an understanding of and practice of its essential values, and a desire to hold on to a genuine, defensible relationship with its church. However, reflecting on perennial attempts to identify the "marks" of the church-related college, Cuninggim argues that diversity in the ranks makes doing so extremely difficult. He even criticizes his own previous attempts to identify such marks, and chides scholars who refuse to relinquish earlier patterns of church relatedness. In the Afterword, we will revisit the matter of how to classify church-related institutions in the twenty-first century.

The last major study of church-affiliated higher education to appear in the 1990s was also the most substantial. James Tunstead Burtchaell's *The Dying of the Light* (1998) continues to be the book everyone concerned with this matter talks about, but few read (it contains nearly nine hundred pages of difficult prose).[90] Helpfully, the book is divided into seven sections corresponding to the various denominations Burtchaell treats (Congregationalists, Presbyterians, Methodists, Baptists, Lutherans, Catholics, and Evangelicals). And though each section treats only two or three colleges, the analysis is so detailed and comprehensive that one can fairly extrapolate from these case studies a history of each denomination's involvement in higher education. Burtchaell's thesis is stated in his preface and reiterated throughout:

> My study . . . discerns the dynamics and rationales at various times whereby the link of mutual patronage between college and church was severed in this century—severed, paradoxically, just at the time when the resources were first in place to allow a vital

synergism, and severed by the hand of ecclesiastics and academics who saw themselves as uniting both identities within themselves, but not within their institutions.[91]

Reviews of Burtchaell's tome have tended to be quite critical and have taken the author to task for purported errors in his interpretation of institutional histories as well as his overall pessimism. But one thing can not be denied: Burtchaell has done his homework. Each of the chapters (the longest of which approaches 30,000 words) is filled with the sort of information that one gleans not only from catalogs and official publications, but from trustee and faculty meeting minutes, legal documents, and personal correspondence and interviews. Because of his thorough research—and his impatience with rhetoric and religious window dressing—one is likely to learn more about an institution from Burtchaell's book than from any official history. For our purposes, two aspects of Burtchaell's contribution to scholarship on church-related higher education are significant. One is the way campus secularization is reflected in the shifting identities and loyalties of faculty members. The other is his sobering realism.

Burtchaell demonstrates in case after case how faculties gradually "lose interest" in an institution's religious tradition. While pious presidents often orchestrate "the critical turn away from Christian accountability," Burtchaell never loses sight of the fact that "whatever presidents and trustees do, whatever be the market forces imposed by those who pay (students and benefactors), the inertial force of these institutions is in their faculties." Thus Burtchaell emphasizes that in the schools he studied, "the faculty was the first constituency to lose interest in their colleges being Lutheran or Catholic or Congregational."[92] They are aided in this process, of course, by many factors. The administration turns campus religious life over to a new class of "religious functionaries"; the emergence of academic disciplines leads to the marginalization of theological discourse; over time, teachers' self-understanding slowly detaches itself from an institution and fastens itself to a discipline or the profession itself. In one paragraph that is characteristic in its careful prose and wry humor, Burtchaell describes the inexorable process by which church affiliation ceases to matter to faculty:

> Because stridency is usually no help to a career, the growing indifference of the professorate to the religious identity of the colleges was usually expressed by silence and absence. At first they took the religious character of the college for granted, or even as a saving grace; but it became an aspect, like the food service, which did not require their management. In that mode they might attend chapel, but no longer be called upon to lead the prayers. Later the religious aspect would take on the weight of a burden, and they would find reasons not to go to chapel. Later still, they needed no reasons. And if in early years they would be chided for it, the chiding rarefied, then ceased. Then it became a matter of indifference in the evaluation of prospective colleagues, though for some years the subject of religion might continue to be raised in the interview with the president or, later, the dean. But those exchanges quickly became stylized: the president's question would be framed in increasingly helpful, i.e., indistinct, terminology, and would lead dialectically to an answer that was an equally indistinct affirmation. As the process worked its way closer toward its term, those conversations brought both affirmations in tones that shifted from assurance to nonchalance, to impatience, and then, to affront. By that time the requisite faculty solidarity with the character of the college would have been significantly reduced as to both noun and verb. The identity would slide from Methodist to evangelical, to Christian, to religious, to wholesome, to "the goals of the college," which by then were stated in intangible terms. The required affirmation would devolve from active membership in the sponsoring church or denomination to nominal membership, to acceptance of the college's own faith statement, to silent tolerance of the ill-specified purposes of the institution.[93]

Burtchaell's second contribution to the debate over the future of church-related higher education is his dogged pessimism, a pessimism anchored firmly in the narratives of self-deception and cowardice that hastened the process of alienation at many of the church-affiliated institutions he has studied. In contrast, the other studies from the 1990s reviewed here exude an optimism regarding the future of church-related higher education that has not been in evidence since the 1950s. This optimism may be based on the arrival of the academic postmodern (De Jong and Marsden), the excellence and notoriety achieved by many church-affiliated institutions (Bass), or the college's new maturity vis-à-vis the church (Cuninggim). But this hopefulness is insidious inasmuch as it tempts us to overlook the real threats to meaningful religious identity that exist at church-related colleges and universities.

By themselves, neither national recognition, freedom from dependence on the church, nor the passing of modernism guarantee a future for church-related higher education. Rather, each represents an opportunity for colleges and denominations to begin the serious theological and practical work that will insure a meaningfully church-related future. These trends do not insure this future any more than did the "religious revival" of the 1950s, the enthusiasm for secularity of the 1960s, or the substantial new funding sources that have appeared since 1970. Church-related institutions may be freer and healthier than ever. But history teaches us that there is no inexorable force guiding them toward a meaningful religious identity. Rather, this goal is as elusive in good times as in bad.

THE FUTURE?

As our survey indicates, twentieth-century scholarship on religiously affiliated higher education in America is simultaneously consistent and varied. From the beginning, the specters of marginalization, obsolescence, and extinction have made proponents of the church-related college anxious. In fact, one has to return to the days prior to America's involvement in World War I to find a study of Christian higher education that does not exude angst about the future.[94] Around mid-century, this anxiety intensified and widespread acknowledgment of an identity crisis for Christian colleges forced advocates of these institutions to enter upon a long season of self-scrutiny.

But while the perception of crisis has been relatively persistent, the themes guiding the resulting self-examination have shifted many times: from an assessment of quality, to a struggle with secularization in higher education and in the larger society, to a focus on serving the public good, to an attempt to identify what, if anything, is distinctive about the educational atmosphere of the church-related college, to acknowledgments of pluralism in society and pleas for diversity within higher education, to a focus on financial realities and the necessity of survival, to calls for a new maturity, to a hearty embrace of postmodernism.

Where is the discussion now, as we stand at the beginning of a new millennium? If past struggles with the role and identity of religiously affiliated colleges have not yielded definitive answers to the questions being asked of these institutions, it is at least heartening to know that American higher education is once again a hospitable environment for conversations about faith and learning. The 1990s witnessed a terrific increase in foundation support for studies of religion and education and a veritable explosion of projects and publications, including some in journals traditionally resistant to religious issues. But even as new published studies appear, conferences are planned, and national and local conversations continue, there are obstacles faced by advocates of the church-related college wishing to enter the broader conversation on religion and education.

Among these is the fact that the intellectual foundation for understanding the American church-related college remains weak. In fact, one striking aspect of the current discussion of the role of religion in higher education is the curious silence of the church-related college. Even recent books and articles treating the segment of higher education in which churches have a historic role concentrate almost exclusively on the larger institutions that are now research universities.[95] What makes this silence particularly conspicuous is the Christian college's historic role as a vociferous participant in these debates. It is hoped that this book will contribute to a resurgence in scholarly interest in church-related higher education.

✠

PART TWO

POSTMODERN OPPORTUNITY

The Habit of Empathy: Postmodernity and the Future of the Church-Related College

Paul Lakeland

The rapid perusal of any history of church-related academic institutions in America should easily persuade the reader that tensions between religious traditions and secular culture are ever-present.[1] In a nation that has always been at one and the same time highly religious yet formally committed to the separation of church and state, such a situation is probably inevitable. The twentieth-century growth of secularization and the increasingly pluralistic cultural and religious landscape only help to intensify the tensions. The more voices in the dialogue, the greater the challenge to each particular voice both to be heard and, perhaps more importantly, to hear itself above the welter of competing voices.

While there have always been tensions in the life of the church-related college, the kinds of tensions have varied with the times. Different times result in different tensions, which present particular challenges. What then, of the specific situation of the church-related college in our times? To offer at least part of an answer to this question, it will be necessary to describe the lineaments of our "postmodern" moment in history. This will lead to the identification of three challenges that our particular historical situation presents to the church-related institution as *college*, as *church* and as *church-related college*. I shall suggest that cultivating what I shall call "the habit of empathy" may be a way of addressing the situation that emerges from the very character of our present-day world. It will be my contention that the parallels between the impulses of postmodern culture on the one hand, and contemporary approaches to academic and religious life on the other, make this a particularly important and hopeful moment for the church-related college.

VARIETIES OF "POSTMODERNISM"

The times in which we now live have come to be called "postmodern," for better or worse. There is no particular value to this label, perhaps even no particular content to it, but as a label it has stuck, and so we will use it. Semantically, of course, it merely suggests that we live *after* modernity, and in itself this too is neither particularly perceptive nor conceptually rich. But it offers us a way to make some initial clarifications, since "modernity," unlike postmodernity, is a relatively well-catalogued phenomenon. What postmodernity means, then, will be a matter of determining the content of the "post" in postmodern.

To take the more pedestrian issue first, "modernity" is normally understood to be that historical epoch in the Western world that stretched from the time of the European Enlightenment to some point in the mid-twentieth century. The Enlightenment itself, while a historical watershed, did not occur out of nowhere, but was in many ways presaged by late-medieval nominalism and early mercantile capitalism.[2] Nevertheless, the two principal motifs of the Enlightenment serve to denote the modern world that followed, namely, the trust in the powers of human reason and the attendant rise in science and technology. Faced with such a secularly empowered culture, post-Enlightenment religion lost confidence in its capacity to address and challenge the everyday "real" world. Three typical forms of modern religion emerged; a deism that kept God out of the world-picture, a privatistic pietism that coexisted somewhat schizophrenically with an attention to the world of mundane affairs, and a ghettoized defensiveness. In each case the religious dimension of life became seriously impoverished, and the world in which it existed played by its own newly fashioned rules.

Precisely because of the post-Enlightenment bifurcation of reason and religion, state and church, world and God, profane and sacred, the church-related college in recent centuries has always been something of a hybrid. While in the age of the so-called "medieval synthesis" learning was sacred and theology was the queen of the sciences, the religious institution of higher learning in the age of modernity would always seem to be trying to meet two incompatible ends: to be faithful to the scripture principle or to the authority of the Church on the one hand, and to pursue the human drive for knowledge of the world in complete freedom on the other. The problems of the church-related college, even in some respects to the present day, all stem from this one dilemma. How can one preserve the character of an institution founded on a religious world-view and yet respect academic freedom? Are there limits on the responsible exercise of academic freedom, and if so, what are they? How much should the life-world of the institution reflect the charisms of the founding religious tradition? How subject to the correction of the academy should the sponsoring religious body be? In some more evangelical contexts questions are still asked about how we can be faithful to scripture and teach evolution or scientific cosmology. Many Catholic colleges struggle with how they can express the values of the Church and teach pluralistic approaches to the question of abortion or make condoms available on campus. These questions and the many others that any reader could add are products of the post-Enlightenment insistence on the autonomy of the secular that has characterized modernity. However, the present day ambivalence towards the legacy of modernity means that the ways of posing these questions may have to change.

The postmodern world into which we have entered is one with many scripts, many narratives, united if at all only in their common agreement that the project of modernity has been seriously flawed. Some postmodern critics will lay stress on the philosophical primacy of subject-centered reason, while others will criticize the emergence of moral relativism and still others will point to the harmful effects of the instrumental rationality that drives scientific and technological advances. In general, however, "postmoderns" espouse one or another of three basic attitudes to modernity. There may be a general regret that it ever happened at all, there may be a sympathy for its objectives coupled with a conviction that it did not achieve its ends, and there may be an embrace of its demise as some kind of new Aquarian moment of unbridled freedom. Thus we have a nostalgic, a critical, and a radical postmodernism.

Whichever variety of postmodernism we engage, and despite the fact that each has its own mix of reasons for criticizing modernity, they all share a suspicion of modernity's commitment to the notion of the transcendental subject, the philosophical apogee of the Enlightenment's confidence in the human. In essence, the notion of transcendental subjectivity makes the human mind, and not God, the measure of all things. In Kant's famous formulation, "our age is in especial degree the age of criticism, and to criticism everything must submit."[3] The subject is then the arbiter of meaning and truth. What comes to be asserted is that the self is an unassailable subject, who is capable of determining a foundation for both metaphysics and morals, and who can master the world, both narratively and technologically.

The nostalgic, critical, and radical forms of postmodern thought can each influence the church-related college's self-understanding. This may occur in one of two ways: through the impact of postmodernity on the conduct of the academic mission or, perhaps more surprisingly, through the influence of postmodernity upon the religious self-understanding of the institution. Nostalgic postmodern thought is socially and politically conservative, the critical variety is liberal, and radical postmodernity names its own ideological orientation. To illustrate this situation, perhaps too simplistically, we could look at the recent debates over the literary canon. Nostalgic postmodern thought would not only be comfortable with the traditional canon of the "dead white males" plus Jane Austen and George Eliot, it would also incline to the idea of a closed canon. Critical postmodern thought, while not uncomfortable with the idea of canonicity, would consider the canon open and currently in need of broadening. Eclectic postmodernity would want to destroy both the canon and the idea of canonicity.

Postmodernity in its three forms can also affect the religious self-understanding of the institution. Thus, a nostalgic inclination leads to the reassertion of premodern understandings of institutional religious identity. Radical postmodern thought, committed as it is to the critique of subjectivity, ethics, reason, and order, seems in the end to be incompatible with the preservation of a genuine religious identity. And the critical attitude will wish to preserve the hard-won victories of modernity, in which religious identity has been compatible with existence in a pluralistic and secularized world, a world in which the intellectual and cultural certainties of modernity have largely evaporated. Obviously, if I am right about these forms of postmodernity, then only the nostalgic and critical are of any further interest in this particular context. In radical postmodernity, there is no future for the church-related college, if that future would entail retaining any serious sense of religious identity. This would not mean, however, that like Nietzsche's churches after the death of God, nominally church-related colleges would not continue indefinitely into the postmodern future.

All three forms of postmodern thought, like the academic institution and the religious tradition, are embodied within a culturally postmodern world. Any attempt at a succinct delineation of the salient characteristics of postmodern culture must be doomed to the charge of rash selectivity and lack of seriousness. While, however, the charge would stick, this should not derail the effort, since the same selectivity and lack of seriousness are themselves two markers of the postmodern temperament. In fact, seen as a cultural phenomenon, postmodernity is much closer to the radical form of postmodern thought than the other two types I have described. The postmodern world is the world of the internet, of cyberspace and sound bites, of ecological awareness and body piercing, of eclectic architecture and an ethics of insouciance. It is not so much that cultural postmodernity is not serious that makes it different from what went before as that its seriousness is not systematic. Structure, system, foundation—most especially any overarching story as to what gives shape and order to my life, this time, and human history—are what postmodernity rejects.

Certain fundamental attitudes shared by much postmodern thought and the thoughtful voices within postmodern culture can be identified. In a recent and more extensive work on religion in postmodernity,[5] I argued that at least the following statements are true as underlying convictions of the postmodern world:

1. No standpoint is neutral or above suspicion. All are rhetorical.

2. The "metanarratives" (or "grand narratives") of modernity have had the effect of erasing otherness by including the other within "my" metanarrative, thereby removing its otherness.

3. The task of understanding or interpreting society, if attempted at all, must be conducted through piecemeal, tactical, pragmatic and tentative means. The philosopher must be the *bricoleur*.

4. The task of changing society, if attempted at all, must be conducted through grassroots, localized (though sometimes networked), tactical, pragmatic, and incremental means. The social activist must be committed to dialogue and consensus-building.

5. Postmodernity contains within it elements both emancipatory and demonic. No theoretical grid is available that will easily allow the discernment of which elements are which, though the kinds of totalizing impulses that would reject points 1 through 4 provide important hints.

If these theses are arguably true of the postmodern world, they are certainly not exhaustive. But taken together they indicate that in the postmodern view of things the world today can no longer be explained by anyone's "grand plan." An enormous number of distinguishable groups tell their own stories of how the world is and offer their own solutions to its problems. Made aware as we all are of this bewildering variety of perspectives through the well-documented phenomenon of the communications explosion, the challenge is to participate, to collaborate, to form alliances, and to tackle our problems bit by bit, one at a time. For all kinds of reasons this is inimical to the standard operating procedures of religiously inspired institutions.

The depiction of the shift to cultural and intellectual postmodernity that I have sketched here suggests three challenges for the church-related college, which I will try briefly to address. First, we must ask what it is that should characterize the academic mission of church-related colleges in this postmodern world and whether this is something specific to institutions with a religious foundation or something common to all academic enterprises. Second, we must examine the Christian tradition for resources that will enable it to address the postmodern world in an open and hopeful spirit. Finally, we shall have to envisage how the religious and academic missions of the church-related college might go beyond mere coexistence to a mutually supportive presence. These are respectively, the academic question, the religious question, and the church-relatedness question.

EMPATHY AND THE PURSUIT OF WISDOM

An academic institution, church-related or secular, cannot function responsibly if it does not enthusiastically pursue excellence. In the world of learning, this level of achievement towards which all ought to be striving requires the cultivation of two important intellectual virtues: critique and empathy. The former is more immediately recognizable in an academic context, requiring as it does the disciplined analysis of the particular object of inquiry. But the latter is at least as significant, while far more frequently missing, in the struggle for intellectual excellence. Moreover, while empathic individuals may be born and not made, and are to be found in the most defiantly secular of colleges and universities, an institutional commitment to the intellectual virtue of empathy is more suitable to a church-related institution, though of course not derivable from

any one specific religious tradition. In other words, the intellectual virtue of empathy is something to which all the faculty
of a church-related institution, believers or not, ought to have
a profound commitment. Such a commitment is deeply appropriate to religiously motivated institutions, as I shall try to
argue below, but not derived specifically from their texts or
history.

While the term *empathy* is most often encountered academically in psychological and therapeutic circles, and while in
popular parlance it is often interchangeable with *sympathy*, even
of a pronouncedly sentimental cast, the intellectual virtue of
empathy is somewhat different. Empathy is the first moment
in the broadly phenomenological approach to academic inquiry
that has always been an option, but is the favored method of
postmodernity. The inquirer as *bricoleur* must let the object of
inquiry show itself as it is. While attention to that which is to
be known will of course be accompanied by a profound sense
of the context-dependency and historicality of knowledge and
the way in which the rhetorical stance of the subject may have
an impact on what can be known, the Kantian transcendental
subject—neutral and omnipotent—is gone. Empathy is then
the necessary condition for such a suspension of judgment;
the virtue, or perhaps better, the *habit* of empathy precludes
premature analysis or critique and does battle against the
strong urge of the academician to place the object of inquiry in
some preapproved taxonomy, system, or metanarrative. While
eschewing sentimentality, the inquirer must in a real way *love*
the object of inquiry; what is to be studied must be respected,
allowed, as it were, to be itself. Only when this happens is there
at least a fighting chance that critique or analysis will in fact
reach the object of inquiry and not remain within the labyrinth of the inquirer's mental pathways. Empathy, in other
words, is profoundly practical.

While the words empathy and love may not be much used
in the postmodern academy, the method that I have described
in these terms is easily recognizable, and it is present to a greater
or lesser degree in all contemporary colleges and universities.
Postmodernity is not much given to abstractions; it suspects
system and is strongly inclined to minimize the role of the sub-

ject in the process of critical inquiry. The academic life of the church-related college, no less than any other, is likely to be affected more and more by such shifts in the intellectual landscape, largely, at least in my estimation, for the better. While empathy may be distinctly less *macho* than system, it makes in the end for less distortion of the object of study.

If I am correct that the academic life of the church-related institution is (or should be) strongly influenced by this "turn to empathy," then there are at least two important corollaries. The first is that the same empathy that the academy employs in its work should be extended to the religious traditions and identity of the church-related institution itself. Is there not a serious inconsistency in a scholar committed to the habit of empathy who makes an exception for the church-relatedness of her or his institution, and in that case and that alone feels perfectly comfortable in an immediate critique or dismissal of the religious character of the school? A frequent and often accurate complaint against faculty in church-related institutions who are critical of that very religious identity is that they do not understand or have any "feeling for" religion or church. But while one ought not to expect them to be religious or to submit to some religious authority, one can expect intellectual consistency. The habit of empathy only exists where it makes no exceptions.

The second corollary relates to the special role of departments of religious studies or theology in the church-related institution. Firstly, the role must flow from the particular situation of the discipline, linking both the dimensions of religion and academy. Second, the department must be as committed as others to the habit of empathy (coupled of course with critique) and thus serve a vital pedagogic function in demonstrating to the rest of the academic community that things religious are not necessarily obscurantist or anti-intellectual. But third and most important, departments of religious studies or theology have a responsibility to the church-relatedness of the institution, namely, to educate it to see more clearly the religious value of the intellectual virtue of empathy. It is the religious studies department that is best placed to teach the church that the virtue of empathy is not only compatible

with, but actually central to, a Christian encounter with
the world.

EMPATHY AND THE THEOLOGY OF RELIGIONS

The fundamental problem of religion in confronting
postmodernity is that while the times dismiss metanarrative,
religion lives by it. All religious traditions, whether militantly
evangelistic or not, are total if not always totalizing systems.
There is no question on any aspect of life (or death) to which a
religion will respond: "Sorry, we don't deal with that issue."
The world of the person of faith is constituted by and structured around the religious story to which he or she is committed. Through its particular blend of offering answers and
invoking mystery, it is accepted by the believer as true.
Postmodern theologies or atheologies may try to shift the
ground of religious reflection, but the communities of faith
remain mostly unaffected. While a metanarrative may not be
possessed of any spirit of aggression or imperialism, it simply
leaves no room for another.

More technically, the problem with metanarrative as a
whole—and thus with religion, which requires metanarrative—
is not so much that it cannot entertain another metanarrative
as that it erases the Other. Consider, for example, Christianity's
encounters with Judaism. While over the centuries the Christian story about Jews and Judaism has often mutated and today, at least in some quarters, is healthier and more respectful
than ever before, it remains the Christian story about Jews.
The Jewish story is erased in the Christian metanarrative, just
as efficiently and perhaps unintentionally as is the woman's
story in patriarchy, the black's story in white liberal reform-
ism, or the story of the poor in society's well-meaning welfare.
It is of the nature of metanarrative to incorporate the Other in
the overall story, and thus to erase the other's story, and so
obliterate the Other as other.

In my view, three methodological imperatives for living religions distinguish our age: the use of the historical-critical
method, the employment of a hermeneutics of suspicion, and
the encounter with the Other. High modernity provided the

first of these, in which the claim is made that truth is given to us only in the wrappings of the historical period out of which it emanates and that sensitivity to such historical and cultural conditioning is the way for that truth to speak more clearly. Late modernity gave us the hermeneutics of suspicion, in which we are enjoined to examine the ideological and cultural presuppositions of both the originating and interpreting subjects of a truth-claim, if we would see what truth is being claimed. Postmodernity presents the third, in which a more radical challenge appears. The world that we hold and that makes us what we are, even informed by historical-critical method and a hermeneutics of suspicion, must look humbly and nondogmatically into the face of the Other and be open to what may emerge from this meeting.

While it was scriptural studies that gave us the historical-critical method, and liberation theologies that uncovered and refined a hermeneutics of suspicion, it is in what is called today "the theology of religions" that we confront most directly the call to the encounter with the Other, a call both threatening and enriching. When, in the theology of religions, the Christian tradition faces the truth-claims of other world religions, it is forced to reexamine itself. It cannot be closed to the Other, and so it must abandon dogmatism. It cannot capitulate to the Other and embrace a pure relativism which is as good as saying that anything goes. And so it embarks on the hard road of uncovering a healthy pluralism through its encounter with the Other. This is incontestably a lesson of postmodernity.

Like the postmodern academy's pursuit of wisdom, the theology of religions—or its close relative, Christian ecumenism—demands the habit of empathy. However, in the practice of either something is learned too. Interreligious dialogue does not require the abandonment of one's particular religious metanarrative, but it most certainly expects that the story not be "foregrounded." In other words, evangelism, in most senses of the term, has no place in the encounter with the religious Other. The first moment of, and essential precondition for, genuine meeting is a willingness to listen to the voice of the Other, at the same time suspending the temptation to insert what is said into a frame of reference provided by one's own thought-world. Clearly, this is the religious face of the intellectual virtue of empathy.

If ecumenism and the theology of religions are where the habit of empathy is most likely to be cultivated by religious communities, what are the specific theological justifications for the abandonment of "foregrounding the metanarrative"? This answer is easier to give for more sacramental and less evangelical Christian traditions, which may explain why schools and colleges in the Catholic and Episcopal traditions seem to find it easier to maintain a religious identity while adopting a distinctly nonsectarian posture towards their academic mission. Liberal Protestant foundations, neither sacramental nor evangelical, seem to possess the most fragile religious identities, while evangelical schools preserve themselves with a more sectarian posture, but often at the price of a less than open academy.[6]

Two "models of the church" underpin an engagement with the world that maintains the metanarrative but places it *behind* rather than *in front of* the community, making it less blueprint and more context.[7] The "sacramental" model sees the church as being in the world as "sign and instrument" of Christ, as he was in his place the sign and instrument of God. This sign and instrument, however, must be patterned according to what it signifies, and this means attention not so much to the proclamation of the gospel of Christ in a narrow sense as to the personal preaching and concrete life-choices of Jesus Christ as servant of the reign of God. This is where the "servant" model becomes important, and where liberal Protestantism enters strongly into the picture (Bonhoeffer, for one, was a strong proponent of a servant model of the church). The servant model stresses the role of the church as existing not for itself but for the world, serving God by serving the world and, by serving selflessly, being the loving presence of God in Christ in the contemporary world. Both models see the church as oriented to the reign of God, but not as identical with it. Moreover, neither model would stress incorporation into the church as its mission. Loving presence in the world, and betterment of the world, are what the church must be and do.

CULTIVATING THE HABIT OF EMPATHY

Thus far I have tried to suggest that in the postmodern world the fragmentation of knowledge, the sidelining of the transcendental subject, the stress on the perspectival, and the new openness to otherness demand from both the academy and the church the cultivation of the habit of empathy. It remains to say something about the implications for the church-related college, which is where church and academy meet. In general terms, it should be apparent that their mutual commitment to empathy ought to clear away the cruder forms of suspicion and confrontation. However, it is possible to go considerably further and be quite specific about the church-related college as the place where the habit of empathy is cherished and cultivated.

In the first place, the habit of empathy dictates that the church-related college be an open place. "Open" here means both open-minded and with an openness of access—at its best, straining to open its doors to every kind of person and its heart to every variety of opinion and idea. But it must be understood that this openness is not a romantic notion, not mere sentimentalizing. It is a hard-nosed application of the fundamental commitments of both church and academy in a postmodern world. The church cannot serve that which is not the church either by closing its doors or minds to the other, or by drowning out the otherness of the Other in some crudely evangelistic din. The academy cannot investigate the new, the unknown, the different, or the alien, if it is not willing to listen attentively.

The openness mandated by the habit of empathy has structural and administrative, even architectural implications. Practices follow from the habit of the virtue. Indeed, they represent an orthopraxis that validates the possession of the virtue. Thus, we should expect the empathic college to be open to the community and to welcome the outsider. Where possible, this should show itself in admissions and scholarships, and although a Catholic school whose student body is only twenty percent Catholic would be distinctly odd, there ought to be questions too about the reality of any commitment to openness possessed by schools with an overwhelming percentage of Catholic students.

A similar remark can be made about the much-discussed questions of hiring practices relative to the confessional perspective of the school: Can a school ignore the religious affiliations of prospective employees and not become secularized? And should it set quotas for faculty who subscribe to its religious identity? And what should those quotas be? While a Methodist school whose faculty is only twenty percent Methodist is much less Methodist than one with a majority of Methodist faculty, a school whose faculty is ninety percent Methodist, one might think, is too Methodist and insufficiently open for its own good. But given that it is more important to have faculty with the appropriate interior commitment to empathy than it is to have those who pay lip-service to some religious identity, it would seem that hiring quotas give no assurance of getting the right kind of people. A surer path would be to be a clearly empathic institution, whose empathy derives equally from its religious character and its academic mission. The chances are that committed Catholic or Methodist academicians would be attracted to rather than repelled by the prospect of working in such an environment.

Administratively, the narrow and often secretive attitudes of hierarchical models ought to have no place in the church-related college. In a learning community and in a church, unlike bureaucratic systems in general and the corporate world in particular, leadership is to be understood as a form of service, and the leaders are accountable *downwards*, not merely to the supervisor in the chain of command.[8] Both church and academy raise up leaders from within, and it is to the grassroots that they are responsible. "Corporate culture" simply has no place in a church-related college, since its product-orientation and narrow understandings of efficiency are out of step with both the religious and academic mission of the institution. To put it in terms of the ruling insight of this paper, while *individuals* in the corporate world may be people whose qualities of sympathy or empathy outshine many who work in academia, the corporate models for organizations cannot make a structural commitment to empathy.

The stress that I have tried to place on empathy is most valuable in addressing that thorniest of issues, namely, the interconnections between church-relatedness and the academic mission of the college. Empathy builds bonds of understanding that are very strong, while suggesting no control of academy over church or church over academy. The religious tradition does not dictate or oversee the academic mission, and the academic purposes of the school need not sideline or distort the religious identity. Rather, church and academy find common ground in the happy coincidence that here in postmodernity both components of the church-related college can and must internalize the habit of empathy if each is to be true to its respective responsibilities. The church is empathic because of what it is, the community as sacrament to/servant of the world. The academy is empathic because of what *it* is, a community devoted to the rigorous discipline of learning, whose first moment is an attention to what is to be understood so that wisdom and not merely knowledge will accrue.

While the emphasis that I have given to empathy in these pages may have led the reader to understand the mission of church and academy to be much the same, there is in fact a substantial difference that, in conclusion, needs to be remarked upon. There is another face to empathy, which in the case of the academy is rightly described as critique. While the first moment in the search for knowledge and wisdom is always one of listening, there is a time for critique, and even judgment. Intellectual inquiry cannot be mere empathy; it must progress to analysis and disciplined assessment. Inquiry conducted in this manner is out of tune with much of cultural postmodernity, which often seems to assume that the juxtaposition of discrete sets of experiences exhausts the process of learning. Wisdom, as the faculty of knowing when—and when not—to pass judgment, goes beyond this.

The other face of empathy in the context of the religious tradition is not the attention to critical inquiry that marks the academic mission of the institution, but the public commitment to a way of seeing the world. Being true to itself as sacrament/servant, the community of faith testifies not so much to the gospel in the narrow sense, as to the importance of faithfulness to the commitments that belief entails. As I suggested earlier, the postmodern church must recognize the legitimacy of the multiplicity of religious perspectives, while it acts out its commitment to one of them. Thus, to the outsider it witnesses to the importance of commitment itself, rather than to the importance of this or that choice. The religious identity of the church-related institution, in the last analysis, is a matter of taking a stand and insisting, in the face of postmodernity's tendency to relativism and indifference, on the importance of commitment. It is radical and countercultural at one and the same time.

Prolegomena to Any Postmodern Hope for the Church-Related College

MARGARET FALLS-CORBITT

INTRODUCTION

The hope that church-related colleges today sit at the cusp of a grand opportunity is premised upon the following set of beliefs:

1. that our culture has shifted from "modernism" to "postmodernism";

2. that the past success of modern epistemology bears significant blame for the last quarter century's secularization of the historically Christian colleges;

3. that postmodern epistemologies, held consistently to their own premises, will prove more favorable to "reprivileging" the Christian tradition at these colleges.

The blame asserted in the second and the trust expressed in the third of these beliefs come from an analysis and assessment of modernism's insistence upon the objectivity of knowledge and postmodernism's rejection of that ideal.

Put very briefly, the story is said to run like this: Under modernism, real knowledge is objective and the methods of the physical and quantitative sciences have proven themselves to be the most truly objective; hence, through these sciences alone is truth obtained. As a result of this conclusion, systems, doctrines, and disciplines that cannot claim such objectivity are put on the defensive to prove they belong in the academy; individual scholars and teachers are discouraged from allowing faith commitments into their work. Thus, the modernized church-related college that wishes to stand for academic excellence is forced increasingly to divorce its religious aims from its academic purposes and programs. Postmodernism, by comparison, insists that all knowledge claims—scientific and otherwise—are inextricably shadowed by the interests, values, and commitments of the knower. This being the case, lack of "objective proof" and the admission of faith commitments should, at the very least, no longer marginalize the believing scholar's work. At the most, justified criticisms of "objective" methods may be clearing the way for epistemologies that articulate the academic enterprise's need for religion and other "qualitative" ways of knowing.[1] Thus postmodernism promises to justify and revitalize the place of religion in higher education.

This essentially epistemological analysis—this concentration upon modernism's and postmodernism's differences of opinion about the possibility and desirability of "objectivity" in knowledge—is crucial, revealing, and promising. I, nonetheless, believe it ignores a vital element in the church-academy debate, especially as it is lived out on the campuses of small church-related liberal arts colleges. That vital element is ethics.

Of course, insofar as ethics investigates our ability to know right from wrong and vices from virtues, a debate about the possibility of objective knowledge incorporates conflicts in ethical theory. And in fact, alongside the literature lamenting modernism's effect on religion, one often finds concern for the status of ethical commitments in educational philosophies. It seems that under modernism's influence, ethics can be judged just as nonquantitative and nonobjective as religion, and that consequently, ethical aims in education, like religious aims, have been forsaken as colleges become universities that become research institutions devoted primarily to the transmission and advancement of knowledge as modernism conceives it.

Despite this trend, the ethical aims of education are still very much alive at small church-related colleges where the focus of the school's mission continues to be on teaching. For example, all of the colleges involved in the Rhodes Consultation have mission statements that, in one way or another, connect education to the development of good values. I observed that all these colleges, no matter their level of dis-ease over church-relatedness, expressed pride in offering an education that did not forget values.

This fact invites a host of questions: Is the commitment to teaching over research for its own sake necessarily a moral aim, requiring the institution to defy modernism's debunking of ethics? Has the church relationship kept these colleges from full entry into the modern world? Are ethical commitments less offensive to modernism than religious ones? Or, have the small church-related colleges been seedbeds of postmodernism after all because they insist upon the place of values in knowledge?

I find each of these questions enticing in its own right. But their very existence suggests to me the need for a more general project: In this paper, I shall seek to add to the epistemological analysis, briefly summarized above, an overtly ethical analysis.

Defining ethical goals for education remains very much a part of life at church-related teaching institutions, and because that is so, the ethical implications and requirements of being church-related shape the debate—even stir up the tensions—over how to relate the college to the church and over whether movement towards secularization is a good thing or a bad thing. Indeed, ethical commitments, I believe, set the terms of the debate more than do epistemological views. This, at least, is certainly the case at Hendrix, "a private undergraduate institution of the liberal arts related to the United Methodist Church."

Thus, for the sake of a more complete assessment of the postmodern opportunity for revitalizing the role of religion at small church-related liberal arts colleges, I offer in this paper: (1) an ethical analysis of the forces for secularization on campuses such as Hendrix and (2) an analysis of whether a shift from modernism to postmodernism can be expected to change the nature or tenor of these ethical forces. At stake in this ethical analysis is the adequacy of the third belief expressed above. To share its confidence, we must be assured that the *ethical* implications of postmodern epistemologies will prove more favorable than have those of modernism to "repriviledging" the Christian tradition. The reasons for doubting that this is so must be taken into account before we can embrace a postmodern solution to secularization.

BACKGROUND FOR THE ETHICAL ANALYSIS OF THE FORCES FOR SECULARIZATION

As indicated above, the ethical analysis I offer is based upon what I find to be the case at my own teaching place. It, therefore, will pertain most formally to those colleges enough like Hendrix for their constituents to find themselves and their situation in the description I give below. This means it applies best to small church-related liberal arts colleges of the liberal Protestant persuasion, though Rhodes Consultation colleagues from Roman Catholic colleges assure me that the analysis applies sufficiently to their institutions.[2]

When discussing secularization at colleges such as Hendrix, one must be careful to note that we have not yet become purely secular institutions with merely a nominal relationship to a church. If Christians on our campus find Hendrix secular, the agnostics and atheists find it "shockingly religious" (that's an actual quote). Yet, by comparison with today's self-consciously "Christian colleges" (as opposed to "church-related") and even by comparison with Hendrix College of 1901, we are undoubtedly secular*ized*. The truth seems to be that although we are secularized, we are not secular.

Clear formal and administrative ties to the United Methodist Church continue at Hendrix. Although nothing "Methodist" or even "religious" carries required participation, the ties to the church shape the *extra*curricular environment in various ways. From opportunities for worship, to sponsorship of lecturers that would be of special interest to Methodist clergy and laity, to special admissions efforts among Methodist youth, to a busy office for the coordination of student volunteers, Hendrix both uses and honors its connections to the United Methodist Church. The *curriculum* may even be said to be effected to some degree by the church relationship. For instance, that relationship is probably a reason for our strong religion department; it is what has attracted some of the faculty with Christian commitments to teach here, and it is what motivates many faculty to call special attention to the religious implications of theories in their field. I, a non-Methodist, have even come to think that the remarkable degree of power held by the faculty is partly due to the colleges' Methodist heritage. And, in ways to be more fully explained later, even the forces for "secularization" have had the church to some degree behind them.

Though far from being a secular institution, Hendrix has an unmistakably secularized academic program. Long gone are the days when specifically Christian purposes could be named and tagged as such in the mission statement, or when commitments to Christian theology and values could unabashedly guide curricular decisions. The faculty recently revised our statement of purpose, and it would be fair to say that, from early on in the process, numerous hours were spent debating how properly to acknowledge our relationship with the United Methodist Church without giving even a hint that the values and goals of the college are uniquely Christian or somehow privilege the Christian perspective.[3] General education requirements are such that a student has some incentive but no requirement to enroll in a religion course. Because we are a liberal arts school that takes interdisciplinary education seriously, any graduating student would certainly have studied religion as social or historical fact and scientific or philosophic quandary. But, religion is treated in a "dispassionate and quasi-scientific manner" by faculty who appear "indifferent to [religion's] truth claims" either because they are indifferent or because they think they should be so in the classroom.[4]

Certainly long, long gone are the days at Hendrix when attending the church-sponsored college meant a student would be mentored by scholar-teachers wedded to Christian belief and doctrine.[5] Religiously, the present-day Hendrix faculty is a hodgepodge of mildly conservative Christians (very few), liberal Christians, eclectic Buddhist-Christians, members of more orthodox non-Christian faith traditions, proud agnostics, shy agnostics, and atheists both quiet and loud. In the hiring process, initiating questions about the candidate's religious beliefs is as anathema as it would be at a secular college or university. Though it was not consistently so in the recent past, candidates today are subjected to standard questions concerning how they feel about the college being church-related, but these are followed quickly by assurances of the presence of academic freedom and the absence of religiosity in the academic atmosphere. As one would expect, the faculty is composed of some who embrace church affiliation, others who are openly uncomfortable with it, and still others who, though not preferring it, have reached a personal peace.

However, what these religiously eclectic professors have in common is ethics. I certainly do not mean that there is unanimity of opinion about major social dilemmas or about the proper set of fundamental moral principles. I would never claim that there is among the Hendrix faculty a shared conception of the good of the kind that either Plato or Aristotle thought necessary for the formation of community. But we are an ethically concerned group, and we openly value that about ourselves, presuming it in everything from faculty meeting debates to lunch-time conversations. Whether we articulate it to ourselves or not, I think we look for a kind of ethical seriousness in the candidates we interview. Blame the church relationship; blame the liberal arts ideal that true scholarship rightly done shall shape a student's character for the good, but Hendrix—like the other church-related teaching institutions of the Rhodes Consultation—accepts and affirms ethical seriousness about the educational process.

Perhaps this is why it is so clear to me that an ethical analysis of secularization must be undertaken. There are values— some of them very intentionally affirmed—that have brought us to this point, and certainly value questions abound if we ask: *ought* Hendrix, having become what it is, redirect itself towards a more overtly religiously guided academic program?

ETHICAL FORCES FOR SECULARIZATION: A MODERN STORY

From the above description of Hendrix's situation, I isolate three practices that are both the primary signs of our having become secularized and are causes of continued secularization: (1) While we check for some assurance that candidates for faculty positions are comfortable with the church relationship, we for the most part hire faculty without regard to their religious allegiances. (2) We resist naming Christian purposes for curricular design and content and, instead, collapse the old Christian mission of "making Christian men and women" into the secularized ideal of the "liberally educated person." In fact, for many in the church and many on campus who care deeply for our church relationship, Hendrix fulfills its duties as a college of the Methodist church by being the best liberal arts college it can be. (3) The intellectual climate of the classroom is inhospitable to exploring faith confessionally because there is a presumed obligation to keep the discussion of religion objective. (Actually, more passion is probably allowed if one is expressing atheism but that is because atheism usually dresses itself in a supposed commitment to objectivity.)

Though distinctly identifiable, these practices are all of a piece and are mutually reinforcing so as to send a college down the path of an ever increasingly secular academic program and environment. Once a college has taken this route there is no way back but by giving up the practices I have named.

No doubt these practices have their source partly in modern epistemology's insistence that good scholarship is objective and devoid of religious commitments. The epistemological analysis outlined at the opening of this paper has part of the story right. But that story does not explain to my satisfaction why so many of my colleagues, believers and nonbelievers, express something very akin to moral indignation when they hear talk of "reprivileging the Christian tradition." Also, it can only partly explain the pressure accreditation agencies and honorary organizations put on colleges to be less "sectarian." For example, is a sectarian faculty less desirable to Phi Beta Kappa because of some remarkable empirically proven link between nonsectarianism and excellence in teaching and research? Or is it because they suspect sectarian colleges of violating certain values of our academic culture?

My suggestion is that the secularizing practices which I have named hold sway on liberal Protestant college campuses such as Hendrix because they have become the acceptable way of expressing the college's commitment to the moral values of fairness, tolerance, and respect for the right of individuals to live by their own best lights. "Oh," says my reader, "that's all you mean. But that's just modernism again." Yes, these are the ethical values of modern political thought, but they deserve a patient analysis: (1) We must be sure we understand how these values become connected with secularizing practices; (2) we need to remind ourselves of just how "Christian" these values seem, why they seem so, and how this complicates their "secularizing" effect; (3) we need to examine exactly the sense in which these values are "modern." And finally, in part II of this paper, we will need to ask whether postmodernism alone or a "postmodern Christianity" is poised to suggest any different set of values or a different way of living these values at a church-related academic institution.

Modern Values and Secularizing Practices. The values of *fairness, tolerance,* and *respect for individual liberty* figure significantly into the ethical theories that underpin modern political theory, and that theory has, in turn, had a pervasive role in shaping the politics and organization of the modern college campus. To understand and assess the influence of these values upon church-related campuses, we must articulate the reasoning by which they have become linked to the sceularizing practices identified above.

Fairness refers to our basic moral duty to treat like cases alike when extending benefits or levying burdens. It does not require us to treat all people alike, but it does require that we be able to give morally relevant reasons for treating otherwise similar cases differently. If two school children have broken the same rule to an approximately equal degree with equal responsibility, then fairness dictates that they receive disciplinary actions of similar kind and degree. A teacher cannot be excused for going lighter on one child because she is better friends with that child's mother. On the other hand, if one of these children were younger and could not have been expected to know better, then fairness would require that the two children be treated differently. Determining exactly what does and does not count as a "morally relevant difference" can get murky. Nonetheless, we can acknowledge a duty to treat like cases alike even while we dispute what makes one case like another in all morally relevant respects.

When we award a job to one candidate rather than another, we treat the two individuals differently in the awarding of a benefit. Typically, differences in desert or merit are understood to be morally relevant differences; hence, fairness dictates that the job be given to the one who merits it. Merit (in the job market) is a measure of the individual's fitness for the job sought. Thus, fairness requires that we not allow factors irrelevant to job performance to enter into our evaluation of candidates. Being exceptionally appealing to the eye is a legitimate standard against which to measure applicants for a modeling job, but not for medical school or a teaching position.

What application does this have to the practice of church-related colleges hiring faculty without regard to their religious allegiances? Cannot a candidate's religion be among the things that fit her for teaching at a church-related college? The answer is of course yes, and this is the justification given by those Christian colleges that require their faculty to sign doctrinal statements.

At Hendrix, on the other hand, we stay judiciously away from direct questions about a candidate's religion. And in fact, if the information surfaced anyway, it would create a ticklish situation in the search committee were a member to argue that, between two equally talented candidates, one should be hired over the other because he was Christian. It would be acceptable to argue that a candidate "was more comfortable about being at a church-related college" or "better understood the dynamics of the church-related college," but not to bring up his actual religious beliefs. It would be considered unfair to do so. Possibly this is because the college, having not advertised any religious requirement, cannot morally, suddenly inject it as a criterion. But I believe part of the reason that we do not make it a criterion from the front end is the seeming unfairness of holding a person's religion against her. If one candidate is hired because he is Christian, the other has been rejected because of her religious beliefs.

Actually, this last claim should be qualified. Insofar as a candidate's religious beliefs are those of an under-represented ethnic group such as Hindu, his religious beliefs would probably be allowed to count in his favor. For at Hendrix, search committees are instructed to look positively upon the fact that a candidate is a woman or a non-Anglo. The reason given is that we need more faculty from both groups in order to carry out more fully our aim of providing a liberal arts education. Giving seeming advantage to a minority member is, of course, controversial. But the important point here is that modern political thinkers who support giving this advantage to minority members, do not do so by giving up fairness as a value. Rather they argue that an expanded, more complete understanding of fairness demands doing so.

A more detailed analysis of this "expanded" version of fairness is important for understanding why a college such as Hendrix would approve choosing a Hindu over a non-Hindu but not approve of choosing a Christian over an atheist.

The expanded version of fairness is based upon several observations. First, there is the reality of social forces that disadvantage individual candidates for reasons beyond their control, thus giving others an unfair advantage, namely one which they did nothing to merit. Second, there is the awareness that the popular prejudices of our culture unfairly disadvantage whole groups and advantage others. Finally, there is the awareness that individual agents of a society have a duty to work towards conditions of fairness in the overarching social order. In combination, these factors are said to justify an institution in choosing, from among its technically qualified applicants, that candidate whose sex, race, or ethnic background best enables the institution to make conditions more fair for its own minority members or to do its part in establishing a generally just social order. In other words, under certain conditions of the social order, a commitment to fairness can allow or require that we take race or sex into account in the hiring process.[6]

Hiring a Hindu is a small step towards righting an imbalance that reinforces unjust prejudices in our own community and the larger society; in addition, it better educates students for living justly in a multicultural world. But one would be hard pressed to convince a search committee at Hendrix that similar reasoning could support hiring the Christian over the non-Christian or atheist. Here we have arrived, I believe, at a significant difference in the perspectives embodied in the hiring practices of liberal Protestant colleges when compared to more conservative Christian colleges. Liberal Protestant denominations work from an assumption of their own majority status. The world is with them, not against them. From such a perspective, requiring candidates for faculty positions to be Christian feels like a prejudicial act, one that contributes to an unfair distribution of the scarce benefit of acceptance into the power structures that be.

Similar dynamics are probably at work in the application of the value of *tolerance*. If the surrounding culture is regarded as hostile to true Christian belief, then being a Christian enclave can be seen as a way of demanding that the world tolerate the true faith. But if one presumes one's institution to represent the Christian majority, then refusing to hire non-Christian believers and atheists is a singularly bold act of institutional intolerance. Both types of academic communities are upholding the value that minority points of view shall be accorded a place in our society, but one group treats itself as the minority that must vigorously protect a place for itself in our culture; the other sees itself as the majority that must be careful not to limit others' access to the power it itself already holds.

Tolerance is an especially vigorously defended value in the academy because it stands for two types of duties at once: a duty of the scholarly vocation and a duty of the moral life. Tolerating the proliferation of unpopular theories may be seen as one's *scholarly duty* because it is necessary for achieving knowledge. J. S. Mill convincingly illustrates in *On Liberty* that we minimize our chances of being stuck with falsehoods if we refuse to censor beliefs repugnant to the majority. Tolerance as a *moral duty* derives from the third value mentioned above:

respect for individual liberty. Allowing those with whom we disagree a "place at the academic table" is one way that we respect others' right to live by their own best lights.

Our duty to *respect individual liberty* might be spelled out more fully as: our duty to respect each individual's right to live in accordance with her own conception of the good. This standard has been viewed as a particularly strong defense against requiring doctrinal statements or faculty participation in religious events. Religion is an arena of the individual's life about which it has seemed most repugnant to be coercive.

Liberal Protestant colleges have interpreted this strong moral duty to leave individuals free in their choice of religious or anti-religious commitments as a moral duty not to discriminate against a candidate because of his religious beliefs. Obviously, rejecting a candidate because of her religious beliefs does not coerce her to do anything and certainly not to give up her religious beliefs. But it does say that the college wills to be a community in which people of her kind are not free to practice and live by their own best lights.

The commitment to respecting individual liberty has implications for college life that go well beyond hiring practices. Taking such a commitment seriously has functioned, I believe, as a strong incentive for church-related colleges to proclaim their educational goals in language that deemphasizes the Christian grounding for their ideals; we substitute instead language that appeals to widely accepted secular values. The more uniquely Christian aims are claimed on the behalf of curricular design and development, the more those who teach and study at the college feel that they must be Christian to be full citizens, that their aims and values which cannot be wrapped in Christian clothing may be censored, and that their non-Christian or non-religious paths to ends common to Christianity will not be allowed expression in concrete acts.

The need to respect individual liberty also undergirds the practice of keeping religious commitments out of the classroom even when handling religiously related topics. The objective stance distances the teacher from the claims being made and offers assurance to the students that there is no intent of imposing religious beliefs. One may wonder how a teacher's confession of a religious commitment could ever be confused with the imposition of belief upon students. But such dynamics are a part of the teacher-student relationship in both its least sophisticated and its more desirable form. The unsophisticated student is prepared to think that she must think as the teacher does to get a good grade. The more sophisticated student knows the objective is for her to think for herself; but even in the mentor relationship the learner feels some obligation to take on the teacher's frame of reference. Sensitive to both ends of the spectrum, faculty use the air of objectivity to allow room for students to mold their own beliefs.

The Sense in Which These Values Are "Christian". Fairness, tolerance, and respect for individual freedom form a moral defense of the liberal Protestant church-related colleges's slide into secularization. Writers critical of this slide harangue such colleges and the liberal denominations that support them for being corrupted by liberalism. The problem with this is that it has not been a one way street of liberal political thought being imposed upon the churches. It has been a two-way street with Christianity shaping the values of our secular culture, then secular culture returning the favor and shaping Christianity. The reason this is important in analyzing the future of the church-related college is this: to the extent that the church has seen its own values in the practices of fairness, tolerance, and respect for individual liberty, the college's commitment to these values is not secular. Embodying these values may lead to practices that then "unprivilege" the founding tradition compared to the college's past; yet it is the theology of the founding church leading the way. A moment from life at Hendrix illustrates this point.

After a faculty meeting to discuss revisions in the statement of purpose, a United Methodist colleague expressed utter frustration at those who seemed to think that academic freedom and diversity of opinion about religion were values that had to be protected from demolition by the church. "Don't they realize," this colleague wondered, "that the Methodist church has a long history of pushing for academic freedom and diversity? Its in our theology to be that way; that's why Hendrix is the open, tolerant community it is."

"It's in our theology." Every denomination has struggled for a theology of revelation. This theory of how God makes Godself known is in part a theory about the place of knowledge in the life of faith. As such, it is also a description of the value or lack of value which that denomination will place on intellect, study, science, and even the discoveries by people outside the church. In the Methodist church's case the guide to authentic revelation is Wesley's Quadrilateral which gives "reason" and "experience" legitimate place alongside Scripture and tradition in interpreting God's ways and God's demands. What exactly it means to appeal to all four—Scripture, tradition, reason, and experience—has of course been such a matter of debate that both inerrantist and liberal have claimed to be at home with Wesley. Fortunately, the aim of this paper does not require me to settle who is most truly Wesleyan. The point need only be that, that strain of Methodism exists and flourishes which understands the quadrilateral as an affirmation of drawing into one's theology the conclusions of human experience broadly and deeply interpreted.

For these liberal Methodists, their theology not only permits but requires openness to the breadth of human experience, including that which would come from those who see with eyes untrained by Christian faith or whose research leads them to conclusions out of kilter with received Christian doctrine. From this theological perspective, it is Methodist to have a religiously eclectic faculty free to experiment and teach as the light of reason guides them. More conservative branches can denounce them for corrupting Wesley with secular values, but whether this is so or not is a *theological* debate that is not furthered one iota by pointing out the mere convergence of liberal Christian values with modern political thought.

The Sense in Which These Values Are "Modern". The values of "modern political thought." In what sense are these values "modern" in the way that the literature on the church and academy in a postmodern era has understood that term? The epistemological analysis of the postmodern opportunity emphasizes modernism's demand for objective knowledge and its claim that only the empirically quantifiable can be objective. Philosophers were hard pressed to fit ethical knowledge into such a criterion, but the sense that some values appeared awfully good in comparison to some others just would not go away. At the risk of oversimplifying, I will boldly assert that the most popular (and hence influential) modernist approaches were that of the Hobbesian family and the Kantian family of theories.

The Hobbesian side grants the lack of objective moral values and asserts that in their absence we are left with no moral authority but the practical, self-interested need to get along with as little damage to each other as possible. It turns out that each person's self-interest is best protected when we submit as a group to live by the rules of playing fair and giving each other as much freedom as is compatible with a like liberty for all. The tricky thing is, that for different reasons, the Kantian approach comes to a similar conclusion.

Kantians acknowledge that *theoretical* reason can only generate empirical knowledge, but insist that *practical* reason reveals a different way of knowing. Practical reason is that in us which asks, "What ought I to do?" whether this is about having tea with supper or telling a lie. Kantians believe that an adequate analysis of what it means to ask about what one "ought to do" demonstrates that every rational agent, qua rational agent, commits herself to the principle that one ought always to respect persons as ends in themselves and not as means only. With some qualifications aside, rules of fairness, tolerance, and respect for individual freedom do this.

In sum, both Christian and modern values undergird academic practices which work towards increasing secularization. Any "reprivileging" of the Christian tradition that backs away from these practices risks doing violence to a deep moral sense held by many believers and nonbelievers on liberal Protestant campuses. One could even say that tacit assent to these values serves as a kind of contract or basis for trust between the two groups.

What Will the Postmodern Story Be?

Does postmodern thought contain resources for challenging the ethical reasoning that has persuaded church-related colleges to adopt practices that have had a secularizing effect on the academic environment of the college?

It seems to me that postmodern thought about ethics is characterized by two strains roughly paralleling differences between Hobbesian and Kantian modernism. Each has something slightly different to say to liberal Protestant colleges.

One strain adds the hermeneutic of suspicion to the relativistic critique of ethical values found already in Hobbesian modernism. All valuing is the taking-up of a perspective; there is no perspective from which the many perspectives can be evaluated, and any move to uphold some values and shut out others is no more than what all valuing is: an assertion of power over others.

An extreme, but perhaps over-simplified, interpretation of this stance is that it is contradictory both to hold a postmodern view of values and to claim that *any* set of ethical prescriptions for a community is better than any other. On such a view, we should hardly hope for any new, postmodern moral guidance for academic policies.

A second extreme, but less simplified, interpretation is seen in those postmoderns who speak as if, from their attack on the objectivity of values, it follows that belief systems that assert the existence of objective values are wrongheaded, and wrongheaded in such a dangerous way that the institutions that grow out of them are especially pernicious and ought, on postmodern grounds, to be denounced. For proponents of this view, the Christian faith, the church, and seriously Christian colleges tend to be the prototypes of what is to be avoided. Thus, we certainly cannot count on this version of postmodern ethics to provide any prescriptions that favor privileging the Christian faith in an academic community.

There is a more moderate version of this Hobbesian-flavored strain under which Christian and church-related colleges may fair better. It still asserts that there are no objective values but tries to avoid both self-contradiction and nihilism by focusing on what it is to live as one who believes there is only perspectival seeing. Living according to such a belief seems to commit one to the practical rule: do what you do if you will, but know that it is only one way among many to go.

Postmoderns may still complain—as a postmodern philosopher colleague of mine always does—that a church college will never pass the test of living by this rule because it is inherent to the Christian faith to claim its own absolute objectivity and rightness. Such a challenge would definitely have to be answered in order to give truly postmodern defenses of privileging the Christian tradition. Let us say for the sake of argument that such defenses could be given. Then, this strain of postmodernism might well offer hope for rejuvenating the church-academy relationship. It seems to say to a secular academic world that it cannot really have anything against the existence of academic communities that try also to be faith communities. It is their way to live out their perspective; secular universities are living out a different perspective. Neither is better than the other. Enough said.

Perhaps reasoning such as this gives postmodern intellectuals more reason than modern intellectuals had to accept the existence of faith-learning communities committed to particular doctrinal perspectives. Maybe postmodernism leaves those of us at liberal Protestant colleges, as well as those at secular universities, less reason to be haughtily and intellectually opposed to "Christian colleges." *But* how can it possibly prescribe new directions for reprivileging the Christian tradition at liberal Protestant colleges? We are one embodiment of a perspective towards faith and learning. What more can be said?

Possibly more can be said if we call upon the second strain of postmodernism. With some intended fun, I say that this one parallels modernism's Kantian strain because it offers postmodern reasons for preferring systems that value "the other." It comes to this by working out the meaning of a hermeneutic understanding, whereby one forgoes the ideal of objective, final knowing but seeks "contextually conditioned knowledge that is necessarily finite."[7] To live with the understanding that all knowing is knowing-for-the-time-being, we must remain open always for the conversation with the other that will give us a new context for knowing. Whatever present understanding we have, we see it as relatively momentary, awaiting the time when our own prejudgments are jostled by conversation with another who has other prejudgments. The

claim is that living by this hermeneutic understanding commits one to be always in conversation with the other in all his
or her otherness. This being-in-conversation-with-the-other
that makes correct understanding possible is tolerance.[8]

Here we have postmodernism willing to make a value assertion that implies something about how an academic community should be. A community committed to the enterprise
of knowing ought to be tolerant. Knowing occurs where there
is disagreement that breaks through old prejudices, makes old
horizons of understanding dissipate and new ones coalesce.
The knowing community, therefore, must be filled with difference and should tolerate as much difference as is possible while
still sustaining the conditions which make conversation possible.[9] This sounds an awful lot like a call to be a community
that respects individual liberty, keeps its doors open to faculty
of all sorts of allegiances and asserts curricular goals acceptable to people of tremendously different perspectives.
This sounds a lot like a well-secularized liberal Protestant
college.

If postmodernism does not give liberal Protestant colleges
reasons to change how they hire and how they state curricular
goals, perhaps it at least gives Christian faculty (and all others, of course) greater room to bring their commitments into
the classroom. This is often thought to be an implication of
postmodernism because it seems to encourage all scholars to
confess the prejudices that inform their knowing. If
postmodernism is to work a change on the liberal Protestant
campus, I think this may indeed be where it will make a difference, namely by making it more intellectually acceptable to
confess being a person of a given religious faith. But I remain
wary of expecting this to bring great change. The postmodern
teacher must be sure she is showing students how to make
that which we call "knowing" into an open-ended conversation with those who will prove her wrong. To do this will she
not have to display something that looks very much like an
"objective" distance from her value commitments?

This then is my challenge to those who see in
postmodernism a promising bulwark against the academy's
slide into secularization. That slide, at least at liberal Protes-

tant colleges, comes from practices undergirded by certain value commitments. The room which postmodernism's suspicion of objective values leaves for an ethical evaluation of these practices is quite limited. In its extreme forms, postmodernism either has nothing prescriptive to say and hence offers no ethical platform from which to reevaluate polices, or it strongly prescribes as much sliding towards secularization as is necessary to distance the church college from the supposed unpostmodern dogmatism inherent to Christianity. In a more moderate form, postmodernism would appear to bring to the discussion the same values as has modernism: a commitment to tolerance, a respect for individual liberty, and a need to teach topics "objectively" as a way of keeping the conversation with "the other" alive and invigorated.

Postmodernism thus seems to reinforce the values that, I have argued, have led liberal Protestant colleges to such policies as hiring without regard to religious allegiance, removing references to religious justifications for curricular decisions, and (perhaps inadvertently) teaching students to seek knowledge by distancing themselves from the truths of Christianity.

CONCLUSION TO THE PROLEGOMENA

I believe that an ethical analysis leads to the conclusion that fairness, tolerance, and respect for individual liberty have strong ethical appeal whether one sees with the eyes of modern political thinker, postmodern advocate, or liberal Christian. This being the case, arguments for changing secularizing practices will have to *disconnect the values from the practices*. That is, arguments will have to be made to the effect that we can uphold these values while forgoing the secularizing practices I described above. But, if we are to count on it being the *postmodern* nature of the present era (and not something else) that offers the promise of reprivileging the Christian tradition in the academy, then we must find and articulate what exactly it is about the postmodern perspective per se that makes it possible to back away from the secularizing practices while retaining the cherished values. And, if there is some such thing within postmodernism, then we must determine whether the church-related college can grasp hold of it and use it while rejecting postmodernism in its extreme forms.

For, a postmodernism that either rejects Christ's church as a hopelessly dogmatic institution or ejects moral aims from legitimate educational processes merely reiterates the very elements of modern epistemology against which the church-related teaching institution has already struggled. As noted earlier, the church-related college that makes teaching the cornerstone of its mission, has lived through the modern era of empiricism with sights still set upon the nonquantifiable, mainly intangible ethical purposes and powers of education. In this sense, such places have been in very serious conversation with their culture's reigning epistemology, but they are not of it. The allusion here to Paul's admonishment to the early Christians is intentional.

FROM PROLEGOMENA TO HOPE

I opened this paper with a summary of the argument used by those who have found in postmodernism's rejection of objectivity some special hope of establishing an epistemological defense for revitalizing religion's role in the academy and "reprivileging" faith traditions in academic settings. In response to that hope I identified specific practices having to do with faculty and curricular development which I believe have the inevitable effect of "unprivileging" a college's founding faith tradition, even though the theology of that very tradition may be used to support those values. And I have thus far argued that postmodern thought does not offer the small church-related college an acceptable, substantial, and weighty critique of the values that have led to and undergird these practices, especially in the ethically sensitive environment that small church-related colleges tend (laudably, in my mind) to be.

As a small step from prolegomena into reasons for hope, consider again this small fact that I have asserted from the beginning of this paper: the flourishing of ethical concerns at small church-related colleges. I have proposed that the small church-related colleges have come through the modern era with an ethical focus to their educational goals even though modern epistemology has made value-neutrality the hallmark of truth. I believe there are two other "going" concerns, well ingrained in the history of such colleges, that suffered hard times under modernism but survive nonetheless. In the paragraphs that follow, I suggest that the legitimate reason many devotees of the church-related college have had their hopes lifted by postmodernism is that postmodernism's critique of modern epistemology has returned these concerns to popularity, making them the concerns of academics generally. My claim is that these issues have been kept alive in church-related colleges despite widespread academic pressure under modernist premises to forgo them, and that in the era of postmodernism the general legitimacy of these concerns is reinstituted within the walls of the secular university, giving church-related colleges the hope of renewed acceptance and rejuvenated relevance.

The first concern I have in mind is the age-old discussion of the relationship of faith and reason. Many of today's college faculty have been educated on modernism's answer to that question and, though that answer has various permutations by which faith suffers to varying degrees in comparison to reason, the net result in the academy is general suspicion of the intellectual merit of faith claims and commitments. While such suspicion runs amuck in many a postmodern writer, the postmodernism's critique of modern epistemology nonetheless lays open the question for new inspection. Once postmodernism makes us sensitive to the way all knowledge claims necessarily bear the markings of the individual knower's prior values and commitments, the question begs to be asked and newly contested in wide academic circles: what makes religious commitments unworthy of invocation in the institutions and enterprises by which we seek understanding of our world?

Thus, postmodern thought renews the place in the academy of the age-old question regarding faith and reason. But in my experience with church-related colleges (four as either teacher or faculty member) this question was never quite so "settled" as the reign of modernism might suggest. Indeed, it seems to me that a church-related college embodies a faith tradition's insistence that there be a vital relationship between faith and knowledge and that the dynamics of one in relation to the other be continually explored, both academically and in individuals' lives. Insofar as postmodernism's critique of objective knowledge motivates a broad spectrum of members in the academic community to reconsider the value of faith to knowledge, it puts a stamp of approval upon one of the central projects of the church-related college.

It also has been my experience that small church-related colleges typically manifest a strong, institutional concern for the teacher-student relationship. "Mentoring" is understood to be a significant part of college teaching. Time with students out of the classroom is encouraged. In both formal and informal faculty discussions, diverse teaching-styles are assessed according to their ability to elicit student involvement in the educational process and to make this process more than a mere route to good grades and a secure job.

Thus, we have yet another way in which small church-related colleges have been a minority voice, standing up against the predominate strains of modern educational philosophy.[10] Reading Mark Schwehn's analysis of the Weberian philosophy of education that has shaped modern education, one readily sees that modern epistemology's emphasis on the value neutrality of real knowledge has been understood as a reason to deemphasize the significance of the teacher-student relationship.[11] The "stuff" of relationships—confession and revelation of character and values on the part of the teacher and the learner—are suspected obstacles to truth- seeking and must be set aside in the learning process; value-neutral truths can be transmitted effectively regardless of the character of the participants and the nature of their relationship.

But if postmodern thought is right, this move has been a mistake. Complementing postmodernism's attack on the ideal of objectivity is its preoccupation with the role of subjectivity in knowing. In denying the existence of objective knowledge, postmodern thinkers declare that all knowing is part confession/part discovery/part revelation of the knower's own values, commitments, and prejudices. If the make-up of those seeking knowledge necessarily infects, tints, or partly constitutes the object that will come to be known, then the make-up of the knowers and their opportunity to be in a relationship of knowing one another becomes a central element in the educational process.

Postmodern thought rejuvenates the academy's interest in what happens between teacher and learner and what each brings into the learning or research environment. Since the church-related college is a place where that conversation has been alive and well all these many years, postmodernism does now present these colleges with the opportunity to display their postmodern relevance. Dare I say that it places the teachers of church-related colleges in a privileged place from which to speak to the post-modern era?

A Sense of Place and the Place of Sense

WILLIAM J. CAHOY

A few years ago the institution where I teach, Saint John's in Minnesota, put together a collection of reminiscences by alumni, faculty, and friends entitled *A Sense of Place*. It is an apt title, for one of the things that comes through loud and clear as a characteristic of our institution and our community is a strong sense of place. Located in the midst of the rolling fields of rural Minnesota, not far from Lake Wobegon, Saint John's property consists of 2400 acres of woods, lakes, and reclaimed prairie that many find peaceful and nourishing. The campus proper is noted for its distinctive architecture that includes some of the oldest major buildings in the state and some striking modern ones by Bauhaus architect Marcel Breuer.

Significant and enriching as all that is, there is more to this sense of place than the physical location. It is intimately connected with the presence and habits of the monastic community that founded the school, continues to own it, and is still a strong presence on campus. In addition to being a college, Saint John's is their home and has been for almost 150 years. It is their place of worship and work; the place where they seek and find God; the place where they are buried; the place where their communal memories and hopes reside. Integral to the monastic life—and our sense of place—is the vow of stability.

A Benedictine is not a wanderer, but pledges fidelity to a particular community in a particular place. Applying this vow to the community as a whole, Benedictines are to sink their roots in their place and be nourished and clothed by it. This is evident at Saint John's in the bricks of the older buildings that were made on the premises from local materials. It is evident in the woodwork and furniture that to this day is made on campus from oak cut from our own forests. More recently, it is evident in the pottery formed from local clays and fired in the country's largest wood-fired kiln. All of this and more, particularly when coupled with the monastic virtue of hospitality, conspires to give us a strong sense of place—a sense of permanence, belonging, rootedness, community.

I mention this not merely to introduce Saint John's or because I think this is somehow unique to us. Quite the contrary, I suspect that something like this sense of place characterizes many small liberal arts colleges. In a host of different ways, these are special places. Moreover, they typically enter the lives of students at special times, providing an extended rite of passage, which is an important element of their significance in the lives and affections of their graduates. Rather, I mention this sense of place because I think we can see something more here than fond remembrances of special places, special times, and special people in our lives. In this essay I will explore the idea of this sense of place as both example and allegory of the importance of location in our knowing and in the way we institutionalize this knowing in colleges and universities. Specifically, place will be used as an allegory for one's location in a particular community and a particular tradition. The thesis of the essay is that this location, the place for sense-making, matters. Where one stands affects what one sees and how one makes sense of what one sees. Would one see different things or, what is not quite the same, would one see things differently, if one stood in the community and tradition of a church-related college than one would in the community and tradition of a non-church-related college? *Should* one see differently? Or is any difference traceable to the church relation, a sign that the college has not yet attained full collegiate status? Of particular interest to its identity as a college, does this located seeing count as knowing?

The essay advances a four-point thesis:

1. The modern university is rooted in a distinctly modern, specifically Enlightenment epistemology that makes the role of place irrelevant.

2. This epistemology makes the idea of a church-related college a virtual oxymoron.

3. The postmodern critique calls into question this modern epistemology, arguing that knowing, sense-making, is always related to one's location, i.e., place.

4. This opens up the possibility of rethinking the idea and rationale of the church-related college.

I

Whatever else they may be, colleges and universities are places dedicated to knowledge: preserving it, expanding it, testing, teaching, and learning it. Their self-understanding and mode of operation are intimately connected with how we understand what it is to know, with epistemology. This is demonstrably the case with the modern university. Typically traced to the founding of the University of Berlin in 1810, its explicit and implicit ideals clearly embody the principles of modern, specifically Enlightenment epistemology. The features of this epistemology most important for the self-understanding of universities and colleges are that reason is objective, neutral, universal, and autonomous.[1] Autonomy is particularly significant, for it is taken to mean that to be rational, scientific, objective (all seen as roughly synonymous and generally desirable), one must be independent of particular local commitments, traditions, and practices, be they national, ethnic, racial, religious or gendered. Such commitments to particular communities or tradition—a sense of place—were seen as obstructions to the universal, neutral, objective nature of reason. To see truly or to see the truth, to be reasonable, these commitments had to be set aside. Obviously this raises significant questions about the legitimacy of a church-related college, at least one that would take its commitments to the church seriously. But to pursue those questions responsibly, we need to establish more firmly this formative, modern epistemology.

The roots of modernity are tangled and deep, going past even the fertile soil of the Renaissance and Reformation. For our purposes, though, we can follow the traditional beginning in Descartes.[2] His basic methodological move of using systematic doubt as the means to truth and certainty, established the hermeneutic of suspicion so characteristic of the modern age. Prominent among the objects of his suspicion were the traditions he had inherited from his culture. They seemed arbitrary and as such were unreliable guides if not actual obstacles to the truth. Only reason was reliable.[3] To establish all on the firm foundation of reason, he engages in a kind of intellectual urban renewal that "raze(s) everything to the ground" and "once and for all . . . get(s) all the beliefs (he) had accepted from birth out of (his) mind."[4] In this way, says Descartes, "I gradually freed myself from many errors that can darken our natural light and render us less able to listen to reason."[5] With reason freed from the obstructions of custom and tradition, Descartes was confident that "there is nothing so far distant that one cannot finally reach nor so hidden that one cannot discover."[6] The first thing he discovers, of course, is the self-evident ground of certainty: the autonomous thinker, the self. On this twin foundation of autonomous reason and the autonomous reasoner the modern project was built.

Building on this foundation, the Enlightenment of the eighteenth century elaborated these norms for knowing and gave them a stronger political edge. The most striking characteristic of this family of thinkers, recognized by champions and critics alike, is their profound sense of the autonomy of reason and of themselves as its liberators. Peter Gay, summarizing his researches into the Enlightenment says that "The philosophes' experience . . . was a dialectical struggle for autonomy."[7] Ernst Cassirer in his influential study, *The Philosophy of the Enlightenment*, makes a similar point, referring to the Enlightenment as "the period which discovered and passionately defended the autonomy of reason, and which firmly established this concept in all fields of knowledge."[8] He also points out that the "permanent results," of the Enlightenment are not any set of "teachings which it develops and tries to formulate into a body of dogma," not content, but its understanding of "the form and manner of intellectual activity in general."[9] It is this understanding of intellectual activity that would prove so influential in the modern university. The classic expression of this understanding from within comes near the end of the century in Kant's famous essay "What is Enlightenment?" It opens with these stirring words: "Enlightenment is man's release from self-incurred tutelage. Tutelage is man's inability to make use of his understanding without direction from another. Self incurred is this tutelage when its cause lies not in lack of reason but in lack of resolution and courage to use it without direction from another. *Sapere aude!* (Dare to know!) 'Have courage to use your own reason!'—that is the motto of enlightenment."[10]

For Kant and the other Enlightenment luminaries the tutelage from which our reason must be liberated is primarily the authority of particular traditions and communities—precisely what I am referring to with the metaphor of "place." As Cassirer puts it, "The philosophy of the Enlightenment . . . opposes the power of convention, tradition, and authority in all the fields of knowledge."[11] Echoing Descartes, he observes that "it does not consider this opposition as merely a work of negation and destruction; it considers rather that it is removing the rubble of the ages in order to make visible the solid foundations of the structure of knowledge."[12] This foundation, of course, is and can only be reason. For the Enlightenment thinkers it was self-evident that reason, pure reason, sense-making, is not affected by place. All reasonable people see the same thing, no matter where they are standing. Cassirer: "The eighteenth century is imbued with a belief in the unity and immutability of reason. Reason is the same for all thinking subjects, all nations, all epochs, and all cultures."[13] The ideal was an epistemological utopia in which all particularities of place are removed or rendered irrelevant to knowing. The sentiment of German *philosophe* Christoph Wieland is typical, "Only the true cosmopolitan can be a good citizen"; for only he can "do the great work to which we have been called: to cultivate, enlighten and ennoble the human race."[14]

By contrast, allegiance to tradition or community—place in our metaphor—looks parochial, arbitrary, partisan, and, in light of persistent sectarian violence since the Reformation, dangerously divisive. With bountiful historical justification, such particular allegiances came to be linked with prejudice, intolerance, and closed-mindedness. They were seen as promoting self-interest at the expense of truth and determining in advance the outcome of any investigation. To the Enlightenment mind it was self-evident that "the falsification of the true standards of knowledge appears as soon as we attempt to anticipate the goal which knowledge must attain and to establish this goal prior to investigation. Not doubt, but dogma, is the most dreaded foe of knowledge. . . ."[15] Ceding authority to dogma, tradition, or community would seem to impose an alien, extrinsic force on reason that obstructs its view and distorts its findings. To be fully rational, to be authentic, reason must be free of all such outside constraints. It must be autonomous, a law unto itself. Only then is it—are we—free to follow the truth wherever it takes us, even to truths that may not support our most cherished beliefs and practices.[16] Only when free can we rely on reason to disclose reality. In general, the assumption is that the less we bring to an encounter with the world, with the facts, the better equipped we are to see clearly, for anything we bring is a potential bias that can distort reality.[17] Hence Descartes' absolutely naked, autonomous self is the model knower. MacIntyre summarizes this Enlightenment position well:

> Rationality requires . . . that we first divest ourselves of allegiance to any one of the contending theories and also abstract ourselves from all . . . particularities of social relationship. . . . Only by so doing . . . shall we arrive at a genuinely neutral, impartial, and in this way, universal point of view, freed from the partisanship and the partiality and onesidedness that otherwise affect us.
>
> . . .
>
> So, it was hoped, reason would displace authority and tradition. Rational justification was to appeal to principles undeniable by any rational person and therefore independent of all those social

and cultural particularities which the Enlightenment thinkers took to be the mere accidental clothing of reason in particular times and places.[18]

Elsewhere MacIntyre describes an impressive and influential example of this neutral, objective reason at work in the ninth edition of the *Encyclopedia Britannica*.[19] As described by MacIntyre, the encyclopaedists understood themselves as the latest and best manifestation of the progress of reason from tutelage to sovereignty. For them, "Descartes symbolized . . . a declaration of independence by reason from the particular bonds of any particular moral and religious community. It is on this view of the essence of rationality that its objectivity is inseparable from its freedom from the partialities of all such communities. It is to allegiance to reason as such, impersonal, impartial, disinterested, uniting, and universal, that the encyclopaedist summons his or her readers and hearers."[20] And it is a testimony to the pervasiveness of the Enlightenment epistemology that writer and reader alike simply took it for granted that "all rational persons conceptualize data in one and the same way and that therefore any attentive and honest observer, unblinded and undistracted by the prejudices of prior commitment to belief would report the same data, the same facts. . . ."[21] It was the task and presumed accomplishment of the *Britannica* to present this data as "a comprehensive synthesis of human knowledge."[22] The subject matter was ambitiously diverse (everything from A to Z), but the criteria of sense and rationality were the same. Their belief that reality in all its diversity can be comprehended with this single method expanded to the stronger position that reality can only be reliably known through this method.[23] The success and prestige of the Encyclopedia that this method produced established all the more firmly the assumption we have seen at work since Descartes, namely that rationality entails "an exclusion of tradition as a guide to truth."[24] As one of the contributors to the Ninth Edition, Henry Sidgwick, wrote in 1865, "Principles will soon be everything, and tradition nothing."[25]

Operative in this assumption and critical for our understanding of the conceptual geography of reason and the university is a fundamental and usually unspoken belief about the nature of freedom; namely, that it is incompatible with commitment. Freedom is generally taken to mean keeping one's options open, being unconstrained. Commitment means picking one option. Obviously, they move in opposite directions in a kind of zero-sum game. The more commitment, the less freedom. The more freedom, the less commitment. In this economy commitment to anything in particular can only be seen as a threat to freedom. Needless to say, this issue is far more complex than we can pursue here, but it is important to recognize the assumptions at work, for ultimately it is this understanding of freedom that justifies, indeed, *requires*, the abandonment of commitment to tradition and community—any sense of place—for the sake of reason.[26] If reasoned inquiry is to be free, the argument goes, it must be unencumbered by commitment. Epistemologically, commitment can only be seen as leading to closed-mindedness. As autonomous, freedom demands sovereignty. Personally, this means the authority of anyone or anything outside oneself is a threat to one's freedom, authenticity, integrity, and maturity. Epistemologically, this means that if reason is made accountable to or dependent on any end outside itself, it has lost its freedom and with that its integrity, authenticity, and maturity. This is the tutelage that must be overthrown if we are to be autonomous, free adults rather than dependent children. Thus the two major goods of the modern age—reason and freedom—conspire to relativize or exclude commitment to a particular tradition or community.

This principle is applied with most vigor to the Christian tradition and the Christian church, which most Enlightenment champions regarded as the primary threat to the free exercise of autonomous reason. Unfortunately, the history of the church offers far too much evidence in support of the charge that it is a force of oppression, intolerance, and closed-mindedness with a stake in perpetuating ignorance and *ancien regimes* of various sorts. Too often has it looked as if one must choose between Enlightenment, with its promise of reason and freedom, and the church, with its call for obedience to authoritative books, institutions and creeds. In this environment it is hardly surprising that the Enlightenment had a distinctly anti-Christian animus. For example, Diderot charged that "the Christian mythology . . . was more productive of crimes than any other" and that "religion retreats to the extent that philosophy advances."[27] Not surprisingly his influential *Encyclopédie* "declares war openly on religion and its claims to validity and truth. It accuses religion, of having been an eternal hindrance to intellectual progress. . . ."[28] In a similar vein, Hume referred to the world beyond that of the Enlightenment and its supporters as the realm of "Stupidity, Christianity & Ignorance" as if these three are generally synonymous.[29] And, of course, there is Voltaire's famous battle cry: *Écrasez l'infâme*, "Crush the villain," where the villain, the filthy thing, refers immediately to superstition but by extension to the church and Christianity. Hence Cassirer can refer in sum to "the great process of secularization of thought . . . which the philosophy of the Enlightenment sees as its main task."[30] Peter Gay goes so far as to identify the tension with or actual rejection of Christianity as one of the defining characteristics of the Enlightenment. He writes enthusiastically of the spirit of the Enlightenment as "a recovery of nerve" in which humanity has come of age in contrast to the failure of nerve he sees in Christianity and the ages dominated by the church.[31] Particularly revealing here is his assessment of Fontenelle as one who, though he "anticipated the philosophes in so much of his work, was not a philosophe in his heart" because—and his reasoning here is significant—"he never made the leap to naturalism" and "he remained . . . a tolerant, cultivated, firmly committed Christian."[32] On this common understanding, to be a true child of the Enlightenment and to be Christian are incompatible.

This all becomes particularly relevant to the church-related college when we recognize the extent to which the modern university and college are institutionalizations of the Enlightenment understanding of reason and freedom. In Marsden's words, these Enlightenment principles "provided the moral rationale for shaping modern higher education."[33] At the heart of this rationale is the principle of free inquiry, the idea that knowledge is to be pursued for its own sake, not for the sake of any other end, secular or religious. David Kelsey makes the Enlightenment connection explicit: "Academic freedom was the direct application to higher education of the central value of the Enlightenment: reason's independence from all authority and its innate responsibility to critically scrutinize any claim to authority."[34] This freedom of inquiry was written into university charters (mission statements) and given legal status through the establishment of faculty tenure.

Until fairly recently this freedom of inquiry worked in concert with the Enlightenment's basic "trust in rationality and its processes" to disclose truth and reality.[35] This process of reasoning was generally referred to as science (*Wissenschaft*) and, it was believed, provided "a basis for all right-thinking people to think alike."[36] Here the epistemological assumptions of the *Britannica*'s Ninth Edition, particularly its belief in the neutrality and universality of knowing, become especially germane to our study; for it reflects the assumptions operative in the university. As MacIntyre points out, "the dominant beliefs in our contemporary academic culture concerning the translatability of alien languages and the intelligibility of alien cultures are . . . a residue, an inherited set of presuppositions which are all the more powerful for being so seldom spelled out, a legacy from successive eighteenth- and nineteenth-century Enlightenments and not least from the culture of the Ninth Edition."[37] This belief is not as prominent as it once was in academic rhetoric but it remains powerfully operative in the curriculum and the pedagogical practice of universities and colleges where "the universal translatability of texts from any and every culture into the language of teacher and student is taken for granted. And so is the universality of a capacity to make what was framed in the light of the canons of one culture intelligible to those who inhabit some other quite alien culture, provided only that the latter is our own, or one very like it."[38] External authority can only confound that process by skewing the inquiry to justify some predetermined results (not to mention—and it usually wasn't—challenging the university's power as arbiter of reason, meaning, and reality).

The history of the institutionalization of this epistemology is most often traced to the German university of the eighteenth century. The University of Halle, founded in 1694 by Lutherans, was the first explicitly to abandon standards of religious orthodoxy to pursue "rational and objective" inquiry. This was followed by Göttingen in 1737, Erlangen in 1743 and, in at least a symbolic watershed, the University of Berlin in 1809. These German universities and their guiding rationale became a model for higher education in the United States. Throughout the nineteenth century a significant number of U.S. faculty studied in Germany and brought that experience back to their American schools.[39] In addition, many of the leaders of American higher education were consciously attempting to implement the German model at their institutions. Among the more influential were Henry Tappan, chancellor of the University of Michigan from 1852–1863, who had, in Marsden's words "an almost mystical reverence for the educational ideals of Prussia and the University of Berlin";[40] Andrew Dickson White, founder and president of Cornell (1868–1885), who was a member of the Michigan faculty during Tappan's time and attributed much of his thinking on education to Tappan's influence;[41] and Daniel Coit Gilman, founder and president of Johns Hopkins University (1876–1901), who early in his career had toured Germany with his friend White to study school systems. Johns Hopkins plays a particularly significant role in the transplantation of the German model to the U.S. Founded specifically as a research university centered on graduate education and granting the Ph.D., it was a Berlin in America and set the standards for the research ideal. Value-free scientific inquiry, pursuit of knowledge for its own sake by faculty and students was the *sine qua non* of authentic knowledge and higher education.

Initially, as these reforms were being implemented in the late nineteenth and early twentieth century, a sharp distinction was made, even by university advocates such as Gilman, between the graduate education of the university and the undergraduate college, be it church-related or not, where there was a more "direct concern to provide for spiritual and moral welfare."[42] But the distinction could not be sustained. With the increasing professionalization of the disciplines, virtually all college faculty were trained in the graduate environment where they learned that authentic knowing is value-free, and required that moral and religious commitments be set aside. As these faculty took up their posts at colleges across the country, how could they not see the traditional collegiate concern for spiritual and moral formation as inappropriate to the educational aims and identity of the college as an institution devoted to higher learning and based on reason? At the college no less than the research university, knowledge was to be pursued for its own sake without regard to the values or prior commitments of the teacher, student, institution, or society. Commitments such as church-relatedness are perceived as biases that must be set aside to participate fully in the academic life and to know and see truly. With this the Enlightenment epistemology was thoroughly institutionalized in the self-understanding of higher education in the United States, church-related no less than non-church-related.

II

In this environment the *idea* of a church-related college is increasingly precarious. The familiar adage that a Catholic (or Baptist or Lutheran or ____) college is an oxymoron turns out to be more than a wagish bon mot. It captures something significant. The college's identity and criteria for success as an institution of higher learning and the church's identity and criteria for success as a community of faith seem to pull in opposite directions. As a community of faith, the church is committed to the authority of revealed truth that *may* transcend reason and that has been articulated in some way in canonical texts, creeds, and doctrines as part of a concrete, historical community and tradition to which one is called to be faithful. This is what I am referring to as a sense of place, a sense of being rooted in a specific community and tradition. On the other hand, the college regards free and autonomous reason unfettered by prior commitments as the *sine qua non* of its pursuit of authentic knowledge. Consequently, for the sake of knowing, i.e., for the sake of the college's identity as a college, commitments such as those expected by the church, legitimate as they may be in their own right, need to be set aside. As one commentator puts it, "How is it possible for an element from a religious mythos to be at all pertinent to a university? The university's formal critical principle was hard won, and the battle left the conviction that knowledge can be freely pursued only if the university does not subject itself to tradition, religious or otherwise."[43]

Ultimately, what is at issue here is the age-old question of the relation between reason and faith, which can be seen as a specification of the relation between freedom and commitment. As Douglas Sloan concludes in his helpful analysis of this issue in relation to Protestantism and higher education in America, "The conception of knowing and of knowable reality that has come during the past centuries to dominate modern culture and education has left little place for the concerns and affirmations of religion."[44] More specifically, "The modes of knowing and the conceptions of knowledge dominant in the university disciplines, and in the worldviews that they also represented and contributed to, left little place for the affirmations of faith."[45] Reflecting this split between faith and knowledge, what Sloan elsewhere refers to as a "faith-knowledge dualism," a specialization of labor arose in which "The church was . . . the sole guardian of faith; the college and university the prime champions of knowledge."[46] Thus the operative epistemology and consequent self-understanding of the modern university rejects as conceptually incoherent what John Paul II identifies as the "privileged task" of a Catholic University, "to unite . . . by intellectual effort two orders of reality that too frequently tend to be placed in opposition as though they were antithetical: the search for truth, and the certainty of already knowing the fount of truth."[47] The search for truth requires that one be open to discovery, including the discovery that one's current beliefs are wrong. The certainty of already knowing the truth entails commitment and fidelity, suggesting that one is not open to all possibilities. It should come as no surprise, then, that "As a consequence of this process of secularization the very right of religious communities to found and maintain universities has often been questioned in various lands."[48] To be sure, in the United States this right is not challenged politically (at least not overtly), but, as we have tried to show, it is challenged conceptually. At bottom, therefore, what is at stake here is nothing less than the conceptual viability of the idea of a church-related college or university.

But what about all those church-related colleges out there (716 by Cuninggim's count)? Does not their long history and continued existence suggest that a marriage between knowing and faith, college and church is possible? Not necessarily. Many would suggest that this mixed marriage is and has always been possible only by compromising the integrity of one or both parties. For most of their history, it is charged, they were able to coexist because the autonomy and integrity of the educational aim was compromised in service of the church. As the academic partner became more self-aware and emerged from this subservience to full autonomy, tensions arose and the marriage seemed destined for divorce or at least separation.

Such a divorce is exactly what we see in the history of church-related universities and colleges in America since the Civil War. As described by Marsden and Burtchaell[49] especially, the last century has seen school after school confront the choice between academic excellence, which invariably was defined in terms of the Enlightenment epistemology described above, and their relation to the church. Once the issue was put that way, the choice to weaken or sever the relation to the church in pursuit of excellence seemed inevitable. History certainly shows that it is the path most often taken.[50] After all, who at a college or university would speak against academic excellence? It seemed necessary, even obviously so, that the school must abandon its relation to a specific community to attain the universal, neutral reason promised and required by the Enlightenment. This, it seemed, was the price of admission to the world of serious, "excellent" academics. This divorce between university and church occurred first at major Protestant universities such as Vanderbilt; but has since spread, especially in the latter half of our own century, to similar Roman Catholic institutions and to church-related liberal arts colleges of all sorts such as are the focus of reflection in this volume.

To understand the dynamics of our own situations, it is important to note that this disestablishment and secularization was not accomplished by anti-Christians in the mold of Voltaire, Hume, or d'Holbach. On the contrary, those directing the move were typically self-identified Christians, often ordained clergy, who understood the changes they were instituting as promoting Christianity.[51] Consistent with the dominant Whig ideal in which "Protestantism was identified with the advances of civilization and the cause of freedom," "the liberal Protestants who constructed the new universities justified the scientific and technological definitions of many university activities on the grounds that such activities simply *were* Christian." In their understanding "Science and Protestant religion went hand in hand, since both stood for free inquiry versus prejudice and arbitrary authority."[52] Hence the freeing of science from the authority of dogma and tradition to follow its own lead was parallel to the Reformation's freeing of individual believers from the power of an authoritarian Roman church. Like the earlier reformation, theirs too would advance the cause of Christianity while also advancing the cause of civilization. These sentiments can be found in the speeches and writings of virtually all the educational leaders of the late nineteenth century, but they could hardly be better expressed than in these words of professor Frederic Henry Hedge addressed to a gathering of Harvard alumni in 1866: "The secularization of the College is no violation of its motto '*Christo et Ecclesiae*.' For as I interpret those sacred ideas, the cause of Christ and the Church is advanced by whatever liberalizes and enriches and enlarges the mind."[53] Whether articulated or not, this general Whig, liberal Protestant confidence is rooted in a theology of creation that sees the world as a place for encountering God. Education, as a study of the world and quest for truth, will, when freely pursued, only lead to encounters with God and thus promote true religion.

While there can be no doubt that these leaders understood their work as promoting Christianity, they were equally clear in their opposition to what they referred to as "sectarianism,"

allegiance to particular communities with their particular doctrines, creeds, and traditions. It was this sectarian allegiance,
not Christianity per se, that was opposed to the Enlightenment
spirit of free inquiry and autonomous reason. They were convinced, therefore, that this sectarianism needed to be opposed
not only for the sake of free inquiry but for the sake of Christianity itself. Thus Christianity in general is endorsed, even
invoked in pursuit of academic excellence, while any connection to a particular community and its tradition, any sense of
being located in a particular spiritual geography, is
marginalized or abandoned. Institutionally, this manifested
itself at school after school in the move from a relationship to a
specific church body to a relationship to generic, non-denominational Christianity. In the quest for an ever more inclusive,
truly universal, utopian framework, even this soon came to
seem too specific, parochial, sectarian. Consequently, in a rhetorical progression that can be traced through the history of
the self-descriptions of many church-related colleges, generic
Christianity was transposed into generic religiosity and then
to a generic affirmation of humanistic values. Thus, whatever
the intentions of those who made the initial moves in the nineteenth century, the net effect has been the disestablishment and
secularization of most major universities in America.

From our historical vantage point, this result may seem inevitable, but there is no reason to think it seemed so to those
making the initial decisions. One thing that makes the effects
of such decisions so difficult to predict is what we might call a
generational lag. As noted above, the decision to move from a
specific church connection to generic Christian values seems
innocent, reasonable, and appropriate, even on Christian
grounds. Initially, all goes along much as before and we seem
to have the best of both worlds, confirming the rationale for
the decision. However, as time passes, usually a generation or
so, this arrangement proves unsustainable. I would submit that
this is no accident. The reason it works initially is that most of
the participants were formed in the old system. Though their
rhetoric may have changed, their fundamental, unspoken,
mostly unrecognized life-shaping mythos remains the same.
In the next generation, in many cases because of the decisions

made a generation before, fewer people have this formation until eventually a majority of the participants no longer share those unspoken assumptions and move further away from what their forebears took for granted.

Mark Schwehn's discussion of Weber's account of the academic vocation makes an interesting case study here.[54] Weber bases his conception of the academic vocation on religious, specifically Christian views of life, but without God. He could perhaps imagine and sustain this vocation because of the religious character of his surrounding culture and his own religious formation, the effects of which were so much a part of him that their source was almost impossible to notice. A generation or two later, however, in part because of changes he helped bring about, his own vision was no longer sustainable and was without a rationale. It is precisely such a story Burtchaell tells about Vanderbilt University and changes in higher education in post-Civil War America. His point, I take it, is to raise the question as to whether many current church-related institutions, particularly Roman Catholic colleges and universities in the post-Vatican II era, might not be in the midst of a similar generational lag. Might the faculty and administration of these institutions, in many cases the fruit of one sort of cultivation by their forebears, be making changes in that cultivation that will make it harder to perpetuate what we value in the institutions? The answer may not be as clear as some suggest, but the question is one the history of the past century forces upon us.

This question is especially pertinent at church-related liberal arts colleges which, despite the pattern of secularization, have maintained a relation of some sort with the church. Even here, where the tension between the Enlightenment norm of autonomy and the commitment to the church has not led to a divorce, it has often led to a separation. On the whole it is amicable, but it is a separation nonetheless. Trading on a standard (and rather simplistic) fact-value distinction parallel to the reason-faith distinction noted earlier, personal commitments and faith are deemed relevant to how one *feels* about what one knows or how one *values* or *evaluates* what one knows; but they can have no bearing on the knowing itself. In this schema the college's church relationship is seen as relevant to such values and is operative institutionally, often to powerful effect, in the domains of campus ministry, student life, or maybe the theology or religion department. However, it is commonly assumed that the religious commitments and the church-relation have no place in the classroom, laboratory, or studio where knowledge is sought and taught. Here, in the academic pursuits that define it as a college, the church-related liberal arts college is no different than its secular siblings. Indeed, many of its advocates celebrate this absence of difference. One frequently hears reassurances from administrators, faculty, and students at such institutions that the relation to the church makes no difference in the classroom. The school is not trying to indoctrinate students, and so on. We might say that what we have here is a separation between church and college in which the parties live on the same premises and have worked out a shared custody arrangement whereby the college is responsible for the students' education, the academics; and the church is welcome to handle or at least participate in the social, moral, and spiritual care of students. Given the Enlightenment framework of the world of higher education, this may be the best we can do. After all, what else could the church-relation mean if knowing must be autonomous in order to be authentic knowing? Moving and important as the sense of standing in the Christian community may be in one's life history, it can have no bearing on what we know—on the proper business of the college *qua* college. When it comes to academics, to thinking and learning, to the facts, one place ought to be much the same as any other.

But to say that the relation to the church, the college's place in a specific community and tradition, is relevant only to issues of personal student development—even if these are in many ways more important than academics—still seems inadequate. The church is left out of the central identity of the college: the use of reason to expand, critique, and pass on our understanding of the world. Thus even here, where the relationship is congenial, we cannot avoid the oxymoron. The Enlightenment understanding of reason as autonomous and its institutionalization in colleges leaves us with few resources for building a sustainable rationale for the relation. The best we can hope for is a division of labor that accepts the church relation as important but ancillary to the *real* academic work of the college. This seems to be the only viable alternative to the pattern of thoroughgoing secularization in which the church-relation is set aside as an obstacle to the rational, scientific, neutral, universal, objective knowledge that is the goal of the college. To be sure, some may set it aside with relish, others with sadness, but it is widely accepted that this is the tuition for genuine higher learning. Indeed, many would suggest that this is the price of maturity both personally and institutionally. In this environment it is hard not to see the church-related college as historically an anachronism and conceptually an oxymoron. Its day has passed and it must adapt. It must modify or abandon its church-relation if it would be a real college.

III

As is well known, the modern Enlightenment understanding of authentic knowing described here is being sharply criticized on a number of fronts by postmodernism. Despite its widespread usage, "postmodernism" remains a notoriously elusive term, used by many different people in many different contexts to mean many different things. As one commentator puts it, "'Postmodern' is a nearly empty tag. Every time I use the word . . . I feel like Warren G. Harding. His speeches were described . . . 'as an army of pompous phrases moving across the landscape in search of an idea'." In another delightful image, "postmodern" is likened to intellectual velcro: a label "so adhesive that it can be used to pick up assorted pieces of lint in our culture (and) to characterize almost anything one approves or disapproves."[55] In many ways, "postmodernism" functions like "existentialism" of a generation past: everyone uses it but to widely different purposes and without a precise definition. For some, postmodernism is synonymous with atheism, relativism, and nihilism; a philosophy in which reality and meaning are whatever we want them to be. For others, postmodernism creates a space for belief in God, tradition, community. While both understandings have a solid basis in the literature, we will be following the second line of thought.

Fortunately, we need not here track all these different postmodernisms, or make any rulings on what is or is not authentic postmodernism. Rather, in the spirit of experimentation appropriate to an essay and the spirit of the collage typical of postmodernism, I will paste together a number of themes generally associated with postmodernism that are particularly germane to our understanding of "knowing" and of the idea of a church-related college. In the end, the point is not what we call this cluster of ideas, whether they are or are not postmodern, but whether they are true. If the critique of the received understanding of knowing is sustainable—and the contention here is that it is—it entails a critique of the standard way of thinking about authentic higher education. This may make room for thinking about the church-related college as something other than an anachronistic oxymoron. That at least is the postmodern opportunity we are exploring here.

So what is this postmodern critique? In terms of our guiding metaphor, we can say that at its heart it is the recognition that knowing, sense-making, has a location. As we have seen, the modern understanding of knowing takes it as axiomatic that considerations of place—one's location in community, culture, history, tradition—are irrelevant if not actual obstructions to knowing. Authentic reason is autonomous, above the fray of partisan disputes. As such it offers a neutral, universally accessible common ground into which all local particularities can be translated and in terms of which their competing claims can be adjudicated. Postmodernism rejects each of these claims as an illusion, disclosing how the Enlightenment's universal, neutral reason is neither universal nor neutral.

Far from universal, the modern understanding of reason, charge the postmoderns, actually limits "reason" to one particular type of reason (scientific, discursive) which is then made synonymous with reason per se and imperialistically imposed as the universal norm for all rationality, truth and reality. This narrow, absolutized notion of rationality distorts not only rationality but reality. In response to this imperialism, postmoderns seek to expand the concept of reason, or what counts as knowing, to include emotions, intuitions, and other traditionally nonrational, often "feminine," avenues as valid paths to knowledge. Inspired by developments in modern physics, hermeneutic theory, and the social sciences, postmodernism maintains that knowledge is not simply a matter of disinterested observation, but has a participatory character. I participate in what I know. Douglas Sloan, who regards this as the one genuine contribution of postmodernism, summarizes it well:

> What seems to be happening is that the objectivistic conception of knowing, which is a mainstay of the mechanical philosophy and the modern mind-set, is being fundamentally challenged. Under broad attack is what Ernst Lehrs once called "the onlooker consciousness," the characteristic mode of modern consciousness. This is the Cartesian view that the knower is simply a detached onlooker, describing a world of self-existent objects as though neither the knower nor the known were mutually and essentially affected in the process. This conception of knowing as involving a detached spectator observing and interpreting a world of mind-independent objects seems to be undergoing massive collapse.[56]

With this, postmodernism also challenges the focus on dispassionate, objective, neutral observation as the sole arbiter of truth, reality, and meaning. The new wrinkle here is not in asking to what extent objectivity is possible, but in asking to what extent objectivity, being disconnected, is desirable. If participation is not merely an emotional side-effect of knowing, an optional overlay, but is a genuine means of knowing; in other words, if there are things known only by participation, then objectivity is not the universal key to knowing. Indeed, there may be times when objectivity obscures rather than discloses reality. In this there is the potential for rethinking the role of autonomy and commitment in knowing.

This critique of the concept of reason as reductionistic also illustrates a broader pattern postmoderns diagnose in modern consciousness; namely, an obsession with commonalities, with sameness. In general, the very idea of the universal is problematic for postmodernism. The concern is that the universal, be it particular concepts or large-scale theories (totalizing discourses), can only be sustained by suppressing anomalies, differences, and the ordinary concrete particularity of the many that comprise the one. In response, the postmodern strategy is to highlight the particular difference, the exceptions to the rule, in hopes of subverting claims to a universal, neutral, objective account of reality. They are willing, at times it seems eager, to sacrifice unity and even coherence for the sake of acknowledging difference. Thus Lyotard closes his short essay, "What is Postmodernism?" by admonishing us to "wage a war on totality . . . activate the differences."[57] While this often involves the deconstruction of the putative universals, it is important to recognize that the aim is not merely to subvert but to disclose realities that have been obscured by the universalizing obsession. In our terms, postmodernism recognizes and affirms the significance of local differences over against the drive of the Enlightenment to discount the local for the sake of universal, global unities, the nonplaced, the utopian, and the disembodied. This, charges the postmodern, is ultimately too removed from the reality in which we live and finally distorts rather than discloses that reality.[58]

Of particular significance in the fight against the limitation of the concept of reason is postmodernism's recovery of narrative as a legitimate form of knowing. This is a central theme of Lyotard's analysis in his seminal work, *The Postmodern Condition*, which he presents as a sharp contrast to the Enlightenment's suspicion of narrative (myth) as primitive, pre-scientific and culturally specific.[59] To be sure, the modern understanding recognizes the importance of narrative as a mnemonic, for cultural bonding or simply for entertainment; but it is confident, in the spirit of Hegel, that any rational content of the narrative, its essence, point or meaning, can be translated from the narrative language to our neutral, universal, scientific language without losing anything important. Similarly, the fact-value distinction is used to explain how narrative may contribute to our interpretation or evaluation of the world, of what we know, but not to our knowing per se. The assumption is that we have a foundational, neutral apprehension of the facts, which is the domain of reason and is to be unaffected by our particular narrative. On top of these facts, if you will, is an interpretive overlay which is often related to a narrative and may vary from culture to culture.

The postmodern turn, which MacIntyre employs so effectively, is simply to point out that this relativization of narrative is precisely the modern narrative. Narrative is inescapable—even for those who would deny it. To make this point, which is central to the possibility of rethinking the church-related college, Lyotard first argues that "scientific knowledge does not represent the totality of knowledge; it has always existed in addition to, in competition and conflict with, another kind of knowledge, which I will call narrative. . . ."[60] As a form of knowing, narrative is linked with "know how," competencies such as knowing how to live, knowing how to listen, to judge, to be happy. Since there is no prima facie, neutral reason not to regard this as knowing, he maintains that "Knowledge (*savoir*) in general cannot be reduced to science, nor even to learning (*connaissance*). . . . Knowledge is not only a set of denotative statements" or that which is arrived at through a process of discursive reasoning. Moreover, as two parallel ways of knowing, science and narrative are not able "to judge the existence or validity" of each other because "the relevant criteria are different."[61] Narrative is not a failed attempt at scientific knowledge nor is science a peculiar attempt at narrative. Knowing simply cannot be reduced to one practice that is the norm for all instances. In particular, against the claims or assumptions of the Enlightenment that science is the neutral normative arbiter of reason, truth, and reality, Lyotard maintains that "Science possesses no general metalanguage in which all other languages can be transcribed and evaluated." Indeed, science is not only "incapable of legitimating other language games," "it is incapable of legitimating itself." Thus science too requires a narrative for its legitimation. "Scientific knowledge cannot know and make known that it is the true knowledge without resorting to the other, narrative, kind of knowledge, which from its point of view is no knowledge at all."[62] In sum, the rationality of the Enlightenment is not the autonomous, neutral knowing it was said to be. Its understanding of knowing, of what is reasonable or makes sense, is also internal to a narrative. Sense has a place—and inescapably so.

The idea that sense-making, our understanding of what counts as rationality, is located in a narrative is developed with particular force by Alasdair MacIntyre. In his aptly titled *Whose Justice? Which Rationality?* he makes it clear that what is at issue between narratives or traditions is nothing less than the concept of rationality itself. "(T)he resources of adequate rationality are made available to us only in and through traditions."[63] "Some problems are indeed shared" between traditions, he observes. "But what importance each particular problem has varies from tradition to tradition, and so do the effects of failing to arrive at a solution. Moreover, what counts as a satisfactory solution and the standards by reference to which different solutions are to be evaluated also differ radically from tradition to tradition. Thus . . . any hope of discovering tradition-independent standards of judgment turns out to be illusory."[64] By locating knowing in narrative, MacIntyre and Lyotard reject the fact-value schema as a misleading map of the epistemological terrain. Narrative here is not merely a secondary or superficial interpretive overlay, a perspective that can be easily put on or removed like a filter or lens. These narratives are deeply formative of one's identity and consciousness, affecting not only the way we interpret or evaluate the world but how we see, experience and know it in the first place.

But we are not yet at the heart of the postmodern use of narrative. For that we must add the contention that there is no grand, totalizing metanarrative by which to adjudicate the competing claims of the various narratives. So central is this idea that Lyotard can say "Simplifying to the extreme, I define *postmodern* as incredulity toward metanarratives."[65] The point here is not so much the comprehensiveness of the narrative but the claim to be above the fray, to be neutral. On this Lyotard is quite clear, "there is no possibility that language games can be unified or totalized in any metadiscourse."[66] MacIntyre, though his own position is ultimately rather different than Lyotard's, makes the same point in discussing three rival versions of moral enquiry: "there is and can be no independent standard or measure by appeal to which their rival claims can be adjudicated, since each has internal to itself its own fundamental standard of judgment."[67] Thus we face the following

situation: Knowing and all our criteria for evaluation are located in a narrative or tradition. There are multiple narratives
with competing claims on a variety of significant questions
such as: What is reasonable? What is just? What is worth knowing? What is good? There is no neutral, nonnarrative position
to which one can appeal to resolve the disputes and there is no
overarching metanarrative into which the particular narratives
can be translated and in terms of which the disputes can be
resolved. There is only the irreducible play of competing narratives. Difference and pluralism are irreducible and
nonadjudicable.

Finally, postmoderns make clear that in speaking of narrative we are also speaking of community. Narratives are told
by communities and in a host of ways live in and bind together
communities. In Lyotard's terms, "What is transmitted through
these narratives is the set of pragmatic rules that constitutes
the social bond."[68] Thus to say that all knowing is located in
narrative or tradition is also to say that it is located in a community and form of life. With this we come to another central
theme of postmodernism; namely, the political character of
knowledge. The contest of narratives is also a contest of communities, in which there is no neutral metacommunity above
the fray just as there is no neutral metanarrative. All are partisan. Thus the identification of one community's narrative of
rationality as universal, neutral, or normative is a powerful
political act. It privileges one community, identifies everyone
else as other, and then discounts them as sectarian, biased, irrational, deviant, and in need of explanation if not therapy.[69]
In this contest, to be accepted as neutral is the ultimate victory,
for it renders one's power virtually invisible and so all the more
effective. This, as MacIntyre points out, is precisely the victory
that has long been enjoyed by the modern, liberal tradition.
The Enlightenment story is one of the contending narratives,
and its claim to be the neutral arbiter of all disputes is not
merely a naive illusion or an innocent mistake, but a clever
subterfuge for power.

Some proponents and opponents of postmodernism conclude that this leaves us with a radical relativism in which
power is everything and there is no truth, no reality, no mean-

ing other than what we give to the world. In one very real and important sense, postmodernism in its various forms is relativistic, for it argues that what we know, see, and perhaps even experience is, at least in part, a function of—and thus relative to—the narrative, tradition, and community of which we are a part. The locatedness of knowing is unavoidable. What we see is relative to where we stand. However, this recognition of the importance and unavoidability of place in what we know does not require the conclusion that there is no truth or that we cannot know it. Some do indeed conclude that, particularly those in what MacIntyre refers to as the genealogical tradition going back to Nietzsche. While in many ways this is the most radical postmodern position, it also seems to be the least *post*modern. Its radical conclusion only follows if it still accepts the modern, Enlightenment premise that knowing must be neutral and autonomous. On that premise, the realization that neutrality is not possible requires the conclusion that we cannot have genuine knowledge of reality or truth. There is an advance here in the honesty and consistency with which the modern critique of tradition-based, located knowing is applied to modernity itself. But there is no fundamental challenge to modernity's norms for knowing. More *post*modern is a position that challenges the assumption that neutrality is necessary for authentic knowing. Local knowledge—knowledge rooted in a place, in narrative, tradition, and community—may be authentic and may disclose reality. The fact that I must stand in a particular place to see some things does not make what I see there untrue.

The charge is also made that recognizing the inescapable location of something as foundational as standards of rationality leaves us shut in on ourselves without a common language in which to speak with other communities, much less assess competing claims.[70] In the final three chapters of *Whose Justice?* MacIntyre argues forcefully that such conversation between incommensurable communities is not only possible but necessary for the vitality of a tradition. "A tradition becomes mature just insofar as its adherents confront and find a rational way through or around those encounters with radically different and incompatible positions which pose the problems of incommensurability and untranslatability."[71] In considering the characteristics of such a conversation, MacIntyre first refines the incommensurability for which he has argued. "It is not . . . that competing traditions do not share some standards," he explains. "All the traditions with which we have been concerned agree in according a certain authority to logic both in their theory and in their practice. Were it not so, their adherents would be unable to disagree in the way in which they do. But that upon which they agree is insufficient to resolve those disagreements."[72] He further points out that such conversation does not require moving to some third language that is natural to neither of the parties. Whatever that would be it would not be the kind of conversation between the two communities that we are seeking. For such a conversation one must learn the other language as a "second first language." One must enter empathetically and imaginatively into the language and form of life of the other community, learning that some things are simply untranslatable. On this basis one can begin to understand the other and even make a case for the rational superiority of one tradition over another.

To make such a comparative evaluation one first uses the understanding one has acquired of the other tradition from within to determine whether it measures up to its own standards. This is significantly different from the standard modern, encyclopedic move of asserting the rational superiority of one's own tradition by invoking the criteria of one's tradition to measure all others. Secondly, one makes oneself and one's tradition vulnerable to the best critiques of the other tradition, to see oneself from its perspective and construct a response. This, he points out, often leads to a crisis in the history of a tradition, offering a significant occasion for creativity and growth or decline. MacIntyre illustrates this in his argument for the superiority of Thomism to the Encyclopaedist and Genealogical traditions.[73] For our purposes, however, the significance in this is not whether his argument is successful, but simply that it is possible. His ability to construct such a comparative assessment without violating the incommensurabil

ity of the competing traditions shows that serious debate between traditions is possible even when standing within a tradition.

A final aspect of the importance of location, of place, in sense-
making, is elaborated by two Christian thinkers not usually
associated with postmodernism or each other: Jaroslav Pelikan
and C. S. Lewis. Each in his own way points to the need or at
least the possibility of seeing *with* tradition, a variation on what
was earlier referred to as "participative knowing." In the last
of his Jefferson lectures, published as *The Vindication of Tradition*, Pelikan takes exception to the way Ralph Waldo Emerson
plays insight against tradition. In what we could call a proto-
typically modern move, Emerson saw tradition as a tyrannical obstacle to insight that needed to be deposed in order to
liberate authentic knowing. Pelikan observes that tradition can
indeed be tyrannical but argues that it can also be and has in
fact been a source of insight and creativity. In the end, says he,
the actual history of human thought does not support
Emerson's simple dichotomy between tradition and insight.
"The condescending attitude" of many modern interpreters
toward tradition "fails to recognize that during most of intellectual history, understanding, . . . insight was achieved by
means of tradition."[74] Participating in the tradition may offer
sources of insight I would not otherwise have seen.

Lewis makes a similar point in a brief essay entitled "Meditation in a Toolshed." He tells of being in a dark toolshed with
a beam of light coming through a crack in the roof. When he
looks *at* the beam of light, he sees one thing and when he
changes his position to enter into the beam of light and look
along it or *with* it, he sees something altogether different. For
one thing, he no longer sees the beam of light. In this case,
literally where he stood affected what he saw. He goes on to
use this as a metaphor for two different ways of knowing—
one observational, from outside, the other participative, from
the inside. For instance, what we might know by "looking at"
Christianity and what we might know by "looking with" Christianity at everything else are not the same. The modern preference, he argues, in line with the position set forth in this essay,
has been for "looking at." The assumption being that this is

objective, and scientific and discloses reality. Undoubtedly, this way of knowing tells us *something* true and important. The point here is simply that it does not tell us *everything* true and important. Moreover, there is no reason to assume that this constitutes the only authentic knowing. Quite the contrary; Lewis observes, in what we might call a very postmodern spirit, that "you can step outside one experience only by stepping inside another. Therefore, if all inside experiences are misleading, we are always misled."[75] If it is the case that one can see *with* tradition and perhaps see some things *only* by looking with and through tradition, then commitment to tradition and the community of which it is a part, does not necessarily obstruct one's view of the world. Recognizing the place of sense may not be antithetical to rationality. Indeed, we could turn the tables and say that if we do see with tradition, then not participating in the tradition, insisting that one must leave traditions behind in order to see, actually obstructs one's view of the world.

IV

The postmodern critique of the Enlightenment has profound implications for how we understand colleges and universities, which, as noted above, have understood themselves almost entirely in terms of the widely discredited Enlightenment notion of autonomous reason. In Marsden's words, "the very principles that provided the moral rationale for shaping modern higher education have proved untenable."[76] Of particular importance for us: it was on the basis of precisely these principles that religious perspectives were excluded from higher education and a relation to the church was deemed incompatible with the academic integrity of a college. Consequently, the failure of these principles opens up the possibility—the necessity—of rethinking the relation of college and church. In general the argument is that if all knowing is rooted in some sustaining community, as postmodernists contend, then the church-related college becomes not an anomaly or even the oxymoron some would claim but a variation on the structure common to all knowing and all colleges.

It is noteworthy that we are not here making a special plead-
ing for the church or the church-related college. The contention is that the strand of postmodernism described in the
previous section offers a better, more accurate conceptual
framework for understanding the relation between colleges
and the communities of which they are a part (of which the
church would be but one example) than does the Enlightenment model. Knowing and its institutionalization in colleges
and universities, say modernity's critics, has always been located in sustaining narratives and communities. The problem
is that this relationship has not been and could not be accounted
for in the rationale of the colleges developed on Enlightenment principles. Where a connection was recognized, it was
typically seen as a vestigial element of an earlier era to be en-
dured and brought into line with the operative rationale. What
the critics help us see is that the inability to eliminate these
communal connections completely was not a problem of implementation, but a problem with the ideal of autonomy itself.
Thus one can say that the place of sense, the relation of knowing to narrative and community, has been one of the factors
repressed for the sake of conforming to the Enlightenment concepts of knowing and the university. As in so many other areas, the contemporary critiques have helped us see that "liberal
universities were never as free from political, commercial, class
and gender interests as their rhetoric implied."[77]

While the full postmodern agenda is diverse and controversial—and is certainly not being endorsed here *carte blanche*—
the central critique of the Enlightenment claim to neutrality
has gained widespread acceptance. In most disciplines professional presentations and papers routinely include a statement of the author's location on a variety of maps: gender,
race, class, sexual orientation, and so on. For the most part,
however, this critique has not been applied to our thinking
about the university as a whole. Here we still act as if location
is unimportant, assuming, it would seem, that colleges are
detached, above the fray, and not significantly affected by relations with narrative, communities, or tradition. There is particular reluctance to apply this sense of location to the influence
of religious communities, whether in the case of individual

scholars or the institution. I suspect that at most colleges one need not listen long to hear faculty members, who in their own disciplines reject the possibility of autonomous, neutral knowing, arguing that any sort of church-relation is inappropriate because it violates the autonomy and neutrality of academic inquiry. We find ourselves in the midst of the not uncommon, but still perplexing situation in which the institutionalization of an idea, in this case the Enlightenment epistemology, is holding on longer than the idea itself—and precisely among people who have explicitly rejected the idea in their own fields.

Thomas Kuhn can help us understand this. In analyzing the dramatic shifts in thought that are scientific revolutions, he noted that even when faced with anomalies in our theories we are reluctant to abandon the old way of thinking until we have a new one to go to (another acknowledgment that we need a place to stand?).[78] At present we see the anomalies in the Enlightenment rationale for the university, but are not sure what the new way of thinking about it would look like. We also may well have a number of well-founded concerns about the alternative: What does it mean for a college to take its location seriously? Is it the end of free academic inquiry? In what sense is it still a college (which of course begs the question of what it means to be a college)? Specifically, what would a college that takes its location in the Christian community seriously look like? Would it be a parochial, narrow-minded, doctrinaire place with only like-minded people interested only in indoctrination? Unfortunately, history gives us abundant reason for concern on these grounds—a point that must never be far from the consciousness of those who would defend the church-related college. Nevertheless, as real as these concerns are, once it is acknowledged that "intellectual inquiry takes place in a framework of communities that shape prior commitments,"[79] as it now widely is, intellectual honesty requires that we also admit that the standard basis for excluding the religious perspective no longer works. It is hardly neutral to invoke neutrality only to eliminate positions one does not like. To be sure, a case may be made for the exclusion of the church from the academy, but it will require more than an appeal to neutrality.

With this we are into precisely the rethinking of the church-college relation the possibility of which it was the task of this essay to demonstrate. So let us take stock. We began by reviewing the Enlightenment claim that authentic knowing is autonomous and thus should be unaffected by relations to particular communities or traditions, detached from any sense of place. As institutionalized in colleges and universities, this claim calls into question the conceptual viability of the idea of a college related to the church. By contrast, the postmodern critique points out the inescapable locatedness of knowing in narrative, tradition, and community. In doing so, it makes the idea of a college related to the narrative, tradition, and community of Christianity *conceptually* viable, thus opening up the possibility of rethinking the nature and mission of the church-related college we set out to demonstrate. QED.

Granting, for the sake of argument, that we have demonstrated the possibility and the need for this rethinking, it is important to recognize that we have not actually done the rethinking. That daunting task now lies before us, but not in this essay. We should note too that the outcome of this rethinking is not given with its possibility. We may have shifted the argument out of the Enlightenment framework, a not insignificant move, but we have not thereby won the argument. Simply because the *idea* of a church-related college is conceptually viable does not mean it is practically viable or a good idea. One may still object on a number of grounds that *this* community and tradition, the Christian church, is incompatible with the life of a college. The difference is that this case can no longer be made on the spurious general principle that a positive relation to community or tradition is incompatible with the nature of a college. Now it must be made by explaining specifically what there is about this community that makes it hostile to free inquiry. As such, this could be a much more productive dialogue for both sides.

While the task of actually rethinking the identity and mission of the church-related college on post-Enlightenment principles must await another time, I would like to give some substance to the possibility we have opened up by indicating briefly the general direction I think this rethinking might take and some of the resources on which it might draw. Since places are always specific and since "there is no such thing as generic Christian higher education,"[80] I will draw more specifically on the Catholic, Benedictine heritage of our place.

Most generally, if our principle is that where I stand affects what I see and everybody stands someplace, the Christian place to stand is with Christ, ultimately at the foot of the cross, mindful of Incarnation and Resurrection. The Christian contention is that from here one sees the world truly (which is not necessarily the same as saying that from here one can see all that is true or even all that is important). Locating a college at this place means that one brings to bear the full weight of rigorous, disciplined, critical thought and discourse on this view of the world. Using Lewis's distinction, what we are talking about here is not looking *at* Christianity, but looking *with* or *through* Christianity at the whole of human experience. Conceptually, this is what authorizes the founding of Christian *colleges* and not only theological seminaries. The broad mission of the church-related college, then, is to explore what it would be like to think rigorously from this place. George Marsden offers an example of this in his recent book, *The Outrageous Idea of Christian Scholarship*, where he describes the dynamics of "scholarship that relates one's belief in God to what else one thinks about."[81] He suggests as a basic form for such reflection the question: "if this religious teaching were true, how would it change the way we look at the subject at hand?"[82]

A second principle guiding our rethinking is that as Christians, we do what we do in order to be faithful and this faithfulness is to extend into our entire being. In our context this means that we establish colleges and pursue a life of rigorous academic inquiry as a way of living out that faithfulness. Far from the anti-rational opiate to human curiosity some would make it out to be, faith seeks understanding—and not just about faith. It impels us to think hard about the world with the best tools available. The fact that historically the Western university arose from within the Christian community is not an accident or the result of some outside, secular forces imposing this institution on the church. In the words of John Paul II, "such an ecclesial origin of the university cannot have been fortuitous. Rather it expresses (the fact that) . . . the faith that the church announces is . . . a faith that demands to penetrate human intelligence, to be thought out by the intellect of the human person."[83]

Michael Buckley adds a significant principle to this line of thought when he explains that the relation between college and church, at least in the Catholic tradition, is to be intrinsic rather than extrinsic. In an extrinsic relation the college and church are understood as two alien entities, one essentially secular the other religious, that occasionally intersect in special programs or events. As such the relationship is inherently schizophrenic or at best an uneasy partnership, to borrow Cuninggim's description. Buckley argues that this way of construing the relationship is "seriously inadequate." Drawing on the Catholic understanding of creation as sacramental, as permeated by the presence of God, Buckley argues instead for an intrinsic relation in which there is a distinction but a mutual completion of grace and nature, faith and reason, church and college.[84] Here the conviction is that "Any movement toward meaning and truth is inchoatively religious" while "At the same time the tendencies of faith are inescapably toward the academic."[85] Understood in this way the college and the church are not essentially opposed to each other or working in opposite directions such that faithfulness to one means the abandonment of the other. Indeed, on these terms, failure to be authentically a college is a failure to be faithful to the community of faith, not just to the academic community.[86]

In this idea that faithfulness impels us toward the academic, we see a significant recurring pattern in the Christian sense of place that provides another principle for our rethinking. As we turn inward to the tradition, to the local, we are propelled outward by the tradition itself to the whole world, to the inclusive and the catholic.[87] All good things have their characteristic temptation and with an affirmation of place that temptation is parochialism. Vigilant as we must ever be to guard against parochialism, it is important to realize that this is a *temptation*. It is not a necessary corollary of an affirmation of place, at least not of *this* place. Indeed, parochialism is a betrayal of the specific character of *this* place, *this* tradition. A prime demonstration of this is the Pastoral Constitution on the Church in the Modern World (*Gaudium et Spes*), of Vatican II. Confident that the Spirit of God is at work throughout creation and not only in the church, the document articulates from within the tradition a mandate to engage the world, culture(s), in genuine dialogue, listening and learning as well as speaking and teaching.[88] As *Ex Corde Ecclesiae*, the 1990 Apostolic Constitution on Catholic Universities, makes clear, this dialogue between church and culture occurs in a special way at the church's colleges and universities.[89]

Beyond the general mandate for dialogue, the tradition also possesses resources that affirm specific academic virtues. For instance, openness to people and ideas from outside the tradition, from other places (so critical to a healthy academic institution) is required by the Christian narrative that commands us to love even our enemies, and to treat all as we would be treated. In the *Rule of Benedict*, which has a particular authority at our college, this is expressed in the simple admonition to receive all as Christ (ch. 53).[90] *Gaudium et Spes* applies this Christian principle of love of others specifically to the kind of diversity that would characterize most colleges or universities: "Those also have a claim on our respect and charity who think and act differently from us in social, political and religious matters. In fact the more deeply we come to understand their ways of thinking through kindness and love, the more easily will we be able to enter into dialogue with them."[91] Clearly, using the sense of place to create a ghetto of like-minded people is a misunderstanding of the specific tradition of this place. Thus the pattern: turning inward we discover an injunction to turn out to the whole world in love, hospitality, and dialogue. Failure to do so, turning in upon ourselves in parochialism or sectarianism, is not only a failure to live up to our ideals as a college, it is a failure to live up to our ideals as a church.

It is of the essence of a college to be open not only to people but to ideas, to be a place of free inquiry, not indoctrination.[92] Here too there are resources within the tradition that impel us to such free inquiry. For one thing, our earlier discussion of the intrinsic relation of faith and reason, church and college enjoins free, rigorous pursuit of truth as a means of understanding not only the world but also God who is at work in the world and is its source and goal.[93] In addition, I would argue that the affirmation of the transcendence of God and the prohibition against idolatry provide an impetus for free inquiry with a warning against indoctrination. The fact that we are to put neither ourselves nor our creations, be they conceptual or material, in the place of God is a profound call for humility that should open us up to new ideas from all sources. The injunction against idolatry applies in a special way to the tradition itself, constituting a warning *from within the tradition* against absolutizing the tradition—or at least our understanding and articulation of it. As Farley observes, "The idolatry of tradition is the characteristic corruption of religion . . . (whereby it comes) to regard what it inherits from the past as an uncriticizable given."[94] In this way the tradition itself encourages a vigorous self-criticism. The biblical narrative is remarkably consistent in portraying the imperfections of its heroes and in its prophetic criticism of the presumptions of its own institutions. To be sure, the prophets were usually not well received by those who saw themselves as the defenders of the tradition, of the sacred place; but the tradition is very clear that it was the critics who were in the right and who were in fact the real defenders of the tradition. *This* tradition, the ideals of *this* place, is not simply one of panegyrics or hagiography for "everyone and everything that is on one's side"[95] but is also critical of its own. Academically this manifests itself in the cultivation of rigorous, intellectual honesty and critical self-examination. Faithfulness to this tradition demands that we pursue the truth vigorously, that we be humble about our own constructs and open to what we learn—even about ourselves.

Even academic freedom, which is often assumed to be alien to a college's church-relation, can draw on the tradition for support. According to a recent study by William Hoye, the first use of the term "academic freedom" in Western literature was by Pope Honorius III in 1220. To the surprise of many, he wrote not to limit it but to affirm it as something of a natural right of the faculty "grounded in the very nature of academic life."[96] Hoye goes on to demonstrate that this defense of academic freedom was not an anomaly but was integral to the self-understanding and the practice of the Medieval universities—universities that had an intimate relation with the church. The church's official endorsement of academic freedom continues to this day, as we can read in *Gaudium et Spes* (59, 62), "The *Declaration on Christian Education*" (10) and *Ex Corde* (12). The theological rationale for academic freedom is perhaps best articulated by John Henry Newman who, as one commentator points out, argues for academic freedom not "on the basis of a liberal theory of individual rights" but on the basis of "a balanced theory of the relation between faith and reason . . . and upon an ecclesiology that knows that freedom is as important as authority if the church is to be able adequately to understand and effectively to communicate the faith to an unbelieving and skeptical culture. It is the church, and not just the individual scholar, that needs academic freedom."[97]

Unfortunately, the church has far too often forgotten that it needs academic freedom or the other academic virtues we have located in the tradition and has worked against them. It would be naive to suggest that this is all in the past, that these academic virtues are not now and will not in the future be threatened by forces of conformity from within the ecclesial community—forces that read the tradition and faithfulness to it differently than here presented. Real and frequent as that fight is, however, the point I want to underscore is that it is a fight *within* the tradition and community of faith in which both sides draw on the resources of the tradition. It need not be understood as a fight between the tradition or the church, the forces of faithfulness, on the one side and the college, the forces of secularism, on the other. The issue here is not to what extent the church and its colleges have or have not lived up to these ideals, but the fact that there are resources within the tradition that establish them as ideals. These resources need to be cultivated as we rethink the nature and mission of the church-related college. While our failures are evident, we need not turn away from the tradition to assess them as failures. A strong sense of being placed in the tradition and community of the church does not turn us in upon ourselves in a kind of smug insular ghetto. It turns us out to receive others as Christ, to engage them in dialogue, to be genuinely open to learn from them, and to be critical of ourselves. In short, it impels us to be a college.

To argue that there are resources within the tradition for establishing academic virtues is not to say that those in the tradition, those who think from this place, have nothing to learn from those outside. Our history shows that we have learned much and suggests that we still have much to learn. Indeed, this is precisely the nature of the dialogue the tradition instructs us to have with the world in which we live. Here MacIntyre's analysis of dialogue between traditions is especially helpful, for it makes clear that in this dialogue a tradition is vulnerable to an epistemological crisis in which it either begins to dissolve in the realization that it is unable to deal with the anomalies confronting it or it breaks through with imaginative conceptual innovation that enables it to understand itself in ways it had not done before. The critical point here, however, is that whatever innovations are adopted, whatever changes occur, they are finally justified on the grounds that the new makes us more faithful to who we actually are, to our defining narrative. New ideas are not adopted simply because forces powerful or popular push us in that direction. Rather, we do what we do, even the new that we do, in order to be faithful. Not to be lost sight of, though, is the fact that it is often this dialogue with the other, a dialogue that involves real listening, vulnerability, and self-examination, that enables us to understand ourselves more fully than we had before and perhaps more fully than we could have had we not entered into the dialogue. Unsettling though it is, such dialogue is necessary for the continuing life of the tradition and the community.

It is the privilege and the responsibility of the church-related college to be the special locus of this dialogue, to exist in the midst of the vulnerability that is its constant companion. Confident that it will be better for it, the Christian community commissions its colleges to engage in dialogue with the world in order to understand both the world and itself better. The religious motivation for this is not simply to convert the world but to discover how God is at work in the world outside the church and to understand more fully how God is at work in the church. Subjecting itself and all around it to rigorous, critical thought, it seeks out the new and reconsiders the old. This is how the church-related college serves the church and the world. Surely, in this place, with roots deeply planted in the Christian community and tradition a college can be a real college. The need is genuine. The idea is viable. It is our task to be in this place a college.

✝

PART THREE

ACADEMIC VOCATION

Conversation and Authority: A Tension in the Inheritance of the Church-Related College

RICHARD KYTE

Let us humble ourselves, therefore, since we are nothing more than a voice and that, of ourselves, we are incapable of doing any good to souls, or even of making the least impression on them, for we are only a voice, a sound, of which nothing remains after it has vibrated in the air.

—*St. John Baptist de la Salle*

How can the wind move the tree when it's nothing but air? Well, it *does move* it; and don't forget it.

—*Ludwig Wittgenstein*

INHERITANCE

Hannah Arendt begins the preface to her book *Between Past and Future* by quoting the poet René Char, commenting on the situation of French postwar society: "Our inheritance was left to us by no testament."[1] It is an aphorism descriptive of many institutions in our day.

Think of almost any church-related college in America.[2] It likely has a rich heritage—an inspiring story of members of a community coming together to bring about a particular vision of the Christian society through higher education. But the story is not adequate to guide the college into the future, nor even to describe (much less justify) its present place in society. In describing its place in society, the church-related college must express its mission, and the mission statement never follows simply from the college's history. Rather, the mission statement finds a way to accommodate the story of the college's past into the description of its present place. The testament—in Protestant colleges typically a creed or confession and in Roman Catholic colleges the living testimony of members of the founding order—originated as something that spoke authoritatively only to those already within the community. It was not designed to justify the place of the institution to society as a whole. But that is what is required now. Mission statements are being rewritten (almost always with a view to a readership of potential customers), and a way is sought to cast the college's historical religious commitment in a manner that is both meaningful and nonoffensive to those who do not identify wholly with the religious tradition. Thus, what once served as a testament is cast as part of the heritage, and what to do with that heritage is an open question.

A couple of examples should help to illustrate the trend.

The opening sentence of the Institutional Mission Statement of Christian Brothers University reads as follows: "Christian Brothers University is a Catholic institution of higher education in the tradition of the Christian Brothers."[3] Right there, in the first sentence of the mission statement, on the first page of the catalog, we find that the Brothers of the Christian Schools, whose presence on campus was once the authoritative and defining voice of the institution, are now instead the presence of a tradition. The Brothers still enrich the institution, but as the number of Brothers who serve on campus diminishes year by year, what is lost is not the identity of the university but rather a daily and visible reminder of the university's heritage.[4]

In the Rhodes College catalog, under the heading, "A Statement of Christian Commitment and Church Relationship," we read the following words: "First, let us look at what [Rhodes' distinctive and extraordinary function as a church-related college] is *not*. Rhodes' commitment to the church and to the Lord of the church does *not* mean that it is a doctrinaire institution requiring intellectual adherence to a creedal religion." Given the creedal nature of Presbyterianism that may seem like a disingenuous claim. As the rest of the Statement makes clear, the Presbyterian Church is looked upon not as an authoritative guide but rather as a source of inspiration and value. In other words the church provides opportunities for worship and demonstrating social concern. The reformed creeds, which at one time carried authoritative weight in the life of the college, now have only the weight of historical relationship. They continue to have a privileged place, but that place is in the church building just across the street, where they may be heard from time to time, but where they may also be ignored.

These are not atypical examples. They are characteristic of colleges that are trying hard to retain the significance of their historical church relationship while at the same time demonstrating an awareness of and justifying their place in a pluralistic society.

The careful and deliberate (if not always self-conscious) exercise of simultaneously drawing attention to and setting aside the core elements of religious identity is an indirect result of the ascendant conception of education as "conversation." The earliest (and the most eloquent) articulation of that conception is to be found in Michael Oakeshott's essay:

> As civilized human beings, we are the inheritors, neither of an inquiry about ourselves and the world, nor of an accumulating body of information, but of a conversation, begun in the primeval forests and extended and made more articulate in the course of centuries. . . . Education, properly speaking, is an initiation into the skill and partnership of this conversation in which we learn to recognize the voices, to distinguish the proper occasions of utterance, and in which we acquire the intellectual and moral habits appropriate to conversation.[5]

Adopting the conversational model of education allows the church-related college to claim a certain kind of legitimacy that has generally been denied it under the earlier conceptions of education as inquiry or transmission of knowledge. The church-related college can justify its distinctive educational mission by stressing its role in ensuring that its denomination's particular mode of discourse remain part of the wider cultural conversation. Thus, church-related colleges, based upon the conversational model of education, are discovering that they can claim a certain authority (a right to speak). It is a form of authority available to any institution that takes upon itself the purpose of articulating a distinctive and traditional voice in a pluralistic society.

TENSION

When an image as rich and powerful as the one we are discussing becomes available, it tends to take over, like an ornamental ivy—partly because it is so attractive and there are so many uses for it, but also because it is impossible to contain. Thus, along with a new conception of educational function, we get a new standard for evaluating its effectiveness: the ability of graduates to speak fluently in diverse voices. If a university conceives its mission too narrowly, it will not adequately prepare students for participation in a pluralistic society. The large research universities are especially susceptible to censure on this score. In her recent memoir, *A Life in School,* Jane Tompkins (who has taught at Temple, Johns Hopkins, and Duke) indicts the educational system for her own and her students' spiritual impoverishment.

> Higher education, in order to produce the knowledge and skills students need to enter certain lucrative professions, cuts students off from both their inner selves and the world around them. By not offering them a chance to know themselves and come into contact with the actual social environment, it prepares them to enter professional school but not to develop as whole human beings.[6]

This is where the church-related college likes to step in and say: "*We* do not neglect the students' development as whole human beings—that is precisely our mission. We preserve in our community the religious voice, but we do not make it the exclusive voice; we allow the student to integrate her spiritual self with the rest of her life and thus develop as a whole person." But where does the religious voice come from on this model? And how does it contribute to integration of the self? It does not automatically do so. The ability to speak fluently in a number of voices is consistent with schizophrenia. If none of the voices in which one speaks carries any weight, a person may develop into a being without any coherent identity.[7]

It is important to note that on the conversational model of education the teacher is above all a facilitator. Her chief function is to help students acquire the skills to articulate a sense of themselves and to communicate effectively with others and thus get along in the world. Again, I think Tompkins gets the description just right (though there is hardly any shortage of voices espousing this model of the teacher):

> From the teacher's point of view, the classroom is a place of opportunity. Here students can enrich themselves, are inspired, motivated, made curious, enlightened by the professor. Here students participate in producing knowledge themselves, since most professors nowadays would agree that students need to be active learners. The great example of student participation in the learning process is class discussion. From the teacher's perspective, class discussion constitutes freedom. It gives students a chance to express themselves. Instead of the teacher talking, the students talk. They air their opinions, exchange ideas; they disagree with one another, and sometimes they even disagree with the instructor. They raise their hands, they speak, their voices are heard.[11]

One frequent criticism of the conversational model of teaching is that it is directionless. Or, that even though the class discussion may develop some direction, it does so by accident and without any authoritative guidance from the teacher, for the teacher (by her own admission) lacks authority to determine the direction. That criticism has a point, but when stated so broadly it goes too far. It overlooks certain conditions of conversation that we customarily take for granted and thus fail to see. Wittgenstein points this out in one of his notebooks.

> In a conversation: One person throws a ball; the other does not know: whether he is supposed to throw it back, or throw it to a third person, or leave it on the ground, or pick it up and put it in his pocket, etc. [10]

To throw a ball is, after all, to author an action with a certain amount of force. It is not possible for the teacher to abdicate all authority in the classroom; even the initial act of engaging the students in conversation presupposes it. The question then is: Whence does the authority of the teacher derive? In many cases the answer is simple and direct: the teacher's authority derives from the mission of the college. Where the mission is clearly stated and clearly received there is perhaps no difficulty. But such cases are exceptional. In most cases the mission of the college or university is not a central matter of concern. What functions in its place is the default mission of the conversational model, which has the advantage of justifying the widely accepted practice of faculty teaching their separate disciplines to the best of their ability. Given such a mission (which is the same as no distinctive mission) the teacher may authoritatively guide classroom discussion in the practice of the particular mode of discourse that constitutes his area of familiarity and expertise. What this means for the church-related college is that room can legitimately be made for a department out of which faculty members speak with a religious voice. But that legitimacy has a price.

The conversational model of education not only provides a kind of authority to religious discourse, it also places severe constraints on that discourse, constraints that create an inevitable and ongoing tension in the life of the church-related college. The professor who sincerely and wholly identifies with the religious tradition of her college—that is, the teacher in whom the religious tradition is alive and present—cannot assume for her teaching the authority that the institution claims on the conversational model of education. To do so would be to renounce or at least diminish the significance of her faith. The teacher for whom a particular mode of religious discourse is not merely one of many possible ways of speaking but is instead the expression of her deepest commitments must necessarily claim for her words the authority of truth—not merely that of respect for a traditional voice. In short, the kind of authority that the institution grants to particular voices within the academy makes no provision for those who would speak out of a religious commitment.

Thus we are led to consider the possibility that (at least in certain cases, and especially in the case of the church-related college) the authority appropriate to the teacher may be distinct from and in tension with the authority appropriate to the institution (or of one who speaks as a representative of the institution). The form of authority appropriate to an institution depends upon cultural norms of recognition and legitimacy. In short, it depends on the notion of a "right"—a right to speak, a right to be heard, a right to be obeyed, etc.[10] But perhaps there is another form of authority appropriate to a teacher in the church-related college, a form of authority that has nothing to do with "rights" but rather with engagement, with the ability to cause others to find one's words compelling. Perhaps the mere fact that a teacher's words do on occasion carry a weight not at all derivable from the legitimacy of the institution out of which they are spoken indicates the presence of a distinct kind of authority—a kind of authority that is *personal* rather than *institutional*.

AUTHORITY

In the figure of St. Augustine we have a clear image of a person who speaks with authority. However, when Augustine's name is invoked in connection with this topic, it is often as someone who exercised an oppressive authority, which teachers in a pluralistic society are advised to avoid. That is unfortunate, not only because the proper use of authority was of great concern to Augustine, but also because there is much to be learned from examining the tension in Augustine's life between the form of personal authority he exercised as a teacher and the institutional authority he carried as bishop. That tension is especially evident in certain depictions of Augustine's role in the Donatist controversy.

Let us take as our conversation piece a painting by Carle Van Loo, *St. Augustin disputant contre les Donatistes*. The event that the painting depicts is the third and final of a series of debates between the Catholic and Donatist bishops that took place in Carthage in the summer of 411 C.E. The debates were a *collatio*, a comparison, of the claims of each party to represent the true Catholic church in North Africa. Hundreds of bishops from each church gathered in the hall of a Roman bath to settle their dispute before a representative of the state. In Van Loo's painting Augustine stands just right of center with one hand raised and the other holding an open book. He faces Petilian, the leading Donatist bishop, whose arms are stretched before him in a gesture of protest. He and the other Donatist bishops are all standing; they refused to sit down during the debate. In the right foreground we see Flavius Marcellinus, the Roman Tribune who is presiding over the debate. He looks upon Augustine with obvious satisfaction and perhaps with some relief that the matter is being settled so decisively. The central figure is a secretary whose task is to record the proceedings of the debate. Van Loo depicts him turning around toward Augustine, *in conversio.*

That Van Loo should depict that particular person *in conversio,* in that particular setting, is curious for a couple of reasons. First, the secretary is sitting next to Augustine, on the Catholic side of the room. The Donatist secretaries are on the other side; one of them can be seen sitting behind Petilian, apparently unaffected by Augustine's words. Thus, Augustine's words are shown to have their strongest effect on a member of the Catholic party; he is converting one of his own. Second, from our knowledge of the debate (which is no better than Van Loo's would have been), Augustine is probably not saying anything of great personal interest. The records indicate that Augustine very skillfully managed to restrict the debate to the legal claims of the Donatists, which he then extemporaneously and decisively refuted.[11]

One explanation of the secretary's posture is that he is simply trying to catch what is being said. In Michael Fried's remarkable study of eighteenth-century French painting, he cites several critics. The first is a contemporary, Abbe Laugier, commenting on the secretary: "He seems to fear that he will not grasp what is said with sufficient accuracy."[12] But that explanation does not account for the centrality of the figure in Van Loo's composition, nor does it take notice of the intensity of the secretary's gaze directed at Augustine. Another contemporary critic, Melchior Grimm, does indeed notice that the secretary "instead of writing, stares at the saint and gazes at him as if gripped by the force of his eloquence,"[13] but then fails to draw the inevitable and peculiar inference that the secretary alone is susceptible to rhetorical charm. A third critic, Abbe Le Blanc, writes: "The strongest attention is so successfully rendered in the eyes of most of those listening to him, and especially in those of the secretary, that one cannot help trying to guess the thoughts with which their minds appear occupied."[14] By saying that we find ourselves compelled to wonder what is going on in the mind of the secretary, Le Blanc is suggesting that Van Loo paints the secretary engaged in a kind of inner turning, a turning around of the soul. And the fact that we are intrigued by the response of the secretary but not by the responses of Marcellinus, Petilian, or the Donatist secretaries draws our attention to the contrast between the two kinds of effect that Augustine is depicted having on his listeners. I want to claim that the contrast is between two kinds of authority, that they compete with one another for effect on the listener, and that Augustine is depicted as possessing both of them.

The contrast between types of authority—what I earlier referred to as *personal* and *institutional* authority—is made a number of times in the Gospels, but most memorably in the concluding lines of Matthew's account of the Sermon on the Mount: "And when Jesus finished these sayings, the crowds were astonished at his teaching, for he taught them as one who had authority, and not as their scribes" (Mt. 7:28–29). If we think of the authority mentioned in this passage as institutional authority—the right or the power to compel obedience, held typically in virtue of one's social position—then surely the scribes had greater authority than Jesus. They had a place in an established tradition out of which to voice their readings of scripture and thus had a legitimate claim upon the assent of their listeners. We therefore must take Matthew to mean that Jesus possessed another form of authority, one that did not depend upon his status in the society but that rather consisted in the fact that the crowd found his words compelling—that he spoke as one who "authored" his own words. Thus, I take the passage to imply that having the ability to cause someone to attend to certain ideas in itself constitutes a form of authority, and that that form of authority is appropriate to the Christian teacher. However, the passage gives us little else to go on. What precisely was it about Jesus' teaching that had such an effect on his listeners?

Perhaps we are faced here with a certain peculiar phenomenon of character—something we may be told about, or that may to some extent be depicted, but which we cannot grasp without being in the presence of the person. Emerson observes in his essay "Character": "We cannot find the smallest part of the personal weight of Washington, in the narrative of his exploits."[15] The same may be said of G. E. Moore, whose writings always seem pale in comparison with his presence, for those fortunate enough to have been acquainted with both. The critic I. A. Richards recollects:

> He was not like any other lecturer I have heard or heard of. He made you sure that what was going on mattered enormously—without your necessarily having even a dim idea as to what it could be that was going on. We were, in truth, undergoing an extraordinarily powerful influence, not one that I would suppose Moore could for a moment conceive. He was not at all interested in that. He was interested in the problem in hand: more interested in it than, I think, I have ever seen anyone interested in anything.[16]

Contrast that with Augustine's recollection of his acquaintance with Faustus, the leader of the Manichean sect. In recounting his experience, he reports that he initially found the Manichean teachings quite reasonable—or at least promising. What eventually turned him away was not only the theological difficulties with Manichean doctrine, but his discovery that Faustus could not "hold the truth of piety."

> The keenness with which I had studied the writings of Manes was thus somewhat blunted; and I was the more hopeless about their other doctors, now that, upon many matters which troubled me, the famous Faustus had shown so ill. . . . all my effort and determination to make progress in the sect simply fell away through my coming to know this man (5.7.2).

That is the severest indictment of a teacher I can imagine—that the teacher cannot support his words and is oppressed by what he professes. Faustus lacked authority, not because his words lacked eloquence or even profundity, but because he did not author them. To teach in the manner of Faustus, to rely on institutional authority as sufficient ground for one's teaching, is to fail as a teacher.

But, then again, such failing is endemic to teaching. Who ever leaves her classroom fully convinced of the justice of her words? It is for precisely this reason that *conversio* is necessary. As teachers, we continually turn inward to re-gather and measure our words, to see if they accurately profess the lives that we would lead. It is this continual *conversio* we see demonstrated in G. E. Moore's teaching, in Van Loo's painting of Augustine, and in those who speak as ones who have authority. It is a sincere and manifest striving to achieve consistency in what one says and how one lives.

CONVERSATION

When we encounter a person who speaks with authority, we do not always realize it at the time. But if we are fortunate, we come to the realization sooner or later. By the time Augustine wrote his *Confessions*, he was quite clear about which person had had the most profound effect on his life and about the means by which that effect was brought about. In at least three places he praises his mother Monica for her "holy conversation" (*sancte* [9.9.22, 9.12.33] or *religiosissimam* [6.2.2] *conversationem*). For example, he writes:

> Such of them as knew her praised and honoured and loved You,
> O God, in her; for they felt Your presence in her heart, showing
> itself in the fruit of her holy conversation (*sanctae conversationis*)
> (9.9.22).

Conversatio is properly translated as "behavior" or "conduct" or "way of living." Its root, *conversari*, means "to dwell with or live with." Earlier uses of the word in English (and French)—until the nineteenth century—retain the original Latin meaning. The *Oxford English Dictionary* cites Marbeck in 1581: "True piete doth not consist in knowledge and talking, but in the action and conversation." A 1611 translation of the Bible into

English has *Philemon* 3:20 read, "For our conversation is in heaven," whereas the Revised Version of 1881 reads, "For our citizenship is in heaven." And Horace Walpole, in his book of 1786 describes Terburgh (whom we know as Gerard Ter Borch the Younger, a Dutch artist and contemporary of Vermeer, renowned for his depiction of intimate domestic scenes) as a painter of "conversations." It is from that genre of painting that we inherit the term "conversation piece."[17]

Augustine's praise of Monica's *conversatio* thus includes, but is not limited to, the way in which she spoke to others, though it is principally her use of words in dealing with others that Augustine remembers and notes. What he learns from Monica is not how to win arguments, but rather how the manner in which one speaks—and refrains from speaking—has an influence that goes beyond the particular meaning of what is said. One passage in particular is especially revealing about the character of Monica and what Augustine found admirable in her manner of interacting with others.

> When she reached the age for marriage, and was bestowed upon a husband, she served him as her lord. She used all her effort to win him to You, preaching You to him by her character, by which You made her beautiful to her husband, respected and loved by him and admirable in his sight. For she bore his acts of unfaithfulness quietly, and never had any jealous scene with her husband about them. She awaited Your mercy upon him, that he might grow chaste through faith in You. And as a matter of fact, though generous beyond measure, he had a very hot temper. But she knew that a woman must not resist a husband in anger, by deed or even by word. Only, when she saw him calm again and quiet, she would take the opportunity to give him an explanation of her actions, if it happened that he had been roused to anger unreasonably (9.9.19).

What kind of authority is there in living a life of "holy conversation" of the sort that Augustine attributes to Monica? Certainly not the kind of authority that can demand obedience, but rather the kind of authority that can draw a person in, turn a person around, effect *conversio*. That is precisely the effect that Monica eventually had on Patricius. Thus when Augustine praises Monica's "holy conversation," he remembers that her way of life—her actions, gestures, and words—were such as to reveal to others the orientation of her life, the habitation of her heart. It was conversation in that sense that gave her words authority, even though he initially found *what she said* about Christianity to be unconvincing, even foolish.

In Van Loo's painting we see Augustine employing certain lessons he has learned from Monica. Since the Donatist bishops are angry, and since they have refused to sit down, he will not engage them in theological disputes. That can wait for other occasions. However, he may rely on his office as bishop, his scholarship, his rhetorical skills, and his reputation, to restrict the scope of the debate to the legality of the Donatists' claims. Thus, Augustine's speech is remarkable not for what he says, but for what he does not say, for passing up the opportunity to express his indignation (which he surely felt) at the recent history of Donatist violence and the propagation of heretical views. Of course, we cannot know what is going on in the mind of the secretary, but perhaps he is drawn to Augustine's restraint—patience exercised where he had expected righteous indignation.

This offers us a possible explanation of personal rather than institutional authority, of why the secretary is turning around toward Augustine, and so begins to answer our question concerning the authority of the teacher. It would suggest that teaching, when it occurs, is always somewhat accidental, at least from the teacher's point of view. And this suggestion is supported by what Augustine himself says about teaching in both the *Confessions* and *De Magistro*. In both of those works we have as the model of the teacher someone who helps others turn to God by means of memory, through a kind of representation. But that task always implies a certain distance (perhaps impassable) between the teacher and the student. Not only because the teacher can only work directly with her own memory, can only represent that which has been present to her; but because learning takes place only when the student's memory is engaged, and the student's representations, although elicited by those of the teacher, are not determined by the teacher.[18] Thus, we have Augustine asserting in *De Magistro* that no human being ever teaches another human being. And in the *Con-fessions* we find Augustine describing how he learned not be-cause of but despite his teachers' misguided efforts:

> I disliked learning and hated to be forced to it. But I *was* forced to
> it, so that good was done to me though it was not my doing. . . .
> Nor did those who forced me do well. . . . But You, Lord, . . . used
> for my good the error of those who urged me to study (1.12).

The lesson we may draw from Augustine's encounter with the Donatists is that the teacher possesses two kinds of au-thority. There is first the authority of the institution that is trans-ferred to him through his position and enhanced by the letters that precede and follow his name, certificates, reputation, etc. Much of what he says will carry weight, will be attended to and noted, just because of the place he occupies in the institu-tion. He may also have a personal form of authority by means of which he may bring about an effect on his students, but it will always be indirect or occasional and therefore, from his point of view, accidental. The student may or may not attend to what he says, may or may not understand or be convinced of the truth of his words. If, by the grace of God, he is able to live a life of holy conversation, any moment, any utterance, any interaction with others may carry infinite weight and be an occasion for another's conversion.[19]

CONCLUSION

If the foregoing conception of the centrality of personal au-thority in teaching is correct, then the distinctive function of the church-related college is to provide two things: a *place* and *time* for holy conversation. When the student engages with a number of other students and teachers who are in holy con-versation with one another, the opportunity for learning is greatly enhanced, and a significant burden is lifted from the individual teacher. It is only when the members of the church-related college come together with a shared purpose—profess-ing and bearing witness in their lives and through their words to the living church in all its multiplicity of relations in the world—that the church-related college becomes distinctive as an institution from a secular college.[20] (Any college or university may have committed Christians teaching in it.) The purpose that members of the church-related college share may be expressed in a number of ways—through creeds, doctrines, or vows—but the expression is always rooted in a shared desire for holy conversation and a corresponding willingness to allow one's personal projects to be constrained by the commitment to associate with one another in the love of Christ and for the sake of the students. (Should we expect those constraints to be any easier to endure than they were for Monica?)

When the conversational model of education is adopted in the church-related college, it may appear that authority is abdicated. In fact, the opposite is true. The teacher assumes for her words a personal authority that she cannot guarantee but that they have for her and that she hopes they will have for her students. The church-related college exists to sustain that hope.

Beyond the Faith-Knowledge Dichotomy: Teaching as Vocation

Elizabeth Newman

How does the language of "vocation" illuminate our understanding of Christian identity and higher education? In this essay, I wish to explore teaching as a vocation in order to shed light on a key issue that has often haunted Christian higher education: the separation between faith and knowledge. Such a separation has often led academics to assume that the classroom is the place to examine and pass on knowledge, while matters of faith belong in the extracurricular spheres of the institution, i.e., campus ministry, service projects, voluntary chapel, or liturgy. From this perspective, the teacher's role (vocation) is not to indoctrinate or impose his or her beliefs on students, but to examine all beliefs with a critical and open mind. Several years ago, Nannerl Keohane, the president of Duke University, nicely reflected these common assumptions at her inauguration when she expressed uneasiness at the university's motto, "*Eruditio et Religio.*" "[T]he emphasis on religion," she stated, "seemed hard to square with the restless yearning for discovery, the staunch and fearless commitment to seek for truth wherever truth may be found that is the hallmark of a great university."[1] It did not seem to her that religious convictions could mix with the *critical* spirit of higher education.

Such assumptions about knowledge and faith reflect the now notorious modern split between knowledge and values, a split that sees knowledge as objective and public, while values are subjective matters of private choice. Yet, as has been extensively documented in the twentieth century, this framework has some glaring flaws. For one, the subject simply cannot achieve the independence from context that this model seems to require. Recent attention to our knowledge as non-foundational, communal, and narrative-based indicates how deeply self-involving our convictions and commitments are. As Charles Scriven, President of Columbia Union College, puts it, "how and what we think at all times reflects a storied past."[2] Thus, those understandings of teaching that imagine we can separate faith convictions from knowledge claims reflect the story of modernity, a story which holds that valid knowledge evolves from "the onlooker consciousness"[3] of a detached spectator. According to this modern mythos, knowledge is reliable insofar as it is universal and freed from particularity. Such knowledge belongs, appropriately, in the public realm (the classroom). Modernity locates faith, on the other hand, in the expressive, ethical, or even irrational sphere. So understood, faith seems quite naturally to belong in the private or subjective realm.

In many ways, it is understandable how this modern story gained such a stronghold over our imaginations. As historian Robert Wilken notes,

> one of the reasons why *faith* has been divorced from *reason* is that by laying stress on the attitude of the believer rather than on the truth of the thing believed, it is easier for people to negotiate our diverse and heterogeneous society. That attitude also discourages religious warfare. If faith is an affair of the believing subject and is self-authenticating, then it is easier for us to tolerate differences and live together in peace and harmony.[4]

Avoidance of religious conflict and openness to pluralism seem to require that we keep our faith convictions private. What is the alternative?

Most of us are by now familiar with postmodern criticisms of the modern story. Chief among these is the observation that any "reason," abstracted from particularity and context, can itself easily become oppressive. What we assume is a universal rationality that everyone shares turns out to be deeply informed by our particular cultures and contexts. Some strands of postmodernism have thus attempted to resolve the problem of difference (and thus conflict) not by upholding objectivistic knowledge, as the modern mythos does, but by endorsing an aesthetic appreciation of otherness. Since knowledge, so this position holds, is inevitably a mode of domination, the resolution lies in aesthetically embracing the plurality of knowledges and the relativity of all truth. Douglas Sloan describes this kind of postmodernism as "putative" or deconstructive: "Extreme expressions of subjectivism, radical relativism, and the deconstruction of everything have often replaced objectivism and hence have been characterized as postpositivist and postmodern."[5]

Such postmodern thinking, however, as I will discuss more fully, remains parasitic on the faith/knowledge dichotomy in that the only alternative to objectivism seems to be a radical relativism, and even nihilism. That is, either knowledge is objectivistic *or* it is open to a chaos of interpretations issuing from one's subjectivity. In this essay, I wish to abandon this dichotomy altogether and describe teaching and knowing in a way that reflects a storied *theological* past rather than a storied *modern* past. What language, practices, and habits of thought from the Christian tradition can inform our understanding of teaching and knowing such that we avoid both a god-like objectivism and a nihilistic relativism? I wish to suggest that reconsidering the notion of teaching and knowing as a vocation, in its full theological sense, gives us a place to stand to avoid the antithesis between faith and knowledge. A Christian conception of "vocation" points to teaching and knowing as fiduciary acts related to a particular way of life that entails certain practices, such as hospitality, testimony, and forgiveness. The language of "vocation" can thus assist us in developing an alternative vision of higher education, one that allows us to recognize how our identities and stories already in fact inform our understandings of knowledge.

MODERN CONCEPTIONS OF TEACHING

First, however, I wish to examine more closely how the story of modernity continues to shape contemporary understandings of teaching. In campus discussions about the future of church-related colleges, one of my colleagues in the economics department stated that he did not wish to impose his personal views on students. After all, he argued, teaching is not indoctrination, and "values" language often serves as a "cloak for one's political bias." Furthermore, he argued, it would be difficult to recommend or advocate one economic theory over another since faithful Christians and others of good will have conflicting views on these matters. Instead, teachers should present students with a variety of theories and students should have the freedom to choose which theory they find most adequate.

We see reflected in my colleague's position a nice example of the privatization of "values" and faith convictions in order to avoid conflict and to support pluralism. Such thinking reflects a broad consensus in the modern university. In his article, "The Disappearing Moral Curriculum," Dennis O'Brien in fact observes that the modern university has "moved beyond *indoctrination* into *choice*." To illustrate, O'Brien cites a statement from the 1997 University of North Dakota catalog:

> Education concerning values is important in general education—not seeking one right way to behave, but recognizing that choices cannot be avoided. Students should be aware of how many choices they make, how these choices are based on values, and how to make informed choices.[6]

In reflecting on this statement, O'Brien points out that students could easily use the belief that values are simply our private choices to *avoid* learning. Students might learn "the lesson of choice and still lack what some would consider morality and practical wisdom: 'I have lots of choices to make in life. My value is to look out for Number One—that's me! Having clarified my value, I will see which curriculum will really pay off. Certainly not philosophy!'"[7]

While we might think that the poor choices students make are simply signs of immaturity (which no doubt they might be), I want to suggest that the problem, represented by University of North Dakota and my colleague, lies much deeper. Ultimately, it rests on a flawed epistemology, or perhaps better stated, a flawed narrative. How can I make this claim? And am I then not guilty of advocating teaching as indoctrination or, worse yet, proselytizing? First, it is important to realize that the story of modernity easily blinds us to the fact that the alternatives are not between proselytizing or not proselytizing. Inasmuch as all teachers and professors teach and profess from a particular place or standpoint, all teaching is proselytizing. Thus, as Wittgenstein once said, we need to place the question mark deeper down. Here I think Stanley Hauerwas's description of our alternatives is more accurate: "In order to really say something, we have to get down to the material convictions that will help us name whether the indoctrination or proselytizing is good or bad."[8]

What are the material convictions that inform the understanding of teaching and education as held by my colleague, and widely shared in the modern university? Alasdair MacIntyre names this position "emotivism," the "doctrine that all evaluative judgments and more specifically all moral judgments are *nothing but* expressions of preference, expressions of attitude or feeling, insofar as they are moral or evaluative in character."[9] For my purposes, it is significant to see that my colleague and the University of North Dakota are "imposing" emotivism on the students. Significantly, emotivism has deeply shaped and been shaped by our modern culture's fascination with consumerism. By selecting which "values" most satisfy her personal needs, the student becomes a consumer in the marketplace of ideas. Thus, Patricia Beattie Jung is right to observe that a supposed neutral style of teaching does not produce students with no biases at all; rather it favors their assimilation to the "prevailing cultural ethos."[10]

Mark Edmundson of the University of Virginia vividly describes this prevailing ethos in his essay, "On the Uses of

Liberal Education, As Lite Entertainment for Bored College Students." He argues that "university culture, like American culture writ large, is, to put it crudely, ever more devoted to consumption and entertainment, to the using and using up of goods and images." As an example of this academic consumerism, Edmundson describes evaluation day at the end of each semester where the students are playing the informed consumer. Evaluation forms are "reminiscent of the sheets circulated after the TV pilot has just played to its sample audience in Burbank." While Edmundson admits to playing the entertaining professor with "off-the-wall questions and sidebar jokes," he is nonetheless disturbed with the idea emerging from student comments that his function is to divert and entertain. "I want some of [my students] to say that they've been changed by the course."[11] Edmundson's poignant comments remind us how practices (in this case consumerism) and stories (in this case modernity) *in fact* shape our habits of thinking. And the conviction that we can chose our values like our shoes underwrites the idea that the vocation of teaching is to offer the consumer a variety of products. Further, the convictions and commitments of the teacher and students are not privatized, as imagined; they clearly fuel the entire educational venture, though they often resist direct scrutiny.[12]

Certainly a number of complex factors have shaped this modern understanding of the academic vocation. We can see the roots of this approach in Max Weber who, in his well-known address, "Academics as a Vocation," expressed his antipathy toward teaching as "indoctrination." He argued that if students want something "more than mere analyses and statements of fact," the academic teacher should resist, and have the intellectual integrity to state only the facts. Questions of value, Weber claimed, do not belong "on the academic platform" but rather with the "prophet or demagogue."[13] Therefore, academics are faithful to their vocation when they *refuse* to address questions about "value," meaning or the purpose of life. Not only did Weber detach the academic vocation from larger questions of meaning but, reflecting his thoroughly modernist assumptions, Weber claimed that one must treat the world itself as disenchanted. "There are no mysterious incalculable forces that come into play, but rather . . . one can, in principle, *master all things by calculation*. This means that the world is disenchanted."[14] Mark Schwehn insightfully observes that because Weber had divested the world and knowledge of meaning, his academic became a kind of solitary and renunciatory hero. As Weber wrote, "Whoever lacks the capacity to put on blinders, so to speak, and to come up to the idea that the *fate of his soul* depends upon whether or not he makes the correct conjecture at this passage of this manuscript may as well stay away from science [academics]."[15]

If how and what we think reflects a storied past, as noted earlier, then we need to situate Weber's understanding of the academic vocation within a larger context. What might this be? Schwehn, among others, points to the deep Puritan influence on Weber's life and thought. For example, Schwehn observes that Weber's conviction that the academic ought not to address larger questions of meaning and purpose (only facts) owes some debt to the Puritan conviction that the larger meaning of their vocations was not their concern but God's.[16] Similarly, we could add that Weber's description of the academic as one called to attend to the details of his or her specialized field, is influenced by the Puritan understanding that vocation occurs in the context of ordinary life. The Puritan preacher, William Perkins, described this "sanctification of the ordinary:

> Now if we compare worke to worke, there is a difference betwixt washing of dishes, and preaching of the word of God: but as touching to please God none at all . . . and whatsoever is done within the lawes of God though it be wrought by the body, as the wipings of shoes and such like, howsoever grosse they appeare outwardly, yet are they sanctified.[17]

Like Weber's academic, the Puritans discovered their vocation in the details of daily living.

Yet Weber's Puritanism lacked the fuller theological vision of earlier Puritan thought, and thus devolves, as Schwehn notes, into a kind of Protestant worldly asceticism:

> Weber's academic was even more acutely lonely than his Puritan precursor. However profound were the depths of the Puritan's spiritual isolation, he at least had intercourse with God. But the

> Weberian academic could merely wait alone, in disciplined attention, for the chance infusion of mundane grace that would lead him to a temporary salvation through his making a correct conjecture in his manuscript.[18]

Weber, in fact, interpreted Christianity as *world-rejecting* and *ascetic*. He saw these as necessary virtues since they offered, along with theocentrism (a sharp separation of divinity from the cosmos), the most potential for a radical disenchantment of the world.[19]

The Puritans, however, while surely displaying strands of asceticism and worldly denial, nonetheless lived by a very different understanding of vocation than that described by Weber. In tracing an alternative story, one that I think gives us a richer understanding of vocation, I wish to turn to Weber's Puritan heritage as reflected in the life and writings of the seventeenth-century Puritan John Bunyan. In his autobiography *Grace Abounding to the Chief of Sinners*, Bunyan vividly describes his own life journey and vocation. We see in Bunyan's story not "autonomous Western man" but rather the story of a tortured soul whose agony dissipates as he moves from isolation into community. Bunyan poignantly describes how the congregation of "the poor people at Bedford" embody a life that might offer hope for his tortured soul. In a particularly moving passage, Bunyan writes:

> I saw as if they [the people of Bedford] were set on the sunny side of some high Mountain, there refreshing themselves with the pleasant beams of the Sun, while I was shivering and shrinking in the cold, afflicted with frost, snow, and dark clouds; methought also betwixt me and them I saw a wall that did compass about this Mountain; now, thorow this wall my Soul did greatly desire to pass, concluding that if I could, I would goe even into the very midst of them, and there also comfort myself with the heat of their Sun.[20]

As Bunyan's account unfolds, the reader discovers that Bunyan comes to see himself as a participant in a drama played out before God. His vocation leads him from being a detached "spectator" into communion with others, the created order (the mountain and the Sun) and ultimately with God; in the final analysis, Bunyan's story is world-affirming.

While we might appreciate Bunyan's poetic words about the journey of the soul, perhaps we are tempted to ask, "How does Bunyan's description of his life journey relate to the *academic* vocation of teaching?" Like Weber, Bunyan, true to his Puritan heritage, makes no distinction between a religious and secular vocation. However, unlike Weber, Bunyan understands that vocation involves a way of life in communion with others. In other words, vocation does not mean simply one's individual job or career. Rather his sense of vocation reflects a wider biblical use of the word. John H. Yoder describes this wider meaning when he observes,

> In the Middle Ages 'vocation' meant religious separateness. With the Reformation it shifts again to 'each serving in his place in the social structure,' so that the prince, the banker, the tradesman, the soldier, are thought of as 'called' to do just what each 'station' involves. The language which in the New Testament meant newness, change, spirit-driven creativity, now means a divine rubber stamp for the present social order.[21]

For Weber, the academic served his place in the social structure by mastering a world of specialized facts. Absent is the fuller biblical notion, one that Bunyan comes to embody, that vocation is above all a creative way of life lived in relation and response to others and God. Thus we see in Bunyan not a Weberian understanding of vocation located in the alienated and autonomous self of modernity, but an understanding of vocation growing out of a way of life in communion with others. I will return to this conception of vocation in the final section of this essay. First, however, further exploration into postmodernism is called for.

POSTMODERNISM AND THE ACADEMIC VOCATION

Postmodernism has rightly recognized that Weber's approach has some serious epistemological flaws. For example, Tina Pippin, in her article "Border Pedagogy," describes her own imagined response to a senior colleague at a faculty meeting who, we can say, maintained a Weberian approach. "In our department," he claimed, "we teach objectively . . . we show the dialectically opposed positions, and *the student chooses the correct position.*" Pippin deconstructs his statement as follows: "We show dialectically opposed positions (which magically are always and only white, male, heterosexual, European-American), and the student chooses (not on her own but with the help of an expert teacher in the information processing model of teaching) *the* correct position (there is only one Truth, and it's not 'politically correct'. . .)." Instead of this Weberian approach, Pippin argues that "the classroom is not a neutral, isolated space but a political space connected with the ideological forces that surround it." She thus encourages listening both inside and outside the classroom and seeks to create an activist classroom, one that "imagines and creates border spaces between the academic institution and cultural workers in the local community." The teacher is called to attend to the social location of her students (race, culture, class, sexuality, religion, age, etc.); the overall purpose or vocation of the teacher is to create "a classroom culture that affirms difference," and to develop a "politics of difference."[22]

Pippin's approach reflects the growing collapse of the Weberian notion of vocation. Political theorist Murray Jardine succinctly describes this devolution as follows:

> In the seventeenth and eighteenth centuries, what is now called "religious belief" conflicted with the model of exact, impersonal knowledge and was relegated to the realm of mere opinion; by the late nineteenth century, morality, which the Enlightenment philosophers had thought could be placed on a firm, secular footing by skeptical rationalism, was well on its way to becoming a matter of subjective value; and by the mid-twentieth century it had become an open question whether even the hardest sciences could meaningfully be described as objective.[23]

Pippin's colleague and Weber reflect the late nineteenth-century position, while Pippin herself the more recent postmodern turn.

In assessing Pippin's description of "border pedagogy," I wish to acknowledge that the approach encourages some innovative pedagogical strategies, especially in the attempt to learn from the local community. In addition, Pippin rightly acknowledges that knowledge itself emerges from the practices of concrete, historical communities rather than abstract principles or universal experience. Even further, such postmodernist strategy recognizes that teaching is already a moral activity, an insight her senior colleague appears not to see. However, inasmuch as border pedagogy shares some of the assumptions of a deconstructive postmodernism, it remains problematic. Deconstructive postmodernism argues that objective truth-claims benefit those in power. That is, the cultural winners have determined the hegemonic boundaries of knowledge, excluding and silencing those who are oppressed. Thus one must expose various knowledge claims for the impostors they are. To avoid privileging any one position, this epistemological and pedagogical strategy endorses an aesthetic, or *noncommittal*, appreciation of "otherness," which bourgeois rationalism—such as Weber's—has silenced. Thus, the purpose of teaching appears to be to ameliorate domination by emphasizing both the relativity of truth, and an aesthetic appreciation of the "other."

The difficulty with this approach, as suggested earlier, is that it leaves unchallenged the gap between faith and knowledge. The modern and deconstructive postmodern approaches to teaching/knowing remain caught in the bind between an objectivist presentation of facts and a relativistic, aesthetic appreciation of difference. Either truth is foundational or entirely relative and a disguise for power. Reflecting this continuity between modernism and some kinds of postmodernism, critics have noted that "postmodernism is not really *post*-modern at all but rather only a kind of disappointed modernism, since . . . it does not really question the Enlightenment conception of valid knowledge but simply draws the conclusion that since no knowledge claims can meet the modern standard of objective truth, there is ultimately no truth."[24] We seem left with a chaos of interpretations, but no way to evaluate them.

Thus, how can we even say what academic vocation means, except one's subjective preference? Any definition beyond this will appear to be hegemonic. Since there is no foundation to secure our epistemological place, as Weber had believed, then our places of knowing/teaching seem to be radically contingent. Here we can see the continuity between the modern and postmodern accounts, since both are tempted to equate meaning with personal preference. What Kathryn Tanner says about modern discourse applies to some postmodern discourse as well: humans "possess the place which they give themselves . . . their identities are not determined by what they have received but by what they make of themselves and their world through the essential human power of active self-assertion."[25] Yet if vocation is merely what we prefer, there is no reason for this preference rather than some other.

TEACHING AS VOCATION:
AN ALTERNATIVE DESCRIPTION

I suggested earlier, in contrast to Weber, that a fuller understanding of vocation—academic or otherwise—involves a way of life in communion with others and ultimately God. Yet I also wish to claim, in sympathy with some forms of postmodernism, that God calls us to a place where there are no "foundations." What do I mean and how does this not lead to the chaos of interpretations described above? Allow me to explain first, by relying upon the thought of Blaise Pascal and Michael Polanyi, and secondly, by turning to specific practices and their implications for an understanding of Christian vocation.

For my purposes, we might describe Pascal as one of the earliest critics of foundationalism. He once asked:

> What is a man in the infinite? He who regards himself in this light will be afraid of himself, and observing himself sustained in the body given him by nature between those two abysses of the Infinite and Nothing, will tremble at the sight of these marvels. . . . For what in fact is man in nature? A Nothing in comparison with the Infinite, an All in comparison with the Nothing. . . .[26]

Engulfed "in the infinite immensity of spaces," Pascal saw clearly that *from a standpoint in Infinite space*—we might say a universal foundation—our particular place becomes radically contingent, even a mere nothing. One place becomes like every other place: "I am frightened, and am astonished at being here rather than there; for there is no reason why here rather than there, why now rather than then. . . ."[27] Such a vivid description of objectivism and its after-image relativism nicely captures the modern/postmodern dilemma, "a nothing in comparison with the Infinite, an all in comparison with Nothing."

Yet this dilemma, as philosopher William H. Poteat rightly notes, owes a certain debt to an understanding of the world as created: "Only in a universe that is viewed not as an eternal cosmos but as a created world that God might have chosen not to create is there a place for a conception of contingency."[28] Poteat is pointing to the idea that ancient thought tended to regard the world as an eternal harmony that was impersonally determined. No contingent act of creation brought the world into being. Any rupture or discontinuity in the world would necessarily return to a harmonious state. In contrast, creation (*ex nihilo*) enables us to conceive of the idea of radical contingency. In fact, Poteat observes that what began as "a belief that my place is contingent in the sense that God might have called me to any of a number of other places . . . becomes the belief that my place is contingent in the sense that I might *choose* any other place—indeed, any place at all—and ends in the belief that my place is contingent in the sense that one place is just like every other."[29] Just as Weber relied upon a kind of weakened Puritanism to inform his notion of the academic vocation, so also we can say that modern/postmodern dilemma relies, at least in part, on a distorted creation story. In fact, as others have noted, this story is one we might well call gnostic. We see gnosticism reflected both in the Weberian escape from the world to a universal foundation, and in the deconstructionist conviction that our created status, our "social location," is inevitably a place of bondage and domination.

At this point, the thought of chemist and philosopher Michael Polanyi is helpful inasmuch as he relies upon a concept of knowing that ultimately endorses our created status in the world. Allow me to explain. In his best known book *Personal Knowledge*, Polanyi describes knowing as "a *fiduciary* act which cannot be analyzed in *non-committal* terms."[30] He argues that in all our knowing efforts we strive under the guidance of antecedent beliefs. Polanyi uses "personal" not to collapse knowing into the merely subjective, but rather to indicate that the knower herself passionately contributes to what is eventually known. This personal coefficient is not a mere deficiency, but a vital component of our knowing. The knower tacitly relies upon various epistemological clues that she has access to by means of her particular place in the world; she comes to know, discover, and even doubt by immersing herself fully or "indwelling" a particular context. Knowledge is true, for Polanyi, to the extent it discloses aspects of reality not even imagined by the original authors. Thus, genuine knowledge has anticipatory powers that reveal clues to future problems, to yet unthinkable further discoveries. Polanyi concludes, "Intellectual commitment is a responsible decision. . . . It is an act of hope, striving to fulfill an obligation within a personal situation for which I am not responsible and which therefore determines my *calling*."[31] For Polanyi, then, knowing is logically an act of trust, hope, and response before it can be an act of doubt or suspicion. And vocation or calling is not self-created, but rests, above all, in our response to a certain givenness.

Nicholas Lash reiterates this Polanyian emphasis when he writes, "Whether in physics or in politics, in psychology or prayer, to grow in knowledge is to grow through trust: trust given, trust betrayed, trust risked, misplaced, sustained, received, and suffered."[32] If Polanyi and Lash are right, as I believe they are, then faith and knowledge are necessarily and always deeply integrated. We cannot privatize faith even if we wish. Further, a reliance upon our created status is not a choice but a necessary fact. Who we are and how we come to know rests in our bondedness to others and to the worlds we inhabit. Even more, such bondedness is not first of all a negative limitation from which we must escape, either through a Weberian objectivism or a postmodern deconstruction. Rather, our created being is the source of all our knowledges. We might call such an understanding of knowledge and vocation "covenantal" in that it proceeds by trust in our bonds with others and, I would argue, ultimately with God. Such an understanding thus shares with the biblical mythos (and ultimately relies upon it) the conviction that vocation is primarily a covenantal concept rather than something the self alone determines.

PRACTICING THE ACADEMIC VOCATION

In the final section of this essay, I would like simply to suggest the kinds of practices that I think would be necessary to sustain a covenantal understanding of vocation. As I discussed earlier, our concepts of vocation and knowing are inevitably sustained by practices. Thus, we saw how the practice of consumerism both continues to shape and be shaped by the modern belief that values are personal choices. Weber himself conceived of the practice of teaching/knowing as essentially an isolated enterprise, one in which the self masters all things by calculation. In contrast to these practices, I would like to point to three alternative practices, each of which I think has the potential to sustain a rich understanding of vocation as covenantal: hospitality, testimony, and forgiveness.

First, I turn to hospitality. It is likely that my colleague's desire not to "impose" his beliefs on his students (certainly a common sentiment) reflects his antipathy toward a kind of Christian triumphalism, an attitude and practice clearly present within the Christian tradition. If we value diversity, should we not maintain harmony by keeping our beliefs "private"? Yet, as previously discussed above, our convictions inevitably "show themselves," and the assumption these can be kept out of the public sphere is a false one. Yet what is the alternative?

The practice of hospitality, I think, stands as an alternative to Christian triumphalism and to imposing anything on another except by means of witness and persuasion. Triumphalism or hegemony is in fact more properly understood as a *distortion* of the Christian mythos. As John H. Yoder notes, ". . . the error in the age of triumphalism was not that it was tied to Jesus but that it denied him, precisely in its power and its disrespect for the neighbor. . . . Its error was not that it propagated Christianity around the world but that what it propagated was not Christian enough."[33] The practice of hospitality, in contrast to triumphalism, calls us to welcome the other in all of his or her particularity, even to the point of being willing to *suffer* at the hands of the other. One of the theological convictions that sustains this risky practice is that the other is a worthy child of God, no matter how much we might fail to see this. Even more, however, hospitality relies upon the conviction and promise that God speaks through "the stranger." Thus hospitality means we welcome the colleague or student who is different from us not because all "values" are relative, but because welcoming the stranger, even the enemy, is one way to practice the conviction that all persons are children of God called to live in communion with each other. So understood, diversity has as its goal not mere coexistence but mutuality and even unity, though a unity made possible not by coercion but by the grace of God.[34]

Surely one aspect of genuine hospitality is speaking the truth as best we can, and truly listening to the truth spoken by another. We might call this related practice "testimony." While testimony often conjures up images of emotionally wrought revivals, rightly understood it can contribute to our ways of thinking about vocation. The practice of testimony gives us space to appear as a "who" before others rather than a "what."[35] Testimony could devolve into mere subjectivism, but it is better understood as embodying a heuristic conception of truth. In other words, the practice of testimony relies upon the notion that truth *unfolds* in those "spaces of appearance" between us, and between ourselves and God. Such a conception of truth, as Polanyi notes, "anticipates an indeterminate range of yet unknown (and perhaps yet inconceivable) true implications."[36] Thomas Hoyt, Jr., describing how testimony has been central in the Black Church tradition, reflects this heuristic understanding of testimony when he notes, "In testimony, people speak truthfully about what they have experienced and seen, offering it to the community for the edification of all. . . . Since testimony is the shared practice of the whole people of God, we may participate in it even when we do not have all the answers."[37] Testimony thus reminds us that knowing is both communal and heuristic.[38] Even more, by allowing a space of appearance for the other, it attends to postmodernism's concern that we not silence the other, but attend to the ways our structures, communities and words have been oppressive. Indeed testimony might well reveal the depths of our own complicity with violence and evil present in the world. Thus the practice of testimony would seem to call for yet another practice which aims at reconciliation: forgiveness.

Postmodernism rightly notes how our words and deeds easily become oppressive, deceptive and hegemonic. Some forms of postmodernism thus conclude that we need constantly to recognize, even relish in, the instability of all discourse. Since words never correspond to a fixed reality, all speech must be deconstructed. While the practice of forgiveness certainly recognizes that our words/deeds oppress, deceive, etc., it nonetheless relies upon some sense of stability. Such stability, however, does not derive from a "correspondence" theory of truth/language, i.e., a foundationalist approach that assumes words have one essential meaning regardless of our use. Rather, stability in the practice of forgiveness rests on the conviction that our words are deeds, ways of acting in the world. Hannah Arendt relies upon just such a conception of speech in her analysis of the irreversibility—we might say instability—of our spoken words and of the chaotic uncertainty of our existence, all of which the postmodernist rightly observes. In *The Human Condition*, Arendt asks (my paraphrase), "How can one reverse or recover from the negative consequences, whether intended or not, of one's words and deeds? Given the unpredictability and contingency of the world in which we live, wherein lies our stability?" Arendt notes:

> The possible redemption from the predicament of irreversibility—of being unable to undo what one has done though one did not, and could not, have known what he was doing—is the faculty of *forgiving*. The remedy for unpredictability, for the chaotic uncertainty of the future, is contained in the faculty to *make and keep promises*. The two faculties belong together in so far as one of them, forgiving, serves to undo the deeds of the past, whose "sins" hang like Damocles' sword over every new generation; and the other, binding oneself through promises, serves to set up in the ocean of uncertainty, which the future is by definition, islands of security without which not even continuity, let alone durability of any kind, would be possible in the relationships between men.[39]

Arendt claims that both of these practices, asking or giving forgiveness and making promises, depend upon a plurality, the presence and action of others. In Arendt's view, our words are not bound by that to which they eternally correspond, but this does not mean they are completely "unhinged." Rather, our words—which Arendt understands as deeds, as ways of acting—are bound or "stabilized" by our promises (made ultimately before God), and unbound or "destabilized" by our acts of forgiveness before others. At this point, Arendt herself is drawing upon a covenantal understanding of the "human condition." Though she does not develop this, she acknowledges her conceptual debt to the biblical understanding of covenant as embodied in Abraham. As she notes, this man from Ur "shows such a passionate drive toward making covenants that it is as though he departed from his country for no other reason than to try out the power of mutual promise [as well as forgiveness] in the wilderness of the world. . . ."[40] Such a biblical concept reveals the contingency of our words, but words nonetheless stabilized by our promises and acts of forgiveness.

In contrast to both modernity and some forms of postmodernity, a covenantal understanding of vocation acknowledges the fiduciary, communal, and heuristic nature of knowing. Such an understanding of vocation thus moves beyond the dichotomy between faith and knowledge, a dichotomy as we have seen that is shaped by a different story (primarily Gnostic), and one that has seriously crippled Christian identity and higher education. I have sought to show how a recovery of a richer theological understanding of vocation can assist us in perceiving more truthfully our vocation in the academic world. Thus Christian identity—embodied in such practices and ways of knowing as hospitality, testimony, and forgiveness—ought not be privatized but apparent even and most especially in the intellectual life of the college or university, where we seek ultimately to love God with our minds.

The Erotic Imagination
and the Catholic Academy

JOHN NEARY

INTRODUCTION: DIVING DEEP

Recently, I was invited to be a mentor at a summer colloquy sponsored by the Lilly-endowed Collegium Institute on Faith and Intellectual Life, an organization that brings together Catholic graduate students and young faculty at Catholic institutions to help them explore the Catholic intellectual tradition and develop a sense of their work as vocation. One of my tasks as mentor was daunting: to make a presentation to the entire group about my own attempts to mesh the spiritual and the intellectual—to tell the story of my own vocation.

Prior to the colloquy, I diligently composed a ten-page speech about my Catholic-school experience, about how I came to major in English and how I began to write about the intersection of literature and theology, and so forth. It was a carefully written little speech, with some attempt at Catholic-school humor, and it was honest and accurate—as far as it went. But then, during mentor training, a fellow mentor (with far more experience in Collegium than I) mentioned that these presentations on career-as-vocation tend to be dull and ineffective unless the speaker "dives deep." And I realized that that was precisely what my written essay did not do. It was chatty and anecdotal, but safe. The true story of the integration of my work with my often-faltering faith is a story not of events but of love—specifically, of my love for three people who have deeply affected me (that is, deeply moved my affections) over the course of my life. I hastily rewrote the presentation, turning it into the story of my relationship with these three people. The presentation went well; clearly this—not some abstract, anecdotal summary—was what the colloquy was longing for.

Using Jungian categories, psychotherapist/theologian Ann Belford Ulanov describes "logos" as the principle of "discrimination, judgment, insight, and relation to nonpersonal truth," while the "concept of eros describes symbolically the psychic urge to relate, to join, to be in-the-midst-of, to reach out to, to value, to get in touch with, to get involved with concrete feelings, things, and people, rather than to abstract or theorize."[1] By these terms, I realized that my academic story is founded less on *logos* than on *eros*. And the fact that the "erotic" rather than the "logical" story was more appropriate at Collegium suggests to me that *eros* may well be a primary value of the Catholic academic world; an important Catholic insight, I suggest, is that the personal story of "concrete feelings, things, and people" precedes abstract, theoretical, "nonpersonal truth." I think it is fitting, then, in this essay on *eros* in the Catholic academy, to begin not theoretically but personally, with the story of my own "erotic" religious education: the story I told Collegium of three crucial relationships.

The first of the three people is my college mentor, an Episcopal priest and Jungian psychologist who taught religion at the Catholic college I attended as an undergraduate; subsequent to my presentation at Collegium I learned that the man was anything but perfect, and I have publicly described his imperfections, calling him "Ronald Foster" (a pseudonym, which I will use here). But despite his unsavory side, it was Ronald who first helped me to integrate the intellectual, the personal, and the spiritual, and to find a settled, grown-up relationship with the Catholic church. As a cradle Catholic who had grown up before Vatican II, I had experienced the beauty and symbolic richness but also the oppressiveness—especially the distrust of physicality—which marked that version of

Catholicism. By the time I began attending college, the church had changed a great deal, and so had I. I was intellectually very skeptical but also personally very confused. I doubted my faith and I longed for personal relationships, and the two needs were somehow linked; my intellectual questions—is there a God? does life have meaning?—and my personal struggles were mixed together. And the great value of Ronald Foster in my life is that he did not try to separate these things. I first encountered him in an academically demanding religion course, with an extensive and sophisticated reading list that surveyed the human quest for a God. This class more than any I have ever taken helped me construct an intellectually viable worldview that has room for a spiritual reality. But as a Jungian, Ronald also approached the divine as a real, immediate experience, deeply entangled with his and his students' everyday lives and personal struggles. He became for me and for many of my classmates a friend, counselor, and mentor, helping us deal with all sorts of psychological, social, and spiritual confusions. And these two dimensions of my relationship with Ronald Foster—the intellectual guidance and the loving human help—were completely of a piece. He taught me what a great teacher is: someone who touches the heart as well as the head; someone who relates not to an abstract general student but to a real, specific person; someone for whom *eros* is at least as important as *logos*.

The second of these three relationships was sweet and sad. I was initially unhappy in graduate school precisely because it largely lacked the *eros*—the particular loving connection—that Ronald Foster had given my undergraduate studies. But then, in my second year, I taught my first literature class, and I loved it; I found that I could carry into the classroom a genuine integration of the intellectual and the affectionate. I had not liked the heady intellectualism of graduate school, but teaching was more like an act of love—clearly a vocation rather than a job. I was only a few years older than my first students, and many of them became my friends. I ended up becoming the best of friends with one of these students, Brian, whom I still think of as having helped me understand what it would be like to have a twin brother: we had a collection of private jokes that were almost our own mind-reading code. But despite his sunny, charismatic personality, and for reasons that even a true twin brother would never have been able to fathom, Brian committed suicide. I sank into a full-fledged depression, and in a wholly negative way experienced the integration of the intellectual and the affective: I no longer cared about *either* aspect of my life. God as *logos* and God as *eros* were both dead.

The final person in the story I told Collegium helped me experience a kind of resurrection: my wife, Laura. I was so obviously depressed that friends, including a graduate-school mentor, nudged me to reenter the human race and reignite my love of teaching by taking a job in an undergraduate dormitory as a graduate-student teacher in residence; once again, the underlying insight here was an integration of work with life and passion and relatedness to others. My experience in that dormitory—where I acted as resident tutor, teacher, and academic-program planner—was positive and powerful. I was able to share my love for learning, and especially for literature, in an atmosphere of friendship rather than of classroom competition. It was in that dorm that I met Laura, to whom I am now married and from whom I have learned most of what I know about love and relatedness. And residence-hall work continues to be a large part of my vocation; I still teach many of my courses in residence halls, sitting on the floor or in a lounge chair rather than standing at a podium. My hope, at least, is that such an atmosphere makes my classes personal and affective rather than just cognitive; *logos* still takes a backseat to *eros* in my work.

In case this sounds sentimental, I need to note something that has always troubled me as a terrible mystery: I quite certainly would not have had that initial dormitory experience, nor would I have met my wife, if my friend Brian had not died. There is a dark religious limit-reality here that resists domestication: an event of deep hopelessness led me to healing and love, and it would be false and offensive to claim that my own more-or-less happy ending compensates for the profound horror that Brian must have experienced. Still, my marriage and family—whom I have been blessed with through this mysterious chain of events—are the most important things in my life, and my attempts at relational rather than coolly objective teaching continue to be very rewarding. And perhaps because of the prevalence and power of that horrific reality in the world, I think that such relationality is precious and necessary; as I have said, *eros* more than *logos* has been crucial to my life as a teacher and a human being, and I wish to argue that *eros* can be one of the great charisms of the Catholic academy.

Of course, *eros* in academe—especially Catholic academe—is hardly a universally positive reality; one manifestation of the "horror" in the lives of too many Catholics and former Catholics is the abuse of the erotic by clergy; indeed, a history of precisely such abusiveness is, sadly, the dark side of the Ronald Foster story. But I think the existence of the abuses proves the potency of the reality that I am exploring here. Readers of John of the Cross's mystical poetry, Dante's *Divine Comedy*, and the *National Enquirer* know that Catholicism has a strongly erotic strain. The fact that Christian *eros* can be dangerous and destructive as well as life-affirming is hardly surprising, and it seems to me that celebrating its virtues rather than suppressing it is the best way to ensure that the virtues prevail. So in the remaining pages I wish to suggest some of the *positive* ways that the Catholic academy—and, I suspect, the larger church-related academy—can make use of an "erotic" Christian way of imagining human relationships with each other and with God.

AGAPE AND EROS

In *Final Payments*, novelist Mary Gordon (a fine contemporary chronicler of the American Catholic experience) depicts a character whose major epiphany is that she needs to embrace the ordinary world of human desire and passion. As a child in a strict, pre-Vatican II Catholic school, the novel's protagonist, Isabel Moore, was taught that such desire and passion are wrong, and that true Christian charity is absolutely selfless; at the time, she had rejected this teaching:

> Love and charity. One was that feeling below the breast, and the other was doing something, anything, to take people's pain away. I remembered the lettering on a bulletin board at Anastasia Hall:

LOVE IS MEASURED BY SACRIFICE. And I remembered thinking how wrong this was, because the minute I gave up something for someone I liked them less.

"Ah," Sister Fidelis had said when I asked her, "you don't
have to like someone to love them in God."

But who wants to be loved in God? . . . We want to be loved
for our singularity, not for what we share with the rest of the
human race. We would rather be loved for the color of our hair
or the shape of our ankle than because God loves us.[2]

In her adulthood, a series of distressing events leads Isabel
temporarily to adopt Sister Fidelis's dispassionate Christian
"charity" after all. As a protection against the pain of relationship, Isabel chooses to love people "now as God loved His
creatures: impartially, impervious to their individual natures."[3]
The novel ends, however, with Isabel's insight that her own
Catholic tradition contains a theological justification for embracing rather than renouncing human passion; Isabel, as a
child, turns out to have been at least as orthodox as Sister
Fidelis. Reflecting on the story of Christ permitting Mary to
anoint his feet, even though the ointment could have been sold
for the poor, Isabel sees that an embrace of the sensuous can
be entirely Christian: "What Christ was saying, what he meant,
was that the pleasures of that hair, that ointment, must be taken,
because the accidents of death would deprive us soon enough.
We must not deprive ourselves, our loved ones, of the luxury
of our extravagant affections."[4] This is Isabel's crucial revelation, a kind of conversion experience. And it is a conversion
precisely away from passionless "charity" and toward passionate, affectionate love: "I knew now I must open the jar of ointment. I must open my life."[5]

What Isabel has been struggling with are two different forms
of love—or rather, conflicting Christian responses to these two
forms of love. For a time she renounces *eros*, love based on
concrete affection and attraction, in favor of an exaggerated
form of *agape*, which Lutheran theologian Anders Nygren—in
his classic book *Agape and Eros*—calls the only genuine form of
Christian love. Nygren describes *agape* precisely as "unmoti-
vated" and "indifferent to value."[6] That is, divine *agape* explains why God can love the righteous and the sinner equally:

God's love is in no way governed by particular attractions or preferences; it is not in any way analogous to human affection. And Christian love, by virtue of divine grace, must be similarly free of the particular desires and appetites that mark the inferior form of love, *eros*: "There is . . . no Christian love that does not derive its character from the Agape that is found in fellowship with God."[7] This is exactly the position that Isabel Moore endorses, prior to her reflection on the story of Christ and the ointment.

But Nygren goes on to explain that medieval Catholicism—especially exemplified by the works of Augustine, Dante, and Aquinas (and embodied in contemporary form in the passion-affirming conclusion of *Final Payments*)—effected a synthesis of *eros* and *agape* as *caritas*. Catholicism, then, attempts to baptize affectionate desire (which for Nygren is always a form of "self-love") as good:

> in Catholicism . . . the idea of acquisitive love is the bond which ultimately holds the whole together. The fact that self-love is at the centre here is most clearly shown in that it is actually located in God, in the Holy Trinity. In self-sufficient blessedness and majesty God is enthroned above the world. God's love means, in the first place, that the Divine being revolves within itself in self-love, and secondly, that it draws the desire of all beings towards itself. In virtue of natural self-love, everything strives upwards. The whole of existence, therefore, presents the spectacle of a ceaseless ascent, an incessant pursuit of that which is higher. Only in God can the desire of created beings for blessedness come to rest.[8]

This is essentially the idea, which Nygren would call thoroughly Catholic, that Isabel Moore comes to: "What Christ was saying, what he meant, was that the pleasures of that hair, that ointment, must be taken."[9] But Nygren applauds Luther's rejection of this "classical Catholic idea of love, the Caritas-synthesis."[10] "Luther," Nygren writes, "has observed how the whole Catholic doctrine of love displays an *egocentric perversion*."[11] In its place, Nygren says, Luther reestablished the dialectic between *eros* and *agape*, which Nygren enthusiastically endorses.

Divine love, for Nygren, is utterly different from human love. God's love, Nygren says, is marked by the radical selflessness of the Cross, the complete emptying of personal desire: "God is Agape. . . . Only at the Cross do we find God, but there we really find Him. 'Theologia crucis' is the only true theology."[12] (The poster in Isabel Moore's school—"LOVE IS MEASURED BY SACRIFICE"—puts this more crudely, but the underlying theology is the same.) Since this dialectical perspective sees no analogy between selfless *agape* and human love, humans themselves can exemplify *agape*, according to Nygren, only "when through faith man becomes open to God."[13] In other words, because fallen humans on their own are incapable of pure, selfless love, they receive access to it only through faith and divine grace.

Nygren's is a severe version of Lutheran theology, and I think a more nuanced reading of Luther would also emphasize Luther's well-known earthiness and his lyrical celebrations of the created world. But Nygren's analysis of *eros* certainly represents a powerful strain within Christianity—and, indeed, the Catholic church itself has often failed to acknowledge the positive value of eroticism implicit in Catholicism's rich imagery. My personal feeling is that the dialectical critique of *eros* and the sacramental retrieval of it are both founded on important insights; each position complements and corrects the excesses of the other. And Nygren's critique perhaps suggests why Catholicism, its literature (Gordon's *Final Payments*, for example), its academic vision (presented by Collegium, for example, which begins each summer colloquy with the lushly festive film *Babette's Feast*), and its colleges and universities may especially embrace a form of *eros*. (I would argue that this is a redeemed form of *eros*, truly generous but also marked by real passion and affection.) Although the positive value of the erotic is by no means an exclusively Roman Catholic insight, the joining together of *eros* and *agape* is related to the Catholic intellectual tradition's tendency to relate seeming opposites: faith and reason, sacred and secular, etc. Contemporary Catholic theologian David Tracy, for instance, demonstrates that the "Caritas-synthesis" criticized by Anders Nygren remains alive and well in the Catholic intellectual tradition. In his book *The Analogical Imagination*, predicated on an affirmation that, even after the Fall, humanity remains a genuine analogy of the divine, Tracy writes: "As grounded in that gift of trust, *eros* will be transformed but not negated by divine *agape*. That transformation is *caritas*."[14]

I suggest, then, that this vision of an *erotic* religious sensibility can inform both the academic content and the communal, pedagogical style of Catholic higher education. (Again, this is not an exclusively Catholic vision, and indeed such a vision might well be one of the Catholic intellectual tradition's best contributions to church-related colleges of all types.) In this essay's next section, I will briefly present a premise underlying my argument for an erotic *imagination*—the premise that the religious is, among other things, a way of *imaging* ultimate reality, and that this imaginative approach to religion can survive and even thrive on postmodern skepticism. Then I will discuss how the erotic religious imagination nurtured by the Catholic intellectual tradition can transform our conception of the teaching-learning process and can nudge Catholic academicians to choose texts that celebrate the erotic. Underlying all of this is a vision of relatedness, in the broadest sense—a vision of connection between humans and each other, humans and the world, humans and God.

THE POSTMODERN BACKGROUND: THE IMPORTANCE OF IMAGINATION

Jacques Derrida declared that awareness of the "structurality of structure"[15]—awareness of humans' access not to things but only to signs—has created a "rupture" in Western metaphysics, one that radically undermines all those words that attempt to affirm a center, a truly *present* being, a religious reality: "*eidos, arche<ebar>, telos, energeia, ousia* (essence, existence, substance, subject), *ale<ebar>theia*, transcendentality, consciousness, God, man, and so forth."[16] In the face of this rupture, it would seem that religious understandings of reality would be merely precious anachronisms; one might assume that the postmodern era is also the postreligious era. Deconstructionist theologian Carl A. Raschke thinks that this is precisely the postmodern realization; he declares that deconstruction "shows that the logos of all our latter-day '——ologies,' including theology, has become nought but a ritualistic and compulsive defense against *to kenon* ('the void')."[17] Raschke goes on to say that deconstruction, "which must be considered the interior drive of twentieth-century theology rather than an alien agenda, is in the final analysis *the death of God put into writing.*"[18]

But deconstructionist literary theorist J. Hillis Miller suggests that postmodern negations may be a way of cracking open the conventional not in order to engage in utter, scornful skepticism but rather to invoke the never-reached ultimate concern or limit, a ground-that-is-not-of-a-ground. This ultimate limit is an unfathomable depth that Miller, quoting William Carlos Williams, calls a radiant gist: "Good reading is . . . productive, performative. Naming the text rightly, it brings the strange phosphorus of the life, what Williams elsewhere calls 'the radiant gist,' back once more above ground."[19] The theological literary critic Kevin Hart goes even further, claiming that negative theology, a mystical theism in which "one gains 'knowledge' of God by successively abstracting God from images of him,"[20] hence guaranteeing "that human speech about God is in fact about *God* and not a *concept* of God,"[21] is actually a form of postmodern deconstruction. What Hart points out is that the postmodern turn reminds us that God-talk always deals with *human images* rather than absolute propositions about ultimate reality. Hence, in the postmodern environment it still makes sense to weave images of God, provided one does so playfully and hypothetically. Fr. Andrew Greeley, who specifically eschews the term "modernist," by which I think he means *post*modernist ("I do not believe," he says, "that symbols can mean whatever we want them to mean"[22]), presents a similar theory of the religious as primarily based on the imagination rather than on propositions: "My contention . . . is that image and experience and story come before formal religious doctrine and are likely to have more raw power than purely propositional teaching can possibly possess."[23] So it is an entirely respectable, intellectually sophisticated, and very valuable enterprise for church-related colleges to attend to the development of a cultural imagination.

This postmodern idea that a religious imagination takes precedence over religious propositions can be drawn from theologians as diverse as David Tracy, with his "analogical imagination," and Sallie McFague, with her "metaphorical theology." My argument in these pages is that the Catholic religious imagination is especially marked by an embrace of *eros* as well as *agape,* a vision of passionate connectedness and relationship.

THE EROTIC IMAGINATION

Over against the dialectical Christian tradition—which stresses the separation of the profane from the sacred and hence views *eros* with suspicion—is, as we have already seen, what Anders Nygren calls the Catholic "Caritas-synthesis." And Andrew Greeley, borrowing heavily from David Tracy, stresses how the Catholic synthesis involves a distinctive form of imagination, what he calls the Catholic or sacramental imagination: "The Catholic 'classics,'" Greeley says, "assume a God who is present in the world, disclosing Himself in and through creation. The world and all its events, objects, and people tend to be somewhat like God."[24] Such a Catholic imagination emphasizes the similarities between the sacred and the secular, the transcendent and the human, the divine and the bodily, *agape* and *eros.* This is the kind of imagination endorsed by Catholic feminist theologian Elizabeth Johnson when she describes the way an incarnational view of the divine affirms *bodiliness*:

> The inner dynamic of the doctrine of incarnation sounds a ringing affirmation of the cherished feminist value of bodiliness, even for God. . . . [T]he living God is *capax hominis,* capable of personal union with what is not God, the flesh and spirit of humanity. . . . Bodiliness opens up the mystery of God to the conditions of history, including suffering and delight. She becomes flesh, choosing the very stuff of the cosmos as her own personal reality forever. She thereby becomes irrevocably, physically connected to the human adventure, for better or worse. Far from functioning as the index of creaturely separation from the divine, human bodiliness is manifest as irreplaceable sacrament of mutual communion between heaven and earth, not only in Jesus' case but ontologically for all.[25]

Such a *bodily* God, which Catholicism's incarnational and sacramental approach to Christianity has long celebrated, is at the heart of the Catholic erotic imagination that I am exploring in these pages. This is a God who experiences delight as well as suffering, who is physically connected to "the very stuff of the cosmos" and to the whole "human adventure," and who is therefore revealed not just in the sacrifice of the Cross but throughout the sensuous creation. As Catholic poet Gerard Manley Hopkins puts it, the grandeur of God will "flame out" everywhere; it oozes from the world like oil pressed from an olive: "The world is charged with the grandeur of God. / It will flame out, like shining from shook foil; / It gathers to a greatness, like the ooze of oil / Crushed" ("God's Grandeur").

Certainly calling this image of God "Catholic" is only a kind of shorthand, since Protestant theologian Sallie McFague uses the metaphor of God-as-lover explicitly to reclaim *eros* as an image of godly love: "This description of eros—that it is a passionate attraction to the valuable and a desire to be united with it—may initially mark it as a strange candidate for a traditional Christian perspective, for expressing God's saving love. It implies that the world is valuable, that God needs it, and that salvation is the reunification of the beloved with its lover, God."[26]

McFague, like Hopkins, Greeley, and Johnson, is imagining here a god who is "somewhat like" the creation and especially humanity; the sacramental or analogical or erotic imagination, therefore, leaps denominational boundaries. Nonetheless, in its rejection of an absolute antithesis between sacred and secular, such an embrace of *eros* surely is markedly Catholic even if not exclusively so. This form of religious imagination is especially interested in connection, a linking love based not on detached agapic benevolence but on active desire, what Mary Gordon calls "the luxury of our extravagant affections."[27] So the Catholic sacramental imagination tells stories of connection: of God's immanent and passionate connection with creation but also of all creatures' connections with each other. Stories of connection, of relatedness, would then be prototypical Catholic stories. The vocation of the Catholic academy could be to incarnate these stories and images of connection, community, and *eros* by adopting an erotic model of teaching and learning, and the Catholic academy could also keep this religious imagination alive by telling and retelling Catholic stories of erotic relatedness.

THE EROS OF TEACHING AND LEARNING

Parker Palmer has argued that the Christian view of truth calls for a style of teaching and learning that is at odds with much of the present-day academy; what Palmer calls for is, in a sense, a retrieval of the *erotic* in education—a reenvisioning of education not as a confrontation between separate atoms but rather a marriage. Palmer criticizes a worship of pure objectivity: "the root meaning of 'objective' is 'to put against, to oppose.' This is the danger of objectivism: it is a way of knowing that places us in an adversary relation to the world. By this view, we are not required to change so that the whole community might flourish; instead, the world must change to meet our needs. Indeed, objectivism has put us in an adversary relation to one another."[28] In place of such atomistic objectivism, Palmer endorses a view of reality as interrelated, married, boundlessly desiring connection: "Reality's ultimate structure is that of an organic, interrelated, mutually responsive community of being. Relationships—not facts and reasons—are the key to reality; as we enter those relationships, knowledge of reality is unlocked. . . . The deepest calling in our quest for knowledge is not to observe and analyze and alter things. Instead, it is personal participation in the organic community of human and nonhuman being, participation in the network of caring and accountability called truth."[29]

This view of reality leads Palmer to espouse a form of knowing, and hence of teaching and learning, that is based not on egoistic domination of the world but rather on love—not a bloodless, abstract love, but a desiring, passionate, erotic love. Such a form of knowing, Palmer says, will aim "not at exploiting and manipulating creation but at reconciling the world to itself."[30] He says that "the act of knowing *is* an act of love, the act of entering and embracing the reality of the other, of allowing the other to enter and embrace our own. In such knowing we know and are known as members of one community, and our knowing becomes a way of reweaving that community's bonds."[31] To know, for Palmer, is not to master some objective, external fact but rather "to become betrothed, to engage the known with one's whole self, an engagement one enters with attentiveness, care, and good will."[32] Such knowledge-as-*eros* is, Palmer says, entirely suited to the Christian view of reality as inherently connected and loving. Since truth passionately desires and loves us, an intense embrace of truth is an entirely appropriate response, and celebrating that embrace of truth should make classrooms loving rather than dull or threatening places. Thus, Palmer compares the activity of good teaching to friendship:

> It depends ultimately on a teacher who has a living relationship with the subject at hand, who invites students into that relationship as full partners. . . .
>
> The metaphor of friendship helps identify some demands of this sort of teaching. The teacher, who knows the subject well, must introduce it to students in the way one would introduce a friend. The students must know why the teacher values the subject, how the subject has transformed the teacher's life. By the same token, the teacher must value the students as potential friends, be vulnerable to the ways students may transform the teacher's relationship with the subject as well as be transformed.[33]

In the face of such a friendly and passionate picture of reality, epistemology, and teaching, it would be foolish for classrooms at church-related colleges (especially, I might add, Catholic colleges, since the Catholic intellectual tradition—as I have been arguing here—is particularly open to passionate, erotic images of the divine) to be cool, objective, fact-based places. Rather, they should be places in which ultimate concerns are real and really explored and in which an appropriate but genuine love between students and teacher and students and each other can thrive. In other words, what Henri Nouwen calls a "violent" teaching process should be eschewed in favor of what he describes as a *redemptive* form of teaching.

Nouwen complains that education is too often seen as a way of "getting things under control"[34] and hence is drenched in competitiveness, is unilateral (the teacher is strong, the student weak), and is alienating (imagined as a preparation for "real" life rather than as truly vital in its own right). The redemptive teaching process that Nouwen prefers is relational—friendly, filled with *eros*—in the ways I have been describing: the redemptive teacher-student relationship is one that is *evocative* (teachers and students evoke in each other their "respective potentials and make them available to each other"[35]), *bilateral* (relational and "open-ended"[36]), and *actualizing* (focused not on some practical, external "real world" but on deep, present relationships and concern[37]).

The classroom behaviors that such a teaching-learning process calls for would likely lean in the direction of "active learning," experiential learning, and discussion-based rather than lecture-based pedagogy. But what I am talking about goes beyond pedagogical technique; as Parker Palmer says, "Practicing obedience to truth in the classroom, practicing listening between teacher, students, and subject, is not finally a matter of technique,"[38] and Palmer calls for "spiritual formation" for teachers rather than technical training.[39] Indeed, active learning can be just a catchy educational trend, and some of the great old lecturers of the past undoubtedly were more deeply in love with truth and more profoundly compassionate toward their students than many faddish practitioners of active learning today. What is at issue is the underlying vision—the way of imaging ultimate reality and our relationship with it and with each other. The Catholic academy, I suggest, can give new, more active pedagogical techniques a depth and resonance by connecting them with *ultimate* rather than merely faddish concerns.

STORIES OF PASSIONATE RELATEDNESS

A view of erotic love as an analogy of divine love should lead the Catholic academy not only to more passionate pedagogies but also to more passionate—dare I say erotic?—texts. The stereotype is that the religious academy would steer clear of erotic texts, or would study them in proud defiance of the stodgy church-related traditions on which religious academic institutions were founded. But I suggest that daring, earthy, perhaps shocking texts should find a home in a Catholic institution because of, not in spite of, its Catholicism. Indeed, I can think

of no better way to undo the damage done to the erotic imagination by our trashy pop culture, which is based, I suspect, on
an underlying notion that the sensuous and the sensual are
dirty. Using Bernini's statue *The Ecstasy of Saint Teresa* ("She is
overcome with pleasure, a woman in a swoon after ecstatic
love"[40]) and Saint Teresa's own poetic mystical texts as examples, Andrew Greeley describes the power of erotic art to
convey a religious vision:

> The point is not that the saint's ecstasy was erotic (though it prob-
> ably was that, too), but that both the saint and the sculptor used
> erotic images to describe what it is like to be caught up in God's
> love. Human passion is a sacrament (as Saint Paul had said long
> before) for divine passion. Bernini's masterpiece (he thought it
> was his best work) is a perfect example . . . of the poetry of Ca-
> tholicism at work, a poetry that no prose prudery can ever undo.[41]

Greeley suggests that the Catholic academy ought to be immersing students in such Catholic imagery, offering courses
on Catholic art, poetry, fiction, and film: "I have the impression that the Catholic college used to be proud to offer such
courses and now is often just a little ashamed to offer them."[42]

My own experience lends credence to Greeley's affirmation
of the power of such texts to deepen students' religious imaginations. For the sake of illustration, I speak from the perspective of my own discipline, literary studies, but I am certain
that the use of Catholic/erotic texts could be adapted to many
other disciplines as well (the communitarian Catholic social
theory, for example, emerges from a deeply relational way of
imagining humans in the world, as do many feminist and ecological theories).

Two of my favorite texts to teach at St. Norbert College have
been D. M. Thomas's *The White Hotel* and James Joyce's *Ulysses*.
The White Hotel begins with a wildly erotic, even pornographic,
journal of sexual fantasies, composed by the novel's central
character while she is in analysis with Sigmund Freud. The
first time I used the book in a class, a young woman expressed
outrage that we would read such smut at a Catholic school,
and she said that if her parents found out they would report
me to the dean immediately. But by the time we finished the

book, in which the initial erotic chapter undergoes multiple repetitions until it eventually is transformed and sublimated into a vision of heaven, the same student was so deeply moved she gave the book to her sister (which worried me as much as the threatened call to her parents, but which for her was a way of passing on a kind of erotically sacred text).

The difficulties of *Ulysses* always drive my students to distraction, and yet the novel grows on them. We have held our discussion of the novel's penultimate chapter—in which the book's protagonists, Stephen Dedalus and Leopold Bloom, finally get together for a comic yet genuine Eucharistic chat over hot cocoa—in the campus church; and the sacramental power of the book's portrayal of friendship comes alive. It is humorously appropriate (and, I think, entirely Catholic) to be in church while I explain to the class that the scene at the end of the chapter—in which Stephen and Bloom urinate, side by side, in the Blooms' garden while Bloom's wife, Molly, who has just had very rowdy sex with another man, hovers above them at a lighted window—is an image of the Trinity and its richly erotic relationality. If I told the students at the beginning of the semester, before they tackled Joyce's difficult and elaborately constructed poetic work, that Bloom, Stephen, and Molly were going to manifest the Father, Son, and Spirit, this concept would mean nothing to them. But having worked all semester with me, with each other, and with Joyce in the kind of erotic collaboration that is the only way most of us can get through this monumentally complicated work, and now sitting in church, the students do get an inkling of the Joycean trinitarian vision—not through *logos*, cognition, but through *eros*, affective experience.

CONCLUSION

In the two pairings that I have invoked—*logos* and *eros, agape* and *eros*—*eros* has traditionally been the inferior, subordinate term. Getting "involved with concrete feelings, things, and people" (*eros*) sounds a great deal less crystalline and rigorous than "nonpersonal truth" (*logos*), and desiring, hungering affection (*eros*) sounds needier and more incomplete and impure than sacrificial selflessness (*agape*). But I began this essay with my own personal story rather than with conceptual ideas precisely to stress that the fabric of our identities is made up of our concrete, affective experience, not just of abstract, selflessly objective beliefs. My life as well as my studies have led me to affirm that a tradition that addresses, blesses, and even arouses the passionate, desiring aspects of the human person—and finds poetic hints of ultimate reality in these earthly and earthy places—is a tradition with much to offer the church-related academy. I suggest that the Catholic tradition, with its sacramental, analogical imagination (which I have been calling an "erotic imagination," because of Catholicism's stubborn defense of the erotic in the face of the Reformation tradition's condemnation of it), can help the academy rediscover a healthy *eros*, just as it helped me give a personal and affective rather than merely factual presentation at the Collegium's summer colloquy. Considering that competitiveness, consumerism, secularism, worship of technology, and fear of sexual abuses are making much of academe sterile and impersonal, such a retrieval of passion and relatedness—of the erotic—would, I think, give church-related higher education a renewed vigor, spirit, and mission.

✠

PART FOUR

PEDAGOGY AND PRAXIS

"Academic" vs. "Confessional" Study of the Bible in the Postmodern Classroom: A Class Response to Philip Davies and David Clines

Julia M. O'Brien

What constitutes academically sound and ethically responsible education in Bible in the postmodern, church-related classroom? I approach this question in earnest, as a scholar of Hebrew Bible and as a teacher—for eight years of undergraduates at a church-related college and now of seminarians at a denominationally affiliated institution.[1] While for most of my own intellectual journey the supposed clash of "faith" and "learning" has been a nonissue (the critical study of scripture enriching my reading of it), I believe that current challenges to the enterprise of faith-informed scholarship, particularly the issues raised by ideological criticism, are substantive ones. My goal in this chapter is to review and to respond to some of those challenges, a task I consider imperative for my own ability to function honestly and responsibly in my institutional context.

OLDER NOTIONS OF THE COMPATIBILITY OF "FAITH" AND "LEARNING"

Numerous scholars have offered diachronic surveys of the evolving conception of the compatibility of "faith" and "learning" in the development of Christian higher education. Noll's scheme, for example, traces an ever-deepening estrangement of the church and the academy. While Puritan ideology perceived the world's wisdom as consistent with biblical orthodoxy, such that Reason (the questionable) was compatible with Christianity (the given), the Revolutionary Generation, under the influence of what Noll terms a "conservative Enlightenment," reversed the formulation, such that Christianity (the questionable) was seen as compatible with Reason (the given). While Samuel Quincy could posit that "Christianity is a rational religion," the new emphasis on the Rational and the Real signaled a change in education's ultimate allegiance.[2]

In Noll's outline, it was the synthesis of these traditions, combined with a staunch belief in America's destiny and in individual freedom, that produced a "Protestant Newtonianism" in which God-ordained laws could be studied by human reason. The reorganization of higher education at the end of the nineteenth century, however, posed the greatest challenge to church-related institutions. The impact of Darwinism, greater emphasis on vocational training, and the adoption of the German model of "electives" within the curriculum brought to higher education a new emphasis on scholarship and professional credentials.[3]

Other surveys complement Noll's schema and elaborate upon late twentieth-century developments. Welch's history of the development of religious studies highlights the years 1945 through 1970 as an "Era of Expansion" in the field, spurred in the secular arena by the Supreme Court's Schempp case decision in 1963, which permitted teaching *about* religion "when presented objectively as part of a secular program of education."[4]

Similarly, the Report of the Task Force for the Study in Depth of Religion identifies the 1960s as a watershed in the development of this secularized discipline: "Faculty set out to design cross-cultural, interdisciplinary studies in religion, without sectarian bias."[5] The Task Force's Report notes with approval this "objective" model of teaching religion:

> Whatever traditions are studied, furthermore, the methods of study are appropriate to the modern university and differ markedly from the various venerable practices of textual study, self-

interpretation, catechesis, and spiritual reflection that have developed within many of the religious communities themselves.[6]

While the Task Force advances the necessity of an empathetic
understanding of the religions being studied (the report maintains that students must understand two traditions well in order to exercise proper comparative work), it argues against
understanding religions from an internal perspective:

> Though they [students of religion] pay close attention to the self-
> interpretations of religious communities, along with other aspects
> of their belief and practice, they do not privilege these self-inter-
> pretations in their own understanding of these communities.[7]

POSTMODERNISM AS SAVIOR

The equation of religious studies with the objective observation of religious phenomena has certainly in rhetoric, if not
reality, served as the self-description of the field within the
modern university—a place where commitments to the material studied have no academic or intellectual value.[8] Such a
paradigm clearly challenges the very basis of church-related
colleges and seminaries, institutions generally founded by
persons of faith and attempting, in various ways, to meet academic standards in the context of Christian witness. From the
objectivist paradigm, the aim of church-related educational
institutions is suspect because their project is grounded within
notions of God, self, and world that are nonempirically based.[9]

It is no wonder, then, given their impugned second-class
status, that by the late twentieth century church-related colleges and seminaries would seek intellectually respectable ar-
ticulations of the legitimacy of their own enterprise. And it is
no wonder that postmodernism would be considered an attractive candidate for appropriation, since postmodernism
shakes the very foundations which support the "modernist"
paradigm.

The modernist pillars, as Phillips describes them, are the
convictions that

    1.   man (*anthropos*) stands as located at the center of
        language, text, world, and meaning; and from this

privileged position grounds, perceives, and judges what is;

2. man as subject grasps what is in the world by the agency of *reason* that lays hold of the ideas, categories, or conceptual tools (critical methods) used to search out, measure, and organize what is;

3. the *telos* of knowledge is to master the positive, to survey regions of the known, to develop and employ critical methods to empower what is useful and efficient, objective and rational, positive and true;

4. explanation is justified finally in relation to *science* and its metadiscourse, philosophy; all is articulated through the "grand narrative" (a *metanarrative*) that legitimates certain forms of knowledge and social institutions—namely the Enlightenment narrative of the emancipation of the rational subject, the acquisition of personal wealth, and the heroic quest for the ethico-political goal of universal peace.[10]

Postmodernism's denial of the subject/object dualism and its exposé of the power dynamics which modernism discourse endeavors (without success) to erase, topples the modernist edifice:

> Exposed is the notion of the critical self as both transcendental, subjective knower and objectively known, a subject who locates self at the point of origin and authentication of language, of text, of social world, of meaning, of history, of structure. Rather, the self of the postmodern epoch is seen as emerging as a product of its local material, historical conditions.[11]

If meaning is produced rather than recovered, then within the postmodernist paradigm there is no intrinsic basis on which to discredit the Christian construction of meaning. Such appears to be the approach of George Marsden, who sees postmodernism as an opportunity for religious scholars to have their voices heard in the academy, as well as the explicit argument of Philip Kenneson's provocatively titled article: "There's

No Such Thing as Objective Truth and It's a Good Thing, Too."[12] In articulating his proposal for the Rhodes consultation, Stephen Haynes raised the same possibility: "How might a new wave of conceptions of knowledge and truth associated with the postmodern—and the receding tide of Enlightenment-inspired models of the academic vocation—affect the ethos of church-related colleges?"[13]

TROUBLE IN PARADISE

On an intellectual landscape which seems to recognize no philosophical battleground on which "objective" and "subjective" religious studies can wage war, new voices are again drawing battle lines or at least arguing that the armistice was naive. The strong insistence of Philip Davies and David Clines that confessional and nonconfessional biblical studies are incompatible in the academic sphere challenges an easy appropriation of the postmodernist paradigm by confessionally minded academics.

Countering recent claims, particularly those of Francis Watson and Brevard Childs, that biblical studies have marginalized theological concerns, Davies argues that the conflation of theological and academic discourses is prevalent throughout biblical scholarship. For example, he well demonstrates that Childs's canonical approach relies on particular configurations of canon that are anachronistically retrojected onto ancient Israel;[14] Davies demonstrates, too, how Childs lays claim to historical discourse while in fact advancing a theological agenda.[15]

In response, Davies utilizes the language of Kenneth Pike to draw a sharp distinction between two very different approaches to studying biblical material. He distinguishes: (1) *emic* discourse about the Bible, which he also calls "bible studies," "scripture," and "confessional discourse." Emic study accepts the text's ideology as its own and reads within confessional bounds; and (2) *etic* discourse about bibles (Davies underscores the multiplicity), also called "biblical studies," "academic" and "nonconfessional discourse." Etic study critiques the literature from an external frame of reference and remains "uninvolved in questions of authority or inspiration, since it has no tools for addressing such matters."[16]

While Davies claims to recognize the value of both types of study, he argues that they are incompatible because their goals and assumptions differ. Because confessional readings assume that truth is known and academic study seeks truth yet to be discovered, they approach texts in different, contesting ways. Hence, while confessional study might be valid within faith communities, it cannot be integrated into academic study, which is the proper purview of the university.

In the similar argument of David Clines, a distinction between the goals of "understanding" and "evaluation" is an important one. Identifying his own interpretive method as ideological critique, Clines maintains that any study which seeks only to explicate a text on its own terms, explicitly or tacitly allowing the text's world view to stand unquestioned, is neither academically rigorous nor ethically responsible scholarship.

> There is, however, yet another distinct project in which I think that we ought to be engaged as readers of the biblical texts: that of 'critique' or evaluation. It is a measure of our commitment to our own standards and values that we register disappointment, dismay or disgust when we encounter in the texts of ancient Israel ideologies that we judge to be inferior to ours. And it is a measure of our open-mindedness and eagerness to learn and do better that we remark with pleasure, respect and envy values and ideologies within the biblical texts that we judge to be superior to our own. . . .[17]

He concludes:

> What it boils down to is this: To be truly academic, and worthy of its place in the academy, biblical studies has to be truly critical, critical not just about lower-order questions like the authorship of the biblical books or the historicity of the biblical narratives, but critical about the Bible's contents, its theology, its ideology. . . . To be critical, you have to take up a standard of reference outside the material you are critiquing.[18]

Clines does not use Davies's language of emic and etic, but the two make similar points: confessionally based readings of biblical texts cannot be truly academic because they assume the inherent truth of the text's own ideologies and because they engage in discourse that is not open to rational or ethical critique.

FALSE DICHOTOMIES

Although, as I will argue below, Davies and Clines raise issues fundamentally important for the church-related classroom, their claims that truly academic interpreters first read a text and then judge it by external standards pose a false distinction between the two enterprises. Davies's language, for example, draws heavily on Enlightenment claims to objectivity and empiricism. He maintains that nonconfessional discourse is "positivistic," based on evidence that is "public and accessible":

> The confessional discourse of 'scripture' has, by virtue of its acceptance of a canon or sacred writings, based its entire procedure on a matter of religious commitment and *not an empirical fact.*

> I do not require any kind of belief, except in the usefulness *of universally agreed rules of evidence and argument* so that we can genuinely seek to persuade or entertain each other.[19]

Davies neither delineates nor defends these "universally agreed rules of evidence and argument." On a practical level, the current methodological and perspectival divisions within the field of biblical studies, even among "secular" scholars, underscore the absence of rules that are "universally agreed." On a philosophical level, Davies offers no criteria by which to assess *what* constitutes evidence—or, more pointedly, *who* gets to determine what constitutes evidence.

Davies recognizes on the level of theory that no reading is objective, but he denies the claim of Christian postmodernists that the abandonment of objectivity places all discourse on equal footing:

The discourse of the academy is value-laden, too, and there will always be those who do not share its humanistic, rational pre-suppositions. But I would resist the suggestion that it is there-fore of the same kind as confessional discourse, or that it is merely a different kind of confessional discourse. It is different in prin-ciple and intent from them. The main feature of this discourse is that it permits and stimulates criticism of its own practices and beliefs. It encourages the expression of any opinion or belief that is amenable to public scrutiny, evaluation, contradiction or con-firmation. It deals not in truths but in hypotheses and paradigms, which can and do change as a result of the discourse itself. . . . It excludes opinions and theories and beliefs that cannot be chal-lenged, tested, critiqued or that insist on an absolute and non-negotiable truth.[20]

Despite his assertion, however, Davies himself cannot consis-tently maintain a distinction between testable and non-test-able hypotheses/assumptions. For example, after presenting the book of Daniel as a celebration of the anti-authoritarian spirit, he offers this self-reflection:

Like the authors of Daniel, I see in history and in texts the story that I want to see. . . . I do not expect any supernatural assur-ances, and I would not believe any of them anyway. . . . In the end, we probably all tend to find in these biblical texts some-thing that we want. But if we can keep our wants as free as pos-sible, there is the chance that the process of reading will reverse and the text will draw some meaning from the reader. And that is when it matters very much "whose bible it is."[21]

Davies's presumption against "supernatural assurances" is no small "want" but rather an *a priori* belief which he recog-nizes as a filter of his own experience. Should he be confronted with a claim of divine care, he would not investigate it scien-tifically, evaluate its worth as an hypothesis, be open to the possibility of change: he simply would not believe it. While his belief position is a valid one, it is not held up to the kind of critique and intellectual testing that he demands of confessional approaches.

Clines does not use the positivistic language of Davies and never claims objectivity, and yet his methodology relies on a distinction between understanding a text on its own terms and evaluating that text from an external set of criteria. Such a distinction between determining meaning and assigning value, however, obscures the way in which prior commitments and values shape reading itself, as is evident in Clines's treatment of the Song of Songs.[22]

The two-part division of the chapter on Songs bespeaks Clines's assumption that one can explicate a text prior to evaluating its ethical import: (1) "Why is There a Song of Songs?" and (2) "What Does it Do to You if You Read It?" In section one, Clines concludes that Songs is a literary contrivance, presenting itself as a prizewinner, arising from the need of a male public for erotic literature. Along with other interpreters such as Trible and Landy he acknowledges that the gender dynamics portrayed in the Song are far more egalitarian than those described in most other biblical literature, but Clines interprets this *apparent* equality as repressing the realities of a patriarchal world:

> the language . . . of mutual possession can only be an attempt, politically speaking, to drive underground the pervasive social reality with pillow talk, to develop, in Jamesonian terminology, a strategy of containment for the social tension, to achieve coherence and closure by shutting out the truth about history. The patriarchal social system not only created the Song of Songs; it needed it.

> What we have in this book is not a woman, not the voice of a woman, not a woman's poem, not a portrayal of female experience from a woman's perspective, but always and only what a man imagines for a woman, his construction of femininity.[23]

While I find Clines's reading plausible and interesting (at points compelling), I question that he has bracketed out evaluative discourse in his opening section. Section 1 is far from a scientific analysis of the text; rather, it relies on numerous assumptions that Clines does not adequately defend. For example,

1. Clines's reading relies on his identification of its author as male, but while he acknowledges that Athalya Brenner, Fokkelien van Dijk-Hemmes, and

others argue the possibility of female authorship
of Songs,[24] the only counter-argument he offers is
the lack of female literacy in ancient Israel.

2. He assumes that a male author is necessarily a party
    to patriarchal hegemony and that we can trust the
    rest of the Hebrew Bible to depict accurately the
    dynamics of that patriarchy.

3. He cites but does not defend a Jamesonian expla-
    nation of the tension between the Songs' egalitar-
    ian vision and the dominant patriarchy of the
    Hebrew Bible: when a party to a hegemonic sys-
    tem imagines a challenge to that system, then the
    imaginative vision *can only be*[25] a deliberate attempt
    to suppress social reality; it never can serve as an
    agent of social change.

Clearly, long before Clines enters into the explicit critique of
section 2, his own values (and the ones he trusts his readers
share) are operative. By portraying a male author imagining
the sexual advances of a subordinate female and by equating
the book's apparent egalitarianism with social control, Clines
disinclines the contemporary interpreter from finding in the
Song any redeeming value—especially if s/he values gender
equality, the equitable resolution of social conflict, and
nonexploitation in real and imagined sexual encounters.

When, in section 2, Clines turns to explicit critique of the
text, he does not presuppose a foundationalist ethic. Explaining that he recognizes no universal standards, he defines "ethical" as "ethical according to me and people who think like
me."[26] Yet, Clines never explicitly articulates what *is* ethical to
him—what he believes about gender, sexuality, and the management of social conflict; and his individualistic definition of
ethics renders as surprising the confidence with which he la-
bels the de-eroticization of the text by various commentators
as "egregious misreadings, strong misreadings."[27] He accuses
male interpreters of Songs of finding the egalitarian message
too hot to handle[28] even while he argues that Songs is not truly
egalitarian. Surprisingly, Clines fails to acknowledge the irony
of his own work: the Clines who lambasts the text's male au-

thor and its male commentators for not allowing women to speak (showing us only male projections of women) is also male and also reflects his society's understandings about what is best for women.

Clines's negative judgment on the text affects what he will see in it. In that regard, his approach differs very little from those informed by assumptions of the Bible's positive value. For example, Trible's reading of Songs as a powerful statement of gender equality seems obviously driven by her own Protestant assumptions of the authority of biblical witness: her self-professed love of the Bible almost guarantees that she will read it in such a way that affirms the causes to which she is committed.[29]

But Clines is no different from Trible. He demonstrates no more "objective" weighing of the evidence than she. My claim is that Clines does not identify the male-projection of the Song and then decide whether he likes the text. Rather, his prior assumption of the text's lack of value guides his choice between various interpretative options. And it is those assumptions—about the Bible, about the church, about himself—that are left unnamed in the discourse of the "read, then evaluate" paradigm.[30]

AN ARGUMENT FOR IDEOLOGICAL CRITIQUE IN BIBLICAL STUDIES

While the distinction that Davies and Clines draw between the etic and the emic (or "understanding" and "evaluation") is difficult to maintain on philosophical and on practical grounds, I believe that their works remain a valid challenge to some traditional practices of confessional biblical studies. Davies and Clines have persuasively shown how often confessional readings fail to engage biblical texts on the level of underlying assumptions, as well as how often confessional readers will forgive in biblical texts the very attitudes and behaviors they refuse to tolerate in other venues. As such, these authors join a larger chorus of voices arguing the value of ideological criticism: a methodology devoted to discerning the power relations inscribed in a text (including those of gender, class, and race), along with the other unspoken assumptions (about God, about humans) on which the text's power to persuade depends.[31]

I share the conviction that texts must be engaged on the level of their ideologies and that the ideologies of biblical texts cannot be assumed to be ethically good. In my own case, as a person especially committed to naming and countering the thought patterns that facilitate the abuse of women and children, I feel compelled to name and critique the patriarchal assumptions on which the "teaching" of Hosea 1–3 relies: Hosea is only a "prophet of love" if the reader assumes the husband's ownership of and right to punish his wife. Hence, should Davies and Clines be correct that biblical study within confessional settings requires assent to the ideologies of the text, then their academic and ethical critique of the church-related institution would be valid.

Both authors *have* made the case that confessional readings often *do* mirror the biblical texts. Davies well demonstrates the "doubling" of the text by Childs and Watson; and Clines's "Metacommentating Amos" masterfully sets forth example after example of how commentators, rarely with any self-awareness, accept the text's diagnosis of Israel's condition as factual and accede to its notions of punishment, even against sound logic.[32] (Are the poor indeed benefited by the destruction of the nation, such as the book of Amos maintains?)[33]

But Davies and Clines have *not* demonstrated that confessional commitments *necessarily* preclude ideological critique. While they may have described accurately certain varieties of confessional biblical study, their scheme ignores (1) those interpreters who take both theological commitments *and* ideological critique seriously, as well as (2) those confessional communities that encourage self-criticism. I acknowledge that the institutional contexts of church-related colleges and seminaries (mission statements, Christian architectural symbols, and the presence of chapels) do indeed privilege certain confessional perspectives; nonetheless, the work of scholars who both claim Christian commitments and also engage in ideological critique challenges a simplistic equation of confessional reading with assent to the text. For example, Carole Fontaine speaks to the necessity (and not just to the possibility) of bringing feminist critique to bear on confessional readings of the Bible.[34] Clines and Davies are fair in challenging any teacher (confessional and otherwise) who fails to engage students in naming and critiquing biblical constructions of gender and power, but they have unfairly assumed that such self-criticism is impossible in confessional educational contexts.

CONCLUSION

I have attempted to demonstrate that, despite their claims, neither Davies nor Clines model a separation between truth/value claims and the reading of biblical texts. This observation does not detract from my grateful appreciation of their insightful, challenging work. Their arguments instead challenge the institution in which I work to name more carefully the assumptions that inform its pedagogy.

Clearly, in the current academic climate, the church-related institution can no longer repeat earlier maxims touting the easy compatibility of faith and learning. Turn-of-the-century notions that an unencumbered search for Truth will lead all people to Jesus are not only theoretically difficult to posit in a postmodern age but also practically difficult to defend. The search for truth has not led Davies, Clines, or countless others into the waiting arms of the church.

But neither does a simple embrace of the postmodern paradigm serve to validate the church-related educational institution. While postmodernism does valorize multiple advocacy positions, it cannot adequately defend the appropriateness of any particular advocacy position within the academic classroom.

The postmodern, church-related classroom must enable students to engage critically the biblical text; along with Davies and Clines, I believe that the ability of students to ask hard questions about the Bible is fundamental—not only to academic study but also to human integrity. But I also maintain that, for students to understand the very nature of the project in which they are engaged, the classroom must also enable them to appreciate the text—an attitude not easily fostered by Davies's and Clines's approaches. Without some sympathetic, or at least empathetic, introduction to the plurality of confessional readings, it will be difficult for a student to understand what the debate (between Davies and Childs, for example) is about—and why anyone would care. To be sure, many who work within a religious studies paradigm claim to practice "informed empathy" (to use Smart's phrase).[35] I am not convinced, however, hearing so little of it modeled. One great strength of the church-related college is its ability to model in powerful ways, inside and outside the classroom, this empathy for the confessional.

Clines and Davies convincingly argue, to those in the church-related college as well as to those in the secular academy, that any approach to texts that rules out critique of the material at hand is academically suspect. And, as such, I believe they have made a much stronger case for the inclusion of ideological criticism as a way of reading texts than they have drawn a demarcation between confessional and nonconfessional readings of the Bible.

Teaching the Conflicts,
For the Bible Tells Me So

Timothy K. Beal

Although we are not always mindful of it, we are always in a time of culture wars. Culture *is* culture war. No matter how cosmopolitan, no matter how sectarian, culture always takes shape through social and symbolic violence: dynamics of exclusion as well as inclusion, writing out as well as writing in. Certainly there are times when we experience culture and cultural identity as seamless, at one with itself, without conflict. But even then, just below the surface, our social organizations, and even our own individual selves, are pervaded by struggles to mend the fractures and erase the otherness within. Cultural hegemonies are not only hard-won but are in fact refought and rearticulated from moment to moment, however subconsciously. There is never a time when cultural identity is not, therefore, under threat, in crisis.

So it is with the current identity crisis experienced by so many church-related colleges. I agree with Stanley Hauerwas and others that our growing *awareness* of this sense of identity crisis is closely related to the breakdown of a certain cultural hegemony that has been maintained and enforced for most of this so-called Christian century by a liberalism "designed to domesticate conflict"[1] and rooted in the larger modern vision of a March of History that will overcome all differences, all otherness, as it progresses toward humanity's universal comprehension of all things.

Without honest, self-reflective acknowledgment of this fundamental sense of institutional instability—that for us it is always "campus life in a time of culture wars"[2]—our responses to the current sense of identity crisis in church-related colleges will tend to fall out in one of two highly problematic ways, both of which involve a kind of violent suppression of the conflict: (1) pretend that there is no problem, and that despite this momentary rough spot we are still moving forward in our grand March of History toward fulfillment of the "Christian century," albeit a little behind schedule;[3] or (2) acknowledge the current crisis, but imagine a time when there was no problem, a pristine origin of unproblematic wholeness, and then to struggle—by whatever means necessary—to get back to that sacred time and place.

As a way of avoiding these two problematic responses to the current sense of identity crisis in many church-related colleges, I would argue, following Mark Walhout (working from Gerald Graff) and Stanley Hauerwas (working from Alisdair MacIntyre),[4] that we need to *teach the conflicts*. That is, we need to create space, in the faculty lounge, in the classroom, in the dorm room, and in the board room, where the profound tensions and dissonances and experiences of alienation that pervade our colleges can be given serious hearing. As honestly and as self-reflectively as possible, we need to give voice to the crisis in which we find ourselves.

At the same time, I suggest that these other calls for teaching the conflicts often do not push far enough, because they presume that individuals and even groups within such a conflictive discourse would hold particular positions and that the conflicts would simply be between those individuals or groups. That is, they have tended to conceive of the conflict to be taught as a kind of back-and-forth dialogical or dialectical relationship between an individual self and an other, or collectively between "us" and "them." Whether it is a matter of individuals or collectives, the cultural subjects in this conflict are presumed to be of one voice with themselves, without inner ambivalence. That would be a very "clean" sort of conflict in which to teach. But such a vision of teaching the conflicts is fantastical.[5] It is fantastical because none of us is of one voice with our own selves in the current crisis. Each of us has *our own* inner conflicts, tensions, and ambivalences when it comes to how we see and how we wish to see the past, present, and future of our colleges. The same goes for the collective cultural "wholes" in which we identify ourselves.

"Teaching the conflicts," then, should also involve serious and honest self-reflection on our various *internal* conflicts and ambivalences. In this regard, the double sense of talking out of place—as talking from a particular social location on the one hand, and as talking oneself out of place, or displacing oneself, on the other hand—is particularly suggestive as a way of redescribing the critical practice of teaching the conflicts. Talking out of place can make one tongue-tied, caught between a speech that locates and a speech that dislocates. As I talk about and from "here" I often feel profoundly "not-here." For when I talk from this place, I am aware not only that I belong here, but also that I am uneasy here, at times feeling distanced from those who share my location even while I identify with those who do not. Thus, without dissolving the differences between myself, in this place, and the other, there (for such liberal dissolvings of difference are equally dangerous fantasies), talking out of place can open reflection on the otherness *within* our individual as well as collective identities.

FOUNDED ON THE ILLEGIBLE

I want to suggest biblical literature as an excellent "place" for church-related colleges to find their way into such discussions of conflict and identity crisis, insofar as that literature provides one of the most deeply and superbly fissured and self-conflicted foundations of identity for such institutions.

Let me begin with a reading of a particularly odd and intriguing version of Scripture: the college insignia Bible. An open Bible is certainly a common feature among church-related (and formerly church-related) college insignias. What I find most interesting is that the Bible on these insignias rarely has any decipherable text—though it will often be framed by text, including a vocabulary of light and truth, usually in Latin (*lux,* *veritas.* . .), sometimes even in Hebrew (*or, emet.* . .). Centered by these words of literal enlightenment we find, strangely enough, an *open and unreadable* Bible. Such an insignia claims a Bible as somehow fundamental in the grounding of an institution's identity even while that Bible is represented as simultaneously accessible and illegible. Of course the alternative of putting text on those open pages would open a huge can of hermeneutical worms: besides the fact that the words would need to be really, really tiny, the institution would need to decide which particular passage to use, anticipating to whatever extent possible the different ways that passage might be understood to comment on the college.

Two other things strike me when I ponder these open and unreadable college insignia Bibles: first, even without any familiar biblical text printed there, it is safe to assume that nearly everyone who sees it will know immediately that the open book is supposed to be a Bible; and second, few who see it would ever ask *which Bible* the image is supposed to represent.[6] For that matter, very few would ever stop to ask anything of such an insignia. That's a Bible; indeed, that's *the* Bible. This college's identity is biblical. What's to question?

It is very common in America for an institution or movement to secure its own identity and to erase any sense of instability within itself by staking its claim on biblical grounds. Why? Because more than any other cultural artifact of American culture, the meaning of "the Bible" is assumed to be self-evident, foundational, of one voice with itself, needing no interpretation. "The Bible" can be used without being opened, or opened without being read. Indeed, when it comes to the work of grounding and securing identity, it is more useful as a closed book, or better still an open closed book. While pretending to be open, the open but unreadable Bible closes out tensions, ambivalences, clashing voices.

Yet anyone who has spent much time reading biblical literature knows that it is anything but univocal. It is, rather, many voiced; indeed, it seems to revel in tensions between and within those many voices. Likewise, anyone who has spent much time studying the history of Bibles—that is, the history of biblical text criticism, translation, and interpretation, as well as the history of authorization of the various biblical canons—knows that "the Bible" is anything but a solid, unambiguous book.

Biblical literature, no matter which Bible you are talking about, resists "impoverishment by univocality"[7]—that is, it resists being reduced to any single message or point. It argues with itself. And so, to open it and to read it is to occupy a site of tension and even conflict. It opens to difference and, I would argue, it always points beyond itself. It pushes beyond its own boundaries. So that, when it is opened and read, honestly and self-reflectively, it will always undermine the desire to use it as a ground for establishing a single, stable, monolithic identity. It does not so much offer a single ground to stand on as it does a place to discuss, to argue, to question together. Thus, although biblical literature, when read and read attentively, may not be very helpful for grounding or regrounding identity, it is an excellent place to begin "teaching the conflicts."

ELIJAH COMPLEX

One biblical opening in which to begin cracking the binding in current discussions of the future of the church-related college might be in the stories of Ahab and Jezebel versus Elijah, which are woven into the books of Kings and which are part of a larger narrative which scholars call the Deuteronomistic History (DtrH). These stories are fundamentally concerned with issues of identity, as is the DtrH as a whole, whose narrative voice is often fiercely polemical as it casts a theological history that moves from the pristine origins of covenant in Deuteronomy down a degenerative path which leads ultimately to exile and dispersion in 2 Kings.

Although Elijah's presence within the larger DtrH narrative is brief and sporadic (1 Kings 17–19; 21; 2 Kings 1–2), he is nonetheless a key narrative figure, providing a prophetic mouthpiece for the Deuteronomistic theological interpretation of Israelite and Judean history. His strong position against the religious syncretism of Ahab and Jezebel, of course, echoes Moses' preaching in Deuteronomy against going after other gods and thereby breaking the covenant and forfeiting divine promise (e.g., Deut. 28). As such, his voice, along with that of the narrator, provides commentary for the reader on where this down-bound-train-of-a-story is heading (i.e., to the horrors of Israelite demise under Assyria and to Judean exile under Babylon).

Elijah's archenemy and the Deuteronomist's quintessential other, or "not-us," is Jezebel, a powerful woman, from another land, representing and serving other gods (hundreds of the prophets of Baal and Asherah eat at her table; 1 Kings 18:19).[8] As the other within, a strong woman married to an often weak and insecure Israelite king, she stands for admixture and emasculation, the ultimate embodiment of threat to Israel's identity.[9]

We all know the story: in the long run Jezebel loses, Elijah wins. And through it all the narrative works very hard to make her unambiguously bad and him unambiguously good, the ultimate and just deserts of their face-off being a glorious assumption for him and a violent, humiliating death for her:

> As they [Elijah and Elisha] continued walking and talking, a chariot of fire and horses of fire separated the two of them, and Elijah ascended in a whirlwind into heaven. Elisha kept watching and crying out, "Father, father! The chariots of Israel and its horsemen!" (2 Kings 2:11–12a)

> As Jehu entered the gate, she [Jezebel] said, "Is it peace, Zimri, murderer of your master?" He looked up to the window and said, "Who is on my side? Who?" Two or three eunuchs looked out at him. He said, "Throw her down." So they threw her down; some of her blood spattered on the wall and on the horses, which trampled on her. Then he went in and ate and drank; he said, "See to that cursed woman and bury her; for she is a king's daughter." But when they went to bury her, they found no more of her than the skull and the feet and the palms of her hands. When they came back and told him, he said, "This is the word of the Lord, which he spoke by his servant Elijah the Tishbite, 'In the territory of Jezreel the dogs shall eat the flesh of Jezebel; the corpse of Jezebel shall be like dung on the field in the territory of Jezreel, so that no one can say, This is Jezebel.'"(2 Kings 9:30–37)

The one rises as the other falls, and the reader is encouraged to revel in both fates.[10]

Reading for internal conflicts and ambivalences in a biblical narrative like this is difficult to do, for two reasons: first, the history of Christian biblical interpretation has trained readers to identify completely and unproblematically with the implied narrator of any biblical story, assuming that narrative voice is completely reliable, omniscient, and authoritative; and second, the narrative voice of this Deuteronomistic text is particularly powerful in its subjection of its readers. That is, this narrative positions them on its own side—on "our" side, "here"—and works very hard to make that subject position completely unproblematic and without alternative. As a result, the history of Christian biblical interpretation has largely shored up the position of the Deuteronomist and further erased any signs of ambiguity or inner conflict within that position.

Yet even in this fiercely polemical us-versus-them narrative, which works so hard to project Jezebel as its quintessential other and Elijah as our Deuteronomistic champion, there is evidence of *internal* ambivalence and conflict as well.[11] Along with many biblical scholars I think we need to read the Elijah-Jezebel story and the DtrH as a whole differently—maybe against the grain a little—and recognize that in fact its supposedly pristine origins were not so pristine after all.[12] That there was struggle, heterogeneity, ambiguity, ambivalence, and tension from the very get-go, and that the oppositional positions marked off for us and them are therefore not so clear and unproblematic either. Even this ideologically overbearing Deuteronomistic discourse, when read very closely, reveals traces of the ambiguities and ambivalences that the DtrH has worked so hard to erase. As Phyllis Trible has recently shown, for example, one can find ambiguities even in the extreme binary oppositions that mark the identity of Elijah as quintessential self and Jezebel as quintessentially other. Indeed, that opposition appears to collapse in on itself at key narrative moments, undermining the narrative's establishment of clear definitions of "us" and "them," and jeopardizing the reader's ability to "make the proper Deuteronomistic choice."[13]

Before ever reading Trible, many students in my "Bible, Gender, and Sexual Politics" course raise questions about this biblical narrative that move our interpretive discussions in a similar direction. Why, they ask, were there so many prophets of Baal and Asherah at Jezebel's table? Could this be evidence of a thriving and long-standing popular movement of Baal and/or Asherah piety among the people of Israel during this time? Were Ahab and Jezebel the only intermarried couple in all Israel? Could such a movement really be all Jezebel's doing? Might some Israelites have worshiped YHWH along with these other gods?[14] Granted, Jezebel was killing the prophets of YHWH (1 Kings 18:4). But the prophets of Baal were not killing anyone, so what justifies Elijah's slaughter of hundreds of them in the valley of Kidron after their god fails to come through for them in a prayer contest (1 Kings 18:17–40; cf. 2 Kings 10:18–27)?[15] At the same time, students are uncomfortable with the gratuitously violent, even misogynistic, description of Jezebel's death at the hands of Jehu in fulfillment of Elijah's prophecy (see above). They are quick to notice, moreover, that Jehu himself is not a model of justice or theological integrity (see, esp. 2 Kings 10:28–31).

Of course these are not new questions for biblical scholars. Nonetheless, there is something about the interpretive context of the college classroom that allows us to experience the internal conflicts found in these narratives in a uniquely dislocating way. On the one hand, as we ask these interpretive questions, we find ourselves unable to revel with the narrator in the blood of Jezebel and the prophets of Baal (some students, reading alone, would), and unable to identify completely with Elijah (some, reading alone, would). On the other hand, neither can we reject Elijah entirely and jump over to Jezebel's side (some, reading alone, would), for she is not always so gracious or just herself (as Naboth's blood gives testimony; see 1 Kings 21). Thus, as we get closer to the text, we find ourselves less and less easily situated within it. Rather, we occupy ambivalent spaces of betweenness.

In the process of our interpretive conversations, moreover, the different cultural locations of the students in the class often become similarly unstable and interstitial, opening new interpersonal relations and identifications between self and other. In one of my recent courses, for example, a theologically fundamentalist student, who had resisted *any* critical questioning of the biblical literature up to that point, found herself identifying in these interpretive discussions with a student who entered the class hating all things biblical without ever having read a single verse. These two students found themselves identifying with each other on one interpretive point, and then another, and then another—often over against their usual allies on either side. This is not to say that any sort of conversion took place on the part of either student; the one did not quit InterVarsity Christian Fellowship, and the other did not join. Without coming to identify or agree completely with one another, these two students experienced moments of highly ambivalent affiliation. Such moments of affiliation break down the supposedly clear oppositions between self and other, us and them. Yet the affiliation is no simple matter of a synthesis or compromise, either. Rather, such relationships emerge in irresolvable tension between identification and difference. And such relationships, which I find to be very common in controversial class discussions on biblical texts, allow us to reflect honestly on conflicts *within* our individual or collective cultural identities.

Although the literary history of DtrH is not at all clear,[16] it is largely agreed that this historical narrative took form in a situation of profound identity crisis, namely the Babylonian exile. And perhaps that is why Jewish and Christian religious institutions and movements often find themselves echoing Elijah and the Deuteronomists when in situations of identity crisis. A Deuteronomistic frame of perception allows for one to interpret the current identity crisis as the result of a fall from pristine origins into tolerance and syncretism, and calling its loyal members to knock down the high places, to get rid of the Canaanites in our midst, to refuse to go to table with the prophets of Baal or Asherah and instead to slaughter them in the valley of Kidron, and to throw Jezebel out the window.

The current sense of identity crisis in church-related colleges seems to be leading some to view themselves as contemporary Elijahs in need of a Deuteronomistic solution: to purge ourselves of otherness (projected, as always, on some unlucky designated other) and get back to our roots. But even those who do not see a public purging of those marked as other to be a realistic solution often tend to see the history of the particular institution in a certain Deuteronomistic light—that is, as being on a downward slide from its pristine covenantal origins into diaspora secularism. It is, after all, a very powerful interpretive framework in the Christian tradition for rendering the past, present, and future.

In keeping with the call for "teaching the conflicts"—conflicts between individuals and groups but also conflicts within individuals and groups—I suggest that we need to interpret our institutional histories (which is also to interpret where we are now and where we are heading) in the same way we need to interpret DtrH: that is, we need to pry at them and at ourselves, to draw attention to the points of dissonance and fracture as well as to the points of association and collective coherence.[17]

To think about the future of higher education today is to find oneself in the wake of lost dreams, especially the lost dream of the university, which was to be the ultimate embodiment and realization of a grand March of History toward humanity's total, encyclopedic comprehension of all things.[18] No such dreams have been realized. Indeed, our dreams have often turned to nightmares. We find ourselves at the end of the twentieth century in a heap of psychosomatic fragmentation in which military marches through towns-become-cinders and death-camp marches of millions of Jews appear as mirrors exposing the shadow side of the grand vision of the March of History. And certainly the theological renaissances of the "Christian century" which have engendered and sustained a certain vision of the church-related college (including the theological renaissance proper of the 1950s and 1960s, discussed by Douglas Sloan)[19] are more or less explicitly theological and ecclesialogical versions of that same modern universalist dream.[20]

As we study and talk and write together, we should allow ourselves honestly and self-reflectively to give voice to the crisis that we find ourselves in. We need to read our histories in the same way we need to read our Bibles and in the same way we need to read all canons: as reflections of culture war, embodiments of irresolvable tensions between functional closure on the one hand and resistance to closure on the other. And we need to read ourselves in the same way—as profoundly conflicted on these matters. I suppose this is both a postmodern condition and a postmodern opportunity.

A Pedagogy of Eucharistic Accompaniment

Dominic P. Scibilia

> The mission of Siena Heights, a Catholic university founded and
> sponsored by the Adrian Dominican Sisters, is to assist people to
> become more competent, purposeful and ethical through a
> teaching and learning environment which respects
> the dignity of all.
>
> —*Siena Heights University Mission Statement*

At the close of the Roman Catholic eucharistic liturgy, a deacon or a celebrant enjoins the community of faith to go in peace to love and serve the Lord. In the Latin Mass, the final commission of the celebrant is *"Ite Missa es."* Those Latin words are more a proclamation of mission—"This is your mission"—than the announcement of the end of a worship service. The community's alleluias or amens affirm our embrace of the mission that is the Mass, an ongoing service in peace and love. Like the Mass, the life of the faithful is eucharistic, a gracious life of invitation, breaking and blessing, giving and transforming.[1] The Mass creates a community in Christ who is able to see in the twenty-first century opportunities for grace.

Much like the community of faith, Siena Heights, a university that claims to be Adrian Dominican Catholic, faces the twenty-first century. If the mission statement of Siena Heights, which became a university in 1998, is anything like the eucharistic mission of the Catholic community of faith, then the faculty and administration of the school must consider who that mission enjoins us to be and what that mission enjoins us to do. We must ask what is the experience rooted in history that enshrines the major hopes and aspirations of the church-related university that names itself Catholic and Adrian Dominican. Who is the author of the storied wisdom that calls faculty and students to be competent, purposeful, and ethical?

One of the great gifts of participation in the Rhodes Consultation on the Future of the Church-Related College is the historical insight gained from a study of the mission statements of church-related schools. Mission statements often reveal that, like the histories of churches in the United States, church-related colleges are caught in recurring cycles of declension and revival, decentering and reprivileging, capitulation and alienation. The struggles of Catholic colleges and universities, especially during the last quarter of the twentieth century, provide ample evidence of the church-related college's experience as outsider who yearns for a place at the table of higher learning. In the grip of alienation from and yearning for a place at this table, church-related universities like Siena Heights become silent about our storied wisdom. Within that silence there is a self-doubting question: Do we have anything wise to bring to the table of higher learning during an age when intellectual trends deconstruct or discount faith testimonies, and when free market ideologies reduce knowledge to an informational commodity and higher learning to social economic domestication?

Eucharistic stories liberate colleges like Siena Heights from our self-doubt and silence. There is a pedagogical wisdom about who a church-related college is and what we do in biblical stories like the Road to Emmaus. Learning and teaching may well be like the disciples' conclusion about their eucharistic encounter with Jesus,

> Now while he was with them at table, he took the bread and said the blessing; then he broke it and handed it to them. And their eyes were opened and they recognized him; but he vanished from their sight. Then they said to each other, "Did not our hearts burn

within us as he talked to us on the road and explained the scripture to us?" (Luke 24:30–32).

Does not the wisdom of our eucharistic encounters with God suggest that higher learning within a church-related college causes our hearts to burn to know and do the good, the true, and the beautiful?

In this particular essay, I invite you to walk with me through a eucharistic pedagogy; to be more than companions on a journey, rather, to be companions of the souls of working-class undergraduates.[2] A eucharistic pedagogy announces that there is something sacramental, something sacred, happening at the table of higher learning. The words of teachers and learners, especially the words of working class undergraduates, make clearly present both the dissonance and promise of church-related colleges in a neoliberal social economy. As I walk with working class undergraduates, I embrace the storied wisdoms that make my soul: the popular Catholic faith of southern Italians, base ecclesial communities and civil societies in Morelos and Chiapas (Mexico), and migrant farm workers in southeast Michigan. For me, the storied wisdoms of working class students and faith communities transform higher learning from a matter of knowing something into an intimate "knowledge that fashions the knower by that which is known."[3] I invite you into a pedagogy of eucharistic accompaniment which celebrates without reservation God's choice to be so close to the creation that we can hear, see, touch, smell, and taste the mystery that we name God.

A pedagogy of eucharistic accompaniment, like the liturgical commission "*Ite Missa es*," enjoins teacher and learner to be as present to each other as Mary and Joseph are truly present with us when we walk with them during the Advent ritual of *La Posada*, or when we walk with Jesus to Golgotha during *La Santa Semana*. As we walk with working class undergraduates in a dialogic, sacramental pedagogy, you and I become with and through their stories subjects of learning. As subjects, we embrace the call of a pedagogy of accompaniment to attend to the geo-political, class, race, gender, and religious dynamics at work where we live; just as Mary, Joseph and Jesus make us critically aware of the impact of Herod, the Sanhedrin, the Canaanite woman, Samaritans, lepers, centurions, and Pilate on their world. We move through a reading of the new U.S. market analysis and interpretation of higher learning in light of a eucharistic social theology. Our reading and assessment lead to a pedagogical action that transforms higher learning from a commitment to the pursuit of self-interest into a commitment to a eucharistic ethic of gracious self-donation. Within the praxis of accompaniment, the church-related college imagines the twenty-first century as a season for transforming and creative graces rather than an accommodation to deterministic cyclical church and college histories.

READING THE PLACES OUT OF WHICH I SPEAK: THE LOSS OF MYSTERY AND THE CRISIS OF MEANING, PRODUCTS OF THE NEOLIBERAL ACADEMY

> And now I looked around a corner of my mind and saw Jack and Norton and Emerson merge into one single white figure. They were very much the same, each attempting to force his picture of reality upon me and neither giving a hoot in hell for how things looked to me. I was simply a material, a natural resource to be used.[4]

For Ralph Ellison's invisible man, revelation is a movement from naiveté to denouncement and announcement. Ellison exposes the *American* illusion: the invisible man realizes that the democratic ideal in which all members of society have access to the opportunities and resources necessary for the pursuit of happiness is waylaid by a stratified, competitive economic system. In our capitalist system, people who dominate capital must deny an increasing number of poor, working, and middle class people access to opportunities and resources in order to maintain control of the economy. Ellison reveals that the *American* free-market capitalist must practice a mean business wherein working poor and working class people are instruments of production.

Migrant workers in southeast Michigan, members of Mexican civil societies like Base Communities and El Barzon (a middle class movement protesting the imposition of World Banking policies on Mexico), and working class undergraduates at Siena Heights University testify to the truth of Ellison's revelation. The stories of stoop laborers on Michigan farms are accounts of continuous struggles against severe wages as well as horrendous living and working conditions. When farm workers press for healthier environments, local church and social agencies answer that they must be mindful of the needs of the farmers and processors. Such chiding induces a silence among farm workers as well as church and civil society.

Gerardo Theissen, liberation theologian and community organizer, invites North Americans to walk with him outside of the United States beside the working poor of Mexico. In that walk, we see and feel the impact of our national economic choices on those people who live on the periphery of our advanced technological world. He calls our commitment to free trade (the unrestrained movement of capital in the Americas) a new *American* liberalism. The new liberalism promises the people of colonias like Flores Magon (Morelos, Mexico) participation in a democratic marketplace with little or no constraints on the pursuit of self-interest. A walk with Theissen reveals, much like Ellison's novel, that the new liberalism serves the interest of the few who control capital, and it dislocates from public life any understanding of nature, person, and society that transcends a materialist ideology. Neoliberal economics induces a public silence on many of the greater issues in the lives of those who struggle to survive. As Manuel Mora of Costa Rica warns, "without profound economic and social changes, democracy will be merely cosmetic, without real content."[5]

Working class students come to our church-related colleges because we offer a neoliberal promise: education will locate our graduates in the job market where they will be able to realize a social and financial security. A common theme in college recruitment literature is the college at the service of the student. A closer listen to undergraduate experiences tells a different story. Even though the literature on student life describes students as customers, experiences teach that "customers" really means financial resources that are necessary for the maintenance of tuition-driven schools. In order to guarantee a dependable flow of financial resources to the college, we must demonstrate that our graduates are marketable products of quality. The location of a high percentage of our products in the regional job market and the testimony of local business managers that our graduates are ideal employees prove our college's claim about product quality. Undergraduates become competent, purposeful, and ethical team players who trust and obey management, and who direct problem-solving skills to the task of corporate fiscal viability. The neoliberal anthropology (human being as product or instrument of production) induces a silence in our university on the greater social issues, because as products, students are objects that others use to make history rather than subjects who create history.

When I turn the critical eye of my theological tradition on my educational context, I experience bewilderment. Such bewilderment, however, is the first step in the walk toward pedagogical and social transformation, the first step in a pedagogy of eucharistic accompaniment.

I am bewildered because the religious and intellectual narratives that form our academic ethos no longer hold the place of definitive authority that we once believed. Whether one waxes eloquent about Catholic identity (a Neo-Thomistic integration of faith and reason) or the civic virtues of the liberal individual like self-sufficiency, each narrative undergirding such perspectives appears to contribute to the alienation so characteristic of the present age. A confidence in the cyberspace university without walls and in the creative forces of the free market marks the administrative vision, policies, and practices in many corners of church-related higher learning. How often have I heard presidential promises that new communication technologies will inculcate a commitment to global community in our students! I am bewildered: on the one hand we discount metanarratives, metaphysics, and an appreciation for embodied reality so central to our vocation, yet on the other hand, our church-relatedness entails a claim to commune with that in which we all move and have our being.

American undergraduates live decentered lives. As Brother Frank Rotsaert (English Department, Siena Heights University) observed, like Yeats, students witness an age in which their cultural centers no longer hold. Things are falling apart. Not even the academic centers of religious communities command students' respect as conveners of a social and moral communion, because students do not find in religious communities and their affiliates the practice of the justice or companionship of which their narratives speak so passionately. All of the six colleges and universities with which I have been in a close working relationship as a graduate or faculty member are deconstructing their liberal arts or general education curricula. Religious schools wrestle with residence life policies and student behaviors that conflict with the ethical orientations of their respective communities of faith. I find that undergraduates seek a golden life (much like our religious ancestors longed for a golden apostolic age) in which the pursuit of self-interest inevitably leads to material happiness. Yet they also express a hunger for a worldview, meaning, and communion that education for a career in the free marketplace cannot deliver. Students grope for an identity larger than the materialist vision. They intuit that there is more to learning than the entrepreneur and the information-age Gnostic tell us.

The use of analogies such as students as customers and graduates as products exposes an alarming turn toward the commercialization of higher learning. Our adoption of marketing and communication images for higher learning is evidence of an epistemological and pedagogical dilemma that calls for critical attention. When one presses commodifying and informational metaphors for knowledge, a material utilitarian ethic surfaces as the moral grounding for educational theories and practices. Seven years of teaching and learning within church-related colleges that purchase a neoliberal interpretation of higher learning introduce me to the highly individuated student of the twenty-first century who learns in silent and insulated uncertainty. Student essays on their family's educational histories (in foundational theology and capstone senior courses) testify to their orientation toward self-interested, non-cooperative learning. Excessively individuated learners make classes cultures of silence, and the church-related college encourages such a learning culture because we remain silent on the greater public issues of life within the college itself. The *student-customer's* resistance to learning in communion with others exposes the loss of both the under-graduate's sense of the sacred and the college's identity as an occasion wherein people act wisely for social justice and peace.

In the religious autobiographies and educational histories that I invite students to write, they document their loss of a critical consciousness of God and self as historical co-creators. When undergraduates deliberate on the political, class, racial, ethnic, and gender dynamics of those narratives, they uncover the causes for both the loss of a God consciousness and their adherence to the culture of silence that infests our classrooms. Students clearly attribute such losses to their immersion in a consumer culture. They resist the exploration of social and theo-logical alternatives to cultures of public silence because their religious traditions have been driven into the private recesses of their lives. Students believe that religious convictions have no place in public spheres such as school and work.

The educational narratives reveal that undergraduates from working class families constitute an academic working class, but with a tragic twist. When they compare their secondary and college experiences, they inform us that the same commercial-ization of learning from high school carries forward, especially in Catholic colleges. Learning focuses more upon the transfer of the information that one needs to attain financial security than the wisdom one cultivates in order to think critically, dis-cern what is good and right, and act accordingly. A Mexican American student writes in her educational history,

> In a community there are doctors, lawyers, teachers and social workers. In our high school, we were not taught about our neigh-bors as humans, but as professionals. Education prepared us for professional life. We did not learn how to live in a multicultural world. We didn't learn about each other's differences, or how to live with and learn from our differences. My education prepared me for a career and what to expect in the business world. Now that I look back on my education as far as relating to human com-

munity, I would have to say that those who were studying and preparing for a profession were in the correct community. Those of us who didn't have professional programs were placed in some other kind of program and they did not interact with us. Learning was more about developing skills for computers, standardized tests, college placement than being a human community.[6]

The epistemological vision of knowledge as an informational commodity calls the working class student to demonstrate his readiness to fit (and marketable fit has become as important for faculty as it is for students) into the structures of neoliberal higher learning. How bewildering: A Catholic college claims a narrative rich with images of transformation yet our own turn toward a materialistic utilitarian ethos calls for conformity. A Catholic college's orientation toward commercial and informational concepts of education is an indication of administrative conclusions about the kind of learning that is appropriate for students with working class backgrounds. Such students will not constitute the elite of our society, but rather a new technical and commercial working underclass. At Siena Heights University, in particular, such conclusions about working class students are the consequences of people who, despite their own working class histories, purchase the new liberal interpretation of higher learning as a marketplace matter.

In *Love and Living,* Thomas Merton writes that

> The purpose of education is to show a person how to define himself authentically and spontaneously in relation to his world. . . . The function of a university is to help men and women save their souls and, in so doing, to save their society: from what? From the hell of meaninglessness of obsession, of complex artifice, of systematic lying, of criminal invasions and neglects, of self-destructive futilities.[7]

The mastery of the marketplace and virtual realities engages the working class student as a subject only insofar as she needs to know and practice the rules for material success. In the college wherein higher learning is run like a business, we think of ourselves as objects for sale in the market. We want to be attractive to customers, to look like the kind of product that makes money. We waste a great deal of time making ourselves over in the image of the affluent society. In the case of Catholic colleges that function with their eyes trained on the promise of a balanced bottom line or on traveling the cybernetic highway, we desacralize being human and higher learning.

Recurring theological themes in undergraduate religious autobiographies are reminiscent of the biblical images of the blessed who hunger and thirst for righteousness. In our course *Biography, Theology and Ethics,* students often write about a desire to connect to learning and something larger than themselves. Even as they express an incipient sense of transcendence, they voice a fear about engaging in religious studies because they share a popular *American* collective suspicion that characterizes religion as the cause for social dissension, a disrupter of the public peace. (Their ability to express that fear is a sign of hope for me. When students are given the chance and skills to think about their histories, they show a promise for critical analysis.) In the throes of that fear, however, students often lapse into a theological autism, the social symptom of which is the insistence that faith and morals are private matters. In conversations about modern scientific studies of religion, like those offered by Robert Wuthnow, Frederick M. Denny, and William Scott Green, undergraduates' infatuation with the reasonableness of neutral objectivity leads to a common conclusion that the matters of the spirit are best treated as historical data rather than plumbed for convictions that form or transform lives. When highly individuated students face postmodern criticisms of religious metanarratives, they offer relativistic reductions of those stories. They write that "the stories are comprehensible to and meaningful only for me." Consequently, when students and faculty encounter the conflicts that come from a society committed to the pursuit of self-interest (as we inevitably do when we engage in service learning), they are unable to draw on our respective wisdom traditions to resolve conflicts. No one can understand the other! In class, our wisdom traditions have no relevance; we are silent citizens.

A PEDAGOGY OF EUCHARISTIC ACCOMPANIMENT: READING THE PLACE OUT OF WHICH I SPEAK AS AN OCCASION FOR TRANSFORMING GRACES

> Faith criticizes the university for failing to nurture the life of the mind. It condemns the rampant commodification of knowledge as simply another instance of mammon worship cloaked in the garb of advancing knowledge. Faith decries the self-aggrandizing instinct of scholars who take a proprietary attitude toward their fields of expertise. Faith asks whether the notion of a community of scholars has any basis in reality on campuses today, or whether it simply masks one more aggregate of consumers, wandering in a marketplace of ideas.[8]

When recruitment materials treat college applicants and their families as consumers and knowledge as a commodity, they betray the Catholic college's commitment to give life and give it abundantly. It is that life-taking that we confront during our walk together in and through higher learning that fuels my commitment to a pedagogy of hospitable, eucharistic accompaniment. Undergraduates testify against the vampiric nature of a neoliberal interpretation of higher learning. When I read seniors' educational histories, I am rattled: for example, an African American athlete describes his experience as indentured servitude. Seniors' testimonies both convict church-related colleges of our sin of institutional self-preservation and announce an opening for pedagogical hope.

During a conversation in a capstone course (1995), students offered breakdowns like the following:

> Teresa Juarez: "We start our education by looking at human experiences, questions and answers."
> I inquired, "Are you referring to Humanities courses?"
> Teresa replied, "Yes, we looked at human conditions."
> Erica Derby added, "Yes, then we got into our majors like accounting where we deal with numbers. But no one asks who do those numbers belong to? Who are they representing?"
> Brandy Lovelady interjected, "We need to realize that our actions have consequences, impact people, our world."
> Teresa concluded, "It is as if our majors moved away from human studies and into professional studies."
> Brandy offered, "Our education is just training."[9]

In eucharistic accompaniment, we transcend the notions of knowledge as a commodity, learners as consumers, and faculty as service providers. For example, in a religious studies course on peacemaking Jennifer Emerson, very much an isolated individual learner (even though she was on "a career path" in education), broke through her wall of silence during a discussion on pedagogies for the non-poor. She became aware of a gnawing discontent when students defined non-poor as those who had the opportunity for higher education. During class break, a colleague encouraged her to give voice to her discontent. When we returned to our conversation, she proposed the following questions:

> The class assumption is that everyone in this class is non-poor because we are here. I wonder how the conversation would change if we were willing to listen to the experience of poor people? How would that listening change non-poor people trying to find pedagogies that liberate them?

I asked her, "What would a poor person make of all of our talk about the non-poor? How would our learning be different?" She seized the invitation to speak of her own history, of the memories and hopes of a poor woman. When she claimed her voice, we began to engage not in a conversation about poverty and liberation for non-poor individuals, but a dialogue between poor and non-poor people. Jennifer brought her enduring self and the wisdom of her traditions to bear upon us. We broke out of the limits of our individuated consumer interests (our concern for our own liberation), and a class in crisis produced a transforming learning moment.[10]

A pedagogy of eucharistic accompaniment relocates higher learning where it belongs—in the struggle to create lives with meaning. Our classrooms are intersections where the struggle for meaning ensues. One who accompanies does not walk the walk of the autonomous individual; rather, accompaniment is a praxis of companionship. It is a walking together in and among each other's communities and families where we meet God and create lives with meaning.[11] Undergraduates like Jennifer and Brandy teach me that higher learning is not a private transaction grounded in the pursuit of one's self-interest. Learning is not personal training.

Higher learning is a public act. It reflects what occurs at the crossroads and intersections of our lives, "where city and home, poor and non-poor, the familiar and stranger, human community and triune community meet."[12] Higher learning does not invoke the image of the formal marketplace of the U.S. style mall like the Plaza de Cuernavaca; rather, it is like the informal marketplace near the Zocalo of Cuernavaca (Mexico). As Dr. Spencer Bennett (Siena Heights University) describes higher learning, "It is a marketplace where exchange is a public, relational, and communal act."

The pedagogy of eucharistic accompaniment reveals that learning is a political and ethical act. The politics and ethics of such a sacramental and transformative act are quite different from the politics and ethics of a neoliberal economic understanding of higher learning. Undergraduates detect that difference from the first day of class. From students' responses to my nonlecture classes, I learn that the initial political and ethical message in the college class is spatial. Students accurately determine from the organization of the classroom who teaches, who learns, who decides what is wise or foolish, what ought to be known or discounted. In the space for accompaniment, learning and teaching are relational and gracious. In a sacramental learning space, we affirm that each of us is a subject, an active participant in determining knowledge and wisdom. The ethics of a transformative pedagogy stresses our personal and communal moral agency. We sit at table together. Each of us brings the wisdom of our respective public lives, and we break open our words in dialogue. We are not the same for it.[13] Each of us is the other and when one understands another in a way that affirms his existence, he comes to a deeper understanding and affirmation of himself as well.[14]

Eucharistic accompaniment has historical and pedagogical ties to popular education because our students have no formal education in academic theology. Even those students who graduate from parochial schools are precritical and preliterate when it comes to religious or theological studies. They bring, however, a rich tradition in popular and civil religions, a religious sensibility, and a theological acumen that develops from familial piety and civic rituals. Undergraduate autobiographies testify to rich ethnic rituals of initiation and development. In my reading of their critical recollections of family life, I taste the festive meals that they associate with familial and community celebrations of baptisms, first communions, saint days, and remembrances of the dead. I hear the music of bands marching through the streets of colonias, barrios, and neighborhoods during holy seasons. I face with undergraduates both their yearning for and distancing of self from such tastes and rhythms. As a nonlecture, interactive teacher, I realize that theology is a critical reflection on daily life (on who the God is that we encounter at the intersections of our lives, on who we are, and how we cocreate lives with meaning).

Eucharistic accompaniment moves from hospitable listening to historical testimonies to analyses of undergraduates' dissonance. From our gracious table of wisdoms broken and shared, we enter a cyclical movement from testimony within our social-educational context to a transformation of that context:

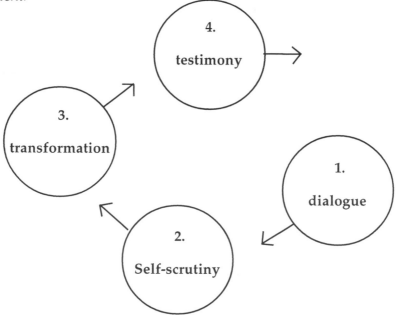

Students' histories are testimonies, occasions "where the believer stands before the community of faith in order to give account of the hope that is in him or her."[15] Just as participation in rituals forms and transforms a community of faith, so undergraduates and faculty participation in the pedagogical ritual of testimony, reflection, and self-scrutiny forms teachers and students into a community of learning. The welcome and affirmation of each person's testimony builds trust that empowers individuals again and again to break open words of wisdom with each other. After listening to each other's testimonies, we enter an ecumenical dialogue that induces self-scrutiny. Our classroom becomes at one time or another like a Methodist Camp meeting, a Catholic Eucharistic liturgy, a Baptist revival, a Cursillo weekend, a familial gathering of elders, the Call and Response movement of the Spirit. Through dialogic self-scrutiny, we become conscious of both the distinctiveness and the limitations of our own perspectives. Each of us realizes that no matter how well we see and understand the mystery in life, we do so only in part. The humility that comes with both affirming what one sees yet recognizing the limitations of one's perspective opens a space for transformative learning. Learners receive the other's affirmation of one's own beliefs as well as the liberation one knows from our inclination to discount lives unfamiliar to us. Dialogic self-scrutiny infuses us with the knowledge that meaning and life are fuller in creative social engagement.

Higher learning within a pedagogy of eucharistic accompaniment, then, is a walk together toward the realization that within the plurality of our perspectives there are related Goods. Rather than a sinful privileging of our own perspectives at the cost of another's perspectives, we break wisdom together. Perhaps in a church-related college, especially a Catholic college, there is no better measure of the authenticity of the praxis of accompaniment than our adherence to the preferential option for the poor. At the church-related college, we must encourage dialogic engagement with the least advantaged in our social-educational systems.

How does a pedagogy of eucharistic accompaniment embody the preferential option for the poor in college theology? If we focus on a foundational theological course, *Biography, Theology and Ethics,* we discover that there is a convergence of three dynamics in learning through accompaniment: the syllabus, an invitation to learn together; the student's questions that compel him or her to participate in a theological course; the faculty and texts (the alter egos of intellectuals who have questions much like the students) as companions. The syllabus is not only an invitation into the journey, it is also a clear and honest description of what the faculty and texts (as voices of people committed to theological reflection) bring to the pilgrimage. The syllabus announces that unlike the political and informational privilege accorded faculty in lecture teaching, a nonlecture learning calls all participants to a place of privilege. The students' and faculty's first essays offer each person's take on the course: the praxis of an interactive pedagogy, and what is required of us, as well as an indication of each person's compelling social, moral, and theological questions.

It is essential to recognize that theological learning with precritical students begins with testimonies rather than introductions to sacred texts or academic theology. Undergraduates need time to recover their human religious imagination, a capacity dulled by the neoliberal definition of religious beliefs as personal sentiments and their location of religious beliefs in the private sphere. In *Biography, Theology and Ethics,* learners move from social, moral, and theological conscientization to a self-understanding as historical subjects. During the first few weeks of the semester, we compose family histories and attend to ethnic, racial, gender, education, class, work, and religious dynamics in those histories. In particular, learners focus upon the social and theological issues of contention within our communities. For example, during the last two years, a significant question in the college's city has been access to clean water. I set a plastic jug of bottled water in the middle of our common space. Students examine it, taste it, read it. We brainstorm what bottled water says about our community—we think in terms of class, race, gender, environment, and creation. Each class member must substantiate her initial claims with concrete support, be it in the form of popular or academic knowledge. Some students are aware of both official letters on the questionable quality of our public water source during the last two years and newspaper reports that the city will market our drinking water as bottled water in other parts of the region. At points in our communal analyses, students assess their responses to the issues and identify the beliefs and sources upon which they base their judgments and proposed actions.

Throughout the semester, scholars like Albert Raboteau, William Scott Green, Jonathan Kozol, Jeanette Rodriguez, and Dorothy Day serve as exemplars of people who engage in the discipline of action and reflection. In the encounters between one's history and immediate experiences of the college community, aided by scholars' analyses, we critically evaluate our social, moral, and theological questions. We also scrutinize the beliefs with which we respond to our community's yearning for life without strife and with meaning. In *Biography, Theology and Ethics,* the full expression of such scrutiny is a theological autobiography. With the postscript of the autobiography, each writer imagines how life together ought to be and how his/ her wisdom tradition inspires social actions toward the realization of one's social hope.

While the students work on histories and autobiographies, they use class cooperatives as a means for giving time and space in which each individual claims and raises her voice. Once autobiographies have been initiated, learners form permanent Base Learning Communities (BLC). BLCs become centers within which we analyze social issues in our immediate community life (Lenawee County, Michigan) in light of our theological beliefs. Each BLC member gives at least twenty hours of service to a community organization; for example, BLC members work in the least advantaged schools in our area, in social service agencies with working poor children and adults, and in county nursing facilities. Anthony Weston's guide, *A Practical Companion to Ethics,* and Michael Himes's journal, *Doing the Truth in Love,* bring to our conversations about community experiences the wisdom of philosophical and theological disciplines that move between action, reflection, and self-scrutiny. A BLC uses time in and out of class to tell each other of

their experiences and to analyze together community questions and responses in light of their readings of Weston, Himes,
and their own wisdom traditions.

Biography, Theology and Ethics concludes with community-
based learning and self-scrutiny. Each BLC composes an assessment of its community work. The learners construct a paper
in which they describe their work, identify the critical social-
moral questions, analyze the communal dimensions of social
struggles, and propose actions to transform such social
struggles from situations that discount people into opportunities in which people count. Each proposal offers justifications
for students' actions based upon their wisdom traditions. Students address issues such as: the difference in a local school
board's allocation of resources between neighborhood schools,
the governor's reduction of property taxes and funding for
public education, the relationship between decreased parental involvement in schools and the transition of the regional
job market from full-time industrial work to part-time service
employment. Every BLC has one class meeting during which
they engage the rest of us in learning from their experiences.
We gain from BLC insights on how our diverse perspectives,
our different convictions, contribute to a life together.

The final self-scrutiny returns to the initial theological questions and statements that learners offered during the first week
of the semester. Participants create critical reflections on those
questions and statements in light of the wisdom traditions that
have surfaced during our walk together. This last self-scrutiny
serves as a postscript to their testimonies. Often these final
pieces tell of conscientization, the revaluation of struggle, and
transformation. Some students commit to continue their community work, maintaining the solidarity that neighbors share
with them, while others explain how self-scrutiny leads to a
reconsideration of their vocational choices in light of sacred
beliefs. I wish that I could write that all of us grow in a wisdom and understanding that leads to social participation, but
I cannot. Yet there is wisdom in silence that remains. Persistent silence or a student's retreat into the promised safety of a
marketable education is itself a testimony. During the Fall semester (1997) of *Biography, Theology, and Ethics,* students' resis-

tance to breaking open wisdom gave us all much to consider. We frequently asked each other: What does our silence say about being human, being moral agents, being citizens? What does our retreat reveal about our understanding of higher learning? What kind of difference does the silence make in our living with our neighbors? What does our silence say about God? I invite students to listen hard to each other's silence.

In a first theological course, a pedagogy of eucharistic accompaniment is, therefore, a cyclical movement from testimony, action/reflection, and self-scrutiny to historical-social, moral agency:

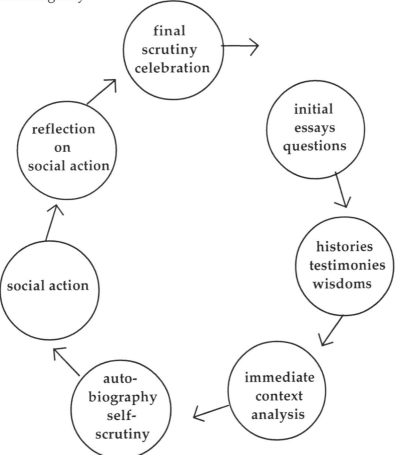

Accompaniment is a pedagogical movement for more than first theology courses. Ultimately, when students and faculty become theological and moral agents the character and life of the college changes. Pedagogical companionship relocates Catholic higher learning in a sacramental wisdom tradition without being politically, morally, intellectually, or theologically hegemonic. The religious privilege of the Catholic tradition in a church-related college is not a privilege of power or primacy over other perspectives. We serve as the host who facilitates the dialogue that seeks understanding between wisdom traditions. The privilege of hospitality emerges from a sacramental imagination that responds to the creation's yearning for relatedness. A Catholic college that practices a pedagogy of eucharistic accompaniment receives the wisdom that working class cultures offer: The critical popular religious insight that human community and triune community meet intimately at the intersections of daily life. The full life of a sacramental college, in its curricular, extracurricular, and administrative dimensions, is companionship: we accompany each other in our struggle to create continually lives that move in, through, and beyond marketability.

POSTSCRIPT

What, then, is a pedagogy of eucharistic accompaniment? It is a sacramental act that transforms a college from an institution of teaching into a community of sapiential learning and action. A colleague in Siena Heights University's Business, Accounting, and Management Division protests, "You are talking about making our students activists!" Yes, I believe that higher learning within the praxis of sacramental accompaniment calls for action. Ultimately, the self-donating act of breaking open the wisdoms of our traditions for the sake of social peace and justice is a hope that we hold for the twenty-first century. Our wisdom traditions compel us to be communities of testimonial dialogue rather than institutions of reprivileged narration. Church-related colleges have a mission to afford each of us the opportunity to commune with the mystery in which the other finds what is true and meaningful, because a sacramental vision sees the twenty-first century as a season for creative and transforming graces.

Ite Missa es.

✞

PART FIVE

Mission and Curriculum

.

A One-Armed Embrace of Postmodernity: International Education and Church-Related Colleges

Keith Graber Miller

> Goshen [College's] identity and national reputation have become so tied to its international program that a few faculty members have asked whether, in the college's communal self-identity and values, international education has not moved above the Mennonite church connection. It is a fair question.
>
> —*Theron F. Schlabach, Goshen College professor of history*[1]

In an increasingly culturally diverse and globally interdependent world, U.S. colleges and universities have recognized the necessity for internationally educating their charges through both curricular alterations and study-abroad programs. Impetus for such education is multiplex. For some, the simple recognition that the U.S. is "behind" other countries in internationalizing its institutions of higher education is sufficient. Although the numbers went up dramatically in the last decade of the twentieth century, still under 80,000 of the 12.5 million U.S. university and college students study abroad each year, compared with 350,000 foreign students studying in the United States. The assumption among advocates of international education is that students with international experience have more marketable abilities and can more effectively function in a world that demands such expertise.

For other higher education institutions, fears of environmental catastrophes have led to efforts to address, often experientially, sustainable development and the relationship of environmental problems, poverty, and economic crises. Federal funding of international education through the National Security Exchange Program has prompted some universities to expand foreign-language offerings and encourage international experiences. For other colleges and universities, philosophical commitments—whether they be rooted in postmodern political praxis or the rejection of metanarratives and the desire to have students experience multiple narratives—have catapulted them into the international arena. For yet others, including Goshen College, which will be the focus of this chapter, attention to study-abroad programs is rooted in religious motivations attached to peacemaking or cross-cultural understanding, breaking down false barriers and learning to know "the other" on his or her own terms.

Whatever the rationale—and usually the motivation is not a singular one—many institutions of higher education are gradually slipping a hip onto the international education bandwagon, an efficacious transport toward the postmodern world. One recent *Academic Year Abroad* directory lists 2,370 programs in eighty countries, many in Latin America, Africa, and Asia. Twenty years ago, most of the study-abroad programs were based in western Europe, in locations considered "safer" and less dissimilar from the experience of white, middle-class U.S. students, who were the primary participants in these educational opportunities.

Church-related liberal arts colleges and universities have been among the leaders in the internationalization of higher education. In this volume, Dominic Scibilia writes, in part, about Catholic-affiliated Siena Heights University's Semester in Mexico program, which models a dialogic pedagogy as a response to postmodernity. Augsburg College, which began in 1869 as a Lutheran seminary and retains its ties to the church, runs a Center for Global Education that organizes short-term travel seminars for community people and semester-long terms for undergraduates. Augsburg's international programs are "grounded in the perspectives of the poor and of others struggling for justice and human dignity," according to the school's catalogue. International education has become part of the identity of Saint Olaf's, another college of the Evangelical Lutheran Church in America. About sixty-five percent of Saint Olaf's graduates have taken a course overseas, either through their own Global Semester, Term in the Middle East, or Term in Asia, or through other multicultural and international offerings. Earlham College, affiliated with the Society of Friends, has fostered a relationship with Japan since the late nineteenth century, and now includes the Institute for Education on Japan among its international programs. All of Earlham's overseas programs require students to complete an ethnographic study of their host culture.[2] Scores of other church-related liberal arts colleges boast study-abroad programs or formally encourage students to experience some type of international education before graduation.

Colleges and universities usually have less control over particular learnings when the international study is experientially based, and that reality frustrates some faculties. Few doubt, though, that international study experiences, with at least minimal supervision, can be mind-opening and life-altering, better preparing participants for thinking critically and living authentically in the multicultural world they are entering. Experiential, international modes of learning seem immensely valid and valuable in a postmodern world, building bridges between the particular communities out of which students come and the multiple, overlapping communities in which they will live. In many cases, perhaps especially at church-affiliated liberal arts colleges, faculty and program administrators make the assumption that students *need* a kind of "conversion" from parochialism toward a broader world perspective; from modern notions of radical individualism toward a recognition of the power (for good or ill) of communities and relationships; from universal rationality toward a critique of such assumptions and realities and a valuing of local wisdoms; and from ethnocentricity toward an appreciation and respect for other cultural and religious traditions.

Such conversions often push out boundaries, both for students and for colleges and universities embedded in particular religious traditions. Here we will examine the international education program at one small, church-affiliated liberal arts college, addressing the motivations for the program's inception, its relationship to the sponsoring denomination, its impact on students, the campus culture and the church, and its promise for appropriately educating twenty-first-century students. Since 1968, all students at Goshen have been required to complete a significant international education component, and most do so through the school's Study-Service Term, which takes students into developing countries in Latin America, the Caribbean, Eastern Europe, Africa, and Asia. For thirteen weeks, students live with middle- to lower-income families; participate in lectures given by nationals on the history, culture, and arts of the country; and work alongside their hosts in short-term, low-key service projects. Although Goshen's religious affiliation and international program create their own distinctive problems and possibilities, such a case study should be illuminating for other church-related schools as well.

GOSHEN COLLEGE AND THE MENNONITE CONTEXT

Goshen College has long had a zesty relationship—what one observer called a "tempestuous love affair"—with the Mennonite Church, which founded the school as Elkhart Institute in 1894. Two recent presidents have compared the church–college union to that of a couple living together without the benefit of marriage, and perhaps in need of premarital counseling. College historian Susan Fisher Miller has evoked the image of a long-suffering parent and a prodigal child.[3] Two decades after its opening, the church shut down the school for one year, fearing that it had immersed itself too deeply in liberal, secularized academia. Although the college reopened the following year, throughout the twentieth century it has experienced a healthy tension with the churches that support its mission. Many faculty, administrators, students, and alumni see the college as faithfully representing the best of the Anabaptist-Mennonite tradition, with its emphases on active discipleship, pacifism, simplicity, humility, and service. If a cultural chasm is developing, some say, it is because both the college and the church have moved away from each other, the former shifting its alliances toward academia and the latter drawing more from popular American religiosity, materialism, and individualism.

Institutionally, however, the college remains deeply embedded in the Mennonite Church, unlike many once religiously affiliated schools that have severed their denominational ties or been set adrift by their founding churches.[4] Goshen College is "owned and operated" by the Mennonite Church. The college's mission statement describes Goshen as a four-year liberal arts college "dedicated to the development of informed, articulate, sensitive, responsible Christians." The statement continues:

> As a ministry of the Mennonite Church, we seek to integrate Christian values with educational and professional life. As a community of faith and learning, we strive to foster personal, intellectual, spiritual, and social growth. We view education as a moral activity that produces servant leaders for the church and the world.

While various advisory boards include other-than-Mennonite representatives, all members of the college's Board of Overseers must be members of the Mennonite Church. The school, and its sister institutions Hesston College and Eastern Mennonite University, are governed by the Mennonite Board of Education, which sets policy and assists in the process of presidential selection. The Board of Education also mandates that at least fifty-five percent of the colleges' students be Mennonite. While Mennonite church membership is not essential for employment, faculty are expected to be sympathetic to the church's understandings of faith and life, and more than ninety percent of Goshen's current faculty are members of Mennonite congregations. A 1995 "Church and College in Partnership" conference, as well as annual meetings on campus for Mennonite church leaders and regular visits by the Indiana-Michigan Mennonite Conference Advisory Board, function as reminders to faculty, administrators, and students of the school's remarkably tight relationship to institutional Mennonitism.

Mennonites trace their origins to the sixteenth-century Anabaptists, part of what is sometimes called the "left wing" of the Reformation. Distinctive emphases of the Anabaptists included the separation of the church from the "worldly" realm of politics; the necessity of voluntary rather than infant baptism, based on an adult commitment to follow in the way of Christ; rejection of "the sword"; and autonomy of the church from the state in matters of worship and religious practice. While many early Anabaptists were highly educated, leaders in the fledgling movement were martyred by the hundreds in the early years, and gradually the Anabaptists became relatively anti-intellectual, a perspective that persisted into the twentieth century. Sociologists from Max Weber to Robert Bellah have identified Anabaptists as classically "sectarian" in their orientation, rejecting compromise, stressing purity, demanding loyalty, and renouncing the goal of world domination, opting instead for intimate intergroup fellowship.[5] Though generally recognized today as a denomination rather than a sect, Mennonites maintain a sectarian-size constituency, with fewer than 200,000 church members in North America.[6]

While small and, until recently, limited primarily to European ethnic ancestry, Mennonites and their institutions have developed a remarkably international perspective. Such internationalism can be traced, in part, to persecution that frequently forced Mennonites to move from their homelands into strange territories—to the American colonies, Russia, Paraguay, Canada, and elsewhere. It is also rooted in the denomination's pacifism. Because members of the church usually seek conscientious-objector status in times of warfare, they have sometimes been referred to as "anti-American." Mennonite ethicist John Richard Burkholder says this response could better be described as "more-than-Americanism." He writes, "Pacifists identify with the entire human community and the long sweep of history. For the pacifist, citizenship in a particular nation-state is just not that important." Pacifists, Burkholder says, "consciously adopt a more global worldview than most Americans. They wear tribal identifications lightly and see themselves as global citizens."[7] Transnationalism is, of course, not the exclusive claim of pacifists. At Saint Olaf College, rich in the Norwegian Lutheran heritage, faculty and students view themselves "as world citizens as well as part of a specific cultural heritage."[8] Some have suggested that religious believers in general should recognize that "religious loyalty transcends national loyalty."[9] In any event, a theologically and ethically grounded international perspective has contributed to study-abroad programs at Goshen College as well as at many other religiously affiliated liberal arts schools.

Mennonite ethicist Ted Koontz writes, in an article titled "Mennonites and 'Postmodernity,'" that "even if parts of the rest of society are moving from modernity to postmodernity, the main agenda for Mennonites is the move from tradition to modernity." This agenda is one that worries Koontz, who—while grateful for the move from the sometimes oppressive and authoritarian nature of traditional societies—seeks to shift Mennonites away from their drift toward the classical liberalism of the modern period, with its emphases on radical individualism, institutionalization and bureaucratization, the language of rights, and procedural justice.[10] In many respects, premodern Mennonites foreshadowed dimensions of postmodernism. While Mennonites are far from anti-foundationalist, they have long been suspicious of universal reason. As a people on the margins throughout most of their history, Mennonites accepted early on that no publicly espoused master narrative was inclusive enough to include them, and that made them distrustful of metanarratives and public rhetoric's potential manipulation. They have been content to remain faithful to their history and religious tradition, perceiving themselves as biblical "salt and light" rather than wielders of power over nature or nations. Their historic commitment to unadulterated honesty, letting "their 'yea' be 'yea' and their 'nay' be 'nay,'" may permit greater fluctuation in seeking after truths. As some developmental theorists suggest, "the greater the truth commitment, the more uncertain the commitment to other attitudes and opinions" since such a commitment provides a dynamism leading to potential revision or overthrow. "The ardent truth seeker shakes up comfortable presumptions, including those of the truth seeker herself," say Anne Colby and William Damon, though they add that not *all* other beliefs may be up for grabs, since "a core commitment of honesty can coexist with other central articles of faith."[11] As pacifists who

only recently added "justice" to their vocabularies, Mennonites generally have contented themselves with working at
local levels at local issues, seeking to serve and empower in
scattered communities around the world rather than in national
power centers. They have rejected the notion of dismembered
individuals, unencumbered selves abstracted from particular
formative narratives, commitments, relationships, and communities. Perhaps—in a bizarre form of postmodern salvation,
just in the nick of time—postmodernism may rescue Mennonites from fully embracing *modernism*. And perhaps international education programs will appropriately school Mennonite
young people, and others who attend Goshen and similar colleges, in the virtues and perspectives of their *petites histoires*
while expediting their entry into a postmodern world with
appreciation for multiculturalism, knowledge of diverse narratives, and commitment to dialogical humility.

In his thorough analysis of Goshen College's church-relatedness, historian Theron F. Schlabach suggests Goshen did not
pass through the stages toward secularization that Marsden
has identified for American universities. In its history, Goshen
did not fuse establishment Christianity with Enlightenment
rationalism, nor did it assume there should be a "unified national culture in which religion ought to play a major supportive part."[12] Instead, says Schlabach, "Mennonites have seen
their educational enterprise as standing largely over against
American thought and culture, not as a transmitter of that culture." While Mennonite educators obviously have drawn from
Protestant educational models and interacted with streams of
modern, Enlightenment thought, Schlabach writes, they have
maintained commitments to counter-values and countercul-
ture.[13] Goshen's president, Shirley Hershey Showalter, observed that the Reformed model for Christian higher education
"tends to be cerebral and therefore transforms living by thinking," while the Mennonite model "transforms thinking by living and by one's commitment to a radically Christocentric
lifestyle."[14]

What this suggests, in pedagogical language, is an emphasis on experiential learning or praxis, an ongoing process of
action and reflection that builds on both social analysis and

cultural immersion. Such a pedagogy recognizes that education is not value-neutral: it is either liberating or domesticating. It also acknowledges the need for learning to be dialogical, and expresses the hope that education be transformative. In theological language, praxis is closely linked with the incarnation. Rodney J. Sawatsky, president of Messiah College, writes that from the Anabaptist-Mennonite perspective, the church is "called to incarnate the Word, to represent—that is, to re-present—the Word in the midst of the world. So, too, the Mennonite college is to be incarnational."[15] Sawatsky then adds further theological support for internationalism by insisting that it is one of six "educational perspectives" emerging from "the Anabaptist incarnational ecclesiology operative in Mennonite colleges."[16]

THE STUDY-SERVICE TERM

Even though the rationale for establishing Goshen College's international education program originally did not include incarnational language, it is undeniable that the school's Study-Service Term (SST) was birthed *because of* Goshen's church-relatedness.[17] In the 1960s, more than half of the college's faculty members had taught or worked abroad for a year or more, and about the same number spoke fluently more than one language. Because of their status as conscientious objectors during World War II, many future Goshen College faculty members or their spouses were required to do Civilian Public Service as an alternative to military service. Although generally CPS assignments were restricted to stateside locations, following the war many Mennonites volunteered to resettle refugees and rebuild Europe and parts of Asia. "In the midst of the emergency," wrote former Goshen College president Victor Stoltzfus, "I doubt that the volunteers considered that the educational byproduct of such service would be language learning and greater cross-cultural sensitivity. The immediate, human reality was hungry, homeless people scarred by World War II."[18] Those who "reached out to a war-torn world" in the 1940s and 1950s included present and later Goshen College faculty members in history, chemistry, psychology, French, English, speech, physics, education, Spanish, Bible and religion, philosophy, economics, nursing, art, and physical education, as well as two business managers, one registrar, two deans, one bookstore manager, and two presidents. They served in France, Germany, Switzerland, Austria, Greece, Paraguay, east Africa, Japan, China, India, Korea, and Thailand. Many others who later joined the faculty studied in European universities, or worked with Mennonite Central Committee (MCC) or other service-oriented, church-related programs overseas.

At the outset of the 1965–1966 school year, Goshen President Paul Mininger appointed a Committee on the Future of the College. At the committee's second meeting, members were thinking creatively about ways to internationalize the college, prompted by a 1965 report by an accrediting team from the North Central Association of Schools and Colleges. The accrediting team noted that Goshen had "an unusual resource" in the fifty percent of the faculty who had lived overseas, but added that "we were not making use of this expertise in any special way," says Henry D. Weaver, then Goshen's provost.[19] By the fall of 1966, faculty members unanimously agreed to implement the Study-Service Trimester, and after trial groups in Haiti, Colombia, and Barbados the following year, SST officially began in the fall of 1968. At that time only three other colleges in the United States sent all of their students abroad: Kalamazoo (Michigan), Lake Erie (Ohio), and Callison (University of the Pacific, California). Goshen was the only undergraduate school to require virtually all of its students to do a full term of both study and service in a developing country.[20]

Mininger initially envisioned SST as a collaborative effort between college and church, with students working alongside Mennonite missionaries.[21] Though such a cooperative effort was not a part of the final SST program, today a number of SST units make links with MCC service workers or with indigenous Mennonite leaders and institutions. By living with host families throughout their SST stay, students are immersed in another language and culture, forced to "break out of the shell" of their own culture and be "exposed to human need" and thereby be "motivated to understand and work at the human problem."[22] Wilbur Birky, director of the SST program since 1994, now proposes that the incarnation can indeed enrich one's understanding of the SST vision:

> Let us propose the Incarnation as an act of divine imagination rooted in a profound realization that even God could not *know and understand* the human condition without *entering into* it, to experience it in the body. That was a true cross-cultural experience. So a description of at least the early parts of Jesus' incarnation applies aptly to the SST experience: it is to give up one's customary place of comfort, to become as a child to learn a new language and eat in new ways, to be received into a new family, to work in the mundane "carpentry shop," to attend the local house of worship, to question and be questioned, to experience frustration and success, and to learn to serve in the very "thick" of life.[23]

Such an intention—and the desire to place students where they are in the minority racially, socially, linguistically, and religiously—necessitates that SST programs be located in Third World countries or places that have been on the receiving end of colonialism.

Each year SST units of twelve to twenty-three students, along with a faculty member and a spouse or assistant, go to one of three or four locations for a full semester. Groups regularly go to the Dominican Republic, Costa Rica, Côte d'Ivoire, and the former East Germany, and occasional units are located in Indonesia and China. Other countries where SST has been based in its thirty-year history include Belize, El Salvador, Guadeloupe, Haiti, Mali, Honduras, Jamaica, South Korea, Nicaragua and Poland. More than six thousand students have participated in one of the more than three hundred SST units, and about fifty present faculty members have led the Study-Service Term. About seventy percent of Goshen's current students complete their international education component through SST, while others transfer credits from various junior-year-abroad programs or special overseas courses of study, and yet others take a series of on-campus international-studies courses to meet the requirement. Over the years, SST has garnered national recognition for the college. Goshen is regularly mentioned among "America's Best Colleges" in *U.S. News and*

World Report and in *Barron's Best Buys in College Education* and the *Making a Difference in College Guide.* It *is* fair to ask whether international education has overshadowed the Mennonite Church connection at Goshen College. However, in light of SST's origins, its embodiment of Mennonite distinctives, and its impact on educating Mennonite and other young people for a postmodern world, Goshen's international program should strengthen rather than harm the church-college relationship.

SERVICE-LEARNING

From the beginning, the service half of the Study-Service Term has been essential in fulfilling Goshen College's religiously based self-understanding. The college's motto is "Culture for Service," and as a recent viewbook says, "The phrase has been on our tongues, but more importantly, in our hearts and minds, for a century. . . . It's only in using our education to serve in the world that our learning has value." In the United States, formal service-learning has been around for more than a century, dating back at least to Morrill & Homestead Act Initiatives which established land grant colleges focused on rural development and education, and to historically black colleges and universities which combined work, service, and learning.[24] In recent years, high schools and colleges across the country have added service to the curriculum.[25] Before his death, Ernest Boyer, president of the Carnegie Foundation for the Advancement of Teaching, also challenged institutions of higher education to see the scholarly interaction between teaching, research, and community service. Quoting Woodrow Wilson, in part, he said, "It is not learning but the spirit of service that will give a college a place in the annals of the nation. . . . Scholarship has to prove its worth, not on its own terms, but by service to the nation and the world."[26]

Most service-learning programs, whether at the college or high school level, are community-based, not international. They also tend to be activist-oriented in some important respects, usually on the liberal-to-left end of the political spectrum. Although not particularly ideological in their approach, those responsible for Goshen College's SST program would argue that service-learning, like all learning, is not and should not be value-neutral. Acts of service need to be connected with critical reflection on contexts, helping students see the links between social policies and homelessness or teen pregnancy or poverty. If students are asked to serve America, they might produce not only George Bush's "thousand points of light," but also "a thousand points of the status quo," say University of Illinois and New York University professors Joseph Kahne and Joel Westheimer.[27] Service learning ought not be solely charity: it is engaged learning, backed by prior and ongoing systematic and critical analysis of social and political realities which establish the context for service. Again, service learning is a form of praxis, a circular activity of action and reflection.

International service programs, including Goshen's, have their own problems. In overseas settings—where histories of colonialism and patronizing, self-interested, First World-initiated development have soured nationals on outside assistance, and where frequently racial, cultural, or religious tensions may be heightened by the appearance of (often white) middle-class American undergraduates—students must "serve" with extraordinary sensitivity.[28] One SST student expressed her frustration with being able to help friends in need back home, but not being able to do the same thing in international settings "without fostering dependence, perpetuating stereotypes of powerful white Americans, and doing more harm than good."[29] Goshen's Study-Service Term students in Dominican Republic regularly take a four-day excursion to the neighboring country of Haiti, where they hear Mennonite Central Committee workers speak about development. In one recent presentation, MCC's country representative evoked the memorable image of "cowboy missionaries," who enter a country like Haiti "with their six-shooters a'blazin'." The MCC service worker reminded the SSTers that they could not truly help their hosts in a brief, six-week period and charged them to "serve" by helping those in their villages believe in themselves, and in what they can accomplish by working together as a community.

Following the trip to Haiti, one perceptive student wrote in his SST journal, which all students are required to keep:

> Going to bed tonight tired, but a good tired that has come from thoroughly extending myself in every intellectual, emotional, and physical way. . . . I pushed so hard to soak up every word from every speaker, pushed my own brain constantly for three days, examining, connecting and critiquing ideas presented to me. . . . And I've never learned so much in three days, never. I think my life/views/opinions have been altered permanently in some areas—like thinking about poverty, and about dependence/service issues, and about entering a culture you have little knowledge of.[30]

Another student wrote later, during his service experience:

> The idea of being part of the community before trying to do anything is powerful. It also runs contrary to many North American models of service (hit-and-run service). Not that it's easy to overcome our acts-based ideology of European Protestantism, but it is surely necessary. To be able to serve we must sacrifice something. . . . It needs to be a sacrifice more than simply the time involved. It needs to be a sacrifice of power. The power of being right.[31]

Prior to leaving for their service assignments, most SST leaders remind students that service includes "being" and "understanding" and "accompanying" as well as "doing." "Your assignment should be less a time of performance than a time of study and reflection upon the meaning of service," says one SST student handout titled "Background for Service Experience."

TOWARD TRANSFORMATION
IN A POSTMODERN WORLD

As already indicated, the six weeks of service are instrumental in achieving SST's goals of "disorienting" and thereby transforming students. During the first six-and-one-half weeks of the term abroad, students study the language and culture of their host country, often at a university or language-training institute and under the tutelage of nationals. They have daily contact with their faculty directors and student peers, however, and meet together regularly as a group to process their experiences. They also are usually located in the capital city, which means communication and transportation are more readily accessible. In service assignments for most SST units, however, students are flung across their host countries, either alone or in pairs, often in remote settings without running water, electricity, or phones or other communication systems. In some villages, no one besides the Goshen student speaks English, so SSTers are forced to communicate in the country's tongue, or to gesture with communicative proficiency. A decade after the Study-Service Term's inception, Director Arlin Hunsberger was charged by the student newspaper with not adequately orienting students for their study abroad. In response, Hunsberger appealed to the program's original design, which he implied "actually proposed a healthy amount of initial disorientation abroad as a primary goal of the undertaking."[32] While students go on SST only after two college courses in the country's language, such study can never fully prepare them for immersion in a host family. Disorientation, when it does not overwhelm, contributes toward humility and receptivity. Disorientation engages students, draws them out, makes them open and vulnerable—teachable.[33] "Newness" in this form temporarily removes traditional foundations, including the safety of home and the certainty of one's cultural truths, teaching students skills essential for entering a postmodern world. In most cases, at least with Study-Service Term students, reorientation comes gradually once they are back in the states, but foundations are less closed, more chastened, than before the study-abroad experience.

With an experiential pedagogy, precise learnings are notoriously difficult to measure, resulting in an unfortunate, perceived dichotomy between experiential learning and academic rigor. Nearly all forms of experiential learning, as with praxis, include substantive, analytical readings and analysis in preparation for or in response to particular actions or experiences. On field trips, through lectures, and in weekly group meetings, SST students process their experiences with their peers and faculty leaders. They also write at least three journal entries each week, ones which focus less on observations than critical reflections about their encounters and learnings. Faculty leaders then read journals weekly, entering into conversation with students, raising additional questions, affirming insights and assisting with providing frameworks and contexts for understanding.

Several studies in the last two decades have confirmed particular types of measurable learnings in international education. In *Students Abroad, Strangers at Home: Education for a Global Society*, authors Norman L. Kauffmann, Judith N. Martin and Henry D. Weaver report their findings regarding personal and intellectual development as well as perspectival changes wrought through study abroad. According to the researchers, students who are less mature when going abroad, but who then immerse themselves in the local culture, are the ones who demonstrate the most personal growth in terms of gaining intrapersonal (self-esteem, autonomy, self-confidence, self-reliance, and self-differentiation) and interpersonal skills, as well as developing values and life and vocational direction. Students who are less mature and who experience another culture only superficially have minimal gains in personal growth and in intellectual development and worldview. Students who are more mature, with a keener sense of who they are and their vocational goals, benefit primarily in intellectual development and expanded worldviews.[34]

Kauffmann et al., drawing on the Omnibus Personality Inventory as well as self-reporting on a questionnaire and extensive interviews, indicated that those who had experienced guided study experiences abroad, such as SST, dramatically increased their interest in and ability for reflective thought in academic activities, and such stimulation continued to climb after the study-abroad experience was over. On SST, critical thought enters into reworking notions of gender norms and roles, wealth and poverty, and justice and injustice. One student who had some background in Latin American liberation theology and in working with issues of faith, justice, and peacemaking prior to her SST experience, wrote in her journal:

> There are three aspects of this *campo* that I think are really valuable—connection with the land, close community and meaning-

ful work. It is because of those things that life here is rich, despite financial poverty. Basing wealth upon only dollars, then, is indeed a deeply engrained myth, because the life in El Rucio and Saladillo has richness that transcends the life that is called poor.[35]

She noted that more education, artistic and musical expression, organized activities for young people, and more efficient water collecting systems could make life in her village more attractive without spoiling its beauty. The journal entry, which then extended over several pages, evidenced an ability to be self-critical about previous attitudes, which she earlier had perceived as somewhat sophisticated, as well as an ability to critique appropriately American materialism and Dominican stratification of wealth. She recognized that she may have an "idealized picture of life in the campo," adding, "Even though I have come to view their lives as really good (and I know that there are millions more who suffer more than they do from hunger, war, mistreatment, etc.), I shouldn't deny that I have an advantage over them, because I have the ability to choose between this life and my life at home."

From the earliest days of SST, the vision for the international education program was that students would be in dialogue with people of other religions. When SST began, most Mennonite students came to the college from rural Mennonite communities, where in the 1960s "ecumenical" meant Mennonites, Methodists, and perhaps Baptists living together in relative peace. Today Mennonites are more urbanized, though for most undergraduates at Goshen College, Mennonite and other-than-Mennonite, contact with other religions is still limited prior to their arrival on campus. In Haiti and Dominican Republic students see voodooism and its syncretistic blend with Catholicism firsthand; in China students encounter atheism, agnosticism, and Buddhism; in Costa Rica and elsewhere in Latin America students experience Pentecostalism and Evangelicalism with an intensity they have not witnessed in North America; in Côte d'Ivoire they see wide-ranging African religions, some mixed with Christian rituals; in Indonesia they experience Buddhism, Islam, and Hinduism; in many settings they have contact with indigenous forms of Mennonitism, some of which look considerably different from what they have known from their home communities. As students worship with their host families in whatever faith is theirs, or avoid organized religion altogether if that is their family's practice, they learn both to critique and value their religious heritage, and also to broaden their views of faith and faithfulness. Already in 1971 one analysis of SST said returning students reported "more tolerance toward religions and a greater understanding of the catholicity of the church."[36] Students also discuss the church's role in colonialism and oppressing and enslaving indigenous people in some of their host countries, recognizing the church's participation in the logics of power.

In many Study-Service Term settings, students also are forced to examine their views of individualism and community. As college students who have been relatively independent for one to three years before going on SST, adjustments to living with gracious and protective host families, returning home at night under culturally defined curfews, attending worship services more frequently than is their practice on campus, and abiding by norms established by external controls, is quite difficult. The move from childhood dependence to relative independence is made prior to SST, but an appreciation for interdependence, or a clearer awareness of socially constructed and socially connected selves, sometimes emerges as a result of the experience abroad. "A small, remote community like El Rucio naturally lends itself to a close-knit community," wrote one student.

> Everyone attends the same church and the same school, rides the *guaguas* together, buys food at the local *colmado*, and knows (or is related to) their neighbors. With this forced closeness comes the attitude of helping each other—watching someone's kids, cutting someone's hair, fixing a neighbor's pair of shoes, sharing food between houses, holding each other responsible, giving someone a ride on a motorcycle, borrowing a tool, lending a hand with a job.[37]

This interdependence includes a recognition that selves are not unencumbered but embedded, selves-in-communities who are shaped by and responsible to and for others. On SST, students' placements in new contexts allow them to recognize formative influences in various locales, and begin the work of critical examination. Students also recognize the interdependence of families in communities, and of communities with other villages, and of countries with other nations. Students recognize the impact their use of resources, and their political views, have on those who have been on the underside of colonialism, and how the rhetoric in their homelands often differs from the realities they experience abroad.

Through studying another language and immersing themselves in another culture, many students also move closer toward becoming multicultural. In orientation sessions prior to going on SST, through contact with faculty leaders and peers, in texts and assignments and journals, students forever are encouraged to be "culturally sensitive," which includes learning to appreciate "otherness." As part of their major "project," a requirement of the SST experience, some students choose to record stories from women in their culture, or take photos of children in their village, or collect recipes of indigenous foods, or create illustrated notebooks of local plants and their fruits. Several years ago, two students in Côte d'Ivoire, Josh Kaufman and Kathy Leidig, spent much of their service experience in Guibéroua with a musician from a nearby village, learning to play Ivoirian instruments. In a convocation after they returned to campus, Kaufman played the stringed *dodo*, speaking the tribal tonal language of Beté into the instrument to create mystical sounds never before heard in Goshen, telling stories and saying words over various rhythms. He drummed the *djimbé*, often used in worship or for dancing, while Leidig played a women's bamboo flute from which sound is coaxed through both blowing and singing pitches. Their performances, and the projects of other SST students, are efforts to value local cultures and to appreciate them on their own terms.

SST Director Wilbur Birky cites a Nigerian proverb from novelist Chinua Achebe which asserts that "there is no story that is not true." Birky says while "the real stories of real people may seem to contradict each other," in reality "they coexist as

expressions of the diversity and the contradictions that tem-
per our lives." One reinterpretation of the biblical story of the
Tower of Babel that has influenced Birky is the notion that
rather than providing many languages and peoples as a *punishment* for hubris, the story may suggest "that many languages
and peoples represent the *remedy* of diversity in the face of the
problem of homogeneity."[38] The interweaving of music and
stories from other cultures into students' lives, and back onto
campus, is a powerful testimony to the crossing of cultural
boundaries. Near the end of her service term, one student wrote
in her journal:

> I just realized how comfortable I am with these people. It's pretty
> incredible to think that in 5 1/2 weeks these relationships have
> formed. . . . I told Rachel that I think if someone goes on SST and
> doesn't come back changed—doesn't have a new understand-
> ing that they will carry with them, then they have abused the
> program. Because this is a very delicate thing. To come into a
> community and live with these people for only six weeks and
> then to leave—most likely forever—is dangerous. . . . The justifi-
> cation is that I use what I have learned, that I use what I know in
> my future to indirectly repay them. I don't know what to do about
> poverty or machismo. I think I've found these problems have
> much deeper roots than are initially apparent. But I do know
> that these are not the problems of the faceless masses. They are
> issues that belong to my family and friends—people who have
> loved me and taken care of me for a month and a half and, thus,
> they belong to me, too. And I can't forget. The most simple part
> of my responsibility is that I can't forget.[39]

Recent research supports the notion that cross-cultural experiences in foreign countries enhance one's multicultural and pluralistic outlook. Direct experience is more effective for
multicultural education than is structured learning, say the
studies.[40] Putting faces on issues, and valuing those people both
for who they are as well as what they represent, creates people
better prepared to live as "Christian world citizens," as former
Goshen College President Paul Mininger hoped, and people
with the ability to be multicultural in a diverse world of multiple, overlapping communities and interwoven stories.

INTERNATIONALISM BACK ON CAMPUS

Back on campus in Goshen, the international culture thrives. At the beginning of every term, from twenty to eighty students return to the campus from their overseas locations, along with other students who have opted for Junior Year Abroad programs or other international study. In both formal and informal ways, recently returned students do much of the orientation for their peers who are about to go on the Study-Service Term. Stories and photo albums about SST abound on campus, and students fairly frequently publish on-campus Pinchpenny Press books out of their experience. Often groups, or persons from groups as illustrated above, do chapel or convocation presentations for the student body. Among the clothing that is "cool" on campus are shirts, skirts, and flowing gowns from parts of Africa, Asia, and Latin America. Each spring the college hosts a growing Ethnic Festival, which draws thousands from a fifty-mile radius around Goshen for a day of food, international dancing, art, and performances. The international culture is so thick that some returning Study-Service Term students complain that they have had the "cliché SST experience," and that no one is willing to hear their stories since they have already heard dozens more about life-changing encounters and cultural differences.

Students wanting to continue developing their language skills or their cross-cultural interactions sometimes volunteer to work with La Casa, a local church-sponsored service agency for lower-income Goshen residents; tutor recently arrived immigrant children in local schools; or seek out relationships with international students on campus. In addition to those students who have traveled overseas, Goshen hosts admirable numbers of international students each year. One 1952 graduate says during his four years at Goshen, he had roommates, classmates, and friends from sixteen countries in four continents. "Almost two decades before the start of SST, Goshen provided me with many opportunities to train for global citizenship," he says.[41] In the 1999–2000 year, seventy-six students enrolled at Goshen College, or just under eight percent of the student body, were from outside the United States and Canada, representing thirty-two different countries. Some were Mennonite, others were from various Protestant, Catholic, or Eastern Orthodox traditions; and yet others were from Muslim, Buddhist, Hindu, and other religious or nonreligious traditions.

An additional spin-off of Goshen's SST program is a Multicultural Education Office, which stimulates discussion about multiculturalism and raises awareness on campus; invites alumni from underrepresented groups back to lecture and meet with students; directs a mentoring program for North American students from underrepresented groups; and gives grants to faculty members to integrate multicultural perspectives into their classes. Most departments include courses with international dimensions: Religious History in the Americas; Asian Religions; Third World Theologies and Liberation Theologies in Bible; Religion, Philosophy, and Peace Studies; as well as occasional Doing Theology Abroad offerings; Transcultural Seminar (Agriculture) in Biology; Communicating Across Cultures in Communication; International Literature in English; Hispanic Culture and Society in Hispanic Ministries; East Asia, First/Third World History, Latin American History and History of Africa in History; Cross-Cultural Aspects of Health and Illness in Nursing; and at least eight courses in Sociology, Social Work, and Anthropology. With half of the faculty having led SST groups, and others having studied or served abroad, many other courses across the curriculum include sections which address international aspects of their disciplines.

The news about Goshen's multiculturalism and internationalism is not all rosy, however. While returning SST students often say they have developed a greater sensitivity to cross-cultural wanderers, since they know what it feels like to be in a minority, cafeteria seating patterns still evidence divisions between international students and the U.S. majority. African-American students on campus have sometimes argued that Goshen's international environment supports those from other, more exotic countries, but ignores those marginalized in the United States.[42] Faculty meetings and on-campus conferences have acknowledged potential tensions between a yearning for multiculturalism and diversity and the Mennonite Board of Education's requirement that at least fifty-five percent of Goshen's students be Mennonite. At a 1995 "Church and College in Partnership" conference on campus, Ernest Boyer made a strong pitch for a significant number of faculty members and students to come out of the Mennonite faith tradition so there can be a common language and common culture on campus. Zenebe Abebe, director of the Multicultural Education Office, and others questioned how one can have both a multicultural campus and a tight community with common languages. Although the Mennonite Church in North America is increasingly diverse, with African-American, Chinese, Vietnamese, Laotian, Hmong, French, and Native American congregations and members, only seven percent of the U.S. Mennonite population is from underrepresented groups. Boyer suggested at the conference that multiculturalism does not all need to happen on campus—some of it happens "out there in the world" through SST.

CHALLENGES FOR SERVICE-LEARNING AND INTERNATIONAL EDUCATION AT CHURCH-RELATED COLLEGES

However imperfectly, international education is one way church-related colleges can prepare students for a postmodern world *and* remain connected to their supportive denominations. This is particularly true in cases where study-abroad programs are integrally related to the religious and cultural ethos on campus. International education may even allow for "conversions" *toward* a church and its distinctive commitments as students critique certain liberal assumptions; come to grips with their self-identity and self-formation; critically examine their communities of origin and their religious traditions; recognize the legitimacies of various truths (even while maintaining some particular religious commitments); and humble themselves as they hammer away at their ethnocentricity by learning to respect other cultural and religious traditions. Through international education, even cautious and skeptical church-related colleges may open themselves to a one-armed embrace of postmodernism. For those denominationally affiliated colleges and universities pushing out students' boundaries through study-abroad programs, several observations emerging from Goshen College's success—and failure—may be instructive.

1. *Where possible, church-related colleges should make clear to students, faculty, and constituencies the historical or theological rationale for their international education programs.* For example, Augsburg College, with its rootedness in ethnic Lutheranism and commitment to intentional diversity, confesses that its Center for Global Education is geared toward working for a more just and sustainable world, grounded in the perspectives of the poor and marginalized. At Goshen, historian Theron Schlabach rightly inquires, "Is Goshen communicating well enough to students and others that its heralded SST program rests on faith commitments? Is the message clearly to invite faith commitment, rather than a relativism that might make all faith commitments seem like mere cultural expression."[43] Moreover, is SST seen primarily as prudent preparation for vocational success in the international marketplace or as an expression of Mennonites' commitments to breaking down boundaries, reaching out to the marginalized, peacemaking, and service. Goshen's public relations materials draw on both religious and secular motivations for the Study-Service Term. One brochure says, "We believe Christ's call to ideals such as peacemaking, living simply, and equality for everyone reach across political boundaries." The brochure adds that graduates "tell us their intercultural experience was the difference in their job search, setting them apart from graduates of other colleges in the hiring process. In the global economy of the 1990s and the 21st century, business and industry need graduates who understand the world around them and international education helps Goshen College graduates fit the bill."[44] Especially as Goshen College prepares its students for SST, faculty need to acknowledge clearly the origin of the experience in Christian discipleship.

2. *In some cases, church-related colleges would be wise to make appropriate connections with overseas mission and service workers*

from their denominations. When Goshen's SST program began, faculty and administrators were reluctant to forge this institutional link too firmly. However, given the international respect organizations such as Mennonite Central Committee have garnered, and given the sensitive and sophisticated perspective of most MCC and Mennonite Board of Missions workers overseas, Goshen's study abroad program has been and will be served well by strengthening these connections. Given that SST is an educational venture, students ought not be co-opted into doing the church's "mission work," but they can learn from lectures by service workers and by observing their manner of graciously relating to and learning from their hosts. In the Dominican Republic, Costa Rica, and Africa students have opportunities to interact with church-related mission and service personnel, and elsewhere SST is connected with indigenous Mennonites, who provide homes for some students. When Mennonite and other students worship with Mennonites in Indonesia or Costa Rica or Germany or the Dominican Republic, they are stimulated to critique what is uniquely "American" about Mennonite churches or their own denominations, and what may be distinctive to particular religious traditions. Other church-affiliated schools with institutional representatives or clusters of congregations in given countries overseas may benefit from tapping into such resources, helping students better understand their own religious origins or those of the college they are attending.

3. *In order for study-abroad programs to effect long-term transformation, colleges and universities must pay close attention to reentry and reintegration.*[45] Where small numbers of students study abroad, reentry may be extraordinarily difficult because the campus culture may not adequately integrate overseas learnings into the classroom context or campus discussions. But even at colleges where a high percentage of students study overseas, reentry is difficult, and students sometimes feel lost in the shuffle or devalue their experience because it does not seem unique. Occasionally students become angry at their families or others who have not shared their experience. After returning from SST, one student said:

> I was frustrated with people in my community. It was like, hey, become aware! There are so many cultures. When I hear people make stereotypical comments about other countries I feel like saying, "No, you don't know. You don't know." It's not like I'm an expert or anything but yet I feel like I try to evaluate things a little more and be a little more open-minded.[46]

In regard to her own reverse culture shock, she added:

> Everybody says that SST is the greatest experience but nobody says that when you come back you are going to be confused. You may not, but you could be really confused. You may have a lot of questions coming to mind. You're going to be sorting through a lot of things. And people around you may not know how to deal with it.[47]

In order for students to do the work of reentry, reintegration, and reconstruction, they need assistance from faculty members and peers who understand the experience. Where groups of students have studied abroad together, this can be done through workshops or brown-bag luncheons, or through the more structured format of a one- to three-hour follow-up course which assists students with processing alterations in themselves, their worldviews, and their faith perspectives. Ideally, faculty leaders would teach such courses to their own groups, though this is not always possible when faculty remain outside the country for more than one term. Single reentry workshops, or later integrative senior seminars in students' various disciplines, are inadequate to do the necessary work of re-entry and reconstruction.

4. *Church-related colleges with strong international programs also need to work at multiculturalism on their home campuses in order to reinforce the learnings overseas.* Attention must be paid to developing diverse student bodies, including international students; students from various Christian denominations as well as those from other religions and nonreligious backgrounds; students from multiple racial and ethnic heritages; and students from other underrepresented groups. Integrity with on-campus multiculturalism helps students better link the multicultural dimensions of their overseas experience with their college and its sponsoring denomination. Forums for cross-fertilization of

ideas should be sponsored, and cross-cultural social relationships should be encouraged through the modeling of administrators and faculty as well as specific programming.

5. *In study-abroad programs, on-site supervision by usually-on-
campus faculty members allows for greater integration of cross-cultural learnings.* Overseas, faculty can work sensitively with
students as they process their own heritage and culture in light
of their new learnings, helping them appropriately critique and
then reappropriate parts of their religious and cultural traditions. While students learn a great deal simply by being thrown
into another culture, guided exercises and activities followed
by group processing with faculty facilitation foster much more
learning and integration. Back on campus, through informal
or more structured interactions, professors who have led SST
can continue the process of integration. By having faculty members from various disciplines lead study-abroad programs, the
campus is doubly impacted: students return stimulated and
transformed, and faculty return similarly moved. Goshen College Professor of Bible, Religion, Philosophy, and Peace Studies Ruth Krall wrote after her SST leadership:

> Previously my conception of teaching and learning was that the
> teacher was responsible to be strong not weak; to be informed,
> not confused, to be loving and perceptive of others, not needful
> of love and perceptivity. . . . But in Costa Rica, I was not an ex-
> pert. I was not always strong. I was not always loving and cul-
> turally perceptive. . . . Honesty about painful feelings and
> confusion did not appear to destroy [students'] inner security
> nor did it seem to cause a lack of trust. Walking the same road as
> they did each day made us co-learners. . . . One enduring result
> of SST in my personal life has been this basic challenge to my
> theories of teaching and learning. I am more committed to rela-
> tional teaching.[48]

Many faculty return from study-abroad experiences with
greater commitment to experiential learning on campus as well.
Experiential learning is one of humans' earliest modes of social and intellectual development, and it breathes life into students' study, making learning both practical and real.[49]
International education which transforms teachers as well as
students should be valued by academic institutions and the

churches which support them, particularly when the experiences open students to lives of service.

6. *As part of their international education programs, church-related colleges may need to give special attention to the issue of cultural relativism.* In some ways, perhaps ironically, programs like SST help balance a relativist position students may develop in college when they are initially exposed to new ideas. In "Confessions of a Former Cultural Relativist," Henry Bagish identifies several behaviors he cannot accept as "just different," including the Danzi of New Guinea's practice of chopping off young girls' fingers to placate certain ghosts; exterminating Jewish people, as in the Nazi holocaust; and ritual clitoridectomies, which still take place in some African and Arab countries. While most study-abroad students do not encounter such extreme practices, they frequently wrestle with machismo and other forms of sexism; with the excessively harsh treatment of children, which sometimes would be classified as abuse in the United States; and with the arrogance of the wealthy or powerful in more highly stratified societies.[50] On campus and in international study, church-related colleges and universities need not seek to remove their charges' religious and moral foundations. The embrace of postmodernism is, after all, a one-armed embrace.

After the first full year of Goshen College's Study-Service Term program, a four-person commission of international-education experts evaluated the program. Among their conclusions was that SST led to "broadened views, tolerance, cultural perspectives, and more liberal or humanistic values." The students' morals, the commission said, were "usually challenged, reviewed, and resecured."[51] Undergraduate students should critique themselves, their worldviews, their congregations and denominations, their faiths, and their ethical frameworks, and can do so effectively through study abroad. They should, in effect, *shake* their foundations, but they need not *discard* them. Some will, no doubt, revise considerably their prior foundational understandings and commitments, and a few will remove them fully. But what may be hoped for is an appropriate shaking that will allow students to value that which is good and truthful about their particular traditions and stories, and to hold to their reconstructed worldviews-in-process with greater humility and more openness than before. International education provides an avenue toward such transformation. Study abroad need neither supersede nor supplant a college's church-relatedness. Nor should the seemingly inevitable movement toward postmodernism—a movement which international education may further—unduly threaten an institution of higher education's religious affiliation. Appropriately embedded and administered, international education in a postmodern world may sustain and even strengthen a church college's ties to its founding denomination.

Religion and the Curriculum at Church-Related Colleges and Universities

Marcia Bunge

Although much has been written about the tendency of academic institutions to marginalize religion and view it as irrelevant to the academic enterprise, at their best, church-related colleges and universities view religion as central to their mission, academic programs, and community life. A strong church-related academic institution recognizes that religious questions are and should be part of the academic conversation. Students and faculty come to these institutions with different religious or even secular backgrounds, and yet all are invited to be part of a campus-wide conversation about religious and ethical issues. Because one aim of many church-related colleges and universities is to generate this kind of lively and informed discussion, they provide a unique public forum for critical reflection on a variety of religious and ethical questions and concerns.

The philosopher Martha Nussbaum recognizes the potential strength and character of the church-related college when she speaks about the University of Notre Dame. She finds that in contrast to secular universities, where religious concerns often have little place apart from the department of religious studies, at Notre Dame "religious and ethical concerns are straightforwardly accepted as part of academic life."[1] Faculty

members may disagree with one another about particular issues. "Nonetheless, there is a remarkable degree of agreement
about which issues are important, and that these issues prominently include issues of ethical and spiritual value."[2] Although
she recognizes some weaknesses in the program at Notre
Dame, Nussbaum congratulates its faculty and administration
for succeeding well in constructing "a distinctively religious
campus that is also a place of genuine inquiry and debate."[3]

One way that church-related colleges and universities have
attempted to create a setting in which religious and ethical issues are taken seriously and in which faith and learning are
intertwined is to incorporate the study of religion into the curriculum, usually in the form of a religion requirement. Although the number of required religion courses has been
declining at church-related institutions, eighty-five percent of
all church-related colleges still have an average requirement
of two or three courses in religion.[4] Of course, the nature of
these requirements greatly varies, even among institutions
within the same denomination. Among colleges of the Evangelical Lutheran Church in America (ELCA), for example,
Muhlenberg requires two courses in "meaning and value" (one
in religion and the other in philosophy), and any religion course
fulfills the first requirement. Roanoke requires only one course
on moral philosophy, called "Values and the Responsible Life,"
which is taken during the junior year and taught by professors in the department of religion and philosophy. Luther College, in contrast, requires a course in Bible as the prerequisite
for a second requirement in religion and a third in either religion or philosophy.

Although it is always important for church-related colleges
and universities to reevaluate the precise ways in which religion is incorporated into the curriculum and the particular aims
of the religion requirement, there are a number of reasons a
serious discussion of the role of religion in the curriculum is
particularly urgent at this time. First, many institutions in the
1990s have experienced tremendous financial difficulties or at
least tightened budgets, creating significant changes in staffing, dwindling resources for departments, and increased competition among colleges for students. In responding to financial

concerns and this competitive market, church-related colleges are searching for new ways to define their goals and academic programs and to articulate the distinctive qualities of their institutions. As church-related colleges address these financial concerns, they must be able to articulate the precise role that religion will play in the way they staff their courses, define their mission, and shape their academic programs and campus community life.

Second, some current academic programs do not take into account that many students today know very little about religion or even about their own religious backgrounds. Many students have a "deep ignorance of religion"[5] and tend to come to college either with no beliefs or "with little knowledge of the religious texts from which their beliefs are drawn."[6] Even students at church-related colleges who were brought up in mainline churches, attended Sunday school, were confirmed, and are confessing Christians remain deeply ignorant about Christianity and are unable to speak with any depth about their own religious convictions. Academic programs established years ago were often built on the assumptions that students held strong religious beliefs and that one aim of the religion courses was to disabuse students of their naive views. Since students today know little about the Christian tradition and have difficulty expressing elements of their faith, this approach is no longer appropriate.

Third, it is essential to discuss and reevaluate the role of religion in the curriculum at church-related colleges and universities because we live in a time of transition in which views of religion in the academy appear to be both "modern" and "postmodern." On the one hand, many students and faculty seem to hold onto the very modern assumption that faith and learning are separate realms and that religion is personal and private and therefore irrelevant to academic life. On the other hand, there appears to be a growing openness to religious perspectives among scholars in several fields that some attribute to the postmodern critique of objectivity and emphasis on pluralism. These differing assumptions about religion and the challenges of postmodernism call for renewed reflection on the role of religion at a church-related college or university.

Precisely because we live at a time when academic institutions are experiencing financial difficulties, students know little about religion, and modern and postmodern assumptions about religion coexist uneasily. Serious conversations about the role of religion in the curriculum are essential and will be, no doubt, both complex and difficult. They will require the discussion of several volatile issues, such as staffing needs and the distribution of often limited financial resources. Faculty members and administrators might also have different assumptions about religion and its importance to the curriculum and the self-understanding of the institution.

The aim of this paper is to help facilitate serious discussions on the campuses of church-related colleges and universities about the role of religion in the curriculum by (1) outlining more fully this modern/postmodern situation in regard to perceptions of religion among students and faculty and (2) outlining some specific suggestions for incorporating religion into the curriculum at church-related colleges and universities. Although this paper cannot suggest a program that fits the needs and aims of the strikingly diverse kinds of church-related colleges and universities, it does argue that there are compelling reasons for them to think more seriously about the role of religion in the curriculum; to include in the curriculum (whether as religion requirements or as part of interdisciplinary programs) a strong introduction to Christianity, an in-depth study of at least one or two other religions, and critical reflection on basic ethical issues; and to foster the discussion of religious and ethical issues through a number of extracurricular programs and events.

THE MODERN/POSTMODERN SITUATION

The view of religion among students and faculty at both church-related and secular academic institutions appears to be at once modern and postmodern. On the one hand, even though we claim to live in a postmodern world, the modern assumption that faith and learning are separate realms and that faith is private still permeates the academic world and the culture in general. As several scholars have recently noted, the church continues to be seen by many as the "sole guardian of faith; the college and the university the prime champions of knowledge."[7] Since modernity defines faith over against knowledge, religion is often seen as marginal to the academic enterprise;[8] "religion has not been able to find a way fully to participate in the intellectual conversation of the contemporary American university."[9] While almost all universities have departments of religious studies, "most discussion of religion is segregated into those departments so that every other discipline is free to ignore religion."[10]

Members of the faculty at both church-related and secular institutions often hold this view that religion is private, marginal, and even irrelevant to the academic enterprise. As Joshua Mitchell notes, "Where at their outset modern universities were, for the most part, unthinkable without religion, today the ivory tower cloisters a new breed of scholars who are often oblivious to or intolerant of religion" and "who are most eager to rule out religion in the university curriculum."[11] As David Hoekema claims, the view that religion is irrelevant to the academic enterprise can be found among both conservative and progressive professors: "Conservatives and progressives seem more than willing to declare a truce in their culture wars in order to close ranks against the encroachment of religion, which belongs in the home and the church, not in the university. The conviction that God has no place on campus is shared even by many religious believers, who regard their faith as a personal matter irrelevant to their role as instructors."[12] Although this conviction might not be stated as loudly among faculty members at church-related academic institutions, some of them hold this opinion and see any emphasis on religion in direct opposition to more important aims, including academic excellence, diversity, or freedom of inquiry.

Many students also assume religion should remain private, and thus they do not see it as an appropriate subject of public debate or academic study. For many of them, religion is something "above" or "beneath" intellectual discussion. In one informal survey of student attitudes about religion courses at a church-related college, one student expressed the sentiment of several others when he or she wrote, "Religious beliefs are extremely private and personal; the idea of expressing and sharing deeply emotional opinions often makes people uncomfortable."[13] Another concluded that the institution "should not require its students to enroll in a class about such a private matter." Partly because students see religion as private and marginal to the academic life, they sometimes view the religion requirement as just one more hoop to graduation and do not understand its relation to their major academic concerns.

It is, in part, this modern notion that religion is private and separate from the academic enterprise that has contributed to the striking ignorance of students not only about religion but also about their own religious traditions. Unless they attended a parochial school, most of them have had few opportunities to discuss religious issues in a public, academic setting.

Even though many students and faculty at academic institutions seem to hold onto the modern assumption that religion is private and that faith and learning inhabit separate realms, in the academy there also appears to be a growing openness to religious perspectives that has been designated "postmodern." Although postmodernism is a complex term that is difficult to define, one of its significant aspects is an awareness of the Other and of human diversity. Postmodernism draws attention to the diversity of rationalities, traditions, cultures, and morals.[14] Furthermore, by calling attention to this diversity, postmodernism challenges one to evaluate critically one's own convictions.

This emphasis on the Other has opened a door to new intellectual perspectives on religion in many fields, creating what some have called a postmodern "boost" to religion in the academy. Alan Wolfe claims that although the academy has tended to leave little room for religion, growing attention is being given to religion among philosophers, literary critics, social scientists, and even natural scientists.[15] Wolfe, a secular scholar, welcomes this "revival of religion" in the academy precisely because "religion can extend the pluralism that liberal values cherish, and it can expand and enrich knowledge."[16] Others claim that this postmodern "boost to religion" comes not only from the need to take religion more seriously but also from the postmodern disillusionment with the sciences and awareness of the finitude of all ways of knowing.[17]

Even as many students hold onto the modern assumption that religion is private, they also reveal a kind of postmodern openness to religion. They are very interested in learning about diverse religious perspectives, such as Buddhism, Native American thought, African religions, and New Age religions. They also express interest in diverse and often neglected voices within the Christian tradition, such as the mystics or Christian traditions of meditation and spiritual formation. Part of this interest can be traced to the simple appeal of religious questions that address human meaning and happiness, but another part of it surely stems from students' growing awareness of other cultures, religions, and ways of conceiving the world that is part of the postmodern mindset.

Although postmodernism has boosted interest in religious perspectives, it has also created a heated debate about the validity of normative claims, which are at the heart of most religious traditions. Because the postmodern emphasis on otherness includes a serious suspicion of so-called metanarratives, universal norms, and absolute truths, it seriously challenges the validity of moral and ethical claims. This suspicion has led some postmodern thinkers to the conviction that all moral claims are relative.

Shaped by this postmodern mindset and the widespread competitive individualism of our culture, many students also hold the position that all normative claims are relative. As several scholars have noted, many students tend to view moral positions as a matter of choice and therefore as relative, and they hesitate to discuss ethical issues. One scholar tells the story of twenty students who were hesitant even to debate the moral acceptability of human sacrifice.[18] These students are not staunch moral relativists with strong philosophical arguments for their position; rather, many of them possess a vague sense that free choice is important, though they cannot articulate what principles guide their own moral choices. They have a kind of fragmented or diffused sense of who they are and what matters to them. As George Dennis O'Brien states, "I do know from long experience in the dean's office that young people do not come to college these days with a big brace of moral dogmas. . . . The sense I receive from college psychiatrists is that contemporary students suffer from identity *diffusion*, not an overdetermined, dogmatic identity."[19] Philosophers and psychologists have tied this diffused sense of self to our postmodern situation and have used various terms to describe it, such as "the saturated self" (Kenneth Gergen), the "fragmented self," or the postmodern "erasure of self."

Although other students do hold strong ethical and religious convictions and long for serious and lively discussions about ethical issues, even they have difficulty articulating the grounds for their views. They have had few opportunities to discuss ethical issues in an academic setting, and they are generally unaware of contemporary arguments (religious and secular) that assert there can still be a place in a postmodern context for the pursuit of truth and the establishment of moral claims. These scholars take seriously the postmodern emphasis on the limitations of human understanding, its concern for the Other and for worlds and voices that have been silenced, and its distrust of universal discourses or metanarratives; yet they do not believe these postmodern insights must lead to radical moral relativism. As Nussbaum has stated, even if we recognize "the search for truth is a human activity, carried on with human faculties in a world in which human beings struggle, often greedily, for power, . . . we should not agree that these facts undermine the very project of pursuing truth and objectivity."[20] She adds that "if we should conclude that our norms are human and historical rather than immutable and eternal, it does not follow that the search for a rational justification of moral norms is futile."[21]

THE ROLE OF RELIGION WITHIN THE CURRICULUM

The heated and serious contemporary debate about the validity of normative claims, the complex mix of modern and postmodern perspectives on religion among faculty and students, widespread ignorance about religion, and the serious financial concerns of church-related colleges and universities call for a reevaluation of the role of religion in the curriculum and the precise nature and aims of the religion requirement. Although one cannot propose a single way to incorporate religion into the curriculum that could fit all church-related academic institutions (or even all institutions within one denomination), there are many reasons for arguing that if they want to become or continue to be institutions in which religious and ethical issues are taken seriously and are part of the broader academic conversation, then they should include within the curriculum: (1) an in-depth study of at least one or two world religions other than Christianity; (2) a comprehensive introduction to Christianity; and (3) a course that explores basic ethical issues, ethical decision making, and diverse normative claims that provide the basis for particular ethical positions. Since institutions have different staffing needs and undergraduate programs, the way to address these topics could vary, such as by requiring specific courses in these areas or by incorporating them into interdisciplinary courses.

One of the reasons for including in the curriculum an in-depth study of at least one or two religions other than Christianity is that it is an exemplary way church-related colleges can take seriously the fact that we live in an increasingly interdependent world with a multitude of cultures, religions, moral claims, and traditions. If one is to understand the diversity found within our own culture and among the various cultures of the world, then one must also gain access to informed perspectives on religion. This is one of the most common reasons scholars have given for arguing that all undergraduate institutions (secular and church-related) should either require one religion course or at least intentionally integrate religious perspectives into the undergraduate curriculum.

Nussbaum, for example, has argued that since we live in a highly plural and interdependent world, and since religion is a significant dimension of human diversity, religion should be a part of the undergraduate curriculum. She rightly claims that religion is of "fundamental importance to all political and economic interactions with the world's varied cultures" and thus "all students should gain some understanding of the major world religions."[22] She claims that this could be achieved in several ways, such as through a world civilization course. Yet she firmly states that religion should be a "nonnegotiable part of the undergraduate curriculum."[23]

Warren Nord, too, proposes that religion be included in a liberal arts education and that all universities require "as an absolute minimum, an introductory course in religion."[24] One of the reasons he cites for a required religion course is its importance for understanding pluralism, including the pluralism within North American culture. He recognizes that our own culture is religiously pluralistic and that "if we are to live together, then we need to understand the diverse religious backgrounds of people in our culture."[25] Furthermore, he claims that religious liberty is an important part of our understanding of America and that it can be preserved only if we understand "the sources, the meaning, and the implications of the First Amendment."[26] Nord's perspectives are echoed in the work of William Scott Green, who argues that education about pluralism and American history is closely tied to education about religion. He believes that "it is highly likely that America's ability to affirm differences as a social benefit derives in some significant way from the constitution's commitment to religious freedom." Thus, "for students to understand what is at stake in religious freedom, they must understand what is at stake in religion itself."[27]

Although Martin Marty does not specifically prescribe a religion course as a required part of the undergraduate curriculum, he does give many grounds for the importance of teaching and studying religion not only in church-related colleges but also "in the higher academy that we often call secular." Like Nord, Nussbaum, and others, Marty believes that understanding religion is an important aspect of understanding pluralism and the Other. "Religion is one of the most revealing dimensions of pluralism," he states, because it serves both to pocket people in enclaves and, at the same time, to help people engage in "criss-crossing between these subcultures."[28] He also strongly encourages the study and teaching of religion for a whole list of additional reasons: it is globally pervasive, has influenced cultures in a number of ways, and "commends itself for study by anyone who wants to understand humans."[29]

There are even stronger reasons for church-related colleges and universities to include in the curriculum an in-depth examination of at least one or two religions other than Christianity. In addition to arguing for the inclusion of a knowledge of world religions on the basis of pluralism, a church-related college can also base its interest in other religions on theological grounds within the Christian tradition itself. Understanding other faiths can be seen as part of an attitude of empathy and compassion for others tied to the Christian mandate "to love thy neighbor." For even though Christians have various views of the possible truth of other religions and disagree about reasons for learning about other faiths, all would agree that compassion involves learning about the situation and beliefs of others. Furthermore, as Pope John Paul II has said (and as Nussbaum points out), learning about the diversity of other faiths can help us understand the mystery of human existence. "To cut oneself off from the reality of difference—or, worse, to attempt to stamp out that difference—is to cut oneself off from the possibility of sounding the depths of the mystery of human life." "Our respect for the culture of others is . . . rooted in our respect for each community's attempt to answer the question of human life . . . every culture has something to teach us about . . . that complex truth. Thus the 'difference' which some find so threatening can, through respectful dialogue, become the source of a deeper understanding of the mystery of human existence."[30]

David Tracy adds that indeed part of the return to otherness in postmodernism is "the return of biblical Judaism and Christianity to undo the complacencies of modernity, including modern theology."[31] The turn to the other disrupts or interrupts "the continuities and similarities masking the increasingly deadening sameness of the modern world view."[32] Here, expressions of otherness include "God's shattering otherness, the neighbor's irreducible otherness, the othering reality of 'revelation,' not only the consoling modern communality of 'religion.' "[33] Attention to forms of theological otherness is, for Tracy, "one way to try to pay serious theological attention to the change all around us—changes determined perhaps by the Divine Spirit who blows whither She will."[34]

In addition to the study of religions other than Christianity, the curriculum at a church-related college or university should include an introduction to Christianity. There are several reasons for including a comprehensive introduction to the Christian tradition at church-related colleges and universities. First, as stated above, many students know very little about Christianity (even when they come with a Christian background or are confessing Christians). Although professors at these institutions might once have assumed that students come with some knowledge of Christianity, this is no longer the case. As a theology professor who has taught at three church-related colleges, I am surprised that many students who were confirmed and are confessing Christians know little about religions and have serious misconceptions about them, including Christianity. For example, in an initial survey given two years ago to sixty students in a course on Christianity, only nine could define the term the "Exodus," not one could define "Babylonian Exile," and less than one-third correctly guessed (in a multiple-choice question) the century in which the Reformation took place. Furthermore, although many of them were science majors, almost all students assumed that all Christians are creationists and reject the theory of evolution, and only five students claimed they had ever participated in a discussion on the relation between Christianity and scientific theories such as evolution.[35]

Second, an introduction to Christianity should be a part of the curriculum at a church-related college because it is important for understanding the Western tradition and, even more particularly, American history and thought. Even when college programs seek to emphasize multiculturalism and an understanding of non-Western cultures, most of them recognize the importance of learning about Western culture and ideas. Christianity has played such a major role in shaping Western thought that it should be included in a liberal arts education.

A third reason for including such an introduction to Christianity in the curriculum at a church-related institution is that an understanding of Christianity is related to its heritage and, in many cases, its mission. Some institutions state this aspect of their mission very clearly. Among the ELCA colleges, for example, the mission of Gustavus Adolphus College states that the educational program aims to foster "a mature understanding of the Christian faith." St. Olaf's mission states that it provides an education that is "committed to the liberal arts, rooted in the Christian Gospel, and incorporating a global perspective" and that it "offers a distinctive environment that integrates teaching, scholarship, creative activity, and opportunities for encounter with the Christian Gospel and God's call to faith."[36] Although some ELCA institutions do not include direct statements about Christian faith in their mission, they typically at least acknowledge the Christian and Lutheran heritage of the school. Roanoke College, for example, states that it "honors its Christian heritage and its founding by Lutherans in 1842, while welcoming and reflecting a variety of religious traditions."[37]

An introduction to Christianity could be designed in a number of ways and could emphasize the Bible, the history of Christianity, or Christian doctrine. It could be taught within a core course of the first-year curriculum or be part of a religion requirement or requirements. However, since students tend to know very little about the Christian tradition and many need a genuine introduction to the subject, it should include the following aims: (1) introduce some central biblical texts and issues of biblical interpretation; (2) introduce selected primary classic or contemporary theological texts; (3) provide an historical framework for understanding Christianity; (4) explore central themes and questions of the Christian tradition as well as aspects of its rich diversity, including an examination of the particular religious tradition that has shaped the college or university and an introduction to diverse ways in which Christianity is being lived out today; and (5) as with any course in religion or ethics, help students think critically about public religious and ethical issues and about their own convictions.

Combining study of the Christian tradition with at least one or two other religious traditions has several merits, particularly for contemporary students. The focus on two or three traditions (instead of none at all or on all "world religions") seems more appropriate for students who tend to have scattered impressions of religious traditions through the media or popular culture, but who have rarely had opportunities to study any religious tradition (even their own) in depth. Further, students will learn more about each tradition and about their own convictions if they are able to compare and contrast two or three religious traditions on selected crucial issues and questions. Finally, by learning how to explore two or three religious traditions in depth, students will gain the tools and the resources necessary to research other religious traditions in the future.

Church-related colleges and universities should also include in the curriculum a way for students to address both classic and current public ethical issues and to explore grounds for their own ethical positions. What is the best way to offer such a course to students today, especially when many of them hesitate to discuss ethical issues or to take a stand on them and have had little or no experience reflecting consciously on moral issues? How does an institution avoid either dogmatism or more commonly, the "value jumble sale" that George Dennis O'Brien claims is so much a part of the contemporary "moral" curriculum?[38] What is the best way for students to test and to sharpen their own convictions and to enable them to contribute to public debate in the future?

O'Brien offers some helpful suggestions for moving students toward "an (educated) attitude of mind toward values—even and especially their most cherished values."[39] He believes it is important for the professor to be "an individual obviously committed to a deep tradition of value."[40] He also suggests having some kind of common curriculum so that students can discuss values with others and extending the program over two years so students have an opportunity to "sift and resift" in order to create "insight and assurance."[41] Finally, he highlights the importance of creating an ambiance on the campus that fosters faculty-faculty, faculty-student, and student-student conversation about values and ethical issues. In addition, since students today easily fall into a position of moral relativism, a course on ethics should introduce them to various ethical theories and to diverse sides of the contemporary debate about the validity of moral and ethical claims.

One approach that some church-related colleges have found helpful and that speaks to many of O'Brien's concerns is designing courses on ethical issues as interdisciplinary and team-taught. In a team-taught setting professors can help create a rich conversation about values by showing students different approaches to ethical issues, by discussing their own differences in regard to an ethical issue, or by outlining the different grounds for the same ethical position. Professors typically enjoy teaching these team-taught courses because they learn about approaches and ideas in other fields, and students appreciate the opportunity to see professors wrestle with difficult moral problems, to learn about the views of other students, and to explore more fully the grounds for their own convictions.

The *Paideia* program at Luther College and the honors program at Christ College (the honors college of Valparaiso University) are models in this respect. In both of these programs all first-year students participate in a two-semester course that focuses on the close reading of selected texts from Western and non-Western traditions. The courses are team-taught by professors representing several disciplines. This first-year course gives all students a chance to discuss a number of religious, literary, and political questions on the basis of a common set of texts, thereby providing a solid basis for upper division courses in both programs. At Christ College, sophomores take two further common courses (one on art, literature, and music and the other on Christianity), and juniors and seniors take seminars that address religious and ethical questions. At Luther, the second part of the program (taken during the junior or senior year) requires students to take a course that focuses on ethical issues and decision-making. The course is team-taught by two or three professors from different fields (including one professor from either philosophy or religion) who design a course that focuses on one of a variety of ethical issues (such as hunger, peace, perspectives on the body, environmental issues, economic justice, and health programs). By using common texts, extending the program over two or three years, and incorporating interdisciplinary courses, both of these programs generate a rich and vital discussion among students and faculty about religious and ethical questions.

In the contemporary context, with tight budgets and many changes in staffing taking place, it is also important to take into consideration the class size and staffing of courses on religion and ethics. Financial concerns at many church-related institutions have already affected class size and staffing in these courses. If religion or ethics are taught as general education requirements, faculty must offer several sections of each course. These sections are often large (with thirty or more students) and frequently taught by adjunct faculty.

Church-related colleges and universities should make a great effort to ensure that at least one of the required courses that addresses religion or ethics is small (about fifteen to eighteen students). Since students are not used to speaking about religious or ethical issues in a public, academic setting, they are much more willing to express their ideas if the class is small and they feel as if they know their classmates. A small class size can foster the kind of "practice of freedom" that writer and educator bell hooks advocates: a classroom in which everyone feels compelled to contribute, there is a shared respect for individual voices, and the particular experiences of all participants are viewed as significant.[42] A smaller classroom also provides a more promising context for practicing the virtue that Parker Palmer finds essential to a more communal way of knowing: the capacity for creative conflict. For Palmer, knowing and learning are communal acts that require members of the community "to confront each other critically and honestly over alleged facts, imputed meanings, or personal biases and prejudices."[43] Although one can nourish this kind of healthy conflict within a large group of students, it is easier to achieve with a group of fewer than twenty students.

Another important reason to ensure that at least one course addressing religion or ethics is small is to enable professors to assign papers that help them gain a clear sense of students' specific questions and the ways in which the students are developing arguments and grounding their own perspectives. Sadly, it is often classes that fulfill the religion requirement at church-related colleges that are some of the largest, and professors are often required to teach several sections of the same course with thirty students in each. Depending on the teaching load at various institutions, this can mean that a professor can have sixty or ninety students in his or her religion classes in one semester. With such a large group of students, it is easy to justify giving objective tests instead of assigning essays or papers. Yet it is only by writing such papers that students can explore more seriously and critically their own religious and ethical convictions and give grounds for their views.

Smaller class sizes in at least one course will also allow professors to require research papers on religious and ethical issues (and not simply short response papers to a text or question). Since students think of religion and ethics as very private and subjective matters, they are often unaware of the long intellectual tradition of Christianity and of the tremendous resources and rich research in the areas of ethics, theology, and religious studies today. By writing a research paper and thereby being "in conversation" with scholars who have thought about a particular issue, students learn to think and formulate their views more critically.

Church-related institutions should also think more carefully about the staffing of required courses in religion and try to ensure that they are taught by qualified professors with records of teaching excellence and a critical appreciation of the Christian tradition. Furthermore, they should be full-time, tenure-track professors who are known by students and with whom students can speak about religious and ethical issues long after the course is over. Often students will continue to reflect on particular issues raised in a religion or theology course and want to discuss them with a professor a semester or even one or two years after a course has ended. Too often, because adjunct labor is inexpensive and religion requirements demand several sections, these classes are taught by adjunct faculty who might only teach at the institution one or two years or might be on campus just two or three days a week, making it more difficult for students to continue a conversation with them.[44]

Furthermore, using temporary appointments (no matter how qualified or gifted) to teach religion requirements sends a message to students that the courses are not important to the faculty or the institution.

Although church-related institutions should include the investigation of Christianity, other religions, and ethical issues into the curriculum, these institutions should not rely on these means alone for fostering meaningful discussion of religious and ethical issues. They should also not depend only on professors of religion or theology to generate this kind of discussion but seek many other avenues as well. For example, they should support a strong chapel program. The excellent chapel program at Gustavus Adolphus, for example, attracts about five hundred students a day for its morning services; the college emphasizes the importance of these services by scheduling no classes or meetings during this twenty-minute period. Other ways to promote discussion about religious and ethical issues include special speakers and events, public debates, service learning projects, and the "natural inclusion" of religious issues in courses outside the religion department.

Because many new faculty come to church-related institutions with little or no background in religion or Christianity, it is also important for the administration to provide an orientation for new faculty that addresses the religious tradition of the college and the ways in which it still informs its mission and aims. The orientation should also point out ways that the religious dimension of the college's mission fits with other stated goals of the college (such as diversity and academic excellence). New members of the faculty are often relieved to discuss these issues (especially if they never attended a church-related college), if they know very little about Christianity in general or about the specific tradition of the college, or if they hold modern assumptions about religion as private and as separate from or inimical to the academic life. Through such orientations new faculty members learn that most church-related colleges and universities seek to affirm academic freedom of inquiry while emphasizing the religious heritage and mission of the college. Once new faculty members learn about the religious tradition of the college and some of the positive

influences of this tradition on campus life, they can more easily become strong advocates for preserving its mission as a
college of the church.

CONCLUSION

The life and mission of any institution is clearly multifaceted,
and academic study can influence students in many more ways
than described above. The aim of this paper has been to reflect
on the curriculum in relation to one goal of many strong church-
related colleges and universities: to create a setting in which
religious and ethical issues are taken seriously and are a vital
part of academic life. If church-related academic institutions
want to sustain or begin a rich campus-wide conversation about
religious and ethical issues, they will need to think more intentionally about the role of religion in the curriculum, especially as they face financial constraints, hire new faculty, and
serve a new generation of students. They will need to incorporate into their academic programs an introduction to Christianity, the study of at least one or two other religions, and
critical reflection on ethical issues. In addition, many existing
avenues for fostering conversation about religious and ethical
issues will need to be strengthened. By doing so, they not only
deepen the education of students but also serve the church
and the wider community by providing a unique public forum for discussing religious and ethical issues. Churches also
need to support church-related colleges and schools by offering financial assistance, encouraging young people to attend
church-related colleges, and recognizing the important and
unique role these institutions can play in fostering serious and
informed conversation about religion and ethics in our mod-
ern/postmodern context.

From the Ties that Bind to Way-Stations: The Dynamics of Religious Commitment among Students and Their Families

D. JONATHAN GRIESER AND CORRIE E. NORMAN

I

The church-related college has undergone renewed scrutiny in recent years. In important books, scholars such as George Marsden have examined the origins of church-related institutions in the religious and cultural history of the United States.[1] Marsden noted the fact that many of the U.S.'s most prominent institutions of higher learning were founded by and for religious denominations, and have since severed all ties with their founding churches. He also called into question the future of church-related colleges. His work and that of a number of other scholars and educational administrators have led to a reexamination of the relationship of the church-related college to its denomination. Most of this reexamination seems to have focused on structural ties. Indeed, one can see in the recent tightening of the relationship between the Roman Catholic Church and its colleges and universities an attempt to codify the relationship between church and school. *Ex corde ecclesia* is only the most obvious example of what has been a wrenching debate in many institutions. How do these colleges and universities embody the ethos of their religious traditions? What is the connection between the principle of academic freedom and the institution's denominational affiliation?

We have found it interesting that much of this talk of strengthening and nurturing the relationship between church and college addressed institutional relationships or faculty identity. What seems to have been less important in the debate is the place of the students themselves. The ever more competitive marketplace of higher education has meant that students choose their colleges for more complex reasons and that they approach their college choices much more self-consciously than their parents or grandparents did. But among those reasons for selecting a college, church-relatedness continues to play a role. We taught at the University of the South, which is owned by the Episcopal Church, for five years. In our time there, we began to notice the many ways in which students dealt with Sewanee's denominational affiliation and we wish to examine in greater detail how students' religious lives shape and are shaped by the church-related college.

When we began discussing this issue, it became clear that what we intended was something different from what other commentators and authors had done. Since James Fowler published his formative work on faith development, it has become common to understand faith in terms of stages.[2] Sharon Parks examined in greater detail the stages through which young adults pass. She makes clear that the years during which young adults attend college are of crucial significance for their overall faith development as they distance themselves from their families, form new attachments, and explore cultural and intellectual worlds that may expand their horizons considerably.[3] It is equally clear that this process exists in tension with the traditional goals of church-related colleges, which were founded to shape young adults as future stalwarts of denominational activities and institutions. Further complicating matters for these colleges, many members of their faculties, having experienced just such an expansion of horizons in their undergraduate days, now see their pedagogical obligation as at least in part subverting their students' denominational commitments.

The reality we encountered at Sewanee was not what we expected. Even those students who seemed to be most committed to the Episcopal Church related to it in ways other than we had anticipated. At the same time, we noticed how easily students from other denominations seemed to find meaning in the religious life of All Saints' Chapel and the various programs offered by the chapel staff. As we sought to understand these religious dynamics among our students, we found most helpful the work of Wade Clark Roof.

In a series of works beginning in 1993, Roof has analyzed the religious ideas and behavior of members of the baby boom generation. In *A Generation of Seekers*, he analyzed data derived from interviews conducted in 1989. More recently, *Spiritual Marketplace* revisited many of the same subjects five years later. His analysis is of enormous significance for understanding the present and future of religious institutions, from the denominational level, down to the local congregation. In both books, Roof demonstrates the continuing importance of the baby boomers' search for meaning, especially spiritual meaning.[4]

According to Roof, the cultural upheavals of the sixties alienated boomers from the institutional church in unprecedented numbers. Surprisingly, this was true even for those who had remained aloof from the counter-cultural movements of the decade. In the eighties, Roof detected a return of baby boomers to the church; though the attitudes and behaviors exhibited by boomers now in their thirties and forties were quite different from those of their parents. They were much more individualistic, much more likely to wander in and out of church attendance, much more distrustful of institutions. Religion had become for them an overwhelmingly personal thing, so much so, that many found the word "religion" itself distasteful because of its institutional connotations. For this group of people, "spirituality" was a term they found much more comfortable.

In interviews conducted in 1988 and 1989, Roof found a significant growth in interest in religious and spiritual matters. Some of this was expected given boomers' interest in Eastern philosophy and religion in the sixties. For many this interest had continued over the years. At the same time, Roof noted an increase in involvement in traditional religious institutions. Many boomers had returned to church after decades of uninvolvement. This return he attributed in large part to boomers' having become parents and wanting to offer religious education and religious experience to their children.

In his follow-up research, Roof discovered that many of those who had returned to church in the late eighties had wandered away again, often as their children grew up and left home. In fact, the percentage of baby boomer church-goers had remained roughly constant. What he learned was that people who had still not returned to church in the late eighties had found their way back in the mid-1990s.

Roof concludes that Americans, and babyboomers in particular, have shifted from "unquestioning belief to a more open, questing mood." The result has been the emergence of a "quest culture" in which he detects "a search for certainty, but also the hope for a more authentic, intrinsically satisfying life."[5] The title of Roof's second book makes clear that he understands boomers as consumers of religion and religious institutions. That metaphor has both negative and positive connotations. On the one hand, it means that boomers will leave an institution that they do not think serves their needs; on the other, it means they often have a clear sense of what they want from religion or spirituality, and they take an active role in seeking it out.

This broad cultural change has had an immense impact on the ways Americans experience and relate to religion. While Roof focused on the effects of these changes for members of the baby boomer generation, he took note as well of the impact on younger Americans. With their parents in this questing mode, the way in which young adults relate to religious institutions and religious questions has also undergone transformation. Roof points out that family plays a decisive role in the transmission of religious commitments across the generations. He identifies a gradient: "a religious script is more easily transmitted from one generation to another where there is strong parental influence and the reinforcement of a religious environment." When parents have moderate commitments, their children are less likely to share their parents' faith; they are least likely to when their parents are secularists.[6]

Roof observes that family exerts its influence on the religious commitments of individuals in several ways. He stresses the importance of symbolic families, by which he means not only the media-constructed images of family, but also the people outside of the immediate family who play an important role. In addition, there is a creative tension between individuals and others (family members or not) who may be role models of religious practice, yet whose behavior for whatever reason, is not emulated.[7] Roof contends that these symbolic families, with their appeal to a nostalgic past and as products of a selective and constructed memory, continue to serve a "stabilizing and boundary-maintaining" function.[8]

Given the importance of family in creating religious identity, we wish to examine the relationship between family, students' religious commitments, and the church-related college. The University of the South's unique character plays a fascinating role in our students' religious development. While other institutions may affect the religious commitments of their students differently, we suspect that administrators, chaplains, and faculty at all church-related colleges would do well to examine the interrelationship of family, church, and college.

II

The University of the South, familiarly known as Sewanee, is set on a 10,000-acre campus atop the Cumberland plateau of middle Tennessee. Rich in academic and religious tradition, Sewanee was founded in 1857 by Southern Episcopalians who wanted to provide their young men with an alternative to the Ivy League schools of the North. After the Civil War, it became a place where Confederate officers and their widows made new lives for themselves.[9] Sewanee is still owned by the Episcopal dioceses of the South. Though much muted now, the school's Southern heritage remains an important part of Sewanee's present and there are ongoing debates about its continued relevance for the university. In these debates, the Episcopalian connection inevitably plays a role. While Sewanee has avoided the doctrinal litmus tests that have faced faculty at other church-related colleges, the meaning of the church relationship for the school, for its academic life, and for the spiritual lives of its students remains unclear. Perhaps because of the Episcopalian emphasis on liturgy, for most members of the academic community the church relationship is embodied in Sewanee's ritual life of convocation, commencement, and worship.

Religion manifests itself in many ways at Sewanee. The Episcopal Church is represented on campus by one of the denomination's thirteen seminaries. A large cross, a war memorial that combines religion, heritage, and nature in a dramatic setting overlooking the valley below is often cited by students as a place of spiritual repose. Most prominently, the geographical and sentimental center of campus is All Saints' Chapel. Built in neogothic style, All Saints' is the site of regularly scheduled worship services throughout the year. It also serves as the location where entering students sign the honor code, the school year's three academic convocations take place, and baccalaureate and commencement are held.

Its association with the rhythms of academic life gives many students a sentimental attachment to the chapel. In addition, the building itself is linked with the school's tradition in significant ways. In the narthex, stained glass windows depict the history of the institution from the laying of the cornerstone in the years before the Civil War, the destruction of that cornerstone by Union Army soldiers, and the building of the school after the war. The university's history is linked to salvation history in the stained glass of the nave and apse, culminating in the window above the high altar which depicts Christ enthroned above the mountain, with a procession below of clergy and laity entering the chapel. The window is a powerful image of the link between the Episcopal Church's liturgical life and the academic life of the institution.

Sewanee has seen considerable change in the thirty years since women were admitted as undergraduates. In the last decade, Sewanee's undergraduate enrollment has grown to 1300. At the same time, it has seen considerable growth in facilities, faculty, and endowment. As a result, its reputation and profile have risen considerably. Recently, it has taken pride in its classification among the top twenty-five national liberal arts colleges in the annual survey produced by *US News and World Report*. This national reputation has helped to diversify its student body beyond its traditional pool of upper-middle class Southerners. While many of its students continue to come from the South, increasingly it has attracted students from other parts of the United States. The percentage of Episcopalian students remains in the mid- to high thirties, while the number of Catholics continues to grow. There are still very few non-Christian students. All of these changes have led to some tensions on campus concerning the relationship of the institution to its past.

In the midst of these transitions, the chapel serves as the locus for a variety of ministries that reflect both continuity and change. Besides the traditional Sunday morning service of Eucharist and the daily office during the week, a well-attended contemporary service on Sunday evening attracts many students of all religious backgrounds. The chaplaincy has a number of outreach programs, from a local chapter of Habitat for Humanity to mission trips scheduled during Spring Break. About the time we arrived at Sewanee, a Catechumenate program was developed for students and others interested in centering themselves more firmly in the Episcopal tradition. While the chaplaincy includes both clergy and nonordained professionals, there are no formal provisions through the chapel to provide ministry for students from other denominations. A Baptist deacon on the university staff has initiated an informal Bible study and prayer group. There is a weekly mass begun by a group of Roman Catholic students and faculty.

III

Before the 1960s, chapel attendance was required. When this requirement was dropped, the curriculum was altered to include a required course in Religion. (Later that requirement was amended to include Philosophy courses.) Many students met this requirement with the "Introduction to Religion" course. We developed the "family religious history project" for our version of this course for a number of reasons. Sewanee's Introduction to Religion course focused on the place of religion in the modern world and sought to introduce students to the general study of religion by having them read authors like Mircea Eliade and help them reflect on the changing nature and role of religion in contemporary society. The family project was initially designed as an opportunity for students to do "fieldwork" on what was assumed to be something quite familiar, the religious commitments and activities of family members across the generations. They were expected to use some of the methodological approaches they had encountered in class as they analyzed their own and their families' experiences.

Over time, we continued to revise the assignment. Eventually it was tied with readings in religious sociology (Bellah's *Habits of the Heart* and writings of Wade Clark Roof) and it usually involved a major rewrite.[10] An initial draft usually provided little more than the raw data and our comments and instructions urged students to work systematically with the scholarly analyses they had read. Occasionally, students would reinterview their subjects and ask questions derived directly from Bellah and Roof.

What was intended to help students understand themselves and contemporary religion became for us a unique window into the religious lives of contemporary students and their families.[11] The best students made the connections between their own histories and Bellah's and Roof's analyses as a means of examining their families' experiences. In addition, we learned a great deal about the changing face of Christianity, especially in the South.

We hoped our students would focus on their families' religious affiliation and practice. While many students followed our instructions carefully, others, no matter how often we dissuaded them, chose to focus on religious belief rather than practice. This was hardly surprising, given that on the first day of class, when asked for a definition of religion, the overwhelming majority of students included belief as the central element. Still, patterns of long-standing family religious involvement did emerge. There were familiar stories of long-time family involvement in a particular denomination, or for some, a specific local congregation. On the other hand, many students described their families' journey in and out of religious communities or from one denomination to another.

In the beginning, we asked them only to interview three members of their family; again, as we revised the project in the five years we used it, we became more specific. We wanted as much generational diversity as possible so we asked that they include a member of their grandparents' generation, their parents', and their own. Eventually, we asked them to provide autobiographical information as well.

Our students were by no means a cross-section of the student body at Sewanee. Most students in our Introduction classes were freshmen or sophomores; but because it was a required course for Religion majors, we occasionally had upper-class students as well. Fifty-four percent of Sewanee students fulfilled the Philosophy/Religion requirement through courses in the Religion department while we were on the faculty; yet we sensed that some students from conservative Protestant denominations avoided the Religion department. Of the projects analyzed in this essay, 39% reflected Episcopalian affiliation; 22% other mainline Protestant; 15% Baptist; 14% Roman Catholic; 3% other Protestant. The remainder either had no religious affiliation or their family's affiliation could not be determined. One Muslim student completed the project. These percentages compare favorably to overall percentages concerning religious affiliation of Sewanee students. Official documents claim 35% of Sewanee students claim Episcopal membership. These numbers contrast sharply with church membership figures for the South as a whole, where Southern Baptists predominate, far outnumbering both mainline Protestant and Catholic.[12]

Of course, as Roof points out in *Spiritual Marketplace*, religious affiliation and commitment is an ever-changing phenomenon. Many of those students we pigeon-holed into one denominational categories could relatively easily fit into another. Their parents, even many of their grandparents, had drifted in and out of active participation in religious institutions. A Catholic grandmother admitted that at an earlier point in her life she had not attended services for over fifteen years. One student marveled that as a teenager, her grandmother had walked several miles to attend church on a bi-weekly basis. At the same time, this student chided herself for allowing her own attendance at Baptist services to lapse while she attended Sewanee. She did not notice that her attendance was almost as regular as her grandmother's had been fifty years earlier, and that they were restricted by the very same reasons—the distance they lived from a Southern Baptist church.

Together these projects provide further evidence of the impact the cultural changes of the last decades have had on traditional religious commitments. What is interesting, however, is the degree to which such religious change is a constant theme across all of the generations. The Baptist subgroup shows considerable movement from other Protestant denominations and almost half of the Catholic families had non-Catholics among the parents or grandparents. The mainline Protestants and Episcopalians are even more mobile, not just from generation to generation, but even within the lifetime of the students themselves. Many students remembered switching churches as children, for reasons they often learned only while working on this project. Some families or family members were involved simultaneously in different churches. One young woman belonged to an Episcopal church but attended a United Methodist youth group while in high school. This is not an uncommon story.

Most of these students' parents are baby boomers, fitting into Roof's "Generation of Seekers." Again, supporting Roof's arguments, while there does not seem to be overwhelming evidence of the parents' participation in the high-profile counter-cultural activities of the sixties, it is clear that cultural transformations have had an enormous impact on families. One father's testimony might be typical. His son reports that "he is fond of saying that the only protest he went to in college was by accident; he simply stumbled into it." Although he identifies his family as politically and religiously conservative, his mother, a convert to Catholicism at her marriage, welcomed the increased participation by women in Roman Catholic worship, a development she attributed directly to cultural change of the sixties.

Rarely is a parent identified as a new-ager, although several students interviewed aunts or uncles precisely because they participated in Eastern religions or new religious movements.[13] The relative absence of New Age activities among our parents may be underreported since we were especially interested in institutional involvement and most students restricted themselves to traditional religious activities. On the other hand, it may also be the case that families with strong New Age tendencies would find an institution like Sewanee a problematic learning environment.

Remarkably, there is little evidence of student involvement in the fastest-growing sectors of American Protestantism—Pentecostalism and the nondenominational mega-church. As we have already noted, this may also reflect the students' self-selection of Introduction to Religion; it may also be due to a larger demographic reality, that Sewanee does not attract students from such traditions. Interestingly, even the students who are most clearly identified with conservative denominations (Evangelical Covenant Church, Presbyterian Church of America) had earlier attended mainline churches (Episcopalian and Presbyterian Church [USA]).

Finally, there is relatively little evidence of the "unchurched." Almost all students report that their family had attended church when they were children, and almost all report that at least one of their parents remains involved, though perhaps only at the most superficial level. At most three or four of the parents interviewed expressed no religious inclination whatsoever. But when students turned to cousins or siblings, the alienation from institutional religion, and from religious experience in general, was much higher. We suspect that siblings were interviewed precisely because they were estranged from institutional religion. A surprising number of interviewed siblings identified themselves as atheists. Often, these students belonged to families that had attended church sporadically while they were children, or whose parents had expressed the importance of their children reaching their own individual religious convictions. At the same time, however, many siblings who were interviewed expressed strong religious convictions and were deeply involved in religious communities (often very conservative churches).

If their parents are religious nomads, even more transient are our students' religious commitments. That is quite to be expected, given both the analysis of families' religious commitments offered by Roof, and the work on stages of faith development by Fowler and Parks. Yet many of our students come to regard Sewanee as something of a home, and given the fierce loyalty to Sewanee exhibited by alumni, Sewanee comes to take on much greater significance in the lives of our students than do many other colleges. Thus we suspect that Sewanee, with its rich ritual life centered on the chapel and its appeal to tradition, comes to play an important role in the religious lives of our students. In a world where so much is in flux—students' personal lives, their values, their futures—the chapel serves as a rock of stability, while they are in school and long after. In fact, two students (among the few who mentioned that one of their parents had attended Sewanee) attributed their families' Episcopalianism to the fact that their parents had become familiar with the denomination while attending college. For other students with Sewanee parents, the same was true. Although they had finally settled on another denominational home, they had attended Episcopal churches for a time because of their exposure to the Episcopal Church as students.

IV

Because Sewanee is an Episcopal institution, we have chosen in this essay to focus on those students identified, however nominally, as Episcopalian. The nature of our data makes it impossible to trace the path of our students' religious journey while at Sewanee but we are able to ascertain how they got where they are. One question of pertinence that we failed to ask was the extent to which Sewanee's religious affiliation contributed to students' decisions to attend. We posit that for Episcopalians there is some correlation between the two, no doubt a higher correlation for those families that show higher commitment to the Episcopal tradition.

The most obvious members of this group come from clerical families. Two students had priests for parents; one's mother was beginning the ordination process at the time of writing. In addition, two had priests for grandparents and one's aunt was ordained. One father was an administrator at an Episcopal prep school. This level of religious commitment in earlier generations certainly had its impact on our students, though one cannot generalize from such a small sample. What is interesting is the relationship of gender and family religious commitment. The Episcopal Church has ordained women to the priesthood only since 1977. Two female priests (and one aspirant) are represented in our sample. Their families show a much higher degree of Roof's "seeker" mentality. Although two of the three women grew up in the Episcopal church, all three went through periods of estrangement from the church. One's siblings include a Unitarian-Universalist and one who describes himself as a "latent Taoist. Occasionally attend Quaker meetings. Hang out with Bahais. Animist, maybe." In this case, the "seeker" mentality extends to the priest's children, one of whom has explored religious traditions from Wicca to Southern Baptist. Interestingly, she found Wicca too ceremonial, but continues to attend Episcopal services occasionally.

On the other hand, the daughter of a male priest exhibits strong conformity to Episcopalianism. Her father is a prominent priest whose family converted from another Protestant denomination when he was a boy. The family exhibits a strong commitment to the Episcopal liturgy and to the institution of the church. Her siblings are as involved in church activities as she is. She and her siblings were active in diocesan youth activities. Now she is a regular attender at Sewanee's chapel services. No doubt the preeminent place of All Saints' Chapel on campus and the familiar rhythms of the liturgy provide a comforting link with the religious life of her childhood and family.

A second group of students have even deeper ties to the Episcopal church than do those with parents and relatives among the clergy. These are cradle Episcopalians, whose families trace their Episcopal roots back for generations. At least two students mentioned by name prominent family members from the colonial period who were Anglican. For three students, "my family has been Episcopalian for as long as anyone can remember," was a common refrain.

Two of these young women traced the Episcopalian heritage through their mothers' families, while the other traced it through the father's. Of the three Episcopalian parents, two of them married spouses whose parents had become Episcopalian; the third spouse converted to Episcopalianism upon his marriage. No doubt these marriage patterns reflect the traditional social status of the Episcopal Church in the South. The student whose father joined this traditional Episcopal family said almost nothing about her father's religious background, because her mother's family seemed "a whole lot easier and quite interesting to follow back." One detects here the construction of a neat package, which may conceal a messier, and for the observer, more interesting past.

From Roof's perspective, however, such strategies fit perfectly into what he calls the symbolic family.[14] For these students, what matters is not so much the fact that a grandparent or parent converted to Episcopalianism; but the inherited memory that "we have been Episcopalian as long as anyone can remember." That these students deliberately selected Episcopalian family members to interview shows how powerful that constructed reality can be.

That students from such families would choose Sewanee is hardly surprising, for some families are as deeply or more rooted in Sewanee as they are in the Episcopal Church. Although students from such families make up a tiny percentage of the students whose families we are examining here, their link to the less institutional aspects of Sewanee's religious life does bear further scrutiny. None of them mentioned Sewanee's Episcopal connection as being of significance when making their college decision. In addition, none of them discussed their own religious commitments or their relationship with the Episcopal Church, or with All Saints' Chapel. It may be that such connections are so ingrained as to be taken for granted; it may also be that none of these students is particularly self-reflective about their religious commitments.

Another group of students fits comfortably into Roof's discussion. These are the children of "seekers," baby boomers whose lives have seen an ongoing quest for spiritual meaning. In Roof's analysis, such seekers, even when they belong to traditional denominations, are highly individualistic in their core beliefs. Their relationship to the church is tenuous; they are concerned to purchase meaning for themselves from the religious marketplace in which they find themselves.

As parents, seekers want to offer as much religious choice to their children as they have experienced. Unlike more traditional believers, they regard it as their child's choice whether to attend church and whether to belong. We have found an interesting dynamic among students whose parents conform to this paradigm. In the first place, it is often the case that students of such parents were heavily involved in church activities in their childhood and youth. They served as acolytes, attended Episcopal summer camps or Episcopal schools; they were active in church youth groups. But often this high level of engagement with the church does not survive the transition to college.

One student described his father in classic seeker terms. The son of generations of Methodist ministers (both his parents were ordained), the father found himself estranged from Christianity after his experiences in the Navy and in college. Reading Whitehead's *The History of the Warfare between Science and Religion* helped him make sense of the conflicts between science and religion that had worried him. He found his way to the Episcopal Church and raised two sons who were highly active in the Church as teens. While the family exhibited a high level of religious activity, the father continued to read widely in religious and theological texts, and passed this habit on to the elder son. After beginning college, the son found himself a very occasional attender of University services. He enjoyed serving as an acolyte at campus worship services, but his inherited intellectual curiosity meant that he had to rethink his religious commitments in light of his intellectual growth.

The poignant conflict between an active past and an awkward relationship with the church during the college years was brought home to us in another way. In an interview conducted for a different project, a young woman recalled fondly the roles she had assumed in her small home parish—from acolyte, to lector, to sexton. When she arrived at Sewanee, she was eager to participate in the religious life of the chapel. But she was a free spirit, inquisitive, nonconformist. In other words, she did not fit the profile of the "chapel brat" and ultimately abandoned all links to chapel programs.

For students like these, we suspect that their parents' relationships to the church have shaped the way they interact with Sewanee's institutional religion. One can see clearly the initial appeal of Sewanee for such students. It offered a college environment in which they could continue to pursue religious activities that had been important to them as teens. Yet when they arrived on campus they discovered that the seeking mentality they had inherited from their parents made them marginal members of the chapel community and they pursued their quests individually.

A third student may provide further evidence. His mother grew up Episcopalian, his father was a seeker, interested in religious matters but deeply cynical of religious institutions. He remembers occasionally attending Episcopal churches as a child, but even then his father's skepticism toward the church was clear. When he grew older, even that tenuous family link with the church eroded. Now his sister, in her mid-twenties, openly identifies herself as an atheist. This student has no ties to the college's religious institutions, yet ironically he chose to major in Religion. The father's quest became the son's academic specialty.

These examples bring home the complexity of students' relationships with their Episcopal past and Sewanee's Episcopal affiliation. The liturgical nature of Anglicanism offers young men and women different ways of relating to the church. Like their counterparts in other denominations, they may find a niche in Sunday School or youth group activities. Alternatively, they may find meaning from participating in the rich liturgical life of the church. But the two groups do not necessarily overlap.

Yet something in the Anglican tradition may overlap with the seeker mentality. The Hookerian sensibility of tolerant, nondoctrinaire truth seeking, articulated in Sewanee's mission statement as "seek[ing] the truth in the light of Christian faith," easily translates in the postmodern world to a personalization or relativization of religion that renders conformity and traditional religious involvement irrelevant. Neither students nor Episcopalians in general express this clearly. But many Episcopalians brought up in *the* faith have learned (perhaps unconsciously) to seek their *own* faith.

One of the important ways students are drawn into the worship life of All Saints' Chapel is through the University Choir, an eighty-member mixed voice group, for which members receive academic credit. The choir sings at the 11:00 Sunday morning service; at important services of the church year; at a monthly Evensong; and at the annual festival of lessons and carols. Choirmembers come from many religious backgrounds, but for many the choir, and the Episcopal liturgy through it, become central elements of their religious life. These students may not become Episcopalian, but their religious sensibilities often do. One Baptist student who enrolled in choir as a freshman was very troubled by the use of wine during "the Lord's Supper," as she put it. We watched that young woman become a gifted cantor and devotee of liturgical worship during her four years at Sewanee.

The impact of Sewanee's Episcopalian heritage on its students is made clear in another student's research. Her family is a paradigm of the seeker mentality. Her parents were raised Methodist and upon their marriage attended the Methodist church her mother had belonged to as a child. When they moved to another city, they explored other religious options, eventually settling into an Episcopal church because "they hoped to find something to serve their religious and spiritual needs." Her father also recalled that he hoped to find in the Episcopal church a community that welcomed doubters and fostered a more intellectual atmosphere. While social connections made the Episcopal church a likely possibility, the fact that her father was a Sewanee alumnus also played a role. For several reasons, the family soon left the Episcopal church and returned to a United Methodist congregation. Her father believed that in order to become a full member of the Episcopal parish he would have to accept completely Episcopal doctrine and practice. Over time, the parents' involvement in the church lessened dramatically. The student and her siblings were not required to attend services or Sunday School. When she interviewed a married older sister, currently an occasional attender at an Atlanta Methodist church, she discovered that the sister hoped to be an active churchgoer as a parent. Both she and her sister, like their father, contemplate becoming Episcopalian. What holds them back is the belief that such a change would reflect a full acceptance of Episcopal doctrine and worship. In this case we see at least some attraction to the church. At the same time, however, none of the family members has perceived in themselves the "comfort" level with Episcopalianism they regard as necessary to make the transition. This despite the fact that the father and two daughters attended Sewanee.

This family represents one side of the seeker experience. The father was uncomfortable changing denominations, but was equally uncomfortable in the church of his youth. While believing that religious education was important for his children, and feeling somewhat guilty for not seeing to their thorough religious upbringing, his alienation from organized religion remains deep. When asked about the place of religion in human life, he mentions its role in helping human beings understand death, suffering, and existence. Again in this case, complex and poignant interactions take place at the crossroads between the Anglican way of being and seeker religiosity.

Another student traces religious and social change through the lives of her parents and grandparents. Raised Baptist, her grandparents left the denomination when their small-town Baptist preacher inveighed against the local country club that employed her grandfather. They immediately began attending the local Episcopal church. After a move to a town in Tennessee that had no Episcopal church, they began attending a Presbyterian congregation with their children. Her father returned to the Episcopal Church when he left for college, and her parents attended an Episcopal church for a time after marriage. Her mother was Methodist, however, and convinced her husband to attend a Methodist church after their children were born. When they divorced, her father returned to the Episcopal church while her mother became estranged from institutional religion. He is a committed supporter of his parish and his daughter attends services with him regularly.

The anguish of divorce cuts fault lines across family religious commitments. In this instance, it is clear that divorce played a central role in the mother's withdrawal from church attendance. Many years after the fact, she now admits the possibility of reestablishing ties with organized religion, but as her daughter reports her mother's words, she retains considerable antipathy toward the church. At the same time, she expressed to her daughter the important role a group for divorced women, sponsored by a local Presbyterian church, had played for her.

In this and other instances, religion plays a role both in the parents' divorce and in the way children relate to their parents. The Episcopal Church seems to have offered many divorced people a spiritual haven after their families broke up and they withdrew from former religious communities. One mother was raised Roman Catholic, married a Protestant, baptized her children in the Catholic Church, but then became Episcopalian and continued attending the Episcopal Church after her divorce. Her daughter remains active in the Episcopal Church, while her teen-aged brother occasionally attends a youth group of another mainline church. What is most interesting about this family is that the grandmother, having been Roman Catholic for more than three decades, joined the Episcopal church. For both mother and grandmother, central in their decision was the Episcopal Church's more egalitarian attitude toward women.

In these two cases, one parent is an active church-goer, while the other is not. The student draws a close connection between her own religious practice and faith and that of the church-going parent. Yet there are important differences. In the second example, all three women assert the importance of individualism. The mother holds a number of nontraditional beliefs, such as reincarnation, while the grandmother expressed her belief in the importance of formulating one's beliefs by exploring a number of religious options before choosing a church home.

That the Episcopal liturgy can offer a bulwark against the ever-changing tides of contemporary American culture is a point made in different ways in many students' projects. But that theme is best expressed by a student whose father, raised Baptist, was exposed to the Episcopal Church while studying at a state university in the 1950s. In spite of divorce and remarriage, he apparently continued to participate in the Episcopal Church. A major shift occurred when his second wife, the student's mother, initiated a change to a parish that continued to use the 1928 *Book of Common Prayer.* This occurred when the student was thirteen. Her mother was raised Catholic but became Episcopal when she was not permitted to marry in the church because her fiancé was divorced. For this family, separated from its moorings in its traditional denominations by social change and divorce, the 1928 *Book of Common Prayer* protects them from the changes in both religion and society. The student comments of her father: "He refers to it as his 'true love' and his greatest happiness now is to see my little sister and I participate and develop our own love for the old prayer book." Ironically perhaps, these lovers of the old liturgy, while attracted to Sewanee's religious affiliation, are often alienated from worship at All Saints, which most often uses the modern Rite II form of the Episcopal liturgy. A few students have even begun attending a parish in the next town that uses the 1928 *Book of Common Prayer.*

V

Sewanee's geographical setting and its architecture have contributed mightily to a sense among students, alumni, and friends that the campus is itself "sacred space." That notion was brought home to us repeatedly in classes as we discussed concepts of sacred space and sacred time.[15] For many students, the natural wonders of the area made the sacred seem more accessible. The prominence of the chapel, too, lent a sense of sacrality, not only to Sewanee's religious life, but to all of life. One sees the importance of the chapel for students' religious lives in a number of ways. For some, the accessibility of the Sunday morning service meant that whatever their denominational affiliation, the chapel became their religious "home" while they were in college. This can be seen even decades later as several of our students remarked that their families were Episcopalian because their father had attended All Saints.

But even among students who retain close ties to their denominations, All Saints exerts a powerful appeal. One student remarked:

> One of my most memorable religious experiences is of my parents and I kneeling together to receive communion in All Saints' Chapel at the beginning of my freshman year. It was almost as if that single act permanently connected them to this place [where] I would be living without them for the next four years.

She comes from a family that is Presbyterian, although her mother was raised Catholic. Interestingly, her mother expresses some regret for having converted; nonetheless, as the daughter puts it, "my mother's desire for a family religion has been the driving force for religious involvement in our family." The student comments that her father was an unwilling church attender while she was a child, and only began to show greater involvement in religious activities in very recent years.

This points to an important characteristic of students whose families belong to other mainline denominations. In many cases, the family's ties to its denomination are quite tenuous. There is a consistent pattern of denomination-jumping, of "mixed" marriages and of unequal participation in religious activities by parents and children. Too, divorce wreaks havoc with religious affiliation. At the same time, there are examples of families whose denominational ties stretch back generations, but often students detect very different attitudes toward the churches in their own or their parents' generation. Not surprisingly, for these families, denominational ties play no role in college selection. Similarly, little mention is made by the student or their family members of Sewanee's religious affiliation.

Within this group, some interesting trends deserve mention. First, these students and their parents often claim to be conservative on moral and political issues. Even when they remain distant from religious institutions, they express the conviction that Christianity remains a bulwark against the moral decay of society. Parents often express the importance of attending church and of providing their children with religious education, and often express guilt feelings for having neglected these duties. These families tend not to exhibit clear evidence of "seeker" activity but they are strong individualists. Again and again, parents say that it is important their children make up their own minds on religious matters, even as they themselves expressed their religious independence from their families.

Many of these families have complex denominational ties. Often, one parent will have grown up in the denomination (Presbyterian, Methodist) in which the family now worships, while the other was raised Southern Baptist. Other couples have compromised by joining yet a third denomination. This has two important effects. A grandmother will continue to serve as a moral and religious beacon for the family, holding her children and grandchildren to a standard of participation, often by attending church with them. The other effect is even more interesting. When it is the father who changes denomination, there is a high likelihood that he will have very weak ties to his new church. That is less likely for the mother. Indeed, one mother who joined her husband's Methodist church upon marriage, continues to be actively involved while her divorced and remarried husband has joined a non-denominational congregation.

For children of religiously blended families, the trend is clear. When both parents are actively involved in the church, children are much more likely to be involved as well. On the other hand, when one or both is little involved, their children are even less active. One student made this clear. Her grandmother remains a devout Presbyterian. Her mother married a Southern Baptist but together her parents joined a Methodist church. She reports that her father was reluctant to attend and that she and her brother resisted attending as children. As a result, she gained relatively little knowledge of Methodist distinctives—

for example, she only discovered from a student's comment in a religion class at Sewanee that the United Methodist Church had bishops.

But there is another group of families from mainline denominations identifiable at Sewanee. These families have ties to their denominations as deep as the "cradle Episcopalians." They can document their families' involvement in a particular denomination back several generations. Some can go even further. One Lutheran student can trace her Lutheran roots back to the generation that emigrated from Germany in the 1850s. A Presbyterian can go even further, to the early eighteenth century. Both of these families have proud traditions of denominational fidelity. The Lutheran student saw little difference in how the generations of her family related to the church. No doubt her close relationship to the church was a product of the close connection between her family, the church, and the community in which she grew up. Her father was a Lutheran pastor, and an ancestor had founded the town which bore the family name.

On the other hand, the Presbyterian detected significant change. Perhaps in part because she comes from Charlotte, North Carolina, which has seen intense social change in the last thirty years, her family is much less committed to the denomination than earlier generations. Her grandfather was the son and grandson of Presbyterian ministers, married a Methodist but remained Presbyterian after a brief time of attending a Methodist church. Her Presbyterian father and Baptist mother apparently alternated churches for some years before settling on a Presbyterian congregation for reasons that were not made clear. For this student, although her father and grandfather identify Presbyterian theological issues such as predestination as factors in their continued involvement, she argues that they are Presbyterian primarily because of the family's traditions. Still, perhaps Presbyterian leaders would take comfort in noting the importance for both men of congregational democracy and a strong preacher.

For these two groups of students the encounter with Episcopal traditions at Sewanee can serve as a prod to reengage their own traditions. Certainly, those whose families are as rooted in their denominations as cradle Episcopalians may have powerful psychological, spiritual, and social reasons for highlighting their own connections to mainline denominations. On the other hand, students with weaker denominational ties might be motivated to seek ways of strengthening their denominational connections in an environment where personal identity is tied closely to affiliation and rootedness matters. With the intense social pressures of a small, isolated college like Sewanee, weak denominational ties might also encourage students to make at least the nominal jump to the Episcopal Church.

In fact, while denominational ties seem to be weakening across the board, some of the traditional movement between denominations recognized by sociologists long ago continues to take place among Sewanee students and their parents. To the extent that college choice is representative of a larger family strategy (conscious or unconscious) of moving up the ladder of social and economic class, Sewanee represents an important stage in that journey. For those students with family roots in traditionally lower-class denominations such as the Church of Christ and even Southern Baptist, Sewanee offers the possibility of putting that past firmly behind and solidifying the family's place in the upper middle class. A student with one set of Baptist grandparents and parents who compromised with the Methodist or Presbyterian Church now seems perfectly comfortable with the social and religious milieu of Sewanee.

While we have not focused much attention on two other large subgroups of our study—Baptists, and Roman Catholics—we suspect that something similar is taking place there. We taught at Sewanee just as the fallout over the fundamentalist "takeover" of the Southern Baptist Convention was becoming clear. For moderate Baptists, Sewanee offered a place where students and their families might avoid the contentious struggles that were taking place in local congregations and in the statewide and national conventions. It was also a way of avoiding the stigma of being identified as fundamentalist.

Among Catholic students, more complex dynamics seem in play. For those old aristocratic Catholic families of the South,

Sewanee is no doubt a relatively comfortable place. It has also attracted a number of conservative upper-class Catholic students from outside the South who are attracted to Sewanee's mythos and ritualism, while wishing to avoid the current tensions and "liberalization" they see in Catholic institutions. The Episcopal affiliation functions only in a negative way. As one student put it, "The heresy is often so subtle in Catholic institutions; at least here, I know that they're heretics."

But other Catholics are attracted to Sewanee as well. For the many third or fourth generation immigrant families, like the Baptists mentioned above, Sewanee is a sign of the family's successful assimilation. Another common theme among those who still identify themselves as Catholic, as well as the many, particularly women, who are either estranged from the church or have joined another denomination, is resistance to the Church's teachings on birth control and its attitude toward divorce and the role of women. Repeatedly these issues have led to a painful break for mothers and grandmothers of our students.

The importance of Roman Catholicism for European immigrants, particularly Italians, is evident in our sample. As Catholic students write about their grandparents, they often describe a situation in which family, church, and ethnic identity are intertwined. What is surprising is the number of intermarriages with non-Catholics even among the eldest generation. For their parents' and their own generation, these students often describe a relationship with the institutional church almost identical to that of mainline Protestants. Thus one student observes that both his parents were raised Catholic, did not attend mass as young adults, returned to the church only when their children were born; and stopped attending again, except for Christmas and Easter, when their children became teenagers. Another student observes that when his Catholic mother married his lapsed Church of Christ father, his father began attending mass, but only converted at the age of fifty. When asked why, he stated that "he was looking for something spiritual that had been missing for years and was not fulfilled by just attending mass."

VI

Roof's findings concerning the attitudes of baby boomers toward denominational institutions have profound implications for the futures of those institutions, whether they be local congregations or national denominational structures. They also have profound implications for church-related colleges. With the ties of boomers to their churches becoming weaker and the expression of their religious commitment more individualistic, the affinity of students and their parents for the church-related college will also become weaker. For a mainline denomination like the Episcopal Church, that has been the case for church-related colleges for a very long time. As for its own colleges, all but Sewanee have dropped their institutional affiliation.

With fewer students choosing colleges based on denominational affiliation, and colleges less committed to their denominational ties, the general prognosis for the future of the church-related college may seem bleak. But there is an alternative. Roof argues that the changes in the ways people relate to religious institutions have led to new structures and new opportunities for education and ministry. If that is the case, then church-related colleges might be able to foster students at the beginnings of their quests, and over the course of their students' lives, to continue to find ways of nurturing the questing mentality for their alumni and friends. For a place like Sewanee, ironically, it may be the most traditional manifestations of religion in ritual and sacred space that speak to the postmodern spiritual quest. Church-related colleges may not provide the ties that bind to denominational affiliation they once did, but they may become important way stations to seekers of all generations.

And what might all this mean for the role of faculty at church-related colleges? Three paradigms for that role have traditionally been offered. One stressed the importance of faculty as helping indoctrinate students into the religious commitments of the denomination. Another sought to break down students' traditional understandings and worldviews. A third argued for dispassionate objectivism in the classroom and outside. It seems to us that none of these three reflects the reality of our students' relationships to religion or, for that matter, to institutions of any sort. They are much more sophisticated than the paradigms would suggest. What does the "seeker" require of a teacher? Perhaps a different model is called for: not the model "churchman," not the dispassionate scientist, or the cultured despiser; but the fellow seeker, grounded in the sources of tradition, immersed in the dynamics of the present, and living out faithful and critical dialogue between the two. Not a master, or an expert, but a seasoned fellow-traveler.

✠

AFTERWORD

A Typology of Church-Related Colleges and Universities

Stephen R. Haynes

Attempts to classify religiously affiliated institutions of higher learning span the twentieth century. The first appeared in 1906 as part of the Carnegie Foundation for the Advancement of Teaching's "First Annual Report,"[1] which developed a five-part typology of church colleges based on the extent of their control by religious denominations. The Carnegie spectrum ranged from "absolute control and ownership" to "no formal . . . but strong sympathetic . . . connection."[2]

Several classification systems were advanced in the 1960s and 1970s, as researchers refashioned the wheel invented by others.[3] The Danforth Commission Study of 1966 distinguished four varieties of church-related institutions: (1) the defender of the faith college; (2) the non-affirming college; (3) the free Christian college; and (4) the church-related university.[4] In 1972, C. Robert Pace offered his own four-pronged schema for grouping Protestant colleges. He distinguished: (1) institutions that had Protestant roots but were no longer Protestant in any legal sense; (2) colleges that remained nominally related to Protestantism but were probably on the verge of disengagement; (3) colleges established by major Protestant denominations which retained a connection with the church; and (4) colleges associated with evangelical, fundamentalist, or interdenominational Christian churches.[5] In 1978, Merrimon Cuninggim offered yet another set of categories: (1) the consonant college, the Ally of its denomination; (2) the proclaiming college, the Witness of its church; and (3) the embodying college, which "is the mirror, almost the embodiment, of the denomination to which it gives fealty."[6]

A new attempt to describe the variants of church-relatedness was advanced in 1992 by William E. Hull of Samford University. Hull outlined "three basic ways in which most denominations have sought to define a Christian dimension in higher education": (1) administrative control; (2) academic components; and (3) campus ethos.[7] Hull concluded that while these approaches to Christian higher education had long influenced the character of denominational colleges and universities, they were insufficient inasmuch as they "marginalize[d] Christianity by entrusting its claims to only a few key administrators, religion professors, or campus ministers." Hull advocated a fourth way of defining the Christian university, one operating "on the boundary between faith and learning, seeking to integrate the entire spectrum of human reason with the entire scope of divine revelation into a living whole."[8]

There is significant diversity among these attempts to develop a typology of Christian higher education. The Carnegie Endowment classification focused on issues of autonomy and control. The Danforth Commission report emphasized college values and adopted a position of neutrality toward the variety of expressions of church-relatedness. Pace illumined the nature of the church connection and the extent to which colleges had moved away from their sponsoring denominations. Cuninggim too focused on collegiate expressions of church affiliation, but his typology was purely descriptive and was not intended to predict the strength or longevity of this connection. For his part, Hull stressed the various modes in which a college's Christian identity may be embodied.

Each of these typologies is useful for illuminating certain aspects of religious affiliation on college campuses; yet each ignores a pivotal dimension of church-relatedness foregrounded in this book. This is the role faculty play in envisioning, articulating, and embodying an institution's affiliation with a religious body. Because faculty have been conspicuously absent from discussions of church-related higher education for at least the past thirty years, it is difficult for many to imagine them exercising such a role. For this reason it is instructive to remember that between 1920 and 1960 many of the pockets of real religious vitality in American higher education were faculty-led.

The Faculty Christian Fellowship, which provided an ecumenical forum for advocates and employees of church-sponsored institutions,[9] is particularly notable, since it was established by and for faculty. Organized in 1952, the FCF's goal was "to uncover the basic presuppositions of the various academic disciplines and to explore the tensions existing between them and those of the Christian faith."[10] To this end, during the 1950s and 1960s the FCF's journal *The Christian Scholar* devoted many articles to the relationship of faith and the academic disciplines. In its heyday, the Fellowship involved nationally recognized scholars and attracted large numbers of faculty to its regional and national gatherings. In 1964, perhaps the apex of its short existence, *The Christian Scholar* had a paid subscription list of about 4,000, while the FCF newsletter *Faculty Forum* had a circulation of 37,000.

Despite its numerical strength, the FCF would not survive the social and intellectual turmoil of the 1960s. Its demise was hastened, Douglas Sloan has shown, by the changing nature of the professoriate. The sheer growth in the number of professors—from 147,000 in 1940 to 509,000 in 1970—was one factor in this transition, as was the growing dominance of the research paradigm. Nor was the FCF reaching younger, more socially diverse faculty members, many of whom sympathized with student critics of the university during the tumultuous 1960s.[11] As Sloan narrates, the Faculty Christian Fellowship succumbed to "collapse and rout" by the end of the decade. He concludes that "the demise of *The Christian Scholar* and of the Faculty Christian Fellowship signaled that the mainstream Protestant churches' critical, scholarly engagement with American higher education was all but over."[12]

Yet we regard the FCF's very existence as a sign of the latent potential of faculty organizations for raising questions of faith and knowledge and building dynamic alliances. In fact, we believe the story of the FCF's short-lived success ought to inspire faculty at church-related colleges to lead the way in engaging questions of religion and higher education in the twenty-first century. We regard this role as so crucial, that we offer a typology of church-related higher education which highlights the role of faculty in envisioning, articulating, and embodying an institution's affiliation with a religious body. We suggest that there are four types of religiously affiliated institutions of higher learning in operation today:

1. Those in which a *majority* of faculty are concerned with their role in helping the institution envision, articulate, and embody its religious identity.

2. Those in which an *active minority* of faculty are concerned with their role in helping the institution envision, articulate, and embody its religious identity.

3. Those in which an *inactive minority* of faculty are concerned with their role in helping the institution envision, articulate, and embody its religious identity

4. Those in which *few if any* faculty are concerned with their role in helping the institution envision, articulate, and embody its religious identity.

In focusing on faculty to the exclusion of other constituencies—for instance, trustees, administrators, staff, alumni, and students—this typology implies that faculty interest and commitment represent the *sine qua non* of meaningful religious identity. We refer to "religious identity" rather than "church affiliation," since faculty generally have little opportunity to determine official relations with church bodies. But once this clarification is made, the faculty role can be stated more explicitly: *Faculty involvement is a necessary condition for meaningful religious identity and in certain situations may be a sufficient condition as well.* That is, without faculty involvement there will be no meaningful religious identity; yet significant faculty concern for religious identity may be sufficient to realize that identity.

Obviously, our analysis of church-related higher education puts a great deal of pressure on faculty hiring and orientation. Increasing the importance of these activities are the significant changes in personal and professional loyalties among teacher-scholars over the past few decades. As many observers have noted, faculty members today are more likely to find their identity in academic disciplines or methodologies than in either a particular institution of higher learning or a religious tradition. This transformation has been gradual, but evidence for it appears in many places. In the first half of the twentieth century, for instance, many commentators on higher education sang the praises of faculty who were deeply committed to their colleges. In 1900, William Rainey Harper opined that the prospects of the small college would "through all time" be boosted by its support among faculty and alumni. He was doxological in his description of faculty members' loyal support for their institutions:

> No greater acts of heroism or self-sacrifice have been performed on battlefield, or in the face of danger, than those which are written down in the book of the recording angel to the credit of the teachers whose very blood has gone into the foundations of some of our weak and struggling colleges.[13]

By mid-century, such altruism was apparently less prevalent. In 1951, an editorial in *The Christian Century* lamented that

> church college administrators often speak with nostalgic regret of the days when faculties in such schools were made up of dedicated idealists who taught for a pittance and the right to tether a cow on the back campus. There are some such left; the total may in fact be as large as was the actual total of these legendary figures now recalled through a romantic haze. But after a teacher has spent the years and the thousands of dollars which are required in these Ph.D.-obsessed days to fit himself for a college position, he is not likely to stay long at a church college unless the working conditions there are as attractive as those in other schools. Moreover, church colleges which are forced in the present emergency to turn off younger faculty members in order to trim their budgets are killing off their future teaching staff by so doing.[14]

By the 1990s, the shift had become nearly complete. In a careful analysis of church-sponsored American universities that over time had become secular, James Tunstead Burtchaell discerned a nine-step path toward the loss of religious identity. The fourth of these steps, according to Burtchaell, was "a transfer of primary loyalty from the church to the 'academic guild,' especially on the part of the faculty."[15] The role of changing faculty loyalties in the secularization process was confirmed in 1997 by Keith Wilson's analysis of theories advanced to explain the secularization of church-sponsored colleges and universities. Wilson analyzed six theorists of collegiate secularization and found that they intersected at one point: changes in religious attitudes among faculty. In Wilson's words, "the admission or employment policy begins to place reduced emphasis upon the majority religion as a selection criterion for enrollment or employment. More and more the religious preferences of the various academic constituencies shift away from a majority faith."[16]

Our own deep interest in the future of church-related colleges notwithstanding, we observe that among many of our faculty colleagues—especially junior and mid-career faculty— evidence of enduring loyalty to church and college is quite rare. And this concerns us. In 1989 Stanley Hauerwas claimed to be "enough of a realist to assume that whoever pays the bills will determine the character, for better or worse, of an institution."[17] We hope Hauerwas is wrong. If he is not, then we must hope that more and more faculty will demonstrate their desire to envision, articulate, and embody religious traditions in ways that will guide others—students, administrators, parents and those who pay the bills—in insuring a relevant and distinctive future for American church-related higher education.

Notes

Preface

[1] Another Lilly-funded program focused on church-related colleges is the Lilly Fellows Program in Humanities and the Arts, headquartered at Valparaiso University. The Lilly Fellows Program has published a *Network Communiqué* since 1992, has hosted a series of national conferences since 1991, and annually publishes its *Directory of the National Network Members of Church-Related Colleges and Universities*.

[2] See Douglas Sloan, *Faith and Knowledge: Mainline Protestantism and American Higher Education* (Louisville, KY: Westminster/John Knox, 1994).

[3] I was commissioned to author a monograph on the presentation of Judaism and the Holocaust in these institutions, and in order to attain the necessary curricular data I designed a questionnaire and mailed it to the chief academic officers of over five hundred church-related liberal arts colleges across America. The results of this research have been published in Stephen R. Haynes, *The Holocaust and the Church-Related College: Restoring Ruptured Traditions* (New York: Greenwood, 1997).

[4] Recent attempts by scholars of religion to describe the postmodern abound. These include David Ray Griffin, William A. Beardslee and Joe Holland, *Varieties of Postmodern Theology* (New York: State University of New York Press, 1989); Stephen D. Moore, *Literary Criticism and the Gospels: The Theoretical Challenge* (New Haven, CT: Yale University Press, 1989); Roger Lundin, *The Culture of Interpretation: Christian Faith and the Postmodern World* (Grand Rapids, MI: Eerdmans, 1993); and Gregory Baum, "Theories of Post-Modernity," *The Ecumenist* 29:2 (Spring, 1991): 4–12. Even evangelical scholars have begun to acknowledge the arrival of the postmodern and have attempted to interpret its meaning for Christianity. See, e.g., J. Richard Middleton and Brian Walsh, *Truth Is Stranger Than It Used to Be* (Downer's Grove, IL: Inter-Varsity Press, 1995).

[5] See Robert Lynn Wood, "'The Survival of Recognizably Protestant Colleges': Reflections on Old-Line Protestantism, 1950–1990," in *The Seculariza-*

tion of the Academy, ed. George M. Marsden and Bradley J. Longfield (New York: Oxford University Press, 1992): 170–94; 171.

[6] Merrimon Cuninggim, *Uneasy Partners: The College and the Church* (Nashville: Abingdon, 1994), 27; Charles E. Peterson, "The Church-Related College: Whence Before Whither," in *The Contribution of the Church-Related College to the Public Good*, Proceedings of the Wingspread Conference on the Contribution of the Church-Related College to the Public Good, December 8–10, 1969, ed. Samuel H. Magill (Washington, D.C.: American Association of Colleges, 1970): 9; Bradley J. Longfield and George M. Marsden, "Presbyterian Colleges in Twentieth-Century America," in *The Pluralistic Vision: Presbyterians and Mainstream Protestant Education and Leadership*, ed. Milton J. Coalter, John M. Mulder and Louis B. Weeks (Louisville, KY: Westminster/John Knox, 1993).

[7] Myron F. Wicke, *The Church-Related College* (Washington, D.C.: The Center for Applied Research in Higher Education, Inc., 1964), 12. Wicke's criteria for church-related colleges were as follows: listed as church-related in one or more of the major college directories; not offering extensive graduate programs or enrolling more than 3,500 students; and not having as their primary function the training of students for the priesthood.

[8] Manning M. Pattillo, Jr. and Donald M. Mackenzie, *Church-Sponsored Higher Education in the United States: Report of the Danforth Commission* (Washington, D.C.: American Council on Education, 1966), 19.

[9] Edgar M. Carlson, *The Future of Church-Related Higher Education* (Minneapolis: Augsburg, 1977), 98.

[10] *Uneasy Partners*, Appendices A and B, 126ff.

[11] It is interesting to compare these numbers with those reported by Merrimon Cuninggim in 1947, who found that only 51.4% of church-related and independent liberal arts colleges and only 60.9% of Catholic colleges had requirements in religion; and the Danforth Commission study of 1966, which discovered that 87% of church-related institutions required formal instruction in the field of religion for graduation. See Merrimon Cuninggim, *The College Seeks Religion* (New Haven, CT: Yale University Press, 1947), 305; Pattillo and Mackenzie, *Church-Sponsored Higher Education*, 140ff.

[12] Cf. William Crawford, "Introduction," in *The Christian College*, ed. Welch et al. (New York: The Methodist Book Concern, 1916): "Religion may be taught in such a way as to prejudice the student against religion" (7).

Haynes: A Review of Research

[1] Albea Godbold, *The Church College of the Old South* (Durham, NC: Duke University Press, 1944), vii.

[2] Winthrop S. Hudson, *The Great Tradition of the American Churches* (New York: Harper, 1953), 197.

[3] "The Church-Related College in American Society," in *The Contribution of the Church-Related College to the Public Good*, Proceedings of the Wingspread Conference on the Contribution of the Church-Related College to the Public Good, December 8–10, 1969, ed. Samuel H. Magill (Washington, D.C.: American Association of Colleges, 1970): 48. In 1972 McCoy asked, "given the context and direction of higher education in the United States, can colleges find a way in which to be uniquely Christian? Within the ecumenical and plural-

istic culture of America and the world, does a place exist for church-related higher education?" Charles S. McCoy, *The Responsible Campus: Toward a New Identity for the Church-Related College* (Nashville: United Methodist Church Board of Education, 1972), 23.

⁴ C. Robert Pace, *Education and Evangelism: A Profile of Protestant Colleges* (New York: McGraw-Hill and the Carnegie Foundation for the Advancement of Teaching, 1972), 14.

⁵ Frederick Rudolph, *The American College and University: A History* (Athens: University of Georgia Press, 1990), 48.

⁶ Ibid., 47.

⁷ Clarence Prouty Shedd, *The Church Follows its Students* (New Haven, CT: Yale University Press, 1938), 3.

⁸ Page Smith, *Killing the Spirit: Higher Education in America* (New York: The Viking Press, 1990), 62.

⁹ Mark A. Noll, "Christian Colleges, Christian Worldviews, and an Invitation to Research," in *The Christian College: A History of Protestant Higher Education in America*, ed. William C. Ringerberg (Grand Rapids, MI: Christian University Press/Eerdmans, 1984): 1–36; 6, 7.

¹⁰ Rudolph, *The American College and University*, 26.

¹¹ In a survey of church-related college catalogs during this period Leslie Karr Patton found "many signs of the battle fought by the defenders of the well-entrenched classical curriculum as they attempted to resist the onslaught of the scientific curriculum protagonists." See *The Purposes of Church-Related Colleges: A Critical Study—A Proposed Program*, Teachers College Columbia University Contributions to Education 783 (New York: Columbia University, 1940), 62.

¹² This historical survey is largely dependent on Mark A. Noll, "Christian Colleges." See also "The Church Institution in the History of American Higher Education," in *Church-Sponsored Higher Education in the United States: Report of the Danforth Commission*, ed. Manning M. Pattillo, Jr. and Donald M. Mackenzie (Washington, D.C.: American Council on Education, 1966): 1–17.

¹³ William Rainey Harper, *The Prospects of the Small College* (Chicago: University of Chicago Press, 1900), 45.

¹⁴ See Dorothy C. Bass, "Ministry on the Margin: Protestants and Education," in *Between the Times: The Travail of the Protestant Establishment in America, 1900–1960*, ed. William R. Hutchison (Cambridge: Cambridge University Press, 1989): 48–71; 48.

¹⁵ Dorothy Bass reports that about fifteen denominational colleges and universities, including Wesleyan, Drury, Drake, Coe, Dickinson, Goucher, Swarthmore, Bowdoin, Rochester, Occidental, Rutgers and Brown, disaffiliated with their churches in order to qualify for the Carnegie pension fund ("Ministry on the Margin," 52).

¹⁶ See Bass, "Ministry on the Margin," 51–56.

¹⁷ Paul M. Limbert, *Denominational Policies in the Support and Supervision of Higher Education*, Columbia Teachers College Contributions to Education 378 (New York: Columbia University Bureau of Publications, 1929), 1. "Proliferation," as it was called, would become a perennial concern in this literature. Suggested methods for dealing with proliferation ranged from voluntary moratoria on the establishment of new institutions to calls for consolidation among existing schools. See, e.g., B. Warren Brown, *Report of the Survey of the*

Educational Work and Responsibility of the Presbyterian Church in the United States (Louisville, KY, 1928); and Myron F. Wicke, *The Church-Related College* (Washington, D.C.: The Center for Applied Research in Higher Education, Inc., 1964).

[18] Bradley J. Longfield and George M. Marsden, "Presbyterian Colleges in Twentieth-Century America," in *The Pluralistic Vision: Presbyterians and Mainstream Protestant Education and Leadership,* ed. Milton J. Coalter, John M. Mulder and Louis B. Weeks (Louisville, KY: Westminster/John Knox, 1993): 106.

[19] Bass, "Ministry on the Margin," 56–57.

[20] Merrimon Cuninggim, *The College Seeks Religion* (New Haven, CT: Yale University Press, 1947), 15–28.

[21] Douglas Sloan, *Faith and Knowledge: Mainline Protestantism and American Higher Education* (Louisville, KY: Westminster/John Knox, 1994), 24–26, 35–36. See also William E. Hull, "Christian Higher Education at the Crossroads," *Perspectives in Religious Studies* 19:4 (Winter, 1992): 441–54; 443–44.

[22] Milton J. Coalter, John M. Mulder, and Louis B. Weeks, *Vital Signs: The Promise of Mainstream Protestantism* (Grand Rapids, MI: Eerdmans, 1994), 69.

[23] Cited in James H. Smylie, "Roads to Our Present," in *Church Related Higher Education: Perceptions and Perspectives,* ed. Robert Rue Parsonage (Valley Forge, PA: Judson Press, 1978): 148.

[24] *The Christian Scholar* 37: 1 (March, 1954): 3. See especially the Symposium entitled "Can and Should a College be Christian?," 12–33.

[25] *The Christian Scholar* 41: special issue (Autumn, 1958).

[26] Sloan, *Faith and Knowledge,* 99. The third and last of these convocations was held in 1962 at St. Olaf College in Northfield, MN. The proceedings were published as *The Mission of the Christian College in the Modern World: Addresses and Reports of the 3rd Quadrennial Convocation of Christian Colleges, June 17–21, 1962* (Washington, D.C.: Council of Protestant Colleges and Universities, 1962).

[27] Sloan, *Faith and Knowledge,* 36. For a discussion of these faculty consultations on religion in higher education, including a list of participating colleges, see Albert C. Outler, *Colleges, Faculties and Religion: An Appraisal of the Program of Faculty Consultations on Religion in Higher Education, 1945–48* (n.p., n.d). For another gauge of interest in religion during this period, see *Religion in the Church College* (n.p.: The Board of Education of the Methodist Church, 1953).

[28] On this movement, see Hull, "Christian Higher Education," 443ff.

[29] Longfield and Marsden, "Presbyterian Colleges," 111.

[30] Dorothy Bass, "Church-Related Colleges: Transmitters of Denominational Cultures?" in *Beyond Establishment: Protestant Identity in a Post-Protestant World,* ed. Jackson W. Carroll and Wade Clark Roof (Louisville, KY: Westminster/John Knox, 1993): 157–72; 162.

[31] Sloan, *Faith and Knowledge,* 101.

[32] Bass, "Church-Related Colleges," 162.

[33] Ben C. Fisher, *The Idea of the Christian University in Today's World* (Macon, GA: Mercer University Press, 1989), 11.

[34] In 1970 Charles E. Peterson, Jr. commented on these colleges' "traditional susceptibility to the ups and downs of the American [economic] scene," and noted that despite the fact that in the nineteenth century most major

denominations had formed agencies for support of their colleges, already by the 1920s the amount of aid rendered by denominations had begun to shrink in relation to the college's budgets. According to Peterson, among the other factors that historically served to diminish denominational financial support for church colleges were institutional desires to qualify for the Carnegie Foundation's 1905 faculty pensions program, and the ecumenical movement in Christian higher education which tended to "weaken doctrinal and dollar ties" between colleges and churches. In Magill, ed., *The Contribution*, 25, 26, Paul Limbert notes that thirty-one separate denominational boards of education were in existence by 1926.

[35] See Harry E. Smith, "The Church's Mission in Higher Education: Renewing our Commitment," *Church and Society* (Jan./Feb., 1998). This article was graciously shared with the author before its publication.

[36] Robert Wood Lynn has referred to this era in the history of the American church-related college as "the Danforth years," an appellation reflecting the prominent role of the foundation in organizing and funding comprehensive studies of church-sponsored higher education. Lynn points out that during the early 1960s the posture of the Danforth Foundation was closely associated with the views of its director. For instance, following Cuninggim's usage, the adjective "church-related" came to be the preferred description of Christian colleges. As Lynn notes, however, this term embodies more than linguistic convenience. It reflects acknowledgment of a growing distance between church and college. See Robert Wood Lynn, "'The Survival of Recognizably Protestant Colleges': Reflections on Old-Line Protestantism, 1950–1990," in *The Secularization of the Academy*, ed. George C. Marsden and Bradley J. Longfield (New York: Oxford University Press, 1992): 180.

[37] This awareness is foregrounded in Richard Baepler et al., *The Quest for a Viable Saga: The Church-Related College in an Age of Pluralism* (n.p.: Association of Lutheran College Faculties, 1977), ch. 1.

[38] Lynn, "Survival," 184–87. As Lynn points out, Cuninggim's typology of church-related colleges in "Categories of Church-Relatedness" (Parsonage, ed., *Church Related Higher Education*, 29–42) represents an attempt to broaden the definition of these colleges.

[39] See, e.g., Arthur F. Holmes, *The Idea of a Christian College* (Grand Rapids, MI: Eerdmans, 1975); and Robert T. Sandin, *The Search for Excellence: The Christian College in an Age of Educational Competition* (Macon, GA: Mercer University Press, 1982). Sandin is particularly concerned with the poor showing of more conservative and sectarian Christian colleges "when measured by the customary bench marks of educational quality" (4).

[40] See George M. Marsden, *The Soul of the American University: From Protestant Establishment to Established Nonbelief* (New York: Oxford University Press, 1994); Sloan, *Faith and Knowledge*; James Tunstead Burtchaell, "The Decline and Fall of the Christian College," *First Things* (April, 1991): 16–29 and (May, 1991): 30–38, and "The Alienation of Christian Higher Education in America: Diagnosis and Prognosis," in *Schooling Christians: "Holy Experiments" in American Education*, ed. Stanley Hauerwas and Jon H. Westerhoff (Grand Rapids, MI: Eerdmans, 1992): 153–83; and Mark R. Schwehn, *Exiles from Eden: Religion and the Academic Vocation in America* (New York: Oxford University Press, 1993).

[41] Although the term "church-related" did not become standard until the

1950s, Patton uses it, he says, because since 1930 it had largely supplanted the term "denominational."

[42] Patton, *The Purposes of the Church-Related College*, 97.

[43] Shedd, *The Church Follows its Students*, xiii.

[44] Ibid.

[45] Dorothy Bass notes that the work of campus ministers "had considerable impact on the perceptions of higher education held by religious leaders in this arena, whose imagination had earlier focused exclusively on church-related institutions. See "Ministry on the Margin," 58.

[46] Cuninggim, *The College Seeks Religion*, 30.

[47] Lynn, "The Survival," 174–75.

[48] It is interesting to note how the analyses of Lowry and other advocates of the Protestant college reflect the theological influence of Paul Tillich rather than the neo-orthodox approach of Karl Barth, which supposedly dominated the thinking of mainstream Protestantism in the 1950s and 1960s.

[49] Alexander Miller, *Faith and Learning: Christian Faith and Higher Education in Twentieth-Century America* (New York: Association Press, 1960), 26. See also Nels F. S. Ferre, *Christian Faith and Higher Education* (New York: Harper and Brothers, 1957); and Lloyd J. Averill, *A Strategy for the Protestant College* (Philadelphia: Westminster, 1966), especially ch. 2, "The Protestant College: The Integrity of Faith and Learning."

[50] Sloan, *Faith and Knowledge*, 97.

[51] "Church Colleges in Trouble," *The Christian Century* (June 20, 1951): 733–35.

[52] "Religion in Higher Education through the Past Twenty-Five Years," in *Religion and Liberal Learning*, ed. Amos N. Wilder (New York: Harper, 1951): 4.

[53] Lynn, "Survival," 179.

[54] Merrimon Cuninggim, *The Protestant Stake in Higher Education* (n.p.: Council of Protestant Colleges and Universities, 1961), 2, 17. It is interesting that Cuninggim regards the term Christian college as "a broader and even vaguer title" than church-related college (2).

[55] Ibid., 30.

[56] In Lynn, "Survival," 182.

[57] Myron F. Wicke, *The Church-Related College* (Washington, D.C.: The Center for Applied Research in Education, Inc., 1964), 2.

[58] Ibid., 42. Wicke was struck by constant reiteration of the claim that these institutions were dedicated to developing both mind and spirit. He also discovered an aspect of the Christian colleges' purpose that had emerged since 1940: "to develop familiarity with, understanding of, and commitment to the Judaeo-Christian tradition."

[59] Pattillo and Mackenzie, *Church-Sponsored Higher Education*. Though the study began with a survey of "the church institution in the history of American higher education," it was heavy with statistics.

[60] Harry E. Smith, *Secularization and the University* (Richmond, VA: John Knox Press, 1968). Smith carefully distinguished between "secularization" and "secularism," embracing the former, which he defined as "a radical reorientation in Western man's understanding of himself in relation to the world, truth, history, and religious institutions . . ." (95).

[61] Ibid., 134.

⁶² Ibid., 133.

⁶³ Ibid., 134.

⁶⁴ Andrew M. Greeley, *From Backwater to Mainstream: A Profile of Catholic Higher Education* (New York: McGraw-Hill, 1969). Other significant studies of Catholic higher education are included in *The Future of Catholic Higher Education: Proceedings of a Panel Discussion Held at the June 24–25, 1980, Meeting of the Foundations and Donors Interested in Catholic Activities* (Washington, D.C: FADICA, n.d.).

⁶⁵ Greeley, *From Backwater to Mainstream*, 3.

⁶⁶ William Graham Cole, "Introductory Remarks," in Magill, ed., *The Contribution*, 2. The book was published by the American Association of Colleges and contained the proceedings of a conference held in December of 1969. On the same topic, see Lloyd J. Averill, *The Church College and the Public Good: A Report on the Status and Prospects of Church-Related Higher Education in the United States* (n.p.: Council of Protestant Colleges and Universities, 1969). The major contributions to the book were a historical survey of church-related higher education by Charles E. Peterson, Jr., a study of the role of these institutions in American society by Charles S. McCoy, and a review of the development of American Catholic higher education by Joseph P. Kelly.

⁶⁷ This volume, along with others published in the 1970s, drew attention to promising curricular innovations that might be new ways of distinguishing church-related colleges. Curricular experiments at Earlham, Davidson, Florida Presbyterian (Eckerd), Maryville, St. Olaf and Redlands were mentioned by commentators during this period. See, e.g., Harry E. Smith, "Commentary," in Magill, ed., *The Contribution*, 43-44.

⁶⁸ McCoy, *The Responsible Campus*, 33, 35.

⁶⁹ Pace, *Education and Evangelism*, 31.

⁷⁰ Ibid.

⁷¹ *A Dialogue on Achieving the Mission of Church-Related Institutions of Higher Learning Hosted by Rockhurst College, Kansas City, Missouri, November 29–30, 1976* (Washington, D.C., 1977). From the same period, see also Edgar M. Carlson, *The Future of Church-Related Higher Education* (Minneapolis: Augsburg, 1977); Richard N. Bender, ed., *The Church Related College Today: Anachronism or Opportunity?: A Symposium of Papers Produced by the Council on the Church-Related College* (Nashville: The Board of Higher Education of the United Methodist Church, 1971); and Woodrow A. Geier, ed., *Church Colleges Today: Perspectives of a Church Agency on Their Problems and Possibilities* (Nashville: Board of Higher Education of the United Methodist Church, 1974).·

⁷² *A Dialogue on Achieving the Mission of Church-Related Institutions of Higher Learning*, 1.

⁷³ Ibid. The conclusion of those participating in the dialogue seemed to be that the special responsibility of faculty members in the area of student formation created a need for "special techniques of recruitment and hiring" (8). The proceedings also indicated agreement that church-related colleges should recruit faculty members who "can heighten the religious atmosphere on campus" and that contracts should specify any "extra dimensions in the religious or value area" expected by the college. Though no consensus was reached, the dialogue even touched on the thorny issue of what proportion of students or faculty must claim membership in, or at least sympathy with,

the sponsoring denomination in order to maintain the religious character of an institution.

[74] Harry E. Smith, "Introduction," in Parsonage, ed., *Church-Related Higher Education,* 9.

[75] Ibid., 74.

[76] James H. Smylie, "Roads to Our Present," in Parsonage, ed., *Church-Related Higher Education,* 169–70.

[77] *Church and College: A Vital Partnership; Volume One: Affirmation: A Shared Commitment for Creative Renewal; Volume Two: A Shared Vision of Educational Purpose; Volume Three: Accountability: Keeping Faith with One Another; Volume Four: Exchange: The National Congress on Church-Related Universities* (Sherman, TX: Center for Program and Institutional Renewal at Austin College, 1980). The congress was underwritten by The Arthur Vining Davis Foundation, The Ford Foundation, and the William and Flora Hewlett Foundation. About the same time appeared several studies treating Lutheran colleges: Baepler et al., *The Quest for a Viable Saga; Lutheran Higher Education in the 1980s: Heritage and Challenge: Papers and Proceedings of the 66th Annual Convention of the Lutheran Educational Conference of North America* (Washington, D.C: LECNA, 1980); and Richard W. Solberg and Merton P. Strommen, *How Church-Related are Church-Related Colleges?: Answers Based on a Comprehensive Survey of Supporting Constituencies of Eighteen LCA Colleges* (Philadelphia: Board of Publication, Lutheran Church in America, 1980).

[78] The exceptions to this rule are few and are for the most part "occasional" writings. Leading examples are the essays on the subject in Stanley Hauerwas, *Christian Existence Today: Essays on Church, World and Living in Between* (Durham, NC: The Labyrinth Press, 1988), and the second section of *Loving God with One's Mind: Essays, Articles and Speeches of F. Thomas Trotter* (Board of Higher Education and Ministry of the United Methodist Church, 1987).

[79] Richard G. Hutcheson, Jr., "Are Church-Related Colleges Also Christian Colleges?" *The Christian Century* (Sept. 28, 1988): 838–41.

[80] Ibid., 839.

[81] Ibid., 840.

[82] F. Thomas Trotter, "The College as the Church's Gift," *The Christian Century* (Nov. 30, 1988): 1098–1100.

[83] Ringerberg, *The Christian College;* Joel A. Carpenter and Kenneth W. Shipps, eds., *Making Higher Education Christian: The History and Mission of Evangelical Colleges in America* (Grand Rapids, MI: Christian University Press, 1987); and Fisher, *The Idea of the Christian University.*

[84] For an example of the former, see Michael G. Cartwright's study of Allegheny College in "Looking Both Ways: A 'Holy Experiment' in American Higher Education," in Hauerwas and Westerhoff, *Schooling Christians,* 184–213. For an example of the latter, see Longfield and Marsden, "Presbyterian Colleges."

[85] In addition to the works of Dorothy Bass and Robert Wood Lynn already cited, see Michael Beaty, Todd Buras, and Larry Lyon, "Challenges and Prospects for Baptist Higher Education," *The Southern Baptist Educator* 61: 4 (April/May/June 1997): 3–6; id., "Christian Higher Education: An Historical and Philosophical Perspective," *Perspectives in Religious Studies* 24: 2 (Summer, 1997): 147–65; id., "Faith and Knowledge in American Higher Education: A Review Essay," *Fides et Historia* 29:1 (Winter/Spring, 1997): 73–80;

and Larry Lyon and Michael Beaty, "Integration, Secularization, and the Two-Spheres View at Religious Colleges: Comparing Baylor University with the University of Notre Dame and Georgetown College," unpublished manuscript. See also Richard Hughes, "Baptists and the Life of the Mind: Reflections on the Baptist Theme of Soul Competency," *The Southern Baptist Educator* 63:2 (1999): 3–7; "Musings on Tuesday's Questions: Luther in the Context of the American Enlightenment," *The Cresset* 62:7 (Special issue, 1999): 26–35; "Our Place in Church Related Higher Education in the United States," *Intersections* 4 (Winter, 1998): 3–9; "Reclaiming a Heritage," *Restoration Quarterly* 37:3 (1995): 129–38; "Can Christian Faith Sustain the Life of the Mind?" *The Southern Baptist Educator* 63:1 (Fall 1998): 3–8; and "Protestant Colleges, 1960–1990," in *Trying Times: Essays on Catholic Higher Education in the 20th Century*, ed. William M. Shea and Daniel Van Slyke (Atlanta: Scholar's Press, 1999): 85–98.

The 1990s also saw a number of articles dealing specifically with Catholic higher education. See especially Phillip Gleason, "American Catholic Higher Education, 1940–1990: The Ideological Context," in Marsden and Longfield, eds., *The Secularization of the Academy*, 234–58; and "A Look Back at the Catholic Intellectualism Issue," *U.S. Catholic Historian* 13 (Winter, 1995): 19–37; David O'Brien, "A Catholic Future for Catholic Higher Education: The State of the Question," *Catholic Education: A Journal of Inquiry and Practice* 1 (Sept., 1997): 37–50; Thomas M. Landy, "Catholic Intellectual Life: Reflections on Mission and Identity," *U.S. Catholic Historian* 13:2 (Winter, 1995): 87–100; "Collegium and the Intellectual's Vocation to Serve," *Conversations on Jesuit Higher Education* 10 (Fall, 1996): 20–29; and Alice Gallin, "Making Colleges Catholic: Bishops and Academics Reach Common Ground," *Commonweal* 124:6 (March 28, 1997): 14–17.

[86] Arthur J. De Jong, *Reclaiming A Mission: New Direction for the Church-Related College* (Grand Rapids, MI: Eerdmans, 1990). Several other books published in the 1990s bear on our topic, though they are not reviewed here. In particular, see Philip Gleason, *Contending with Modernity: Catholic Higher Education in the Twentieth Century* (New York: Oxford University Press, 1995); and Richard T. Hughes and William B. Adrian, eds., *Models for Christian Higher Education: Strategies for Success in the Twenty-First Century* (Grand Rapids, MI: Eerdmans, 1997). See also William McInnes, *Perspectives on the Current Status of and Emerging Policy Issues for Church-Related Colleges and Universities*, AGB Occasional Paper No. 8 (Washington, D.C.: Association of Governing Boards of Universities and Colleges, 1991); J. Patrick Murphy, *Visions and Values in Catholic Higher Education* (Kansas City, MO: Sheed and Ward, 1991); Bridget Puzon, ed., *Women Religious and the Intellectual Life: The North American Achievement* (San Francisco: International Scholars Publication, 1996); Alice Gallin, *Independence and a New Partnership in Catholic Higher Education* (Notre Dame, IN: University of Notre Dame Press, 1996); and *Negotiating Identity: Catholic Higher Education since 1960* (Notre Dame, IN: University of Notre Dame Press, 2000). The results of a briefer study are reported in Diane Winston, "The Mission, Formation and Diversity Report: Adult Degree Programs at Faith-Based Colleges" (Princeton, NJ: Center for the Study of Religion, 1999).

[87] Merrimon Cuninggim, *Uneasy Partners* (Nashville: Abingdon, 1994), 109.

[88] Ibid., 125.

[89] Marsden, *The Soul of the University*; and Sloan, *Faith and Knowledge*.

[90] James Tunstead Burtchaell, *The Dying of the Light: The Disengagement of Colleges and Universities from their Christian Churches* (Grand Rapids, MI: Eerdmans, 1998).

[91] Ibid., ix.

[92] Ibid., 828–29.

[93] Ibid., 829–30.

[94] See, for example, Herbert Welch, Henry Churchill King, and Thomas Nicholson, *The Christian College*, Introduction by William H. Crawford (New York: The Methodist Book Concern, 1916), a book whose authors (two college presidents and a denominational board secretary) are brimming with self-confidence. On the influence of philanthropic foundations, see Smylie, "Roads to Our Present," in Parsonage, ed., *Church-Related Higher Education*, 146–47; and Bass, "Ministry on the Margin."

[95] For example, Burtchaell, "The Decline and Fall of the Christian College"; John W. Dixon, Jr., "What Should Religion Departments Teach?" *Theology Today* 46:4 (Jan., 1990): 364–72; David H. Kelsey, *Between Athens and Berlin: The Theological Education Debate* (Grand Rapids, MI: Eerdmans, 1993); Marsden and Longfield, eds., *The Secularization of the Academy*; George M. Marsden, "The Ambiguities of Academic Freedom," *Church History* 62:2 (June, 1993): 221–25; Parker J. Palmer, *To Know as We Are Known: A Spirituality of Education* (San Francisco: Harper and Row, 1983); Schwehn, *Exiles From Eden*; and "The Once and Future University," a symposium in *Cross Currents: The Journal of the Association of Religion and Intellectual Life* (Winter, 1993–1994).

Lakeland: The Habit of Empathy

[1] Merrimon Cuninggim, *Uneasy Partners: The College and the Church* (Nashville: Abingdon Press, 1994); David O'Brien, *From the Heart of the American Church: Catholic Higher Education and American Culture* (Maryknoll, NY: Orbis Press, 1994).

[2] Louis Dupré, *Passage to Modernity: An Essay in the Hermeneutics of Nature and Culture* (New Haven, CT: Yale University Press, 1993); Fernand Braudel, *Civilization and Capitalism, 15th–18th Century*, 3 vols. (New York: Harper and Row, 1982–1984).

[3] Immanuel Kant, *Foundations of the Metaphysics of Morals* and *What is Enlightenment?* (Indianapolis: Bobbs-Merrill, 1959), 85–92.

[4] Though Jürgen Habermas has argued quite convincingly that in essence it is neoconservative. Jürgen Habermas, "Modernity: An Incomplete Project," in *The Anti-Aesthetic: Essays on Postmodern Culture*, ed. Hal Foster (Port Townsend, WA: Bay Press, 1983): 3–15, and *The Philosophical Discourse of Modernity: Twelve Lectures* (Cambridge, MA: MIT Press, 1987).

[5] Paul Lakeland, *Postmodernity* (Philadelphia: Fortress Press, 1998).

[6] Though there is surprising aid to the evangelical position in the teaching of the Roman Catholic bishops at the Second Vatican Council that love is "a preparation for the gospel." In other words, provided we are dealing with socially conscious evangelicals (the *Sojourners* movement, for example) and not the purely kerygmatic kind, evangelical schools can also come on board the empathy wagon!

[7] Avery Dulles, *Models of the Church* (Garden City, NY: Doubleday, 1974).

[8] Robert K. Greenleaf, *Servant Leadership: A Journey Into the Nature of Legitimate Power and Greatness* (New York: Paulist Press, 1977).

Falls-Corbitt: Prolegomena to Any Postmodern Hope

[1] See for example, Douglas Sloan, "Protestantism and Its Postmodern Prospect: Some Reflections on the Present and Future," in *Faith and Knowledge: Mainline Protestantism and American Higher Education* (Louisville, KY: Westminster/John Knox, 1994): 212–43.

[2] For reasons that will become clear below, I cannot say that the ethical forces for secularization that operate at Hendrix function similarly in "Christian Colleges" bearing more conservative Protestant identities.

[3] Compare 1901 catalog copy: "Hendrix College, founded and maintained by a Christian Church, is intended to be in the highest sense a Christian institution."

[4] Isaac Kramnick and R. Laurence Moore, "The Godless University," *Academe* (Nov.–Dec. 1996): 21.

[5] From the 1901 catalog again: "[Students] will not be committed to teachers whose skeptical views or careless life may destroy confidence in the faith and hopes of religious parents, but teachers will be found who endeavor, by precept and example, to lead ever towards the ideals of the Great Teacher, the Way, the Truth, the Life of the spiritual world."

[6] This, of course, is a quick survey of a typical justification of "affirmative action" policies. It is not, by any means, a full defense. My purpose here is simply to show how taking a person's religion into account is in fact sometimes justified by appeal to fairness.

[7] Lawrence K. Schmidt, "Tolerance: From a Hermeneutic Perspective," *Existentia* 6–7 (1996–1997): 83.

[8] Ibid., 83–85.

[9] Ibid., 86.

[10] It is appropriate to wonder whether this attention to relationship is due to such colleges' relative small size or, in the case of many, to such goals as being liberal arts colleges. I am prepared to argue that, while small or liberal arts secular colleges may also have this emphasis, at church-related colleges the emphasis on student-teacher relationships is strongly driven by the historical relationship to a church and by the wishes of present laity in the founding denomination that this emphasis be retained.

[11] Mark R. Schwehn, *Exiles from Eden: Religion and the Academic Vocation in America* (New York: Oxford University Press, 1993). A similar strain can be found in recent books by Sloan, Willimon, and hooks.

Cahoy: A Sense of Place

[1] The risk of oversimplification is very real, as Richard Bernstein points out in criticism of those, usually critics of the Enlightenment, who speak of it "as if it were a unified whole with a common essence." Rather, says he, if we actually read the writers of the Enlightenment "we will be extremely

wary of facile universal claims. . . . There is no single platform, no set of substantive claims, no common essence that the thinkers of the age of Enlightenment share" ("Are We Beyond the Enlightenment Horizon?" in *Knowledge and Belief in America: Enlightenment Traditions and Modern Religious Thought*, ed. William M. Shea and Peter A. Huff, Woodrow Wilson Center Series [Cambridge: Cambridge University Press], 335–36). While I take this to heart, it is also the case that for the most part those shaping higher education in America in the nineteenth century were guided by the more unified sense of the Enlightenment vision with the traits described above. It is this not the scholarly accuracy of their understanding that is of concern to us.

[2] Dupré offers a helpful study of the complexity and antiquity of the roots of modernity. See *Passage to Modernity: An Essay in the Hermeneutics of Nature and Culture* (New Haven, CT: Yale University Press, 1993).

[3] Given the subsequent history of these ideas, it is important to note that Descartes himself did not take this to require the abandonment of faith or as incompatible with the belief that revelation might disclose truth. In his own words "I revered our theology and desired as much as the next man to go to heaven; but having learned . . . that the revealed truths leading to it are beyond our understanding, I would not have dared to subject them to my feeble reasonings" (*Discourse on Method* and *Meditations on First Philosophy*, 3d ed., tr. Donald A. Cress [Indianapolis: Hacket, 1993], 5/8.) Elsewhere he refers to having set aside from his doubt "the truths of the faith, which have always held first place in my set of beliefs" (Ibid., 16/28). Nevertheless, it must also be noted that Descartes' praise and insulation of faith does have the effect, intended or not, of setting theology and faith outside the realm of reason. In its own way this too contributes to the problematic status of a college's church-relation.

[4] Ibid., 59/17, 8/13.

[5] Ibid., 6/10.

[6] Ibid., 11/19.

[7] Peter Gay, *The Enlightenment: An Interpretation*, 2 vols. (New York: Knopf, 1966), 1:xi.

[8] Ernst Cassirer, *The Philosophy of the Enlightment*, tr. Fritz Koelln and James Pettergrove (Boston: Beacon, 1951), xi.

[9] Ibid., vi, ix.

[10] Immanuel Kant, "What is Enlightenment?" tr. Lewis White Beck. In *Foundations of the Metaphysics of Morals* (Indianapolis: Bobbs-Merrill, 1959): 85.

[11] Cassirer, *Philosophy*, 234.

[12] Ibid.

[13] Ibid., 6.

[14] Gay, *The Enlightenment*, 1:13. MacIntyre, writing from a critical stance, identifies the same "rootless cosmopolitanism . . . aspiring to be at home anywhere" as "the fate toward which modernity moves precisely insofar as it successfully modernizes itself and others by emancipating itself from social, cultural, and linguistic particularity and so from tradition" (*Whose Justice? Which Rationality?* [Notre Dame, IN: University of Notre Dame Press, 1988] 388).

[15] Cassirer, *Philosophy*, 161. He goes on to note that "Bayle is the first thinker to become an out-and-out advocate of this truth. In his *Historical and Critical Dictionary* he laid the foundation on which all later attempts at its justification and realization have been based. (In his words) 'the obstacles to a good examination come (not) so much from the fact that the mind is void of knowledge as that it is full of prejudice'." It is from this prejudice that reason needs to be liberated in order to ascertain the truth.

[16] The fact that many of these beliefs and practices had long been enforced with the authority of the state and church gave these epistemological reflections a sharp political edge that was not lost on its advocates or their foes.

[17] Voltaire goes so far as to say that if we want to see things as they really are in themselves, "We must never make hypotheses" because we then run the risk of distorting the facts to suit our hypothesis (quoted in Cassirer, *Philosophy*, 12).

[18] MacIntyre, *Whose Justice?*, 3, 6.

[19] For good reasons, the French *Encyclopédie* of Diderot and other *philosophes* is often taken to be the prototypical Enlightenment work. MacIntyre makes a compelling case for the Ninth Edition as a no less complete embodiment of Enlightenment principles. Moreover, its milder tone and extensive use as a standard reference work in the English-speaking world indicates just how widely accepted these principles had become by the end of the nineteenth century. MacIntyre notes that the most systematic difference between the eighteenth-century Enlightenment and the Ninth Edition is that the latter takes a more developmental, evolutionary approach to reality whereas the *philosophes* have a more timeless understanding (*Three Rival Versions of Moral Enquiry: Encyclopedia, Genealogy, and Tradition* [Notre Dame, IN: University of Notre Dame Press, 1990], 176). However, this difference need not concern us here as it does not appreciably affect the basic epistemological position they share.

[20] MacIntyre, *Three Rival Versions*, 59.

[21] Ibid., 16–17.

[22] Ibid., 19.

[23] Elsewhere MacIntyre refers to this as "one of the central characteristics of cosmopolitan modernity: the confident belief that all cultural phenomena must be potentially translucent to understanding, that all texts must be capable of being translated into the language which the adherents of modernity speak to each other" (*Whose Justice?*, 327).

[24] MacIntyre, *Three Rival Versions*, 65.

[25] Quoted in ibid., 78.

[26] In addition to the epistemological implications being considered here, there are obvious and momentous political, relational (how is one to understand marriage other than as threat to and compromise with one's freedom), and spiritual/theological implications of this concept of freedom. Indeed, one could argue that this is the fundamental mistake of modernity.

[27] Quoted in Gay, *The Enlightenment*, 1:399.

[28] Cassirer, *Philosophy*, 134.

[29] Quoted in Gay, *The Enlightment*, 1:20.

[30] Cassirer, *Philosophy*, 97.

[31] Gay, *The Enlightenment*, 2:3–8.

[32] Ibid., 1:318.

[33] George M. Marsden, "Introduction," in George M. Marsden and Bradley J. Longfield, eds., *The Secularization of the Academy* (New York: Oxford, 1992), 6.

[34] David Kelsey, *To Understand God Truly: What's Theological About a Theological School* (Louisville, KY: Westminster/John Knox, 1992), 81.

[35] Jaroslav Pelikan, *The Idea of the University: A Reexamination* (New Haven, CT: Yale University Press, 1992), 50.

[36] Marsden, "Introduction," 30.

[37] MacIntyre, *Three Rival Versions*, 172.

[38] Ibid., 171.

[39] Marsden reports that "between 1815 and 1914 about nine to ten thousand Americans studied in Germany" and that in general "Americans stood in awe of the German universities." "It would be rare to find either a university leader or a major scholar who had not spent some years studying in Germany" (*The Soul of the American University: From Protestant Establishment to Established Nonbelief* [New York: Oxford University Press, 1994], 104).

[40] Ibid., 106.

[41] White's educational ideals are evident in a letter he wrote to his friend Gerrit Smith in 1862 expressing his goals for a new university. It should be "'an asylum for *Science*—where truth shall be sought for truth's sake,' not stretched or cut 'exactly to fit Revealed Religion'; and should foster 'a Moral Philosophy, History, and Political Economy unwarped to suit present abuses in Politics and Religion'" (quoted in "White, Andrew Dickson," in *Dictionary of American Biography*, ed. Dumas Malone [New York: Charles Scribner's Sons, 1936], 89). These ideals were later implemented in the Cornell charter.

[42] Marsden, *The Soul of the American University*, 153.

[43] Edward Farley, *The Fragility of Knowledge: Theological Education in the Church and the University* (Philadelphia: Fortess, 1988), 27.

[44] Douglas Sloan, *Faith and Knowledge: Mainline Protestantism and American Higher Education* (Louisville, KY: Westminster/John Knox, 1994), viii.

[45] Ibid., 50.

[46] Ibid., 213, 1.

[47] John Paul II, *Ex Corde Ecclesiae: Apostolic Constitution on Catholic Universities* (Washington: U.S. Catholic Conference, 1996 [1990]).

[48] Jaroslav Pelikan, *The Vindication of Tradition* (New Haven, CT: Yale University Press, 1984), 47.

[49] Marsden offers what his subtitle suggests, a review of the move from the establishment of Protestantism in American higher education, even at state schools, to disestablishment, secularization, and now the establishment of nonbelief ("The Soul of the American University: A Historical Overview," in *The Secularization of the Academy*, ed. George M. Marsden and Bradley J. Longfield [New York: Oxford University Press, 1992]). Burtchaell makes a similar point through an examination of Vanderbilt's history as a case-study, which he then compares to American Catholic higher education since Vatican II ("The Alienation of Christian Higher Education in America: Diagnosis and Prognosis," in *Schooling Christians: Holy Experiments in American Education*, ed. Stanley Hauerwas and John H. Westerhoff [Grand Rapids, MI:

Eerdmans, 1992]). Gleason traces a similar history in Roman Catholic higher education in this century ("American Catholic Higher Education, 1940–1990: The Ideological Context," in *The Secularization of the Academy*, ed. George M. Marsden and Bradley J. Longfield [New York: Oxford University Press, 1992]. Cf. also his *Contending with Modernity: Catholic Higher Education in the Twentieth Century* [New York: Oxford University Press, 1995].) Burtchaell's account of the events at Vanderbilt, as well as the views on secularization offered by him, Marsden, and others, are challenged by Cuninggim (*Uneasy Partners: The College and the Church* [Nashville: Abingdon, 1994], esp. 63–76). David O'Brien offers a comparable Roman Catholic alternative interpretation to that of Burtchaell and Gleason (*From the Heart of the American Church: Catholic Higher Education and American Culture* [Maryknoll, NY: Orbis Books, 1994]).

⁵⁰ As Sloan puts it, "In this approach, Christian faith and values have at most a tangential relationship to knowledge and, hence, to 'academic excellence.' Whatever is variously conceived under Christian faith and values is, therefore, subjected to constant pressure to give way before the institutional, ideological, and individual career demands of 'academic excellence' . . ." (*Faith and Knowledge*, 232). He goes on to observe, "That 'academic excellence' in its present, dominant form has little intrinsic place for faith and human values of any kind is a problem still seldom brought to consciousness by either college or church much less seriously addressed."

⁵¹ On the whole the Enlightenment in America was not as radical, skeptical, or anti-religious as it was in Europe, especially France. Or, to be more precise, the radical group in the Enlightenment in America was significantly smaller and less influential than it was in Europe. In the words of one historian of the era, "Some eighteenth-century intellectuals may have dabbled in skepticism and radicalism, but for the most part the Enlightenment ideology that prevailed in America was committed to order and stability . . . that shored up traditional Christian truths while freeing Christianity from tradition" (D. G. Hart, "The Protestant Enlightenment Revisited: Daniel Coit Gilman and the Academic Reforms of the Modern American University," *The Journal of Ecclesiastical History* 47:4 [Oct., 1996]. Cambridge University Press Online Journal. Internet, accessed 27 Jan. 1998, 12). In particular, "Those who won the battle to dominate American higher education had won against the forces of the skeptical Enlightenment" (Marsden, *The Soul of the American University*, 92).

⁵² Marsden, *The Soul of the American University*, 84, 16–17, 85.

⁵³ Quoted in Marsden, "The Soul of the American University," 9. For examples of statements to this effect by various university presidents, see Sloan, *Faith and Knowledge*, 23. This is even true of Gilman whose Johns Hopkins is commonly regarded as marking a decisive move in the secularization of American universities. As Hart explains, Gilman "regarded his own work as the culmination of a Christian calling and strove in a variety of ways to make Johns Hopkins a Christian university" ("The Protestant Enlightenment Revisited," 3). Gilman "was convinced that the university's goals of extending the benefits of science to society were synonymous with the teachings of Christianity" (Ibid., 5). "(H)is defense of the Christian character of the university movement rested upon an understanding of science which flowed from the Protestant appropriation of the Enlightenment" (Ibid., 8) Among

recent writers the strongest proponent for this liberal Protestant understanding of the church-related college is probably the late Merrimon Cuninggim. See especially *Uneasy Partners*.

54 Mark R. Schwehn, *Exiles from Eden: Religion and the Academic Vocation in America* (New York: Oxford University Press, 1993), 9–16.

55 Tyron Inbody, "Postmodernism: Intellectual Velcro Dragged Across Culture," *Theology Today* 51 (1995): 524.

56 Sloan, *Faith and Knowledge*, 215.

57 Jean-François Lyotard, "Answering the Question: What is Postmodernism?" tr. Régis Durand. In *The Postmodern Condition: A Report on Knowledge* (Minneapolis: University of Minnesota Press, 1984): 82.

58 Applied to postmodernism itself, this uneasiness about universals helps to explain the difficulty in capturing postmodernism in a single definition. Quite consistently it is not one thing and the risk in a single definition is precisely that it fails to do justice to the individual particularities of the various proponents.

59 "The scientist questions the validity of narrative statements and concludes that they are never subject to argumentation or proof. He classifies them as belonging to a different mentality: savage, primitive, underdeveloped, backward, alienated, composed of opinions, customs, authority, prejudice, ignorance, ideology. Narratives are fables, myths, legends, fit only for women and children" (Jean-François Lyotard, *The Postmodern Condition: A Report on Knowledge*, tr. Geoff Bennington and Brian Massumi. Theory and History of Literature, 10 [Minneapolis: University of Minnesota Press, 1984], 27).

60 Ibid., 7.

61 Ibid., 18, 26.

62 Ibid., 64, 40, 20. He goes on: "Without such recourse it would be in the position of presupposing its own validity and would be stooping to what it condemns: begging the question, proceeding on prejudice. But does it not fall into the same trap by using narrative as its authority?" (29).

63 MacIntyre, *Whose Justice?*, 369.

64 Ibid., 348.

65 Lyotard, *The Postmodern Condition*, xxiv.

66 Ibid., 36.

67 MacIntyre, *Three Rival Versions*, 4.

68 Lyotard, *The Postmodern Condition*, 21.

69 Feminist critiques of the tradition as androcentric are a good example of this analysis. Michel Foucault is also especially good at demonstrating the connection between power and knowledge. His studies of those things that reason typically excludes—madness, chance, discontinuity—demonstrate how the social sciences play into a political drive for power and control.

70 E.g., Sloan, *Faith and Knowledge*, 216–18.

71 MacIntyre, *Whose Justice?*, 327.

72 Ibid., 351.

73 MacIntyre, *Three Rival Versions*, 181–85.

74 Pelikan, *The Vindication of Tradition*, 74.

75 C. S. Lewis, "Meditation in a Toolshed," in *God in the Dock: Essays on*

Theology and Ethics, ed. Walter Hooper (Grand Rapids, MI: Eerdmans, 1970): 215.

[76] Marsden, "Introduction," 6.

[77] Marsden, *The Soul of the American University*, 6–7.

[78] Thomas Kuhn, *The Structure of Scientific Revolutions*, 2d ed. (Chicago: University of Chicago Press, 1970), 52–91.

[79] Marsden, *The Soul of the American University*, 430.

[80] Richard Hughes makes this observation in his "Introduction" in *Models for Christian Higher Education: Strategies for Success in the Twenty-first Century.* . . ., (3), a comparative study of fourteen institutions in seven different Christian traditions. It includes accounts written by people from each school of how their institution has managed its relation to the church and a theological essay on how each tradition understands its contribution to higher education. One of the things that emerges clearly is how a particular tradition's ecclesiology and understanding of the relation of grace and nature affects how it envisions the relation between church and college and what counts as a successful relation.

[81] George M. Marsden, *The Outrageous Idea of Christian Scholarship* (New York: Oxford University Press, 1997), 4.

[82] Ibid., 52–53. The book also includes a useful bibliography of such scholarship in various fields.

[83] Quoted in Michael Buckley, "The Catholic University and the Promise Inherent in Its Identity," in *Catholic Universitites in Church and Society: A Dialogue on Ex Corde Ecclesiae*, ed. John P. Langan (Washington, D.C.: Georgetown University Press, 1993), 83. Historically, the institutionalization of this drive to understand the world and ourselves from within the Christian community can be seen in monasteries and cathedral schools well before the first universities were established.

[84] While a distinctive rationale for this intrinsic relation can be traced in the Catholic tradition, it is certainly not uniquely Catholic. For discussions from the Protestant perspective of the relation between faith and reason as it bears on higher education, see Schwehn, who explores the possibility of an "integral" relationship between religion and higher education through the cultivation of "spiritual values that have always been essential to the process of learning" (*Exiles from Eden*, 40–64); Sloan, who examines the neo-orthodox theological renaissance of the mid-twentieth century and its influence on the way we think of the church-college relation; and Farley, who explains why we must reject any schema that would suggest that the drive for ordered learning came from the secular, Greek side of our heritage as distinct from the Jewish-Christian side (85–92). For a good, brief discussion of major themes of the Catholic theological tradition as they bear on higher education with an eye to the issue of uniqueness, see Hellwig.

[85] Buckley, "The Catholic University," 82.

[86] Interestingly, what Buckley advances as a distinctively Catholic position sounds much like that of liberal Protestantism in the nineteenth century, which is precisely Burtchaell's worry about post-concilliar Roman Catholic higher education. While I share this worry, I also agree with Buckley that this understanding of the intrinsic relation between faith and reason is part of the Catholic identity and should be cultivated at Catholic institu-

tions. Catholicism is not sectarian. But we must, therefore, be all the more vigilant that it not dissipate into a generic religiosity and secularism—a scenario Buckley also recounts and cautions against.

[87] In this sense Christianity offers a totalizing discourse that is incompatible with some postmodernisms. Nevertheless, it remains significantly different from the Enlightenment model in that it makes no claim to neutrality. This totalizing account of the world only makes sense from a particular place: the foot of the cross.

[88] *Gaudium et Spes, The Pastoral Constitution on the Church in the Modern World*. Documents of Vatican Council II. Ed. Austin Falnery, O.P. Northport, NY: Costello Publishing, 1975: esp. 1–4, 28–45, 53–62.

[89] See John Paul II, *Ex Corde Ecclesiae. Gaudium et Spes* also refers to the work of colleges and universities; see esp. 36 and 57.

[90] *Rule of Benedict*, ed. Timothy Fry (Collegeville, MN: Liturgical Press, 1981). Also relevant here is the famous opening word of the *Rule*: "Listen." For further consideration of the connection between charity and learning see Schwehn, *Exiles from Eden*, 50–53; and Marsden, *The Outrageous Idea*, 53–55.

[91] *Gaudium et Spes*, 28.

[92] For simplicity's sake we will address this distinction between free inquiry and indoctrination as it is usually stated, since it reflects a long-standing and important distinction between advocacy or proselytizing on the one hand and inquiry on the other. However, it should not go unnoted that in disclosing the illusion of neutrality, postmodernism also discloses the incipient advocacy in all positions, particularly the dominant ideology, where it may be least noticeable. In doing so, it calls into question the legitimacy of the very distinction between advocacy, which looks essentially partisan, and inquiry, which looks essentially neutral. Having said that, however, I would also say that I do not think this means the distinction must be abandoned, only that it must not be absolutized. It does call attention to a significant difference. Recognizing the illusory claim to neutrality does not authorize the substitution of proselytizing for inquiry.

[93] *Gaudium et Spes*, 36, 57.

[94] Farley, *The Fragility of Knowledge*, 26. Pelikan, in his *Vindication of Tradition*, makes a similar point in calling attention to the difference between tradition as idol, token, and icon. As an idol it points to itself rather than beyond itself. As a token it points beyond itself but "is an altogether accidental representation that does not embody what it represents" (the primary Enlightenment understanding). As an icon—the understanding he endorses—tradition embodies what it represents but also points beyond itself so we look "through it . . . to that living reality of which it is an embodiment" (55). Farley points out that this idolatry is what the Enlightenment saw—correctly—as a threat to knowledge. Its response was to reject tradition per se. Farley, Pelikan, and others within the tradition would urge the rejection of the idolatry, not the tradition itself. However, by calling attention to our idolatry, the Enlightenment critics performed a valuable service to Christianity, calling us to be more faithful to our own traditions.

[95] Marsden, *The Outrageous Idea*, 54.

[96] William J. Hoye, "The Religious Roots of Academic Freedom," *Theological Studies* 58 (1997): 414–15.

[97] Joseph A. Komonchak, "The Catholic University in the Church," in *Catholic Universities in Church and Society: A Dialogue on Ex Corde Ecclesiae*, ed. John P. Langan (Washington, D.C.: Georgetown University Press, 1993): 48.

Kyte: Conversation and Authority

[1] Hanna Arendt, *Between the Past and the Future* (New York: The Viking Press, 1961), 3.

[2] The use of the term "church-related college" (which in these pages may denote either a college or a university) is a capitulation to pluralism that leaves us without an adequate term to describe ourselves. I take it that our very discomfort with the term—with its vagueness, generality, and awkwardness—goes some way towards supporting the claim of this paper.

[3] The Institute of the Brothers of the Christian Schools was founded in France in the eighteenth century by John Baptist de La Salle. For an account of his life, see Luke Salm, *The Work is Yours: The Life of Saint John Baptist de La Salle* (Romeoville, IL: Christian Brothers Publications, 1989).

[4] I am not suggesting that the Brothers serve only as reminders of a heritage. Rather, the mere fact that a member of the faculty or staff is a Brother no longer carries the authority it once did. The Brothers have for the most part the same role in the life of the university as the lay faculty and staff, bringing to the institution whatever gifts they may have in terms of talent, training, attention, service, and so forth. They bring those gifts in abundance.

[5] Michael Oakeshott, "The Voice of Poetry in the Conversations of Mankind," in *Rationalism in Politics, and Other Essays* (New York: Basic Books, 1962).

[6] Jane Tompkins, *A Life in School* (Reading, MA: Addison-Wesley, 1996), 223. Here we find the conversational image not only to describe education's place in society as a whole, but also to describe relationships within the college or university. In this case, the university itself is conceived as a representative conversation, representing some of the modes of discourse that a student is likely to encounter in the world and thereby preparing students for participation in it.

[7] See David Denby's article, "Buried Alive" (*The New Yorker* [15 July 1996]: 48–58) in which he describes the effects of his sons' immersion in pop culture, most notably their tendency to switch instantly from one character's voice to another's: "Whooha! Whooha! It is *you*, Luke Skywalker, who are mistaken. Alrightee then! Power and the money, money and the power. Minute after minute, hour after hour. Thank you, come again!" [Apu, Darth Vader, Snoop Doggy Dogg, Ace Ventura] (51).

[8] Tompkins, *A Life at School*, 209.

[9] Ludwig Wittgenstein, *Culture and Value*, tr. P. Winch (Oxford: Blackwell, 1980), 74e.

[10] It is the form of authority Hannah Arendt claimed has disappeared from the world. The closest thing we get to such authority now is tolerance, which is not so much the right to speak as no right to stop someone from speaking.

[11] Peter Brown, *Augustine of Hippo* (Berkeley: University of California Press, 1967), 334.

[12] Michael Fried, *Absorption and the Theatricality: Painting and Beholder in the Age of Diderot* (Chicago: University of Chicago Press, 1980), 20.

[13] Ibid.

[14] Ibid., 19–20.

[15] Ralph Waldo Emerson, "Character," in *Essays and Lectures,* ed. Joel Porte (New York: The Library of America, 1983 [1844]): 495.

[16] Stanley Cavell, *The Claim of Reason: Wittgenstein, Skepticism, Morality and Tragedy* (New York: Oxford University Press, 1979), 327.

[17] *Oxford English Dictionary* (1971): 941.

[18] Take the famous story of stealing the pears. Either Augustine's recounting of that event answers to my experience or it does not. If it does not, I cannot learn from it. If it does, I already (in some sense) know it.

[19] That is why the chief virtues of the Christian teacher (think again of Monica) are humility and hope: humility because she must be willing to have her private interests constrained by the interests of living together in the community and hope because she seldom gets to see the ripened fruits of her work.

[20] Cf. the first paragraph of John Baptist de La Salle's *The Rule of the Brothers of the Christian Schools*: "That which is of the utmost importance, and to which the greatest attention should be given in an Institute is that all who compose it possess the spirit peculiar to it; that the novices apply themselves to acquire it; and that those who are already members make it their first care to preserve and increase it in themselves; for it is this spirit that should animate all their actions, be the motive of their whole conduct; and those who do not possess it and those who have lost it, should be looked upon as dead members, and they should look upon themselves as such; because they are deprived of the life and grace of their state; and they should be convinced that it will be very difficult for them to preserve the grace of God" (http://www.catholic.org/delasalle/1.2.7.0.html [15 Jan. 1998]: 1).

Newman: Beyond the Faith-Knowledge Dichotomy

[1] As quoted in Michael J. Baxter and Frederick C. Bauerschmidt, "*Eruditio* without *Religio*?: The Dilemma of Catholics in the Academy," *Communio* 22 (Summer, 1995): 284.

[2] Charles Scriven, "Schooling for the Tournament of Narratives: Postmodernism and the Idea of the Christian College," in *Theology Without Foundations, Religious Practice and the Future of Theological Truth,* ed. Stanley Hauerwas, Nancey Murphy, and Mark Nation (Nashville: Abingdon, 1994): 227.

[3] A phrase used by Ernst Lehrs, quoted in Douglas Sloan, *Faith and Knowledge: Mainline Protestantism and American Higher Education* (Louisville, KY: Westminster/John Knox, 1994), 215.

[4] Robert Wilken, "The Christian Intellectual Tradition," *First Things* 14 (June/July, 1991): 14.

[5] Sloan, *Faith and Knowledge,* 216.

[6] Cited by Dennis O'Brien, "The Disappearing Moral Curriculum," *The Key Reporter* 62:4 (Summer, 1997): 4.

[7] Ibid. Stanley Hauerwas has often observed how such an approach to education would never be an option in medical schools. Whereas in divinity

schools, for example, students might think they can choose not to take a class on the trinity on the assumption that it would not make much difference in their professional life, any medical student who chose not to take a course in anatomy would simply be dismissed.

[8] Stanley Hauerwas, personal correspondence.

[9] Alasdair MacIntyre, *After Virtue* (Notre Dame, IN: University of Notre Dame Press, 1984), 11–12.

[10] Cited by Scriven, "Schooling for the Tournament of Narratives," 280.

[11] Mark Edmundson, "On the Uses of Liberal Education, As Lite Entertainment for Bored College Students," *Harper's* (Sept., 1997): 39 and 40.

[12] For similar kinds of observations, see David Burrell, "A Catholic University," in *The Challenge and Promise of a Catholic University*, ed. Theodore M. Hesburgh, C.S.C. (Notre Dame, IN: University of Notre Dame Press, 1994), 35–44.

[13] Max Weber, "Science as a Vocation," in *From Max Weber: Essays in Sociology*, H. H. Geth and C. Wright Mills, tr. and ed. (New York: Oxford University Press, 1977): 149.

[14] Ibid., 139, emphasis added.

[15] Ibid., 135, emphasis added.

[16] Mark Schwehn cites several authors who discuss how Weber's conception of the academic vocation draws from his Puritan heritage. Among these are Arnold Eisen and Sheldon Wolin. See Schwehn, *Exiles from Eden: Religion and the Academic Vocation in America* (New York: Oxford University Press, 1993), 12–14.

[17] Cited by Charles Taylor, *Sources of the Self: The Making of the Modern Identity* (Cambridge, MA: Harvard University Press, 1989), 224.

[18] Schwehn, *Exiles from Eden*, 15–16.

[19] For a fuller description of Weber's disenchantment, see Nicholas Wolterstorff, "Theology and Science: Listening to Each Other," in *Religion and Science: History, Method, Dialogue*, ed. W. Mark Richardson and Wesley J. Wildman (New York: Routledge, 1996): 95–96.

[20] John Bunyan, *Grace Abounding to the Chief of Sinners*, in *The Pilgrim's Progress and Grace Abounding*, ed. James Thorpe (Boston: Houghton Mifflin Co., 1969 [1666]): paragraph 53.

[21] John H. Yoder, *The Priestly Kingdom* (Notre Dame, IN: University of Notre Dame Press, 1984), 210 n. 9.

[22] Tina Pippin, "Border Pedagogy: Activism in a Wymyn and Religion Classroom," *The Council of Societies for the Study of Religion Bulletin* 4:1 (Feb., 1995): 5–8.

[23] Murray Jardine, *Speech and Political Practice: Recovering the Place of Human Responsibility* (New York: State University of New York Press, 1998), 2–3.

[24] Ibid., 5–6. Nicholas Lash describes this modern/postmodern dilemma: "it is as if the ideals of the seventeenth century [have] been *reversed*. . . . we find ourselves enmeshed in endless labours of interpretation, all discourse seemingly unstable, pregnant with possibility and unforeseen disaster, heavy with allusions, dreams, and nightmares. . . ." in "Contemplation, Metaphor, and Real Knowledge," unpublished paper, delivered at "Knowing God, Christ and Nature in the Post-Positivistic Era," Symposium, University of Notre Dame, April 14–17, 1993, 17, emphasis added.

[25] Kathryn Tanner, *God and Creation in Christian Theology* (New York: Basil Blackwell, 1988), 125.

[26] These passages from Pascal's *Penseés,* tr. W. F. Trotter (London, 1932) are quoted by William H. Poteat, "Persons and Places: Paradigms in Communication," in *The Primacy of Persons and the Language of Culture,* ed. James M. Nickell and James W. Stines (Columbia: University of Missouri Press, 1993): 32–33.

[27] Ibid., 40.

[28] Poteat, "Persons and Places," 32–33, 40.

[29] Ibid.

[30] Michael Polanyi, *Personal Knowledge, Towards a Post-Critical Philosophy* (Chicago: University of Chicago Press, 1958), 294, emphasis added.

[31] Ibid., 65. Emphasis added. Poteat observes that Polanyi shares Augustine's emphasis on the "relying upon" character of all our knowing and being, the persistence of Platonic elements in Augustine's own imagination notwithstanding. Augustine writes: "Whoever doubts that he lives, and remembers, and understands, and wills, and thinks, and knows, and judges. For indeed even if he doubts, he lives; if he doubts, he remembers why he doubts; if he doubts, he understands that he doubts; if he doubts, he knows that he does not know; if he doubts, he judges that he ought not to give his consent rashly. Whosoever therefore doubts about anything else, ought not to doubt about all these things; for if they were not, he would not be able to doubt about anything." As Poteat notes, "A more sweeping statement of the fiduciary structure of knowing and being can hardly be imagined," in William H. Poteat, *Polanyian Meditations: In Search of a Post-Critical Logic* (Durham, NC: Duke University Press, 1985): 185.

[32] Lash, "Contemplation," 4.

[33] John H. Yoder, *The Royal Priesthood: Essays Ecclesiological and Ecumenical* (Grand Rapids, MI: Eerdmans, 1994), 257.

[34] I have developed the relation between hospitality and higher education further in "Who's Home Cooking? Hospitality, Christian Identity and Higher Education," *Perspectives in Religious Studies* 26:1 (Spring, 1999): 7–16, and "The Politics of Higher Education: Hospitality as a Counter Practice," paper presented at the Baylor Pruit Memorial Symposium: Cultivating Citizens, Soulcraft and Citizenship in Contemporary America, Baylor University, Oct. 28–30, 1999.

[35] Hannah Arendt writes that such "spaces of appearance" are by no means a matter of course in a society which readily objectifies others, and defines people in terms of their work or "contribution." She maintains, however, that this "is not to say that [we] are free to dispense with a public realm altogether, for without a space of appearance and without trusting in action and speech as a mode of being together, neither the reality of one's self, of one's own identity, nor the reality of the surrounding world can be established beyond doubt," in *The Human Condition* (Chicago: University of Chicago Press, 1958), 208. Reinhold Niebuhr likewise distinguishes between "external observation" which can easily debase another, and listening to another speak in his or her own words: "This person, this other 'Thou' cannot be understood until he speaks to us. . . . This word spoken from beyond

us and to us is both a verification of our belief that we are dealing with a different dimension than animal existence; and also a revelation of the actual and precise character of the person with whom we are dealing," in *The Nature and Destiny of Man*, vol. 1 (New York: Charles Scribner's Sons, 1941), 130.

[36] Polanyi, *Personal Knowledge*, viii.

[37] Thomas Hoyt, Jr. "Testimony," in *Practicing Our Faith: A Way of Life for a Searching People*, ed. Dorothy C. Bass (San Francisco: Jossey-Bass, 1997): 92 and 99.

[38] I have further discussed the significance of testimony for our postmodern times in "The Practice of Testimony in a 'Postmodern' Context," *Perspectives in Religious Studies* 25:1 (Spring, 1998): 81–92.

[39] Arendt, *The Human Condition*, 237. Emphasis added.

[40] Ibid., 243.

Neary: The Erotic Imagination

[1] Ann Belaford Ulanov, *The Feminine in Jungian Psychology and in Christian Theology* (Evanston, IL: Northwestern University Press, 1971), 155.

[2] Mary Gordon, *Final Payments* (New York: Ballantine Books, 1979), 175.

[3] Ibid., 260.

[4] Ibid., 298.

[5] Ibid., 299.

[6] Anders Nygren, *Agape and Eros* (Philadelphia: Westminster, 1953), 75–77.

[7] Ibid., 93.

[8] Ibid., 739–40.

[9] Ibid., 298.

[10] Ibid., 722.

[11] Ibid., 683.

[12] Ibid., 740.

[13] Ibid.

[14] David Tracy, *The Analogical Imagination: Christian Theology and the Culture of Pluralism* (New York: Crossroad, 1981), 432.

[15] Jacques Derrida, *Writing and Difference*, tr. Alan Bass (Chicago: University of Chicago Press, 1978), 278.

[16] Ibid., 279–80.

[17] Carl A. Raschke, "The Deconstruction of God," in *Deconstruction and Theology*, ed. Thomas J. J. Altizer et al. (New York: Crossroad, 1983): 3.

[18] Ibid.

[19] J. Hillis Miller, "Presidential Address 1986, The Triumph of Theory, the Resistance to Reading, and the Question of the Material Base," *PMLA* 102 (1987): 282.

[20] Kevin Hart, *The Trespass of the Sign: Deconstruction, Theology, and Philosophy* (Cambridge: Cambridge University Press, 1989), 190.

[21] Ibid., 192.

[22] Andrew M. Greeley, *The Catholic Myth: The Behavior and Beliefs of American Catholics* (New York: Macmillan, 1990), 13.

[23] Ibid.

[24] Ibid., 45.

[25] Elizabeth Johnson, *She Who Is: The Mystery of God in Feminist Theological Discourse* (New York: Crossroad, 1987), 168.

[26] Sally McFague, *Models of God: Theology for an Ecological, Nuclear Age* (Philadelphia: Fortress Press, 1987), 131.

[27] Gordon, *Final Payments*, 298.

[28] Parker J. Palmer, *To Know As We Are Known: Education as a Spiritual Journey* (San Francisco: HarperSanFrancisco, 1993 [1983]), 68.

[29] Ibid., 53–54.

[30] Ibid., 8.

[31] Ibid.

[32] Ibid., 31.

[33] Ibid., 103–4.

[34] Henri J. M. Nouwen, *Creative Ministry* (Garden City, NY: Doubleday, 1971), 4.

[35] Ibid., 11.

[36] Ibid., 12.

[37] Ibid., 13–14.

[38] Palmer, *To Know As We Are Known*, 103.

[39] Ibid., 106–25.

[40] Greeley, *Catholic Myth*, 272.

[41] Ibid., 273.

[42] Andrew M. Greeley, "The Catholic Imagination and the Catholic University," *Current Issues in Catholic Higher Education* 12 (1992): 39.

O'Brien: "Academic" vs. "Confessional" Study of the Bible

[1] From 1989–1997, I taught at Meredith College in Raleigh, North Carolina, an undergraduate college for women, at the time formally related to the Southern Baptist denomination through the North Carolina Convention. I now hold the position of Paul H. and Grace L. Stern Professor of Old Testament Studies at Lancaster Theological Seminary in Lancaster, Pennsylvania, a seminary of the United Church of Christ that serves persons from a variety of denominational and life contexts.

[2] Mark A. Noll, "Christian Colleges, Christian Worldviews, and an Invitation to Research," in *The Christian College: A History of Protestant Higher Education in America*, ed. William C. Ringenberg (Grand Rapids, MI: Christian University Press/Eerdmans, 1985): 3–16.

[3] Ibid., 24–32.

[4] Claude Welch, "The Twentieth Century American Development of Programs for the Study of Religion," a paper prepared for the Berkeley/Chicago/Harvard Summer Workshop (June 18, 1985).

[5] Task Force, "Report of the Task Force on Study in Depth of Religion," in *Liberal Learning and the Religion Major: A Report to the Profession*. Completed in conjunction with the Association of American College National Review of Arts and Sciences Majors (American Academy of Religion, 1990): 3

[6] Ibid., 4–5.

[7] Ibid., 16.

[8] Such a climate gives rise to the critique of the secular classroom by John W. Dixon, Jr.: "Departments of religion are the only departments forbidden

to be committed to their own subject, compelled to act as though it did not exist. We can do anything we want to do with the study of religion except for one thing: we cannot, professionally, take it seriously, believe that it is true, or act on that belief." See "What Should Religion Departments Teach?" (*Theology Today* 46 [Jan., 1990]: 364–72; 364).

[9] Numerous, heated debates about the "scientific" nature of religious studies have appeared in *The Bulletin of the Council of Societies for the Study of Religion*. The November 1999 issue, for example, runs critiques of Donald Wiebe's *The Politics of Religious Studies* (New York: St. Martin's Press, 1999). Richard Miller (111–12) challenges Wiebe's assumption that religious studies can be objective, and Steven Sutcliffe (113–15) notes, among other issues, Wiebe's "sidestepping of postmodernism" (114).

[10] Gary Phillips, "Exegesis as Critical Praxis: Reclaiming History and Text from a Postmodern Perspective," *Semeia* 51 (1990): 21.

[11] Ibid., 23.

[12] Charotte Allen provides an overview of other appropriations of postmodernism by evangelical Christians. See "Is Deconstruction the Last Best Hope of Evangelical Christians?" *Lingua Franca* 9:9 (2000): 46–59.

[13] Stephen Haynes, "Will the Paradox Endure? American Church-Related Colleges and the Postmodern Opportunity," proposal submitted to Lilly Endowment Inc., 1995: 2.

[14] Philip R. Davies, *Whose Bible Is It, Anyway?* JSOTS 204 (Sheffield: JSOT Press, 1995), 30.

[15] Ibid., 31.

[16] Ibid., 21.

[17] David J. A. Clines, *Interested Parties: The Ideology of Writers and Readers of the Hebrew Bible*, JSOTS 205 (Sheffield: JSOT Press, 1995), 19–20.

[18] Ibid., 109–10.

[19] Davies, *Whose Bible Is It?*, 27, 53.

[20] Ibid., 48.

[21] Ibid., 140–1.

[22] Clines, *Interested Parties*, 94–121.

[23] Ibid., 102, 117.

[24] A. Brenner and F. van Dijk-Hemmes, *On Gendering Texts: Female and Male Voices in the Hebrew Bible* (Leiden: E. J. Brill, 1993), 71–93; see also Athalya Brenner, ed., *A Feminist Companion to the Song of Songs* (Sheffield: JSOT Press, 1993).

[25] Clines's language (*Interested Parties*, 102); as cited above.

[26] Ibid., 109.

[27] Ibid., 111.

[28] Ibid., 117.

[29] Phyllis Trible, *God and the Rhetoric of Sexuality* (Philadelphia: Fortress Press, 1978). Similarly, Ilana Pardes deems Trible's 1973 attempt to find strong statements of gender equality in Genesis 2–3 as the effort to make the Bible into a "feminist manifesto." See *Countertraditions in the Bible: A Feminist Approach* (Cambridge, MA: Harvard University Press, 1992), 24.

[30] In this regard, I disagree with Ninian Smart's quip, "Anyway, anyone who can't distinguish between descriptive studies and value judgements is, in my view, unprofessional." See "Religious Studies and Theology," *Bulletin of the Council of Societies for the Study of Religion* 26 (1997): 66–68; 68.

[31] While I am aware of the argument of Stephen Fowl that ideologies are in readers rather than in texts, I maintain that a reader must share certain assumptions with the writer of a text in order for the text to be persuasive rhetorically. See "Texts Don't Have Ideologies," *Biblical Interpretation* 3 (1995): 15–34.

[32] Clines, *Interested Parties*, 76–93.

[33] Feminist scholars consistently have exposed the complicity of commentators with the power and gender assumptions of biblical texts. Among many examples, I cite Danna Fewell's look at commentators on Judges 1:11–15 and Pardes's exploration of the assumptions of feminist interpreters of Genesis 2–3 (*Countertraditions in the Bible*, 13–28). See Fewell, "Deconstructive Criticism: Achsah and the (E)razed City of Writing," in *Judges and Method: New Approaches in Biblical Studies*, ed. Gale Yee (Philadelphia: Fortress Press, 1995): 119–45.

[34] My own attempt to deal with the possibility—and personal necessity—of not assenting to a text's ideology is found in Julia O'Brien, "On Saying 'No' to a Prophet," *Semeia* 72 (1997): 111–24.

[35] Ninian Smart, "Religious Studies and Theology," *Bulletin of the Council of Societies for the Study of Religion* 26 (1997): 67. So, too, the statement of the AAR Task Force on Study in Depth of Religion: "If criticism is uninformed by an empathetic understanding of the criticized, it chiefly serves to confirm the moral or cultural superiority of the critic." See *Liberal Learning and the Religion Major*, 13.

Beal: Teaching the Conflicts

[1] Stanley Hauerwas, "A Non-violent Proposal for Christian Participation in the Culture Wars," *Soundings* 75 (1992), 477.

[2] This is the title of the article by Beverly Asbury (*Soundings* 75 [1992] 464–75) that provoked Hauerwas's "Non-violent Proposal."

[3] For discussions of the violence of modern metaphysics of history, see esp. Emmanuel Levinas, *Totality and Infinity*, tr. Alphonso Lingis (Pittsburgh: Duquesne University Press, 1969), 42–48; and Jacques Derrida, "Violence and Metaphysics: An Essay on the Thought of Emmanuel Levinas," in *Writing and Difference*, tr. Alan Bass (Chicago: University of Chicago Press, 1978): 79–153. On theological dimensions of this metaphysics of history, see Mark C. Taylor, "Denegating God," *Critical Inquiry* 20 (1994): 592–610; and Gianni Vattimo, *The Transparent Society*, tr. D. Webb (Baltimore, MD: The Johns Hopkins University Press, 1992), 41.

[4] Mark D. Walhout, "Beyond the Wars of Religion: How Teaching the Conflicts Can Desecularize American Education," *Profession* (1996): 139–45, working from Gerald Graff, *Beyond the Culture Wars: How Teaching the Conflicts Can Revitalize American Education* (New York: Norton, 1992); and Stanley Hauerwas, "Non-violent Proposal," 485–90, working from Alisdair MacIntyre, *Three Rival Versions of Moral Inquiry: Encyclopedia, Genealogy and Tradition* (Notre Dame, IN: University of Notre Dame Press, 1990). See also Graff's "Response to Mark Walhout," *Profession* (1996): 145–48; and Beverly Asbury's "A Reply to Hauerwas," *Soundings* 75 (1992): 493–97. It should be noted that all these writers except Walhout are focusing not on the church-related college but on the university and the current sense of identity crisis

in higher education more generally. See my discussion in the "Collegial Post-script" to this chapter.

[5] Homi Bhabha, "Editor's Introduction: Minority Maneuvers and Unsettled Negotiations," *Critical Inquiry* 23 (1997): 431–59, has made a similar critique of the "binary relationship that consists of unitary (individual and collective) cultural subjects" assumed in Charles Taylor's recent essay on mutual recognition in a context of multiculturalism, in which "difference is constituted and totalized *within* each culture," thereby leaving the illusion of cultural wholes without internal ambivalence. On the location of culture as interstitial, see esp. Homi K. Bhabha, *The Location of Culture* (London and New York: Routledge, 1994). For Charles Taylor's argument, see "The Politics of Recognition," *Multiculturalism*, ed. Amy Gutman (Princeton, NJ: Princeton University Press, 1994).

[6] My implication is not simply that one must choose which canonical list (e.g., Jewish Tanakh, Protestant, Catholic). Moreover, it is not simply a matter of which translation to choose. More to the point would be to ask which text(s) to translate. We have no original(s). If text critical scholarship has made anything clear it is that, despite its goal of establishing the most reliable text, the further we go back in text history the more variants there are. For a provocative and informative discussion on these matters and the deeply frustrated desire in biblical studies for a pristine textual origin, see esp. David M. Gunn, "What Does the Bible Say? A Question of Text and Canon," in *Reading Bibles, Writing Bodies: Identity and The Book*, ed. Timothy K. Beal and David M. Gunn (London and New York: Routledge, 1996): 242–61.

[7] The phrase is from Jacques Derrida, "Living On/Border Lines," tr. James Hulbert, in *Deconstruction and Criticism*, ed. Harold Bloom et al. (New York: Continuum, 1979), 90.

[8] I am using the term Other here in the sense described by Simone de Beauvoir in *The Second Sex*, tr. H. M. Parshley (New York: Vintage, 1953)—that is, as the one marked socially and politically and intellectually as the privileged representation of oppositional difference to "us," the quintessential not-self. This use of the term diverges significantly from its use in the context of negative theology and neo-orthodox theology, on which see Taylor, "Denegating God."

[9] See esp. Danna Nolan Fewell and David M. Gunn, *Gender, Power, and Promise: The Subject of the Bible's First Story* (Nashville: Abingdon, 1993), 164–73 and 182–85.

[10] The Hebrew pointing of her name gives it the meaning "dung," which obviously adds another level of gratuitousness to the literary play on her death here. See John Gray, *1 and 2 Kings* (Philadelphia: Westminster, 1978), 368.

[11] Likewise, on a canonical level, other voices can be found within Hebrew Scriptures that are in explicit and deep conflict with the Deuteronomistic interpretation of that crisis. For an in-depth discussion of Job as a critique of the moral universe of Deuteronomy, for example, see Timothy K. Beal, "Facing Job," *Semeia* (forthcoming); see also Tod Linafelt, "The Undecidability of *barak* in the Prologue to Job," *Biblical Interpretation* 4 (1995): 1–18.

[12] Indeed, there are ethical reasons for reading this narrative against the grain as I am proposing. How can we identify unquestionably with the Deuteronomistic point of view and its champion Elijah in a time of so-called

ethnic cleansing—driven by the similar fantasies of "our" pristine origins—and of prophetic reformers like Yigal Amir, who did no more than Elijah would have wanted when he assassinated Israeli Prime Minister Yitzhak Rabin for entertaining conversation and compromise with modern Israel's other, the Palestinian Liberation Organization?

¹³ Phyllis Trible, "Exegesis for Storytellers and Other Strangers," *Journal of Biblical Literature* 114 (1995): 3–19; see also "The Odd Couple: Elijah and Jezebel," in *Out of the Garden: Women Writers on the Bible*, ed. Christina Büchmann and Celina Spiegel (London: Pandora, 1994).

¹⁴ Besides supportive details in the biblical text itself, the legitimacy of such a question might be supported by the recent discovery of a broken pythos, found at the excavation of Kuntillet 'Ajrud in northeastern Sinai and dated to the eighth century BCE, which depicts two figures with arms locked together and a third figure in the background, along with the inscription (in Hebrew), "I bless you by yhwh of Samaria [another name for the northern kingdom of Israel] and his Asherah." For a sketch of the image, along with a discussion of its possible significance as evidence of a divine consort for YHWH in ancient Israel, see Athalya Brenner, "The Hebrew God and His Female Complements," in Beal and Gunn, ed., *Reading Bibles, Writing Bodies*, 65-68.

¹⁵ Compare Jehu's murderous trick on the prophets of Baal after Ahab's death in 2 Kings 10:18–27.

¹⁶ For a helpful recent survey of scholarly theories on the literary history of DtrH, see esp. Steven L. McKenzie, "Deuteronomistic History," *Anchor Bible Dictionary* 2: 160–68.

¹⁷ For a recent discussion between Ernesto Laclau and Judith Butler on hegemony that is suggestive with regard to this point, see *Diacritics* 27 (1997): 3–19.

¹⁸ Jean-François Lyotard, *The Postmodern Condition: A Report on Knowledge*, tr. Geoff Bennington and Brian Massumi (Minneapolis: University of Minnesota Press, 1984), 31–37. See the subsequent discussion.

¹⁹ Douglas Sloan, *Faith and Knowledge: Mainline Protestantism and Higher Education* (Louisville, KY: Westminster/John Knox, 1994), 91–97, 179, 212 *et passim*.

²⁰ Indeed, the "liberal Protestantism" and "post-Protestantism" described by George M. Marsden is a Hegelian modernism linked with American nationalism. See, e.g., "The Soul of the American University: An Historical Overview," in *The Secularization of the Academy*, ed. George M. Marsden and Bradley J. Longfield (Oxford: Oxford University Press, 1992), 22–25, 34.

Scibilia: A Pedagogy of Eucharistic Accompaniment

¹ Henri J. M. Nouwen, *With Burning Hearts* (New York: Orbis Books, 1996), 81.

² Ibid., 58.

³ Robert Wilken, *Remembering the Christian Past* (Grand Rapids, MI: Eerdmans, 1995) citing Maximus the Confessor in *Knowledge of God*, 156.

⁴ Ralph Ellison, *Invisible Man* (New York: Vintage International, 1990), 508.

[5] "Poverty, Corruption and Slow Demilitarization Process Threatens Governability in Central America," *Central America/Mexico Report* 3 (June 1997): 2.

[6] Dominic Scibilia et al., "Conscientizing the Culture of Silience," paper presented at the Pedagogy of the Oppressed Conference, University of Nebraska at Omaha (Feb. 6, 1995): 3.

[7] Thomas Merton, *Love and Living* (New York: Harcourt, Brace and Co., 1985), 3–4.

[8] Albert Raboteau, *Fire in the Bones* (Boston: Beacon, 1995), 11.

[9] Scibilia, "Conscientizing," 4.

[10] Ibid., 9–10.

[11] Roberto Goizueta, *Camineos Con Jesús* (New York: Orbis Books, 1995), 5–17.

[12] Ibid., 191ff.

[13] bell hooks and Cornel West, *Breaking Bread* (Boston: South End Press, 1991), 18f.

[14] Raboteau, *Fire in the Bones*, 10.

[15] hooks and West, *Breaking Bread*, 1.

Miller: A One-Armed Embrace of Postmodernity

[1] Theron F. Schlabach, "Goshen College and Its Church Relations: History and Reflections," in *Models for Christian Higher Education: Strategies for Survival and Success in the Twenty-First Century*, ed. Richard T. Hughes and William B. Adrian (Grand Rapids, MI: Eerdmans, 1997): 209.

[2] Fuller descriptions of some of these and twenty other programs can be found in Ann Kelleher, *Learning from Success: Case Studies in International Program Development* (New York: Peter Lang, 1996).

[3] Most of these descriptions were given at the Goshen-sponsored conference "The Church and College in Partnership: A Vision for the Future," 23–26 March 1995.

[4] At the first meeting of the Rhodes Consultation on the Future of the Church-Related College, each participant described his or her institution's relationship with its sponsoring denomination. With tale after tale of quite tenuous linkages and occasional wistfulness about past interconnectedness, I felt strangely out-of-place, as though I had entered the wrong room.

[5] Robert N. Bellah, Richard Madsen, William M. Sullivan, Ann Swidler and Steve Tipton, *Habits of the Heart* (San Francisco: Harper and Row, 1985), 245.

[6] I'm speaking here of the Mennonite Church and the General Conference Mennonite Church, the two largest Mennonite denominations which are now in the process of integrating into one denomination, the Mennonite Church. There are a score of other Mennonite and Amish groupings under the larger Anabaptist umbrella, with a total of just over one million members around the world.

[7] John Richard Burkholder, "Pacifist Ethics and Pacifist Politics," in *Betrayed? Essays on Pacifism and Politics*, ed. Michael Cromartie (Washington, D.C.: Ethics and Public Policy Center, 1990): 198.

[8] Kelleher, *Learning*, 209.

[9] On this, see Robert N. Bellah et al., *The Good Society* (New York: Knopf, 1991), 217.

[10] Ted Koontz, "Mennonites and 'Postmodernity', " *Mennonite Quarterly Review* 63:4 (Oct., 1989). See also the quite differently structured and argued thesis of Elaine K. Swartzentruber, "Marking and Remarking the Body of Christ: Toward a Postmodern Mennonite Ecclesiology," *Mennonite Quarterly Review* 71:2 (April, 1997): 243–65.

[11] On this, see Anne Colby and William Damon, *Some Do Care: Contemporary Lives of Moral Commitment* (New York: The Free Press, 1992), 77.

[12] The quote is from George Marsden, "The Soul of the American University: A Historical Overview," in *The Secularization of the Academy*, ed. Marsden and Bradley J. Longfield (New York: Oxford University Press, 1992): 30.

[13] Schlabach, "Goshen College," 202–3.

[14] Richard T. Hughes, "Introduction," in Hughes and Adrian, *Models*, 5–6.

[15] Rodney J. Sawatsky, "What Can the Mennonite Tradition Contribute to Christian Higher Education," in Hughes and Adrian, *Models*, 194.

[16] Sawatsky, "What Can the Mennonite Tradition," 196. Sawatsky says Mennonite colleges hire only Christian faculty for incarnational reasons as well. "The professors are both to teach and to model their Christian faith."

[17] Schlabach says that "at the risk of making a false dichotomy, it seems fair to say that Goshen's SST resulted more from the kind of church that sponsored the college than from the college itself." Schlabach, "Goshen College," 209.

[18] Victor Stoltzfus, "Faculty Experience Factor in SST Origin," *Goshen College Bulletin* (Nov., 1988): 24. See also Susan Fisher Miller's description of the impact of Civilian Public Service in *Culture for Service: A History of Goshen College, 1894–1994* (Goshen, IN: Goshen College, 1994), 170–76.

[19] Henry D. Weaver, "The Goshen Faculty Create SST," *Goshen College Bulletin* (July, 1988): 2–3.

[20] See Allan O. Pfnister, "Everyone Overseas! Goshen College Pioneers," *International, Educational, and Cultural Exchange* 8:2 (Washington, D.C.: U.S. Advisory Commission Staff, Department of State, 1972): 1. Kalamazoo and Lake Erie sent their students to European universities, and Callison sent its sophomores to the University of Bangalore in India. Nearly two hundred other American colleges and universities sent at least some students abroad at the time. One hundred sixty-four sent students to Europe; fourteen to Asia; ten to Central America and the Caribbean; six to South America; and four to Africa. See "The Study-Service Trimester Abroad at Goshen College: A Summary," 7, available in the Mennonite Historical Library, Goshen College.

[21] From Ann Martin, "An International Legacy," *Goshen College Bulletin* (March, 1985): 2.

[22] "The Study-Service Trimester Abroad" (March, 1971): 11, available in Mennonite Historical Library.

[23] Wilbur Birky, "SST: Vision, History, and Ethos," *1999–2000 SST Faculty Handbook*, Goshen College. Emphasis in original.

[24] See Robert L. Sigmon's "A Service Learning Timeline," Appendix A in Sigmon et al., *Journey to Service Learning* (Washington, D.C.: Council of Independent Colleges, 1996): 158–67.

[25] Thirty-seven percent of U.S. high schools are either operating or planning programs in which students are "required to perform a specific number of hours of community service," according to one recent report cited in Chester E. Finn, Jr., and Gregg Vanourek, "Charity Begins at School," *Commentary* (Oct., 1995): 46. Maryland has a statewide service-learning requirement for high schools.

[26] Ernest Boyer, "Creating the New American College," *The Chronicle of Higher Education* (9 March 1994): A48. The article has been cited by many service-learning proponents, including John W. Eby in "Linking Service and Scholarship," in Sigmon et al., *Journey*, 87–97; and Robert G. Bringle and Julie A. Hatcher, "Implementing Service Learning in Higher Education," *The Journal of Higher Education* (March/April, 1996): 221–39. A 1994 survey of Goshen College alumni indicated that of seven factors influencing them toward volunteer/service work, next to the church, Goshen College and its SST program had provided the most impetus.

[27] Joseph Kahne and Joel Westheimer, "In the Service of What? The Politics of Service Learning," *Phi Delta Kappan* (May, 1996): 596.

[28] About the time Goshen's SST program was initiated, Ivan Illich gave a provocative address to the Conference on Inter-American Student Projects at Cuernavaca. In the speech, titled "To Hell with Good Intentions!," Illich told his listeners voluntarily to "renounce exercising the power which being an American gives you (as 'vacationing do-gooders') to impose American benevolence on Mexico." He entreated his audience to "use your money, your status and your education to travel in Latin America. Come to look, come to climb our mountains, to enjoy our flowers. Come to *study*. But do not come to *help*." Cited in Alexander A. Kwapong, "Some Reflections on the Role of International Education in the '90s," in *The Role of Service-Learning in International Education*, ed. Stuart W. Showalter (Goshen, IN: Goshen College, 1989): 16.

[29] Rachel Eash, SST Journal, Summer 1997. Most of the student journals I'm drawing on here are from the Dominican Republic, where my spouse and I have led four Study-Service Term units, two in 1989 and two in 1997. I draw from this material because it is most familiar to me, but many other sources from student journals over the past thirty-two years confirm the basic trajectories and sensitivities noted here.

[30] David G. Roth, SST Journal, Summer 1997.

[31] Peter Wiens, SST Journal, Summer 1997. According to a 1971 Goshen College analysis, the values best taught on SST were "international perspective, service, and social concern" and the values most poorly taught were "purity and academic excellence." See "The Study Service Trimester Abroad of Goshen College" (March, 1971): 48, available in Mennonite Historical Library.

[32] Miller, *Culture for Service*, 270. The encounter between Hunsberger and *Goshen College Record* staffers took place in the 28 January 1977 and 4 March 1977 issues.

[33] On disorientation, see, e.g., William A. Beardslee, "Stories in the Postmodern World: Orienting and Disorienting," in *Sacred Interconnections: Postmodern Spirituality, Political Economy and Art*, ed. David Ray Griffin (Albany: State University of New York Press, 1990): 163–75. See also Hebrew Scripture scholar Walter Brueggemann on personal development changes

coming about through discontinuity, displacement, and disjunction rather than in stages of equilibrium. Brueggemann, *Hope within History* (Atlanta: John Knox Press, 1987), 9. As my colleague Marcia Bunge rightly notes in her essay for this volume, many students arriving on our campuses—including Goshen College—now come without a coherent foundation or a clear sense of their moral-ethical tradition. Therefore, the need for many forms of "disorienting" is considerably less than it may have been in 1968.

[34] Norman L. Kauffmann, Judith N. Martin, and Henry D. Weaver, with Judy Weaver, *Students Abroad, Strangers at Home: Education for a Global Society* (Yarmouth, ME: Intercultural Press, 1992). The authors, two of whom were long-time administrators at Goshen College and based some of their research on interviews with returned SST students, note that findings vary depending on research methodology, and on what terms such as "interpersonal skills" mean. Many other studies confirm the basic results reported here.

[35] Amy Thut, SST journal, Spring 1997. Among the stated goals for SST are "appreciation of the integrity of a culture other than one's own," "critical evaluation of one's own culture," and "acknowledgment of the intellectual and artistic contributions of world cultures." See "Final Report, Common Experience Committee, SST Review Group" (13 May 1993): 2.

[36] "The Study Service Trimester Abroad," 46. Among the stated goals for SST are "entering into dialogue with people of other religious traditions and being able to express one's own beliefs in a culturally sensitive manner" and "maturation in spiritual faith and personal religious commitment." See "Final Report, Common Experience Committee," 2.

[37] Amy Thut, SST journal, Spring 1997.

[38] "Vision for SST—Wilbur Birky—October 1995," 1. In a 1994 survey of Goshen College alumni, graduates were asked what impact their Goshen College education had on helping them meet Goshen's "Ten Desired Outcomes." The outcome rated highest by students was "intercultural openness with the ability to function effectively with people of other worldviews."

[39] Lisa Koop, SST journal, Summer 1997.

[40] See, e.g., June Noronha, "International and Multicultural Education: Unrelated Adversaries or Successful Partners?," in *Promoting Diversity in College Classrooms: Innovative Responses for Curriculum, Faculty and Institutions*, ed. Maurianne Adams (San Francisco: Jossey-Bass, 1999): 53–61; Janet Marie Bennett and Milton James Bennett, "Multiculturalism and International Education: Domestic and International Differences," in *Learning Across Cultures*, ed. Gary Althen (NAFSA: Association of International Educators, 1994), 145–72; and Elaine Razzano, "The Overseas Route to Multicultural and International Education," *The Clearing House* (May–June, 1996): 268–70.

[41] Edgar Metzler, "International Orientation Decades Old," *Goshen College Bulletin* (Nov., 1988): 3. For a refined understanding of how cultural differences are manifest on campuses with foreign students, see Gary Althen's "Cultural Differences on Campus," in Althen, ed., *Learning Across Cultures*, 55–71.

[42] See Susan Fisher Miller, *Culture for Service*, 271–72, regarding earlier tensions between the college and its African-American students. Other tensions have emerged in the last decade as well. Nonetheless, in the spring of 2000,

Goshen College received the first Racial Harmony Award given by the Council for Christian Colleges and Universities.

[43] Schlabach, "Goshen College," 215. Kelleher also notes that "successful, sustainable international programs are identified with the existing values already in the minds of faculty and administrators." Kelleher, *Learning from Success*, 11.

[44] "International Education at GC," two-page Goshen College flyer, 1997.

[45] On this, see Kauffmann et al., *Students Abroad*, 157–60.

[46] "DZ," in Cynthia Hockman, *Returning Home: SSTers Talk about the Re-Entry Experience* (Goshen, IN: Pinchpenny Press, 1989): 24. The Hockman book is required reading for most SST groups.

[47] "DZ," in Hockman, *Returning Home*, 14.

[48] Ruth Krall, "Leading SST Convinces Krall Relational Teaching Is Best," *Goshen College Bulletin* (Nov., 1988): 5.

[49] SST leaders function as teachers, counselors, substitute parents, friends, physicians and pastors for students. The international setting allows for the development of intimate, empathic teaching and learning of the sort that other colleagues have addressed in this volume. Some of these methods of relating and teaching can and should be brought back into the classroom on campus.

[50] This listing, which corresponds with observations made by many SSTers, can be found in Althen, "Recurring Issues in Intercultural Communication," in Althen, ed., *Learning Across Cultures*, 188. Althen also cites the Bagish statement from a presentation at the University of California at Santa Barbara.

[51] Stuart Showalter, "A Bold Experiment in Education," *Goshen College Bulletin* (March, 1985): 3.

Bunge: Religion and the Curriculum

[1] Martha C. Nussbaum, *Cultivating Humanity: A Classical Defense of Reform in Liberal Education* (Cambridge, MA: Harvard University Press, 1997), 264.

[2] Ibid., 265.

[3] Ibid., 278.

[4] According to a survey conducted by Stephen Haynes (Associate Professor of Religious Studies, Rhodes College), the average is 2.4 courses.

[5] Alan Wolfe, "A Welcome Revival of Religion in the Academy," *Chronicle of Higher Education* (Sept. 19, 1997): 2.

[6] Ibid., 2. Wolfe adds that they also lack three dispositions associated with religious belief: "a tragic view of life, grounding in a particular set of ethical maxims, and a sense of wonder."

[7] Douglas Sloan, *Faith and Knowledge: Mainline Protestantism and American Higher Education* (Louisville, KY: Westminster/John Knox, 1994), 1.

[8] See George M. Marsden, "The Soul of the American University: A Historical Overview," in *The Secularization of the Academy*, ed. George M. Marsden and Bradley J. Longfield (New York: Oxford University Press, 1992).

[9] William Scott Green, "Religion within the Limits," *Academe* (Nov.–Dec., 1996): 26.

[10] Warren A. Nord, *Religion and American Education: Rethinking a National Dilemma* (Chapel Hill: University of North Carolina Press, 1995), 3.

[11] Joshua Mitchell, "Religion in the Academic Life," *Academe* (Nov.–Dec., 1996): 30–31.

[12] David Hoekema, "Politics, Religion, and Other Crimes Against Civility," *Academe* (Nov.–Dec., 1996): 35.

[13] Informal survey given to students in the course "Studies in Religion" at Gustavus Adolphus College (Spring, 1997).

[14] As David Tracy has said, "The real face of postmodernity, as Emmanuel Levinas sees with such clarity, is the face of the other, the face that commands 'Do not kill me,' the face that insists, beyond Levinas, do not reduce me or anyone else to your grand narrative" ("Theology and the Many Faces of Postmodernity," *Theology Today* 51 [1994]: 108).

[15] Wolfe, "A Welcome Revival," 1.

[16] Ibid.

[17] Isaac Kramnick and R. Laurence Moore, "The Godless University," *Academe* (Nov.–Dec., 1996): 22.

[18] Kay Haugaard, "Result of Too Much Tolerance?"; see also Robert Simon, "The Paralysis of 'Absolutophobia'." Both articles are in *The Chronicle of Higher Education* (June 27, 1997).

[19] George Dennis O'Brien, *All the Essential Half-Truths about Higher Education* (Chicago: University of Chicago Press, 1998), 68.

[20] Nussbaum, *Cultivating Humanity*, 40. Here she also cites the work of Hilary Putnam, W.V.O. Quine, and Donald Davidson.

[21] Ibid., 54.

[22] Ibid., 145.

[23] Ibid.

[24] Nord, *Religion and American Education*, 212.

[25] Ibid., 207. He also argues for the inclusion of religion in a liberal arts education by emphasizing that religion is an important aspect of human experience: It has significantly shaped human affairs and contemporary culture, it has influenced moral beliefs and actions, it addresses questions of ultimate concern (204–12).

[26] Nord, *Religion and American Education*, 206.

[27] William Scott Green, "Religion Within the Limits," *Academe* (Nov.–Dec., 1996): 27.

[28] Martin Marty, "You Get to Teach and Study Religion," *Academe* (Nov.–Dec., 1996), 17.

[29] Some of the other reasons he gives: "religion is hard to define, and thus a tantalizing subject"; "religion, however defined, helps explain many human activities"; "religion is protean, so discovery in its zone demands many specialties" (you cannot "disentangle religion from the manifold forms of human expression"); "religion gets to be studied because it is practical"; and "religion as a subject matter or a dimension of culture has attracted a scholarly cohort of experts" ("You Get to Teach," 14–17).

[30] Address to the United Nations General Assembly, Oct. 1995. Quoted from Nussbuam, *Cultivating Humanity*, 259.

[31] Tracy, "Theology," 108.

[32] Ibid., 109.

[33] Ibid., 108.

[34] Ibid., 109.

[35] Nord claims that "the great majority of students know very little about religion. They learn nothing about it at school, and increasingly, they learn nothing about it at home or in church or synagogue" (*Religion and American Education*, 200). He also gave students a short exam of thirty questions dealing with the Bible, Western religious history, and world religions, attempting to test their "religious literacy." Not one of the one hundred and fifty students who took the exam passed with a score of seventy percent or above; the average score was twenty-eight percent (199).

[36] St. Olaf Academic Catalogue (1996–1997), 27.

[37] Roanoke College Academic Catalog (1996–1997), 1.

[38] O'Brien, *All the Essential Half-Truths*, 67.

[39] Ibid., 190.

[40] Ibid., 199.

[41] Ibid., 198.

[42] bell hooks, *Teaching to Transgress: Education as the Practice of Freedom* (New York: Routledge, 1994).

[43] Parker J. Palmer, "Community, Conflict, and Ways of Knowing," *Change* (Sept./Oct.): 25. See also Parker J. Palmer, *To Know as We Are Known: Education as a Spiritual Journey* (San Francisco: HarperSan Francisco, 1983).

[44] For a description of the current situation of adjunct and temporary appointments, see *Will Teach for Food: Academic Labor in Crisis*, ed. Cary Nelson (Minneapolis: University of Minnesota Press, 1997).

Grieser and Norman: From the Ties that Bind to Way-Stations

[1] George M. Marsden, *The Soul of the American University: From Protestant Establishment to Established Nonbelief* (New York: Oxford University Press, 1994).

[2] James Fowler, *Stages of Faith: The Psychology of Human Development and the Quest for Meaning* (San Francisco: HarperSanFrancisco, 1995 [1981]).

[3] Sharon Parks, *The Critical Years: Young Adults and the Search for Meaning, Faith and Commitment* (San Francisco: Harper and Row, 1986).

[4] The works by Wade Clark Roof are: *A Generation of Seekers: The Spiritual Journeys of the Baby Boom Generation* (San Francisco: HarperSanFrancisco, 1993) and *Spiritual Marketplace: Baby Boomers and the Remaking of American Religion* (Princeton, NJ: Princeton University Press, 1999).

[5] Roof, *A Generation of Seekers*, 10.

[6] Roof, *Spiritual Marketplace*, 229.

[7] Ibid., 227.

[8] Ibid., 228.

[9] For a fascinating discussion of Sewanee's role in the religious life of the South after the Civil War, see Charles Reagan Wilson, *Baptized in Blood: The Religion of the Lost Cause 1865–1920* (Athens: University of Georgia Press, 1980), 145–51, 160.

[10] Robert N. Bellah et al., *Habits of the Heart: Individualism and Commitment in American Life* (Berkeley: University of California Press, 1985), 219–35.

[11] After reading the first set of projects, we became aware of their value as primary sources and we asked for students' permission to use them in future research and publications.

¹² Most recent census figures give the following: for the regions from which Sewanee derives most of its students, the percentage of Southern Baptists among all who identified religious affiliation ranged from 27.1% for the South Atlantic region to 45.4% for the East South Central (which includes Tennessee). Catholic membership varied from 7.4% in the East South Central to 29.6% in the West South Central. By contrast, Episcopal membership is at the highest in the South Atlantic, where it reaches 2.7% of the total number of people who claim membership in Christian churches. Martin B. Bradley et al., eds., *Churches and Church Membership in the United States 1990: An Enumeration by Region, State and County Based on Data Reported for 133 Church Groupings* (Atlanta: Glenmary Research Center, 1991), 7–9.

¹³ One of the most remarkable transformations involved a student's grandmother, born in Ireland, a devout Roman Catholic wife and mother, who began to attend services at a Hindu monastery (identified by the student as "Rama Krishna") after the death of her husband.

¹⁴ Roof, *Spiritual Marketplace*, 227.

¹⁵ Mircea Eliade, *The Sacred and the Profane: The Nature of Religion*, tr. Willard R. Trask (New York: Harcourt Brace and Co., 1959).

Haynes: A Typology

¹ "First Annual Report of the President and Treasurer" (1906), cited in Leslie Karr Patton, *The Purposes of Church-Related Colleges: A Critical Study—A Proposal Program*, Teachers College Columbia University Contributions to Education 783 (New York: Columbia University, 1940): 7.

² The foundation utilized this typology in determining eligibility for its faculty pension program, excluding colleges in the first four categories and requiring those in the fifth "to certify by trustee resolution that no distinctly denominational tenets influenced admission, instruction, or the choice of trustees, officers or faculty."

³ Dorothy C. Bass, "Ministry on the Margin: Protestants and Education," in *Between the Times: The Travail of the Protestant Establishment in America, 1900–1960*, ed. William R. Hutchison (Cambridge: Cambridge University Press, 1989): 52.

⁴ Manning M. Pattillo, Jr., and Donald M. Mackenzie, *Church-Sponsored Higher Education in the United States: Report of the Danforth Commission* (Washington, D.C.: American Council on Education, 1966), 31.

⁵ See C. Robert Pace, *Education and Evangelism: A Profile of Protestant Colleges* (New York: McGraw-Hill and the Carnegie Foundation for the Advancement of Teaching, 1972), vii.

⁶ Merrimon Cuninggim, "Categories of Church-Relatedness," in *Church-Related Higher Education: Perceptions and Perspectives*, ed. Robert Rue Parsonage (Vallege Forge, PA: Judson Press, 1978): 32–35.

⁷ William E. Hull, "Christian Higher Education at the Crossroads," *Perspectives in Religious Studies* 19:4 (Winter, 1992): 442.

⁸ Ibid.

⁹ See Bass, "Church-Related Colleges."

¹⁰ Douglas Sloan, *Faith and Knowledge: Mainline Protestantism and American Higher Education* (Louisville: Westminster/John Knox, 1994), 84. This

discussion of the Faculty Christian Fellowship is dependent on Sloan, 84–86 and 179–85.

[11] Ibid., 180. Sloan also notes "the disappearance of any strong theological support for a critical dialogue with the university disciplines."

[12] Ibid., 185.

[13] William Rainey Harper, *The Prospects of the Small College* (Chicago: University of Chicago Press, 1900), 8.

[14] "Church Colleges in Trouble," *The Christian Century* (June 20, 1951): 733–35; 734.

[15] James Turnstead Burtchaell, "The Alienation of Christian Higher Education in America," in *Schooling Christians: Holy Experiments in American Education*, ed. Stanley Hauerwas and John Westerhoff (Grand Rapids, MI: Eerdmans, 1992): 153–83; 153.

[16] Keith Wilson, "The Secularization of the Academy: Is There a Theory that Maps the Process?," paper presented at Conference on the Church-Related College's Postmodern Opportunity, Rhodes College, May 2–4, 1997, 9.

[17] Stanley Hauerwas, *Christian Existence Today: Essays on Church, World and Living in Between* (Durham, NC: Labyrinth Press, 1988), 223.

Bibliography

Allen, Charlotte. "Is Deconstruction the Last Best Hope of Evangelical Christians?" *Lingua Franca* 9:9 (2000): 46–59.

Althen, Gary, ed. *Learning Across Cultures.* NAFSA: Association of International Educators, 1994.

Arendt, Hannah. *Between the Past and the Future.* New York: Viking Press, 1961.

———. *The Human Condition.* Chicago: University of Chicago Press, 1958.

Asbury, Beverly. "A Reply to Hauerwas," *Soundings* 74:4 (Winter, 1992): 493–97.

Augustine. *Confessions.* Tr. F. J. Sheed. Indianapolis: Hackett, 1993.

Averill, Lloyd J. *The Church College and the Public Good: A Report on the Status and Prospects of Church-Related Higher Education in the United States.* n.p.: Council of Protestant Colleges and Universities, 1969.

———. *A Strategy for the Protestant College.* Philadelphia: Westminster, 1966.

Baepler, Richard et al. *The Quest for a Viable Saga: The Church-Related College in an Age of Pluralism.* n.p.: Association of Lutheran College Faculties, 1977.

Bass, Dorothy C. "Church-Related Colleges: Transmitters of Denominational Cultures?" In *Beyond Establishment: Protestant Identity in a Post-Protestant World.* Ed. Jackson W. Carroll and Wade Clark Roof. Louisville, KY: Westminster/John Knox, 1993.

———. "Ministry on the Margin: Protestants and Education." In *Between the Times: The Travail of the Protestant Establishment in America, 1900–1960.* Ed. William R. Hutchison. Cambridge: Cambridge University Press, 1989.

————, ed. *Practicing Our Faith: A Way of Life for a Searching People.* San Francisco: Jossey-Bass, 1997.

Battersby, W. J. *Lasallian Meditations.* London: Waldegrave, 1964.

Baum, Gregory. "Theories of Post-Modernity." *The Ecumenist* 29:2 (Spring, 1991): 4–12.

Baxter, Michael J. and Frederick C. Bauerschmidt. "*Eruditio* without *Religio*?: The Dilemma of Catholics in the Academy." *Communio* 22 (Summer, 1995): 284.

Beal, Timothy K. "Facing Job," *Semeia* (forthcoming, 2002).

Beal, Timothy K. and David M. Gunn, eds. *Reading Bibles, Writing Bodies: Identity and The Book.* London and New York: Routledge, 1996.

Beardslee, William A. "Stories in the Postmodern World: Orienting and Disorienting." In *Sacred Interconnections: Postmodern Spirituality, Political Economy and Art.* Ed. David Ray Griffin. Albany: State University of New York Press, 1990: 163–75.

Beaty, Michael, Todd Buras, and Larry Lyon. "Challenges and Prospects for Baptist Higher Education." *The Southern Baptist Educator* 61: 4 (April/May/June, 1997): 3–6.

————. "Christian Higher Education: An Historical and Philosophical Perspective." *Perspectives in Religious Studies* 24:2 (Summer 1997): 147–65.

————. "Faith and Knowledge in American Higher Education: A Review Essay." *Fides et Historia* 29:1 (Winter/Spring 1997): 73f.

Beauvoir, Simone de. *The Second Sex.* Tr. H. M. Parshley. New York: Vintage, 1953.

Bellah, Robert N., et al. *The Good Society.* New York: Alfred A. Knopf, 1991.

Bellah, Robert N., Richard Madsen, William M. Sullivan, Ann Swidler and Steve Tipton. *Habits of the Heart.* San Francisco: Harper and Row, 1985.

Bender, Richard N., ed. *The Church-Related College Today: Anachronism or Opportunity?: A Symposium of Papers Produced by the Council on the Church-Related College.* Nashville: The Board of Higher Education of the United Methodist Church, 1971.

Bernstein, Richard. "Are We Beyond the Enlightenment Horizon?" In *Knowledge and Belief in America: Enlightenment Traditions and Modern Religious Thought.* Ed. William M. Shea and Peter A. Huff. Woodrow Wilson Center Series, 35–45. Cambridge: Cambridge University Press, 1995.

Bhabha, Homi K. "Editor's Introduction: Minority Maneuvers and Unsettled Negotiations," *Critical Inquiry* 23 (1997): 431–59.

————. *The Location of Culture.* London and New York: Routledge, 1994.

Boyer, Ernest. "Creating the New American College." *The Chronicle of Higher Education* (9 March 1994), A48.

Bradley, Martin B., et al., eds. *Churches and Church Membership in the United States 1990: An Enumeration by Region, State and County Based on Data Reported for 133 Church Groupings.* Atlanta: Glenmary Research Center, 1991.

Braudel, Fernand. *Civilization and Capitalism, 15th–18th Century,* 3 vols. New York: Harper and Row, 1982–1984.

Brenner, Athalya, ed. *A Feminist Companion to the Song of Songs.* Sheffield: JSOT Press, 1993.

Brenner, A., and F. van Dijk-Hemmes. *On Gendering Texts: Female and Male Voices in the Hebrew Bible.* Leiden: E. J. Brill, 1993.

Bringle, Robert G. and Julie A. Hatcher. "Implementing Service Learning in Higher Education." *The Journal of Higher Education* (March/April, 1996): 221–39.

Brown, B. Warren. *Report of the Survey of the Educational Work and Responsibility of the Presbyterian Church in the United States.* Louisville, KY: Presbyterian Church in the United States, 1928.

Brown, Peter. *Augustine of Hippo.* Berkeley: University of California Press, 1967.

Brueggemann, Walter. *Hope within History.* Atlanta: John Knox, 1987.

Bunyan, John. *Grace Abounding to the Chief of Sinners,* in *The Pilgrim's Progress and Grace Abounding.* Ed. James Thorpe. Boston: Houghton Mifflin Co., 1969 [1666].

Burkholder, John Richard. "Pacifist Ethics and Pacifist Politics." In *Betrayed? Essays on Pacifism and Politics.* Ed. Michael Cromartie. Washington, D.C.: Ethics and Public Policy Center, 1990.

Burrell, David. "A Catholic University." In *The Challenge and Promise of a Catholic University.* Ed. Theodore M. Hesburgh, C.S.C. Notre Dame, IN: University of Notre Dame Press, 1994.

Burtchaell, James Turnstead. "The Decline and Fall of the Christian College." *First Things* (April, 1991): 16–29 and (May, 1991): 30–38.
———. *The Dying of the Light: The Disengagement of Colleges and Universities from their Christian Churches.* Grand Rapids, MI: Eerdmans, 1998.

Butler, Judith P., Ernesto Laclau and Reinaldo José Ladagga, "The Uses of Equality." *Diacritics* 27:1 (Spring, 1997): 3–19.

Carlson, Edgar M. *The Future of Church-Related Higher Education.* Minneapolis, MN: Augsburg, 1977.

Carpenter, Joel A. and Kenneth W. Shipps, eds. *Making Higher Education Christian: The History and Mission of Evangelical Colleges in America.* Grand Rapids, MI: Christian University Press, 1987.

Cassirer, Ernst. *The Philosophy of the Enlightenment.* Tr. Fritz Koelln and James Pettergrove. Boston: Beacon, 1951.

Cavell, Stanley. *The Claim of Reason: Wittgenstein, Skepticism, Morality and Tragedy.* New York: Oxford University Press, 1979.

Childs, Brevard. *Introduction to the Old Testament as Scripture.* Philadelphia: Westminster, 1979.

The Christian Scholar 37:1 (March, 1954) and 41: special issue (Autumn, 1958).

Church and College: A Vital Partnership; Volume One: Affirmation: A Shared Commitment for Creative Renewal; Volume Two: A Shared Vision of Educational Purpose; Volume Three: Accountability: Keeping Faith with One Another; Volume Four: Exchange: The National Congress on Church-Related Universities. Sherman, TX: Center for Program and Institutional Renewal at Austin College, 1980.

"Church Colleges in Trouble." *The Christian Century* (June 20, 1951): 733–35.

Clines, David J. A. *Interested Parties: The Ideology of Writers and Readers of the Hebrew Bible.* JSOTS 205. Sheffield: JSOT Press, 1995.

Coalter, Milton J., John M. Mulder, and Louis B. Weeks. *Vital Signs: The Promise of Mainstream Protestantism.* Grand Rapids, MI: Eerdmans, 1994.

Colby, Anne and William Damon. *Some Do Care: Contemporary Lives of Moral Commitment.* New York: The Free Press, 1992.

Connor, Steven. *Postmodernist Culture: An Introduction to Theories of the Contemporary.* Oxford: Blackwell, 1989.

Cuninggim, Merrimon. "Categories of Church-Relatedness," In *Church Related Higher Education: Perceptions and Perspectives.* Ed. Robert R. Parsonage. Valley Forge, PA: Judson Press, 1978.

———. *The College Seeks Religion.* New Haven, CT: Yale University Press, 1947.

———. *The Protestant Stake in Higher Education.* n.p: Council of Protestant Colleges and Universities, 1961.

———. *Uneasy Partners: The College and the Church.* Nashville: Abingdon Press, 1994.

Davies, Philip R. *Whose Bible Is It, Anyway?* JSOTS 204. Sheffield: JSOT Press, 1995.

De Jong, Arthur J. *Reclaiming a Mission: New Direction for the Church-Related College.* Grand Rapids, MI: Eerdmans, 1990.

Denby, David. "Buried Alive." *The New Yorker* (15 July 1996): 48–58.

Derrida, Jacques. "Living on/Border Lines." Tr. James Hulbert. In *Deconstruction and Criticism.* Ed. Harold Bloom, et al. New York: Continuum, 1979.

———. *Writing and Difference.* Tr. Alan Bass. Chicago: University of Chicago Press, 1978.

Descartes, Rene. *Discourse on Method* and *Meditations on First Philosophy,* 3d ed. Tr. Donald A. Cress. Indianapolis: Hacket, 1993.

A Dialogue on Achieving the Mission of Church-Related Institutions of Higher Learning Hosted by Rockhurst College, Kansas City, Missouri, November 29–30, 1976. Washington, D.C.: American Association of Colleges, 1977.

Dixon, John W., Jr. "What Should Religion Departments Teach?" *Theology Today* 46:4 (Jan., 1990): 364–72.

Dulles, Avery. *Models of the Church.* Garden City, NY: Doubleday, 1974.

Dupré, Louis. *Passage to Modernity: An Essay in the Hermeneutics of Nature and Culture.* New Haven, CT: Yale University Press, 1993.

Edmundson, Mark. "On the Uses of Liberal Education, As Lite Entertainment for Bored College Students." *Harper's* (Sept., 1997), 39–49.

Eliade, Mircea. *The Sacred and the Profane: The Nature of Religion.* Tr. Willard R. Trask. New York: Harcourt Brace and Co., 1959.

Ellison, Ralph. *Invisible Man.* New York: Vintage, 1990.

Emerson, Ralph Waldo. "Character." In *Essays and Lectures.* Ed. Joel Porte. New York: The Library of America, 1983 [1844].

Farley, Edward. *The Fragility of Knowledge: Theological Education in the Church and the University.* Philadelphia: Fortress Press, 1988.

Ferre, Nels F. S. *Christian Faith and Higher Education.* New York: Harper and Brothers, 1957.

Fewell, Danna Nolan and David M. Gunn. *Gender, Power, and Promise: The Subject of the Bible's First Story.* Nashville: Abingdon Press, 1993.

Finn, Chester E., Jr., and Gregg Vanourek. "Charity Begins at School." *Commentary* (Oct., 1995): 46–48.

Fisher, Ben C. *The Idea of the Christian University in Today's World.* Macon, GA: Mercer University Press, 1989.

Flannery, Austin, ed. *Vatican Council II: The Conciliar and Post Conciliar Documents.* Northport, NY: Costello, 1981.

Fontaine, Carole. "The Abusive Bible: On the Use of Feminist Method in Pastoral Contexts." In *A Feminist Companion to Reading the Bible: Approaches, Methods and Strategies.* Ed. Athalya Brenner and Carole Fontaine, 84–113. Sheffield: Sheffield Academic Press, 1997.

Fowl, Stephen. "Texts Don't Have Ideologies." *Biblical Interpretation* 3 (1995): 15–34.

Fowler, James. *Stages of Faith: The Psychology of Human Development and the Quest for Meaning.* San Francisco: HarperSanFrancisco, 1995 [1981].

Fried, Michael. *Absorption and Theatricality: Painting and Beholder in the Age of Diderot.* Chicago: University of Chicago Press, 1980.

The Future of Catholic Higher Education: Proceedings of a Panel Discussion held at the June 24–25, 1980, Meeting of the Foundations and Donors Interested in Catholic Activities. Washington, D.C: FADICA, n.d.

Gallin, Alice. *Independence and a New Partnership in Catholic Higher Education*. Notre Dame, IN: University of Notre Dame Press, 1996.

———. "Making Colleges Catholic: Bishops and Academics Reach Common Ground." *Commonweal* 124:6 (March 28, 1997).

———. *Negotiating Identity: Catholic Higher Education since 1960*. Notre Dame, IN: University of Notre Dame Press, 2000.

Gaudium et Spes. The Pastoral Constitution on the Church in the Modern World. In *Vatican Council II: The Conciliar and Post Conciliar Documents*. Ed. Austin Flannery, 903–1001. Northport, NY: Costello, 1981.

Gay, Peter. *The Enlightenment: An Interpretation*. 2 vols. New York: Knopf, 1966.

Geier, Woodrow A., ed. *Church Colleges Today: Perspectives of a Church Agency on Their Problems and Possibilities*. Nashville: Board of Higher Education of the United Methodist Church, 1974.

Gleason, Philip. *Contending with Modernity: Catholic Higher Education in the Twentieth Century*. New York: Oxford University Press, 1995.

Godbold, Albea. *The Church College of the Old South*. Durham, NC: Duke University Press, 1944.

Goizueta, Roberto. *Caminemos Con Jesús*. New York: Orbis Books, 1995.

Gordon, Mary. *Final Payments*. New York: Ballantine Books, 1979.

Graff, Gerald. *Beyond the Culture Wars: How Teaching the Conflicts Can Revitalize American Education*. New York: Norton, 1992.

———. "Response to Mark Walhout." *Profession* (1996): 145–48.

Gray, John. *1 and 2 Kings*. Philadelphia: Westminster, 1978.

Greeley, Andrew M. "The Catholic Imagination and the Catholic University." *Current Issues in Catholic Higher Education* 12 (1992): 36–40.

———. *The Catholic Myth: The Behavior and Beliefs of American Catholics*. New York: Macmillan, 1990.

———. *From Backwater to Mainstream: A Profile of Catholic Higher Education*. New York: McGraw-Hill, 1969.

Green, William Scott. "Religion within the Limits." *Academe* (Nov.–Dec., 1996).

Greenleaf, Robert K. *Servant Leadership: A Journey Into the Nature of Legitimate Power and Greatness*. New York: Paulist Press, 1977.

Griffin, David Ray, William A. Beardslee and Joe Holland. *Varieties of Postmodern Theology*. New York: State University of New York Press, 1989.

Habermas, Jürgen. "Modernity: An Incomplete Project." In *The Anti-Aesthetic: Essays on Postmodern Culture*. Ed. Hal Foster, 3–15. Port Townsend, WA: Bay Press, 1983.

———. *The Philosophical Discourse of Modernity: Twelve Lectures*. Cambridge, MA: MIT Press, 1987.

Harper, William Rainey. *The Prospects of the Small College*. Chicago: University of Chicago Press, 1900.

Hart, D. G. "The Protestant Enlightenment Revisited: Daniel Coit Gilman and the Academic Reforms of the Modern American University." *The Journal of Ecclesiastical History* 47:4 (Oct., 1996). Cambridge University Press Online Journal.

Hart, Kevin. *The Trespass of the Sign: Deconstruction, Theology, and Philosophy*. Cambridge: Cambridge University Press, 1989.

Hauerwas, Stanley. *Christian Existence Today: Essays on Church, World and Living in Between*. Durham, NC: Labyrinth Press, 1988.

———. *Loving God with One's Mind: Essays, Articles and Speeches of F. Thomas Trotter*. Board of Higher Education and Ministry of the United Methodist Church, 1987.

———. "A Non-violent Proposal for Christian Participation in the Culture Wars." *Soundings* 75:4 (Winter, 1992): 477–92.

Hauerwas, Stanley and John H. Westerhoff, eds. *Schooling Christians: Holy Experiments in American Education*. Grand Rapids, MI: Eerdmans, 1992.

Haugaard, Kay. "Result of Too Much Tolerance?" *The Chronicle of Higher Education* (June 27, 1997).

Haynes, Stephen, R. *The Holocaust and the Church-Related College: Restoring Ruptured Traditions*. New York: Greenwood, 1997.

———. "Will the Paradox Endure? American Church-Related Colleges and the Postmodern Opportunity." Proposal submitted to Lilly Endowment Inc., 1995.

Hockman, Cynthia. *Returning Home: SSTers Talk about the Re-Entry Experience*. Goshen, IN: Pinchpenny Press, 1989.

Hoekema, David. "Politics, Religion, and Other Crimes Against Civility." *Academe* (Nov.–Dec., 1996).

Holmes, Arthur F. *The Idea of a Christian College*. Grand Rapids, MI: Eerdmans, 1975.

hooks, bell. *Teaching to Transgress: Education as the Practice of Freedom*. New York: Routledge, 1994.

hooks, bell, and Cornel West. *Breaking Bread*. Boston: South End Press, 1991.

Hoye, William J. "The Religious Roots of Academic Freedom." *Theological Studies* 58 (1997): 409–28.

Hudson, Winthrop S. *The Great Tradition of the American Churches*. New York: Harper, 1953.

Hughes, Richard T. "Baptists and the Life of the Mind: Reflections on the Baptist Theme of Soul Competency." *The Southern Baptist Educator* 63: 2 (1999): 3–7.

———. "Can Christian Faith Sustain the Life of the Mind?" *The Southern Baptist Educator* 63:1 (Fall, 1998): 3–8.

———. "Musings on Tuesday's Questions: Luther in the Context of the American Enlightenment." *The Cresset* 62:7 (Special issue, 1999): 26–35.

———. "Our Place in Church Related Higher Education in the United States." *Intersections* 4 (Winter, 1998): 3–9.

———. "Protestant Colleges, 1960–1990." In *Trying Times: Essays on Catholic Higher Education in the 20th Century.* Ed. William M. Shea and Daniel Van Slyke. Atlanta: Scholar's Press, 1999.

——— "Reclaiming a Heritage." *Restoration Quarterly* 37:3 (1995): 129–38.

Hughes, Richard T. and William B. Adrian, eds. *Models for Christian Higher Education: Strategies for Success in the Twenty-First Century.* Grand Rapids, MI: Eerdmans, 1997.

Hull, William E. "Christian Higher Education at the Crossroads." *Perspectives in Religious Studies* 19:4 (Winter, 1992): 441–54.

Hutcheson, Richard G., Jr. "Are Church-Related Colleges Also Christian Colleges?" *The Christian Century* (Sept. 28, 1988): 838–41.

Inbody, Tyron. "Postmodernism: Intellectual Velcro Dragged Across Culture." *Theology Today* 51 (1995): 524–38.

Jardine, Murray. *Speech and Political Practice, Recovering the Place of Human Responsibility.* New York: State University of New York Press, 1998.

John Paul II. *Ex Corde Ecclesiae: Apostolic Constitution on Catholic Universities.* Washington, D.C.: U.S. Catholic Conference, 1996 [1990].

Johnson, Elizabeth A. *She Who Is: The Mystery of God in Feminist Theological Discourse.* New York: Crossroads, 1987.

Kahne, Joseph and Joel Westheimer. "In the Service of What? The Politics of Service Learning." *Phi Delta Kappan* (May, 1996).

Kant, Immanuel. *Foundations of the Metaphysics of Morals* and *What is Enlightenment?* Indianapolis: Bobbs-Merrill, 1959.

Kauffmann, Norman L., Judith N. Martin, and Henry D. Weaver, with Judy Weaver. *Students Abroad, Strangers at Home: Education for a Global Society.* Yarmouth, ME: Intercultural Press, 1992.

Kelleher, Ann. *Learning from Success: Case Studies in International Program Development.* New York: Peter Lang, 1996.

Kelsey, David H. *Between Athens and Berlin: The Theological Education Debate.* Grand Rapids, MI: Eerdmans, 1993.

———. *To Understand God Truly: What's Theological About a Theological School.* Louisville, KY: Westminster/John Knox, 1992.

Koontz, Ted. "Mennonites and 'Postmodernity'." *Mennonite Quarterly Review* 63:4 (Oct., 1989).

Kramnick, Isaac and R. Laurence Moore. "The Godless University." *Academe* (Nov.–Dec., 1996).

Kuhn, Thomas. *The Structure of Scientific Revolutions.* 2d ed. Chicago: University of Chicago Press, 1970.

Lakeland, Paul. *Postmodernity*. Philadelphia: Fortress Press, 1998.

Landy, Francis. *Paradoxes of Paradise: Identity and Difference in the Song of Songs*. Sheffield: Almond Press, 1983.

Landy, Thomas M. "Catholic Intellectual Life: Reflections on Mission and Identity." *U.S. Catholic Historian* 13:2 (Winter, 1995): 87–100.

———. "Collegium and the Intellectual's Vocation to Serve." *Conversations on Jesuit Higher Education* 10 (Fall, 1996): 20–29.

Langan, John P., ed. *Catholic Universities in Church and Society: A Dialogue on Ex Corde Ecclesiae*. Washington, D.C.: Georgetown University Press, 1993.

Levinas, Emmanuel. *Totality and Infinity*. Tr. Alphonso Lingis. Pittsburgh: Duquesne University Press, 1969.

Lewis, C. S. "Meditation in a Toolshed." In *God in the Dock: Essays on Theology and Ethics*. Ed. Walter Hooper. Grand Rapids, MI: Eerdmans, 1970.

Limbert, Paul M. *Denominational Policies in the Support and Supervision of Higher Education*. Columbia Teachers College Contributions to Education 378. New York: Columbia University Bureau of Publications, 1929.

Linafelt, Tod. "The Undecidability of *barak* in the Prologue to Job." *Biblical Interpretation* 4 (1995): 1–18.

Longfield, Bradley J. and George M. Marsden. "Presbyterian Colleges in Twentieth-Century America." In *The Pluralistic Vision: Presbyterians and Mainstream Protestant Education and Leadership*. Ed. Milton J. Coalter, John M. Mulder and Louis B. Weeks. Louisville, KY: Westminster/John Knox, 1993.

"A Look Back at the Catholic Intellectualism Issue." *US Catholic Historian* 13 (Winter 1995): 19–37.

Lundin, Roger. *The Culture of Interprtation: Christian Faith and the Postmodern World*. Grand Rapids, MI: Eerdmans, 1993.

Lynn, Robert Wood. "'The Survival of Recognizably Protestant Colleges': Reflections on Old-Line Protestantism, 1950–1990." In *The Secularization of the Academy*. Ed. George M. Marsden and Bradley J. Longfield, 170–94. New York: Oxford University Press, 1992.

Lyotard, Jean-François. "Answering the Question: What is Postmodernism?" Tr. Régis Durand. In Jean-François Lyotard, *The Postmodern Condition: A Report on Knowledge*, 71–82. Tr. Geoff Bennington and Brian Massumi. Theory and History of Literature 10. Minneapolis: University of Minnesota Press, 1984.

———. *The Postmodern Condition: A Report on Knowledge*. Tr. Geoff Bennington and Brian Massumi. Theory and History of Literature 10. Minneapolis: University of Minnesota Press, 1984.

MacIntyre, Alasdair. *After Virtue*. Notre Dame, IN: University of Notre Dame, 1984.

————. *Three Rival Versions of Moral Enquiry: Encyclopedia, Genealogy, and Tradition.* Notre Dame, IN: University of Notre Dame Press, 1990.

————. *Whose Justice? Which Rationality?* Notre Dame, IN: University of Notre Dame Press, 1988.

Magill, Samuel H., ed. *The Contribution of the Church-Related College to the Public Good.* Proceedings of the Wingspread Conference on the Contribution of the Church-Related College to the Public Good, December 8–10, 1969. Washington, D.C.: American Association of Colleges, 1970.

Marsden, George M. "The Ambiguities of Academic Freedom." *Church History* 62:2 (June, 1993): 221–25.

————. *The Outrageous Idea of Christian Scholarship.* New York: Oxford University Press, 1997.

————. *The Soul of the American University: From Protestant Establishment to Established Nonbelief.* New York: Oxford University Press, 1994.

Marsden, George M. and Bradley J. Longfield, eds. *The Secularization of the Academy.* New York: Oxford University Press, 1992.

Marty, Martin. "You Get to Teach and Study Religion." *Academe* (Nov.–Dec., 1996).

McCoy, Charles S. *The Responsible Campus: Toward a New Identity for the Church-Related College.* Nashville: United Methodist Church Board of Education, 1972.

McFague, Sallie. *Models of God: Theology for an Ecological, Nuclear Age.* Philadelphia: Fortress Press, 1987.

McInnes, William. *Perspectives on the Current Status of and Emerging Policy Issues for Church-Related Colleges and Universities.* AGB Occasional Paper No. 8. Washington, D.C.: Association of Governing Boards of Universities and Colleges, 1991.

Merriam, Thorton W. "Religion in Higher Education through the Past Twenty-Five Years." In *Religion and Liberal Learning.* Ed. Amos N. Wilder. New York: Harper, 1951.

Merton, Thomas. *Love and Living.* New York: Harcourt, Brace and Co., 1985.

Middleton, J. Richard and Brian Walsh. *Truth is Stranger Than It Used to Be.* Downer's Grove, IL: Inter-Varsity Press, 1995.

Miller, Alexander. *Faith and Learning: Christian Faith and Higher Education in Twentieth-Century America.* New York: Association Press, 1960.

Miller, J. Hillis. "Presidential Address 1986, The Triumph of Theory, the Resistance to Reading, and the Question of the Material Base." *PMLA* 102 (1987): 281–91.

Miller, Susan Fisher. *Culture for Service: A History of Goshen College, 1894–1994.* Goshen, IN: Goshen College, 1994.

The Mission of the Christian College in the Modern World: Addresses and Reports of the 3rd Quadrennial Convocation of Christian Colleges, June 17–21, 1962. Washington, D.C.: Council of Protestant Colleges and Universities, 1962.

Mitchell, Joshua. "Religion in the Academic Life." *Academe* (Nov.–Dec., 1996).

Moore, Stephen D. *Literary Criticism and the Gospels: The Theoretical Challenge.* New Haven, CT: Yale Universtiy Press, 1989.

Murphy, J. Patrick. *Visions and Values in Catholic Higher Education.* Kansas City, MO: Sheed and Ward, 1991.

Nelson, Cary, ed. *Will Teach for Food: Academic Labor in Crisis.* Minneapolis: University of Minnesota Press, 1997.

Newman, Elizabeth. "The Practice of Testimony in a 'Postmodern' Context." *Perspectives in Religious Studies* 25: 1 (Spring, 1998): 81–92.

———. "Who's Home Cooking? Hospitality, Christian Identity and Higher Education." *Perspectives in Religious Studies* 26: 1 (Spring, 1999): 7–16.

Niebuhr, Reinhold. *The Nature and Destiny of Man.* Vol. 1. New York: Charles Scribner's Sons, 1941.

Noll, Mark A. "Christian Colleges, Christian Worldviews, and an Invitation to Research." In *The Christian College: A History of Protestant Higher Education in America.* Ed. William C. Ringenberg, 1–36. Grand Rapids, MI: Christian University Press/Eerdmans, 1984.

Nord, Warren A. *Religion and American Education: Rethinking a National Dilemma.* Chapel Hill: University of North Carolina Press, 1995.

Noronha, June. "International and Multicultural Education: Unrelated Adversaries or Successful Partners?" In *Promoting Diversity in College Classrooms: Innovative Responses for Curriculum, Faculty and Institutions.* Ed. Maurianne Adams, 53–61. San Francisco: Jossey-Bass, 1999.

Nouwen, Henri J. M. *Creative Ministry.* Garden City, NY: Doubleday, 1971.

———. *With Burning Hearts.* New York: Orbis Books, 1996.

Nussbaum, Martha C. *Cultivating Humanity: A Classical Defense of Reform in Liberal Education.* Cambridge, MA: Harvard University Press, 1997.

Nygren, Anders. *Agape and Eros.* Tr. Philip S. Watson. Philadelphia: Westminster, 1953.

O'Brien, David J. "A Catholic Future for Catholic Higher Education: The State of the Question." *Catholic Education: A Journal of Inquiry and Practice* 1 (Sept., 1997): 37–50.

———. *From the Heart of the American Church: Catholic Higher Education and American Culture.* Maryknoll, NY: Orbis Press, 1994.

O'Brien, Dennis. "The Disappearing Moral Curriculum." *The Key Reporter* 62:4 (Summer, 1997): 4.

———. *All the Essential Half-Truths about Higher Education*. Chicago: University of Chicago Press, 1998.

O'Brien, Julia. "On Saying 'No' to a Prophet." *Semeia* 72 (1997): 111–24.

Oakeshott, Michael. *Rationalism in Politics, and Other Essays*. New York: Basic Books, 1962.

Outler, Albert C. *Colleges, Faculties and Religion: An Appraisal of the Program of Faculty Consultations on Religion in Higher Education, 1945–48* (n.p., n.d).

Pace, C. Robert. *Education and Evangelism: A Profile of Protestant Colleges*. New York: McGraw-Hill and the Carnegie Foundation for the Advancement of Teaching, 1972.

Palmer, Parker J. *To Know as We Are Known: A Spirituality of Education*. San Francisco: HarperSan Francisco 1993 [1983].

Pardes, Ilana. *Countertraditions in the Bible: A Feminist Approach*. Cambridge, MA: Harvard University Press, 1992.

Parks, Sharon. *The Critical Years: Young Adults and the Search for Meaning, Faith and Commitment*. San Francisco: Harper and Row, 1986.

Parsonage, Robert Rue, ed. *Church Related Higher Education: Perceptions and Perspectives*. Valley Forge, PA: Judson Press, 1978.

Pascal, Blaise. *Penseés*. Tr. W. F. Trotter. London: J. M. Dent and Sons, 1931.

Patton, Leslie Kerr. *The Purposes of Church-Related Colleges: A Critical Study—A Proposed Program*. Teachers College Columbia University Contributions to Education 783. New York: Columbia University, 1940.

Pelikan, Jaroslav. *The Idea of the University: A Reexamination*. New Haven, CT: Yale University Press, 1992.

———. *The Vindication of Tradition*. New Haven, CT: Yale University Press, 1984.

Phillips, Gary. "Exegesis as Critical Praxis: Reclaiming History and Text from a Postmodern Perspective." *Semeia* 51 (1990): 7–49.

Phillips, Timothy R. and Dennis L. Okholm, eds. *Christian Apologetics in the Postmodern World*. Downer's Grove, IL: Inter-Varsity Press, 1995.

Pike, Kenneth. "Towards a Theory of the Structure of Human Behavior." In *Language in Culture and Society*. Ed. D. Hymes, 154–61. New York: Harper and Row, 1964.

Pippin, Tina. "Border Pedagogy: Activism in a Wymyn and Religion Classroom." *The Council of Societies for the Study of Religion Bulletin* 4:1 (Feb., 1995).

Polanyi, Michael. *Personal Knowledge, Towards a Post-Critical Philosophy*. Chicago: University of Chicago Press, 1958.

Poteat, William H. "Persons and Places, Paradigms in Communication." In *The Primacy of Persons and the Language of Culture.* Ed. James M. Nickell and James W. Stines. Columbia: University of Missouri, 1993.

——. *Polanyian Meditations, In Search of a Post-Critical Logic.* Durham, NC: Duke University Press, 1985.

Puzon, Bridget, ed. *Women Religious and the Intellectual Life: The North American Achievement.* San Francisco: International Scholars Publication, 1996.

Raboteau, Albert. *Fire in the Bones.* Boston: Beacon Press, 1995.

Raschke, Carl A. "The Deconstruction of God." In *Deconstruction and Theology,* ed. Thomas J. J. Altizer, et al., 1–33. New York: Crossroads, 1983.

Razzano, Elaine. "The Overseas Route to Multicultural and International Education." *The Clearing House* (May–June, 1996): 268–70.

Religion in the Church College. n.p.: The Board of Education of the Methodist Church, 1953.

Ringerberg, William C., ed. *The Christian College: A History of Protestant Higher Education in America.* Grand Rapids, MI: Christian University Press/Eerdmans, 1984.

Roof, Wade Clark. *A Generation of Seekers: The Spiritual Journeys of the Baby Boom Generation.* San Francisco: HarperSanFrancisco, 1993.

——. *Spiritual Marketplace: Baby Boomers and the Remaking of American Religion.* Princeton, NJ: Princeton University Press, 1999.

Rudolph, Frederick. *The American College and University: A History.* Athens: University of Georgia Press, 1990.

Rule of Benedict. Ed. Timothy Fry. Collegeville, MN: Liturgical Press, 1981.

Salm, Luke. *The Work Is Yours: The Life of Saint John Baptist de La Salle.* Romeoville, IL: Christian Brothers Publications, 1989.

Sandin, Robert T. *The Search for Excellence: The Christian College in an Age of Educational Competition.* Macon, GA: Mercer University Press, 1982.

Schüssler-Fiorenza, Elizabeth. *Bread Not Stone.* Boston: Beacon Press, 1984.

Schwehn, Mark R. *Exiles from Eden: Religion and the Academic Vocation in America.* New York: Oxford University Press, 1993.

——. "The Once and Future University." A symposium in *Cross Currents: The Journal of the Association of Religion and Intellectual Life* (Winter, 1993–1994).

Scriven, Charles. "Schooling for the Tournament of Narratives: Postmodernism and the Idea of the Christian College." In *Theology Without Foundations, Religious Practice and the Future of Theological Truth.* Ed. Stanley Hauerwas, Nancey Murphy, and Mark Nation. Nashville: Abingdon Press, 1994.

Shedd, Clarence Prouty. *The Church Follows its Students*. New Haven, CT: Yale University Press, 1938.

Showalter, Stuart, ed. *The Role of Service-Learning in International Education*. Goshen, IN: Goshen College, 1989.

Sigmon, Robert L., et al. *Journey to Service Learning*. Washington, D.C.: Council of Independent Colleges, 1996.

———. "The Paralysis of 'Absolutophobia'." *The Chronicle of Higher Education* (June 27, 1997).

Sloan, Douglas. *Faith and Knowledge: Mainline Protestantism and American Higher Education*. Louisville, KY: Westminster/John Knox, 1994.

Smart, Ninian. "Religious Studies and Theology." *Bulletin of the Council of Societies for the Study of Religion* 26 (1997): 66–68.

Smith, Harry E. "The Church's Mission in Higher Education: Renewing our Commitment." *Church and Society* (Jan./Feb., 1998): 58–66.

———. *Secularization and the University*. Richmond, VA: John Knox Press, 1968.

Smith, Page. *Killing the Spirit: Higher Education in America*. New York: Viking, 1990.

Solberg, Richard W. and Merton P. Strommen. *How Church-Related are Church-Related Colleges?: Answers Based on a Comprehensive Survey of Supporting Constituencies of Eighteen LCA Colleges*. Philadelphia: Board of Publication, Lutheran Church in America, 1980.

Swartzentruber, Elaine K. "Marking and Remarking the Body of Christ: Toward a Postmodern Mennonite Ecclesiology." *Mennonite Quarterly Review* 71:2 (April, 1997): 243–65.

Tanner, Kathryn. *God and Creation in Christian Theology*. New York: Basil Blackwell, 1988.

Task Force on Study in Depth of Religion. *Liberal Learning and the Religion Major: A Report to the Profession*. Completed in conjunction with the Association of American College National Review of Arts and Sciences Majors. American Academy of Religion, 1990.

Taylor, Charles. "The Politics of Recognition." In *Multiculturalism*. Ed. Amy Gutman. Princeton, NJ: Princeton University Press, 1994.

———. *Sources of the Self: The Making of the Modern Identity*. Cambridge, MA: Harvard University, 1989.

Taylor, Mark C. "Denegating God." *Critical Inquiry* 20 (1994): 592–610.

Tompkins, Jane. *A Life in School*. Reading, MA: Addison-Wesley, 1996.

Tracy, David. *The Analogical Imagination: Christian Theology and the Culture of Pluralism*. New York: Crossroads, 1981.

———. "Theology and the Many Faces of Postmodernity." *Theology Today* 51 (1994).

Trible, Phyllis. "Eve and Adam: Genesis 2–3 Reread." *Andover Newton Quarterly* 13 (1973): 251–58.

———. "Exegesis for Storytellers and Other Strangers." *Journal of Biblical Literature* 114 (1995): 3–19.

———. *God and the Rhetoric of Sexuality.* Philadelphia: Fortress Press, 1978.

———. "The Odd Couple: Elijah and Jezebel." In *Out of the Garden: Women Writers on the Bible.* Ed. Christina Büchmann and Celina Spiegel. London: Pandora, 1994.

Trotter, F. Thomas. "The College as the Church's Gift." *The Christian Century* (Nov. 30, 1988): 1098–1100.

Ulanov, Ann Belford. *The Feminine in Jungian Psychology and in Christian Theology.* Evanston, IL: Northwestern University Press, 1971.

Vattimo, Gianni. *The Transparent Society.* Tr. D. Webb. Baltimore, MD: The Johns Hopkins University Press, 1992.

Walhout, Mark D. "Beyond the Wars of Religion: How Teaching the Conflicts Can Desecularize American Education." *Profession* (1996): 139–45.

Watson, Francis. *Text, Church and World.* Edinburgh: T & T Clark, 1994.

Weber, Max. "Science as a Vocation." In *From Max Weber: Essays in Sociology.* Ed. and Tr. H. H. Geth and C. Wright Mills. New York: Oxford University Press, 1977.

Welch, Herbert, Henry Churchill King, and Thomas Nicholson. *The Christian College.* Introduction by William H. Crawford. New York: The Methodist Book Concern, 1916.

"White, Andrew Dickson." In *Dictionary of American Biography.* Ed. Dumas Malone. New York: Charles Scribner's Sons, 1936.

Wicke, Myron F. *The Church-Related College.* Washington, D.C.: The Center for Applied Research in Education, Inc., 1964.

Wiebe, Donald. *The Politics of Religious Studies.* New York: St. Martin's Press, 1999.

Wilken, Robert. "The Christian Intellectual Tradition." *First Things* 14 (June/July, 1991): 14.

———. *Remembering the Christian Past.* Grand Rapids, MI: Eerdmans, 1995.

Wilson, Charles Reagan. *Baptized in Blood: The Religion of the Lost Cause 1865–1920.* Athens, GA: University of Georgia Press, 1980.

Winston, Diane. "The Mission, Formation and Diversity Report: Adult Degree Programs at Faith-Based Colleges." Princeton, NJ: Center for the Study of Religion, 1999.

Wittgenstein, Ludwig. *Culture and Value.* Tr. P. Winch. Oxford: Blackwell, 1980.

Wolfe, Alan. "A Welcome Revival of Religion in the Academy." *The Chronicle of Higher Education* (Sept. 19, 1997).

Wolterstorff, Nicholas. "Theology and Science: Listening to Each Other." In *Religion and Science, History, Method, Dialogue.* Ed. W.

Mark Richardson and Wesley J. Wildman. New York: Routledge, 1996.

Yee, Gale, ed. *Judges and Method: New Approaches in Biblical Studies.* Philadelphia: Fortress Press, 1995.

Yoder, John H. *The Priestly Kingdom.* Notre Dame, IN: University of Notre Dame Press, 1984.

———. *The Royal Priesthood: Essays Ecclesiological and Ecumenical.* Grand Rapids, MI: Eerdmans, 1994.

CONTRIBUTORS

Timothy K. Beal (Ph.D., Emory) is Harkness Associate Professor of Biblical Literature and co-director of the Interdisciplinary Initiative on Religion and Culture at Case Western Reserve University in Cleveland, OH. Before coming to CWRU, he was Assistant Professor of Religion at Eckerd College in St. Petersburg, FL. He is the author of *The Book of Hiding: Gender, Ethnicity, Annihilation, and Esther* (Routledge, 1997), a commentary on Esther (Liturgical, 1999), and *Religion and Its Monsters* (Routledge, 2002).

Marcia J. Bunge (Ph.D., Chicago) is Associate Professor of Theology and Humanities at Christ College, the Honors College of Valparaiso University. She taught at Gustavus Adolphus College, Luther College, and Luther Seminary before joining the Christ College faculty in 1997. She is the author of several articles and two books. She edited, translated, and introduced a selection of J. G. Herder's writings entitled *Against Pure Reason: Writings on History, Language, and Religion* (Fortress Press, 1993). In addition, from 1998 to 2000 she directed a project on theological perspectives on children, funded by the Lilly Endowment, and edited a collection of essays based on that project entitled *The Child in Christian Thought* (Eerdmans, 2001).

William J. Cahoy (Ph.D., Yale) is Dean of the School of Theology and Seminary at Saint John's University, Collegeville, Minnesota, where he has taught since 1990. Prior to that he was a member of the Religious Studies Department at Saint Mary's University.

Margaret Falls-Corbitt (Ph.D., Vanderbilt) is Professor of Philosophy at Hendrix College where she has taught since 1987. She has authored articles in the areas of philosophy of religion and ethics, with particular attention to Kantian theories of punishment and moral responsibility. In January of 2002 she began serving as the Director of the Hendrix-Lilly Vocations Initiative.

D. Jonathan Grieser (Th.D., Harvard) currently teaches at Furman University. He publishes regularly in the history of Christianity and religious studies and is active in the Episcopal Church.

Stephen R. Haynes (Ph.D., Emory) holds the A. B. Curry Chair of Religious Studies at Rhodes College in Memphis, TN, where he has taught since 1989. Since 1996 he has directed the Rhodes Consultation on the Future of the Church-Related College, a national network of teacher-scholars at religiously affiliated institutions of higher education. His publications include *Reluctant Witnesses: Jews and the Christian Imagination* (Macmillan, 1995) and *Noah's Curse: The Biblical Justification for Slavery in America* (Oxford, 2001).

Richard Kyte (Ph.D., Johns Hopkins) is Director of the D. B. Reinhart Institute for Ethics in Leadership and Associate Professor of Philosophy at Viterbo University. His recent research has been on topics in the field of moral psychology, including forgiveness, hospitality, and character formation. He and his wife Cindi have two children and are members of the First Presbyterian Church in La Crosse, Wisconsin.

Paul Lakeland (Ph.D., Vanderbilt) is Professor and Chair of the Department of Religious Studies at Fairfield University in Connecticut, where he has taught since 1981. He is the author of five books, including *Theology and Critical Theory: The Discourse of the Church* (Abingdon, 1990) and *Postmodernity: Christian Identity in a Fragmented Age* (Fortress, 1997). He currently serves as Chair of the Theology and Religious Reflection Section of the American Academy of Religion, and is Co-director of the Workgroup for Constructive Theology, an independent national body of systematic and constructive theologians.

Keith Graber Miller (Ph.D., Emory) is Professor of Religion and Philosophy at Goshen College in Goshen, IN, where he taught from 1987-89 and again since 1993. He is the author of *Wise as Serpents, Innocent as Doves: American Mennonites Engage Washington* (Tennessee, 1996), editor of *Teaching to Transform: Perspectives on Mennonite Higher Education* (Pinchpenny, 2000), and a regular contributor of essays to other edited texts and academic journals.

John Neary (Ph.D., California—Irvine) is Associate Professor of English at St. Norbert College in Wisconsin, where he recently completed a term as chair of the Division of Humanities and Fine Arts. He is the author of two books: *Something and Nothingness: The Fiction of John Updike and John Fowles* and *Like and Unlike God: Religious Imaginations in Modern and Contemporary Fiction*. He currently serves on the board of directors of the Collegium Institute on Faith and Intellectual Life.

Elizabeth Newman (Ph.D., Duke) is Associate Professor of Theology and Ethics at Saint Mary's College, Notre Dame, IN. She has written articles on Christian identity and higher education, theology and science, and a variety of ecclesial practices such as testimony, eucharist, and hospitality. She also has research interests in Orthodox theology and ecumenism. She is co-editor of the Studies in Baptist Life and Thought series and is currently co-authoring a book on hospitality and the Christian college.

Corrie E. Norman (Th.D., Harvard) is Assistant Professor of Religion at Converse College in Spartanburg, SC. She publishes studies in the history of Christianity and is currently working on a book project on food and religion. She is active in the Episcopal Church.

Julia Myers O'Brien (Ph.D., Duke) is Howard and Grace Stern Professor of Old Testament at Lancaster Theological Seminary in Lancaster, PA. From 1989 to 1997 she taught at Meredith College in Raleigh, NC, where she also served as head of the Department of Religion and Philosophy. Dr. O'Brien holds a B.A. in Religion from Wake Forest University, an M.Div. from Duke Divinity School, and a Ph.D. in Hebrew Bible and Semitic Studies from Duke University.

Dominic Scibilia (Ph.D., Marquette) is on the Religion Faculty of St. Peter's Preparatory School in Jersey City, NJ, where he has taught since 1999. He has several published articles on lay and religious Catholics in the American labor movement and teaching college theology. His continuing work with the Rhodes Consultation on the Future of Church Related Colleges began in 1995. Currently, he also serves as a consultant for the Lilly Endowment Project on Mentoring College Junior Faculty, contributing to the chapters on the theology and spirituality of mentoring for that project's book.